COUNTRY REPORTS ON TERRORISM 2012

Table of Contents

Chapter 5. Terrorist Safe Havens (Update to 7120 Report)
Terrorist Safe Havens
Countering Terrorism on the Economic Front
Multilateral Efforts to Counter Terrorism
International Conventions and Protocols Matrix
Long-Term Programs and Initiatives Designed to Counter Terrorist Safe Havens
   -Countering Violent Extremism
   -Capacity Building
   -Regional Strategic Initiative
Support for Pakistan
Collaboration with Saudi Arabia
Broadcasting Board of Governors Initiatives: Outreach through Foreign
   Broadcast Media
Basic Education in Muslim Countries

Chapter 6. Terrorist Organizations
Abdallah Azzam Brigades (AAB)
Abu Nidal Organization (ANO)
Abu Sayyaf Group (ASG)
Al-Aqsa Martyrs Brigade (AAMB)
Ansar al-Islam (AAI)
Army of Islam (AOI)
Asbat al-Ansar (AAA)
Aum Shinrikyo (AUM)
Basque Fatherland and Liberty (ETA)
Communist Party of Philippines/New People's Army (CPP/NPA)
Continuity Irish Republican Army (CIRA)
Gama'a al-Islamiyya (IG)
Hamas
Haqqani Network (HQN)
Harakat ul-Jihad-i-Islami (HUJI)
Harakat ul-Jihad-i-Islami/Bangladesh (HUJI-B)
Harakat ul-Mujahideen (HUM)
Hizballah
Indian Mujahedeen (IM)
Islamic Jihad Union (IJU)
Islamic Movement of Uzbekistan (IMU)
Jaish-e-Mohammed (JEM)
Jemaah Ansharut Tauhid (JAT)
Jemaah Islamiya (JI)
Jundallah
Kahane Chai
Kata'ib Hizballah (KH)
Kurdistan Workers' Party (PKK)
Lashkar e-Tayyiba
Lashkar i Jhangvi (LJ)
Liberation Tigers of Tamil Eelam (LTTE)
Libyan Islamic Fighting Group (LIFG)

Moroccan Islamic Combatant Group (GICM)
National Liberation Army (ELN)
Palestine Islamic Jihad – Shaqaqi Faction (PIJ)
Palestine Liberation Front – Abu Abbas Faction (PLF)
Popular Front for the Liberation of Palestine (PFLP)
Popular Front for the Liberation of Palestine-General Command (PFLP-GC)
Al-Qa'ida (AQ)
Al-Qa'ida in the Arabian Peninsula (AQAP)
Al-Qa'ida in Iraq (AQI)
Al-Qa'ida in the Islamic Maghreb (AQIM)
Real IRA (RIRA)
Revolutionary Armed Forces of Colombia (FARC)
Revolutionary Organization 17 November (17N)
Revolutionary People's Liberation Party/Front (DHKP/C)
Revolutionary Struggle (RS)
Al-Shabaab (AS)
Shining Path (SL)
Tehrik-e Taliban Pakistan (TTP)
United Self-Defense Forces of Colombia (AUC)

Chapter 7. Legislative Requirements and Key Terms

Chapter 1.
Strategic Assessment

The al-Qa'ida (AQ) core, under the direction of Ayman al-Zawahiri, has been significantly degraded as a result of ongoing worldwide efforts against the organization. Usama bin Laden's death was the most important milestone in the fight against AQ, but there have been other successes – dozens of senior AQ leaders have been removed from the fight in the Afghanistan-Pakistan region. Ilyas Kashmiri, one of the most capable AQ operatives in South Asia, and Atiya Abdul Rahman, AQ's second-in-command, were killed in Pakistan in 2011. AQ leaders Abu Yahya Al-Libi and Abu Zaid al-Kuwaiti were killed in 2012. As a result of these leadership losses, the AQ core's ability to direct the activities and attacks of its affiliates has diminished, as its leaders focus increasingly on survival.

Leadership losses have also driven AQ affiliates to become more independent. The affiliates are increasingly setting their own goals and specifying their own targets. As avenues previously open to them for receiving and sending funds have become more difficult to access, several affiliates have engaged in kidnapping for ransom. Through kidnapping for ransom operations and other criminal activities, the affiliates have also increased their financial independence.

While AQ affiliates still seek to attack the "far enemy," they seem more inclined to focus on smaller scale attacks closer to their home base. Both al-Qa'ida in the Arabian Peninsula (AQAP) and al-Qa'ida in the Islamic Maghreb (AQIM) have taken steps to seize land and impose their brutal authority over local populations.

The AQ core still has the ability to inspire, plot, and launch regional and transnational attacks from its safe haven in Western Pakistan, despite its leadership losses. Along with AQ, the Afghan Taliban, the Haqqani Network, Tehrik-e Taliban Pakistan, and other like-minded groups continue to conduct operations against U.S., Coalition, Afghan, and Pakistani interests from safe havens on both sides of the Afghanistan/Pakistan border. Other South Asian terrorist organizations, including Lashkar e-Tayyiba (LeT), cite U.S. interests as legitimate targets for attacks. LeT, the group responsible for the 2008 Mumbai attacks, continues to pose a serious threat to regional stability.

In Yemen, the fight against AQAP is a work in progress, but the trend lines are positive. Yemeni forces have had success pushing AQAP out of its southern strongholds over the last year, leading AQAP to turn increasingly to asymmetric tactics in a campaign of bombings and targeted assassinations against government targets, pro-government tribal militias known as Popular Committees and their leaders, soldiers, civilians, and foreign diplomatic personnel.

After more than two decades of strife, autumn 2012 marked the beginning of political transition in Somalia, with a new provisional constitution, parliament, and president. These are hopeful signs of a new era in this long-suffering country. This success was made possible because Somali National Forces and the AU Mission in Somalia – with strong financial support and training from the United States and Western partners – expelled al-Shabaab from major cities in southern Somalia. Though al-Shabaab is carrying out attacks against the new government, it is fragmented by dissension and much weakened.

Though the AQ core is on a path to defeat, and its two most dangerous affiliates have suffered serious setbacks, tumultuous events in the Middle East and North Africa have complicated the counterterrorism picture. The dispersal of weapons stocks in the wake of the revolution in Libya, the Tuareg rebellion, and the coup d'état in Mali presented terrorists with new opportunities. The actions of France and African countries, however, in conjunction with both short-term U.S. support to the African-led International Support Mission to Mali and the long-term efforts of the United States via the Trans-Sahara Counterterrorism Partnership, have done much to roll back and contain the threat.

In Libya, the security vacuum in the aftermath of the 2011 revolution provided greater opportunity for terrorists to operate. This vacuum, combined with the weakness of Libya's nascent security institutions, allowed violent extremists to act, as we saw too clearly on September 11 in Benghazi, when J. Christopher Stevens, the U.S. Ambassador to Libya, and three staff members, died during attacks on U.S. facilities.

In Syria, AQI seeks to establish a long-term presence under the pseudonym of al-Nusrah Front. The Nusrah Front has denounced the Syrian Opposition Coalition's founding, rejected the vision statement that the opposition issued in Cairo, and says it is fighting to establish an Islamic caliphate encompassing the entire Levant.

In Gaza, a sharp increase in the number of rocket attacks launched by Hamas and other Gaza-based violent extremist groups led Israel to launch Operation Pillar of Defense in November 2012. During the course of the eight day operation, Israeli forces targeted more than 1,500 terrorist sites. Since the Egypt-brokered November 21 ceasefire, the United States has engaged with our Egyptian and Israeli counterparts to strengthen and sustain the peace.

In West Africa we are seeing a loosely-organized collection of factions known as Boko Haram (BH) – some of them with ties to AQIM – exploiting the grievances of northern Nigerians to gain recruits and public sympathy. The number and sophistication of BH's attacks are increasing, and while the group focuses principally on local Nigerian issues and actors, there are reports that it is developing financial and training links with transnational violent extremists.

The year 2012 was also notable in demonstrating a marked resurgence of Iran's state sponsorship of terrorism, through its Islamic Revolutionary Guard Corps-Qods Force (IRGC-QF), its Ministry of Intelligence and Security (MOIS), and Tehran's ally Hizballah. Iran and Hizballah's terrorist activity has reached a tempo unseen since the 1990s, with attacks plotted in Southeast Asia, Europe, and Africa. On February 5, 2013, the Bulgarian government publically implicated Hizballah in the July 2012 Burgas bombing that killed five Israelis and one Bulgarian citizen, and injured 32 others. On March 21, 2013, a Cyprus court found a Hizballah operative guilty of charges stemming from his surveillance activities, carried out in 2012, of Israeli tourist targets, while Thailand was prosecuting a Hizballah member for his role in helping plan a possible terrorist attack in that country. The IRGC-QF is suspected of directing planned terrorist attacks in Georgia, India, Thailand, and Kenya in 2012, and is also implicated in a 2011 plot to assassinate the Saudi ambassador to the United States in Washington, DC. And both Iran and Hizballah are providing a broad range of critical support to the Asad regime, as it continues its brutal crackdown against the Syrian people.

While terrorism from non-state actors related to AQ and state-sponsored terrorism originating in Iran remained the predominant concern of the United States, other forms of terrorism undermined peace and security around the world. In Turkey, the Kurdistan Workers' Party remained active in 2012. Anarchists in Greece and Italy launched periodic attacks, targeting private businesses, foreign missions, and symbols of the state. In Colombia, terrorist attacks occurred almost every day until the declaration of a unilateral cease-fire by the Revolutionary Armed Forces of Colombia in November. In Northern Ireland, dissident Republican groups continued their campaigns of violence. "Lone Wolf" violent extremists also remain a concern, as we saw in March 2012, when violent extremist gunman Mohammed Merah went on a multiday killing spree in Toulouse and Montauban, France. Seven people, including three children, lost their lives before he was killed by police.

Chapter 2.
Country Reports on Terrorism

AFRICA

In the Trans-Sahara region, al-Qa'ida in the Islamic Maghreb (AQIM) took advantage of a renewed Tuareg rebellion in northern Mali and a coup d'état in Bamako to overrun northern Mali by joining with violent extremist mercenary fighters returning from Libya in the wake of the revolution there. Alongside regional efforts to contain and marginalize AQIM and its allies in northern Mali, the international community urged Mali's interim government to restore an elected government to Mali, negotiate with groups in northern Mali that reject terrorism and accept Mali's territorial integrity, and respond to the humanitarian crisis.

Conflict in Nigeria continued throughout the northern part of the country, with hundreds of casualties as indigenous terrorist attacks increased. The Nigerian violent extremist group, Boko Haram, claimed responsibility for some of these attacks.

In East Africa, the Somalia-based terrorist group al-Shabaab remained the primary terrorist threat. Along with progress on government formation, Somalia saw significant progress in 2012 on security as Somali National Security Forces and the AU Mission in Somalia along with Ethiopian and allied Somali militia forces battled al-Shabaab and drove them out of many population strongholds in south-central Somalia. Most notably, Kenyan forces gained control of the port city of Kismayo in late September. Al-Shabaab continued to employ indirect assaults and asymmetric tactics in Somalia, as well as claim credit for some attacks in Kenya.

Various East African countries continued to enhance domestic and regional efforts to bolster border security; detect, deter, disrupt, investigate, and prosecute terrorist incidents; and create integrated and dedicated counterterrorism practitioners.

TRANS-SAHARA COUNTERTERRORISM PARTNERSHIP (TSCTP)

Established in 2005, the Trans-Sahara Counterterrorism Partnership (TSCTP) is a U.S.-funded and implemented multi-faceted, multi-year effort designed to counter violent extremism and contain and marginalize terrorist organizations. TSCTP's core goals are to enhance the indigenous capacities of governments in the pan-Sahel (Mauritania, Mali, Chad, Niger, Nigeria, Senegal, and Burkina Faso), to confront the challenge posed by terrorist organizations in the trans-Sahara, and to facilitate cooperation between those countries and U.S. partners in the Maghreb (Morocco, Algeria, and Tunisia).

TSCTP has been successful in building capacity and cooperation despite setbacks caused by coups d'état, ethnic rebellions, and extra-constitutional actions that have interrupted work and progress with select partner countries. For example, U.S. training and equipment have assisted Mauritania to monitor its border with Mali and sustain professional units during operations against AQIM, similarly, training and equipment have supported Niger's efforts to protect its borders and interdict terrorists attempting transit through its territory. Several TSCTP programs have worked to counter the pull of violent extremism on youth, including educational and training courses in Algeria and Morocco in the Maghreb, and extensive youth employment and outreach programs, community development and media activities in Niger and Chad.

In March 2012, assistance to Mali under TSCTP was suspended following a military coup that overthrew Mali's democratically elected government.

THE PARTNERSHIP FOR REGIONAL EAST AFRICAN COUNTERTERRORISM (PREACT)

PREACT, formerly known as the East Africa Regional Strategic Initiative, is the East Africa counterpart to the Trans-Sahara Counterterrorism Partnership (TSCTP). First established in 2009, PREACT is a U.S.-funded and implemented multi-year, multi-faceted program designed to build the counterterrorism capacity and capability of member countries to thwart short-term terrorist threats, counter violent extremism, and address longer-term vulnerabilities. It uses law enforcement, military, and development resources to achieve its strategic objectives, including reducing the operational capacity of terrorist networks, expanding border security, enhancing and institutionalizing cooperation among the region's security organizations, improving democratic governance, and discrediting terrorist ideology. PREACT member countries include Burundi, Comoros, Djibouti, Ethiopia, Kenya, Rwanda, Seychelles, Somalia, South Sudan, Sudan, Tanzania, and Uganda. In 2012, in concert with political developments in Somalia and elsewhere in the region, the U.S. government continued to help PREACT member countries to address near-term threats as well as build strategic counterterrorism capacities and bolster international counterterrorism cooperation.

BURKINA FASO

Overview: In 2012, the Government of Burkina Faso was vigilant and responsive to the threats and dangers posed by terrorist organizations, specifically al-Qa'ida in the Islamic Maghreb (AQIM). The government continued to stress that regional cooperation is imperative to combat and defeat terrorism. It proactively issued notices to the diplomatic community regarding the AQIM threat.

In recent years, the Government of Burkina Faso has been instrumental in securing the release of Western hostages from AQIM and other organizations in the region. In April and July, Burkinabe officials successfully negotiated three separate agreements to release hostages held by AQIM, Ansar al Dine, and the Movement for Unity and Jihad in West Africa (MUJAO). The first release, on April 17, was of an Italian citizen who had been held hostage for 14 months. The second release, on April 24, was of a Swiss hostage who had been kidnapped earlier in the month by a private militia, handed over to AQIM, and then transferred to Ansar al Dine. The third release, on July 19, included one Italian and two Spanish citizens who had been kidnapped by MUJAO in Algeria in October 2011. The Government of Burkina Faso did not release information to the public regarding the terms of these hostage releases.

These three cases highlighted earlier comments, made by the Minister of Foreign Affairs to reporters, that Burkina Faso had contacts to secure the release of Western hostages held by AQIM and other unidentified groups in the region. The Foreign Minister acknowledged that Burkina Faso has been spared so far from terrorist activities, but that the threat is real and Burkina Faso is not immune. In October 2012, Burkinabe President Blaise Compaore ordered the deployment of 1,000 combat troops to the northern region of the country bordering crisis-hit Mali, to guard against kidnappings.

While the Burkinabe government's counterterrorism capabilities remained limited, the continued delivery of U.S. training and equipment, as well as Burkina Faso's participation in regional counterterrorism conferences and training opportunities, were important benchmarks for 2012.

Legislation, Law Enforcement, and Border Security: Burkinabe prosecutors have not developed expertise in terrorism investigations due to the lack of substantive terrorism cases in the country. Prosecutors continued to be included in both bilateral and regional counterterrorism training opportunities to enhance their capacity and develop a rapport with the National Police and National Gendarmerie. Despite financial constraints, the Burkinabe government increased armed patrols in the capital and along the border in response to the crisis in Mali.

Burkina Faso received substantial training support for counterterrorism, intelligence, and border security issues through the International Law Enforcement Academy and the Antiterrorism Assistance (ATA) Program. More than 160 Burkinabe law enforcement officials attended and graduated from ATA courses in 2012. The primary beneficiaries of ATA training remained the National Police and National Gendarmerie. Customs, the Municipal Police of Ouagadougou, and criminal prosecutors also participated. The Burkinabe government, with the assistance of ATA training, developed and refined response plans for a kidnapping for ransom (KFR) operation.

In October, Burkina Faso agreed to implement and support the installation of the Terrorist Interdiction Program/Personal Identification Secure Comparison and Evaluation System (TIP/PISCES) at the International Airport of Ouagadougou.

Countering Terrorist Finance: Burkina Faso is a member of the Inter-Governmental Action Group against Money Laundering in West Africa, a Financial Action Task Force-style regional body. The Burkinabe Financial Intelligence Unit, CENTIF, collects and processes financial information on money laundering and terrorist financing. Since its 2008 inception, CENTIF has participated in an extensive training program on combating money laundering and terrorist financing. In 2012, CENTIF completed a research trip to Monaco and participated in training in St. Petersburg, Russia. The Burkinabe government continued to provide financial institutions with the names of UN-listed terrorist individuals and entities. There were no known terrorist financing prosecutions in 2012. For further information on money laundering and financial crimes, we refer you to the *2013 International Narcotics Control Strategy Report (INCSR), Volume 2, Money Laundering and Financial Crimes*: http://www.state.gov/j/inl/rls/nrcrpt/index.htm.

Regional and International Cooperation: Burkina Faso's continued participation in the Trans-Sahara Counterterrorism Partnership provided border training, two-way radios, and vehicles to Burkinabe gendarme units in the Mali-Niger-Burkina Faso tri-border area. Burkina Faso participated in the Global Counterterrorism Forum's Sahel Working Group. The Burkinabe government remained responsive to U.S. government requests for military and security assistance. It participated in regional and international counterterrorism conferences and training exercises, including with regard to KFR.

Countering Radicalization and Violent Extremism: The Burkinabe government encourages regular and ongoing interfaith dialogues as a way to mitigate violent extremism. Religious leaders regularly denounced violence and called for the peaceful coexistence of all religions.

BURUNDI

Overview: Burundi has shown an interest in addressing international terrorism and has contributed troops to the AU Mission in Somalia (AMISOM). A counterterrorism cell, formed in 2010, consists of elements of the police, military, and the National Intelligence Service. The cell's physical security recommendations have been put into operation but the cell has not yet implemented a comprehensive counterterrorism plan.

Legislation, Law Enforcement, and Border Security: Burundi has provisions in its penal code defining all forms of terrorism. Sentences for acts of terrorism range from 10 to 20 years or life imprisonment if the act results in the death of a person. Burundian law enforcement continued its participation in the Department of State's Antiterrorism Assistance program and the International Law Enforcement Academy.

Countering Terrorist Finance: Burundi is not considered a significant center for terrorist financing. The government has created counterterrorist financing laws but has yet to commit funding, provide training, or implement policies. Burundi is not a member of a Financial Action Task Force-style regional body. For further information on money laundering and financial crimes, we refer you to the *2013 International Narcotics Control Strategy Report (INCSR), Volume 2, Money Laundering and Financial Crimes*: http://www.state.gov/j/inl/rls/nrcrpt/index.htm.

Regional and International Cooperation: Burundi is a member of the Partnership for Regional East African Counterterrorism, and as such, has received funding for counterterrorism training. Burundi has cooperated with neighboring countries to exchange information on suspected terrorists. Burundi has also contributed troops to AMISOM to stabilize the situation in Somalia and to counter terrorism.

Countering Radicalization and Violent Extremism: The Burundian government does not have any formal programs to counter violent extremism. Several international organizations fund vocational training and economic development programs designed to provide positive alternatives for populations vulnerable to radicalization and recruitment into terrorist organizations.

CAMEROON

Overview: The Government of Cameroon considers counterterrorism a top security priority and worked with the United States to improve the capacity of its security forces. Cameroon's prospects for preventing terrorism also rested on the ability of the government to address humanitarian concerns in its northern regions (following a slow response to catastrophic flooding in September and October 2012) as well as socio-economic and political challenges such as widespread youth unemployment, poor transportation infrastructure, inadequate public service delivery, endemic corruption, and political marginalization.

Legislation, Law Enforcement, and Border Security: Cameroon does not have specific counterterrorism legislation, but rather relies on various provisions in its penal code to respond to possible terrorist acts. These include sanctions for efforts to undermine state authority, threats to public and individual safety, the destruction of property, threats to the safety of civil aviation and maritime navigation, hostage taking, and the regulation of firearms and explosive substances.

Cameroon participated in targeted U.S. capacity building projects to improve its counterterrorism and law enforcement capacities, including training in the areas of airport security, border control, cyber security and cyber crimes, fraudulent document detection, and small arms trafficking. Significant political will to counter terrorism exists in Cameroon, but efforts were hampered by corruption and a lack of coordination among Cameroonian law enforcement and security forces.

Countering Terrorist Finance: Cameroon is a member of the Central African Action Group against Money Laundering, an entity in the process of becoming a Financial Action Task Force (FATF)-style regional body. As a member of the Economic and Monetary Community of Central African States (CEMAC), Cameroon shares a regional Central Bank (Bank of the States of Central Africa) with other member countries that have ceded banking regulatory sovereignty to CEMAC. It established a financial intelligence unit, the National Financial Investigation Agency (ANIF), to process suspicious transaction reports and initiate investigations; ANIF is a member of the Egmont Group. No terrorist assets were identified, frozen, or confiscated in 2012. For further information on money laundering and financial crimes, we refer you to the *2013 International Narcotics Control Strategy Report (INCSR), Volume 2, Money Laundering and Financial Crimes*: http://www.state.gov/j/inl/rls/nrcrpt/index.htm.

Regional and International Cooperation: Cameroon is an active participant in the UN and has been supportive of UNGA resolutions related to terrorism. It is also active in counterterrorism-related activities in the AU and the Economic Community of Central African States.

Countering Radicalization and Violent Extremism: Cameroonian authorities have taken a series of measures to counter violent extremism, including forming partnerships with local, traditional, and religious leaders to monitor preaching in mosques; and participating in meetings with local administrative and religious officials.

CHAD

Overview: The Government of Chad was a strong counterterrorism partner in 2012. Countering terrorism threats in Chad was a priority at the highest levels of Chad's government, with a particular focus on countering potential terrorist threats from across the Sahel region. Special Operations Command Africa, through the Joint Special Operations Task Force-Trans-Sahara, maintained a Special Operations Forces Liaison Element in Chad to support Chadian counterterrorism forces with training and logistical support. This element worked primarily with the Chadian Special Anti-Terrorism Group, which has the mandate to conduct national security and counterterrorism operations with a specific focus on border security and interdiction of those trafficking in illicit goods.

Legislation, Law Enforcement, and Border Security: Chadian criminal law does not explicitly criminalize terrorism. However, certain general provisions of the Penal Code (1967) have been used to prosecute acts of terrorism.

Chad formed a joint border commission with Sudan to better control its eastern border. It also began talks with Niger and Libya to form a tripartite border commission, and with Cameroon and Nigeria to form a bilateral border commission.

Nearly all Chadian law enforcement agencies and officers were poorly resourced and under-trained, particularly in the areas of complex investigations and border security – especially along the Chari River, bordering Nigeria and Cameroon, and Lake Chad.

The United States provided Chad with training and technical assistance through the State Department's Anti-Terrorism Assistance program, ranging from the donation of forensic investigative equipment to courses such as Border Control Management. Chad worked on the implementation of a biometric screening program at N'Djamena Airport as part of the Terrorist Interdiction Program/Personal Identification Secure Comparison and Evaluation System.

Countering Terrorist Finance: Chad is a member of the Central African Action Group against Money Laundering, an entity in the process of becoming a Financial Action Task Force (FATF)-style regional body. As a member of the Economic and Monetary Community of Central African States (CEMAC), Chad shares a regional Central Bank (Bank of the States of Central Africa) with other member countries which have ceded banking regulatory sovereignty to CEMAC. Chad's Financial Intelligence Unit is the National Financial Investigative Agency (ANIF). ANIF is hindered by serious resource constraints, and law enforcement and customs officials need training in financial crimes enforcement.

Chad's financial systems are basic and largely informal. ANIF works directly with the few formal banks in Chad to prosecute money laundering cases; however, it is limited in its capacity to monitor the financial system effectively because of a low number of trained personnel to investigate and prosecute financial crimes. Funding sources of non-profit organizations are not subject to monitoring by ANIF. For further information on money laundering and financial crimes, we refer you to the *2013 International Narcotics Control Strategy Report (INCSR), Volume 2, Money Laundering and Financial Crimes*: http://www.state.gov/j/inl/rls/nrcrpt/index.htm.

Regional and International Cooperation: In May, Chad participated in the Global Counterterrorism Forum's (GCTF's) Sahel Region Capacity Building Working Group meeting in Niamey, Niger; and served on the committee that made recommendations to strengthen the capacity building of member states. Chad also attended GCTF conferences in Algiers, Algeria; Addis Ababa, Ethiopia; and Abuja, Nigeria. Chad's President, Idriss Déby, spoke out in favor of supporting the December 20 UNSCR authorizing the International Mission of Support in Mali and worked toward seeking National Assembly approval to deploy troops to assist Mali in military operations to regain territory lost to terrorist groups.

Countering Radicalization and Violent Extremism: As a member of the Trans-Sahara Counterterrorism Partnership, Chad participated in targeted projects to counter violent extremism. Specific activities have included building the capacity of civil society organizations;

community engagement and youth empowerment; promoting interfaith dialogue and religious tolerance; and media and outreach work. President Déby instructed the High Council for Islamic Affairs to closely monitor religious activities in mosques in order to counter violent extremism.

Every December 10 is celebrated as the day of Peace in Chad. Instituted in 2011, this Peace Day is intended to bring together Chadians from different religious groups to celebrate living in peace, as well as to raise awareness of the threat of violent extremism. In his address to the nation, President Déby regularly advocated for peaceful cohabitation of Chadians from different religious backgrounds.

DEMOCRATIC REPUBLIC OF THE CONGO

Overview: There was no credible evidence to indicate a significant presence of al-Qa'ida (AQ)-affiliated groups in the Democratic Republic of the Congo (DRC). The DRC is a vast country bordered by nine neighbors. The Government of the DRC lacked complete control over some areas of its territory, especially in the east where numerous armed groups operated with impunity and had very limited capacity to monitor and disrupt potential terrorist threats. Starting in April 2012, the rebellion of the newly formed M23 armed group in North Kivu against the Government of the DRC and the armed forces (FARDC) required the complete military and political attention of the government and the UN Organization Stabilization Mission in the DRC (MONUSCO), as FARDC and peacekeeping forces were redeployed in vast numbers to North Kivu. The resulting vacuum of authority and lack of security forces in areas not under M23 control allowed multiple other armed groups greater freedom of action to expand their territory and retake the offensive against traditional rivals in land disputes.

Counterterrorism was not a priority issue for the government. There were ongoing efforts by the International Conference of the Great Lakes Region (ICGLR), the AU, and the UN to bring stability to eastern DRC and the region. Steps to counter activities of the Democratic Forces for the Liberation of Rwanda (known by its French acronym, FDLR) were an element of these efforts.

The most active terrorist group in the DRC was the LRA, a rebel movement formed in Uganda in the late 1980s and early 1990s which continues to operate and find safe haven in the northeastern DRC along the border with South Sudan and the Central African Republic. The LRA's propensity for attacking civilians and using fear as a weapon prompted the State Department to designate the armed group as a Terrorist Exclusion List organization under section 212 of the Immigration and Nationality Act, as amended by the USA PATRIOT Act in 2001. By designating these groups, the Secretary strengthened the United States ability to exclude supporters of terrorism from the United States or to deport them if they are found within U.S. borders. In 2008, the U.S. Department of State designated Joseph Kony, the leader of the LRA, pursuant to Executive Order 13224, as a "Specially Designated Global Terrorist." Despite an ICC arrest warrant for crimes against humanity and U.S.-supported, regionally-led anti-LRA operations, Kony and much of his cadre remain at large in the DRC and the region. In 2012, most LRA activities were restricted to Orientale Province.

The ADF/NALU is made up of Ugandan opposition forces, and operates in North Kivu province. The Ugandan government asserts that the ADF/NALU constitutes an Islamist armed group with potential ties to AQ. However, these alleged links have not been substantiated. The ADF/NALU remained an active security threat to the population of North Kivu, in part due to the increased instability caused by the M23 rebellion. (M23 leadership had been sanctioned by the U.S. Department of Treasury for its abuses in the eastern DRC and its leader was wanted by the International Criminal Court.)

2012 Terrorist Incidents: The year witnessed 162 attacks by the LRA, FDLR, and ADF; 22 people were killed and 131 were abducted.

Legislation and Law Enforcement: The DRC has no comprehensive counterterrorism legislation, but a 2001 presidential decree established a National Committee for the Coordination of Anti-International Terrorism within a counterterrorism office in its Ministry of Interior. Yet, the DRC government has made statements indicating that denying safe haven to the LRA remains a matter of great importance. The DRC government has supported international efforts to eradicate the LRA in the DRC, and made some progress on its border security management program. In collaboration with the Organization for International Migration (IOM), the Government of the DRC established national and provincial oversight committees to further develop the program's implementation. The Congolese National Police was equipped with biometrics, and the Director General of Migration established a personal identification and recognition system, developed by IOM, that was used at eight strategic border posts.

Additionally, the United States has worked with the FARDC and the Ugandan People's Defense Forces to bolster regional capacity for anti-LRA operations.

Countering Terrorist Finance: The DRC has anti-money laundering/combating the financing of terrorism legislation and a Financial Intelligence Unit (CENAREF). The DRC is not a member of any Financial Action Task Force-style regional bodies. There were no legal restrictions in the DRC prohibiting the sharing of financial account information with foreign entities. CENAREF occasionally shared information with the United States on money laundering and terrorist financing cases, and in 2012 expressed interest in signing a memo of understanding with the Financial Crimes Enforcement Network, FINCEN, to increase bilateral cooperation. In 2011, the DRC signed a mutual assistance agreement with Belgium's CTIF (Cellule des Traitements des Informations Financières). At year's end, CENAREF had received 157 suspicious transaction reports, including 29 reports from banks and other financial institutions and eight from several DRC government agencies, including the National Intelligence Agency (ANR). In 2012, the Government of the DRC had one money laundering prosecution underway, but no convictions. For further information on money laundering and financial crimes, we refer you to the *2013 International Narcotics Control Strategy Report (INCSR), Volume 2, Money Laundering and Financial Crimes*: http://www.state.gov/j/inl/rls/nrcrpt/index.htm.

Regional and International Cooperation: The FDLR and LRA threats have a regional impact on security. Affected countries have cooperated in the past to counter the threat and ensure regional stability. The Government of the DRC continued to cooperate with neighboring states, especially the Central African Republic, South Sudan, and Uganda under the African Union Regional Task Force framework. The DRC government provided some limited support to UN efforts against the LRA.

The DRC is a member of numerous regional organizations and has diverse cooperation agreements – with the South African Development Community, the Economic Community of the

Great Lakes Countries, and the Economic Community of Central Africa – to exchange information and enhance border security. The DRC is a member of the International Conference of the Great Lakes Region and will head this organization for the next five years.

DJIBOUTI

Overview: Djibouti remained an active and cooperative counterterrorism partner. Increased training for police and military members and deploying soldiers to the AU Mission in Somalia (AMISOM) campaign was the focus of Djibouti's 2012 efforts to counter terrorism.

Legislation, Law Enforcement, and Border Security: Due to its geographic location and porous borders, counterterrorism remained a high priority for all Djiboutian law enforcement entities. Djibouti tries terrorists in criminal courts using its penal code, but in 2012, its legislature was in the process of adapting its existing laws to reflect the current terrorist threat. Djibouti's most visible counterterrorism efforts were *ad hoc* checkpoints within the capital city and an increased emphasis at border control points to screen for potential security threats.

Djibouti continued to process travelers on entry and departure at its international airport and seaport with the Personal Identification Secure Comparison Evaluation System (PISCES). Djibouti has not fully implemented the PISCES fingerprinting collection feature, however. While the airport and seaport are important entry points, the vast majority of travelers cross into Djibouti by land at one of three land border points, including one point on the border with Somalia. Djibouti regularly issued passports to non-citizen Somalis with close personal or business relationships to the Djiboutian government, as well as to residents of Somalia with no legal claim to Djiboutian citizenship.

Djibouti received significant counterterrorism training and equipment provided by the United States through a variety of courses and programs.

Countering Terrorist Finance: The Central Bank of Djibouti houses a Financial Intelligence Unit (FIU), known as the Fraud Investigation Unit. Given its very limited resources including lack of staff, however, it is focusing on outreach to the private sector but is unable to perform the core functions of an FIU. For further information on money laundering and financial crimes, we refer you to the *2013 International Narcotics Control Strategy Report (INCSR), Volume 2, Money Laundering and Financial Crimes*: http://www.state.gov/j/inl/rls/nrcrpt/index.htm.

Regional and International Cooperation: Djibouti is a member of the AU and has deployed troops to AMISOM. Djibouti has been supportive of UNGA resolutions related to terrorism. Djibouti hosts Camp Lemonnier, the largest U.S. military presence in Africa, which serves as headquarters to approximately 4,000 U.S. troops, including those serving with the U.S. Africa Command's Combined Joint Task Force-Horn of Africa.

Countering Radicalization and Violent Extremism: Most of the Government of Djibouti's strategic communications efforts focused on youth, a group widely-recognized as susceptible to violent extremism. In response to a growing youth violence problem, members of Parliament and representatives from the Ministry of Islamic Affairs held monthly meetings in Djibouti's low-income neighborhoods. The Ministry of Youth and Sports organized sports leagues to engage youth in positive activities. In addition, the Government of Djibouti approves themes for Friday prayer services to ensure the sermons do not incite to violence.

ERITREA

Overview: There was limited dialogue between Eritrea and the United States regarding terrorism in 2012. The Government of Eritrea stressed that it wanted to be a partner in international counterterrorism efforts, and it cooperated in providing over-flight clearance to U.S. military aircraft engaged in regional security missions.

Still, its poor relations with surrounding nations, potential African partners, and the United States reduced opportunities for cooperation. Lack of transparency on how governing structures function meant that there is not a clear picture of methods the government used to track terrorists or maintain safeguards for its citizens. For a number of years, members of the police have refused to meet with security officials of western nations, closing off opportunities for information-sharing and dialogue. The Eritrean government's national doctrine of self-reliance and disinclination to accept international assistance prevented the United States from providing training, technology, or other counterterrorism assistance.

In May, the United States re-certified Eritrea as "not cooperating fully" with U.S. counterterrorism efforts under Section 40A of the Arms Export and Control Act, as amended. In considering this annual determination, the Department of State reviewed Eritrea's overall level of cooperation with U.S. efforts to combat terrorism, taking into account U.S. counterterrorism objectives and a realistic assessment of Eritrean capabilities.

Eritrea has been under UNSC sanctions since December 2009. UNSCR 1907 imposed an arms embargo on Eritrea and a travel ban and asset freeze on some military and political leaders, calling on the nation to "cease arming, training and equipping armed groups and their members, including al-Shabaab, that aim to destabilize the region." In December 2011, UNSCR 2023 was adopted, strengthening the provisions of the earlier resolution and establishing guidelines for use of the "diaspora tax" that the government levies on Eritreans living overseas.

Legislation, Law Enforcement, and Border Security: The Government of Eritrea closely monitors passenger manifests for any flights coming into Asmara, and scrutinizes travel documents of visitors, but does not take fingerprints. The government did not share information gathered at ports of entry with the United States. Eritrea's borders with Ethiopia and Djibouti are tightly controlled, whereas the border with Sudan is porous in some places, resulting in considerable movement across by persons who are not recorded as coming or going.

As U.S. relations with Eritrean law enforcement entities were extremely limited, we do not know what capabilities the Eritrean government had in terms of special response units. In September, however, the Eritrean government cooperated effectively with the Embassy, Federal Bureau of Investigation, and Department of Justice in denying a work permit to a third-country national suspected of terrorist affiliation.

In 2011, the government ceased providing police protection to diplomatic missions, claiming Asmara to be safe. The Embassy periodically requested and received extra police for special events, however, but the numbers deployed were usually small. On occasion the police asked for transportation, fuel, or extra pay.

Countering Terrorist Finance: Eritrea is not a member of any Financial Action Task Force-style regional body. Eritrea's general lack of transparency on banking, financial, and economic matters made gathering of definitive information difficult. Eritrea does not adhere to international standards for monitoring or regulation of remittance services. It extensively monitored remittances and money transfers of the Eritrean diaspora, members of whom are required to pay a two per cent foreign income tax to the government to receive passport and other services, and it extensively monitored transfers of money out of the nation to ensure than an artificially high exchange rate is not undercut by black market exchanges. Eritrea does require the collection of data for wire transfers; however, this is more for tracking the "Diaspora Tax" and hard currency outflows than for counterterrorism. For further information on money laundering and financial crimes, we refer you to the *2013 International Narcotics Control Strategy Report (INCSR), Volume 2, Money Laundering and Financial Crimes*: http://www.state.gov/j/inl/rls/nrcrpt/index.htm.

Regional and International Cooperation: Eritrea is a member of the AU, and would like to reactivate its membership in the Intergovernmental Authority on Development in Eastern Africa, but this is opposed by Ethiopia and host nation Djibouti, both of whom have had military conflicts with Eritrea in recent years. Eritrea's relationship with the UN (particularly the UNSC's Somalia/Eritrea Sanctions Committee) is antagonistic, as Eritrea resents being placed under economic and other sanctions. Eritrean government officials regularly accused the Somalia/Eritrea Monitoring Group of bias and inadequacy.

ETHIOPIA

Overview: The Government of Ethiopia's counterterrorism cooperation with the United States included military, intelligence, and security aspects. The Ethiopian government viewed instability in Somalia as a critical national security threat and maintained a defensive military presence along the Somali border to stem potential infiltration of violent extremists into Ethiopia.

Ethiopian military forces continued counterterrorism operations in Somalia and were instrumental in combating al-Shabaab in southern and central Somalia. Within Ethiopia's borders, the Ethiopian government successfully identified an al-Qa'ida (AQ) cell, and then arrested and convicted cell affiliates. The government remained concerned about groups such as the Ogaden National Liberation Front (ONLF), Oromo Liberation Front, and Ginbot 7, which its parliament designated as terrorist groups in 2011.

2012 Terrorist Incidents: In January, five European tourists were killed and two were kidnapped by the Afar Revolutionary Democratic Unit Front (ARDUF), a violent extremist group the Ethiopian government claimed was backed by Eritrea. In retaliation, the Ethiopian military made incursions into Eritrea in March to target "subversive groups," including ARDUF, and a military base. In April, an attack by armed gunmen on a farm operated by Saudi Star Development in the Gambella region killed at least five people. The Government of Ethiopia regarded the January attack on tourists and the April attack on the Saudi Star compound as terrorist attacks.

Legislation, Law Enforcement, and Border Security: Ethiopia's National Intelligence and Security Service (NISS) has broad authority for intelligence, border security, and criminal investigation and is responsible for overall counterterrorism management. The Ethiopian Federal Police worked in conjunction with the NISS on counterterrorism. Ethiopia continued to use the Personal Identification Secure Comparison and Evaluation System, PISCES, biometric security measures at immigration enforcement stations at Bole and Dire Dawa International Airports, as well as other points of entry throughout the country.

In February, the Government of Ethiopia announced that it had arrested eight AQ operatives in the Bale area of the Oromia Region in December 2011. Those arrested had links to Kenya, Sudan, the Philippines, Saudi Arabia, and South Africa. A verdict in the trial of self-confessed cell leader Hassan Jarso – a Kenyan national – and other cell members, had not been reached by year's end.

The Government of Ethiopia convicted 46 people, 24 of whom were tried in absentia, under its 2009 Anti-Terrorism Proclamation, including an 11-person AQ cell and three members of the ONLF.

Also among those convicted were 12 journalists, opposition political figures, and activists whose trials were deemed by several international human rights organizations and foreign diplomatic missions to be politically motivated and based on evidence indicative of acts of a political nature rather than linked to terrorism. The government also invoked the Anti-Terrorism Proclamation in charging 28 Muslims in connection with protests that alleged government interference in religious affairs, and accused one Muslim of accepting funds illegally from a foreign embassy.

Countering Terrorist Finance: Ethiopia is not a member of a Financial Action Task Force-style regional body (FSRB), but is an observer to the Eastern and Southern Africa Anti-Money Laundering Group, an FSRB, which it hopes to become a member of in 2013. The Ethiopian government froze assets allegedly used in planning terrorist acts, pending investigation as to whether those assets can be legally confiscated. The Government of Ethiopia's Charities and Societies Agency is responsible for monitoring non-profit organizations to prevent misuse of funds and terrorist financing. NGOs were monitored, but the Ethiopian government has limited expertise in the area of terrorist financing. The Government of Ethiopia routinely distributed the UN list of designated terrorists and terrorist entities to financial institutions. For further information on money laundering and financial crimes, we refer you to the *2013 International Narcotics Control Strategy Report (INCSR), Volume 2, Money Laundering and Financial Crimes*: http://www.state.gov/j/inl/rls/nrcrpt/index.htm.

Regional and International Cooperation: Ethiopia is a member state of the Inter-Governmental Authority on Development and participated actively in its Security Sector Program, which builds the capacity of its member states to mitigate, detect, and deter advances by terrorists. Ethiopia was an active participant in the AU's counterterrorism efforts and participated in its Center for Study and Research on Terrorism and in meetings of the Committee of Intelligence and Security Services of Africa.

Countering Radicalization and Violent Extremism: The Ethiopian government and the Ethiopian Islamic Affairs Supreme Council continued to implement a controversial training program for Muslims on the subject of violent extremism; the program led to ongoing protests by some members of the Muslim community who alleged government interference in religious affairs.

KENYA

Overview: 2012 was a significant year for Kenyan counterterrorism efforts. Despite Somali refugee issues, preparation for 2013 national elections, the threat of al-Shabaab, and ethnic, political, and economic tensions, the Kenyan government demonstrated persistent political will to secure its borders, apprehend terrorists, and cooperate in regional and international counterterrorism efforts. Notably, a decade of debate culminated in the long-awaited passage of Kenya's Prevention of Terrorism Act. At home, Kenyan authorities successfully disrupted several large-scale terrorist plots, though small-scale terrorist incidents continued, especially in North Eastern Province, but also in Nairobi and Mombasa. Abroad, Kenyan military operations against al-Shabaab, initially independent and later under the auspices of the AU Mission in Somalia, resulted in the capture of the key port city of Kismayo, al-Shabaab's last major stronghold.

2012 Terrorist Incidents: More than three dozen presumed terrorist incidents were reported in Kenya during 2012 – mostly grenade attacks – that the Kenyan government generally attributed to al-Shabaab or its supporters, though few were formally claimed by any terrorist group and several were specifically denied. The number and severity of attacks in the Dadaab refugee camp decreased, but attacks on police and civilians in the nearby city of Garissa increased, including a July 1 church attack with guns and grenades that left 17 dead and 40 injured. Deadly grenade and improvised explosive device attacks in Nairobi targeted bars, restaurants, churches, a bus station, and a mosque, hitting the predominantly Somali district of Eastleigh especially hard. A November 18 minibus explosion in Eastleigh left 10 dead and 34 injured. Total reported casualties from possible terrorists incidents were 34 dead and over 145 injured, though many of the incidents remained unattributed.

Legislation, Law Enforcement, and Border Security: Kenya's Prevention of Terrorism Act, passed by Parliament in September and signed into law by President Kibaki in October, marked a key legislative milestone in the fight against terrorism. Combined with the 2009 Proceeds of Crime and Anti-Money Laundering Act and the 2010 Prevention of Organized Crime Act, Kenyan prosecutors have a robust suite of tools for bringing individuals and organizations to justice, tools which will also greatly facilitate international cooperation and mutual legal assistance in terrorism cases. Even prior to the passage of the new law, Kenyan authorities began prosecution of two ongoing high-profile terrorist cases against Iranian citizens and alleged Islamic Revolutionary Guard Corps-Qods Forces persons Ahmad Abolfathi and Sayed Mansouri on explosives charges, and against British citizen Jermaine Grant on charges of plotting to kill Western tourists on behalf of al-Qa'ida.

Kenya was an active law enforcement partner and participated in the Department of State's Antiterrorism Assistance (ATA) program. ATA programs focused on strengthening border security, enhancing investigative capacity, promoting respect for human rights, and building critical incident response capacity through training, mentoring, advising and equipping Kenyan counterterrorism-focused law-enforcement agencies. Kenya also continued its partnership with the United States on expanding Personal Identification Secure Comparison and Evaluation System, PISCES, border controls to additional ports of entry.

Countering Terrorist Finance: Kenya is a member of the Eastern and Southern Africa Anti-Money Laundering Group, a Financial Action Task Force (FATF)-style regional body. The FATF had previously highlighted the deficiencies in Kenya's anti-money laundering/combating the financing of terrorism regime and intimated possible countermeasures against Kenya. In response, Kenyan authorities developed and made significant progress on an action plan to address those deficiencies, including the establishment of the Financial Reporting Center (FRC) in April and adoption of the Prevention of Terrorism Act (POTA) in October.

By December, the FRC was up and running with investigators receiving and reviewing suspicious transaction reports and investigating potential money laundering violations. The establishment of the FRC combined with the passage of the POTA demonstrated a strong enough commitment on the part of the Kenyan government that FATF did not invoke countermeasures. Nonetheless, FATF emphasized, and Kenyan authorities acknowledged, that Kenya still has much work to do on its Action Plan with the FATF, most notably in developing the institutional capacity and regulatory structures to implement the POTA as well as track, seize, and confiscate the assets of al-Shabaab and other terrorist groups. FATF has also identified some concerns with the new law. For further information on money laundering and financial crimes, we refer you to the *2013 International Narcotics Control Strategy Report (INCSR), Volume 2, Money Laundering and Financial Crimes*: http://www.state.gov/j/inl/rls/nrcrpt/index.htm.

Regional and International Cooperation: Kenya is a member of the AU, the Inter-Governmental Authority on Development, the Community of Eastern and Southern Africa, and the East African Community. The Kenyan government coordinated with these groups significantly during its military campaign against al-Shabaab militants in Somalia. Kenyan law enforcement agencies worked closely with the international community, including the United States, to increase their counterterrorism abilities, secure porous land borders, and improve maritime security. Kenya hosted numerous trainings involving law enforcement professionals from neighboring nations to build counterterrorism capacities and increase regional cooperation. Kenya also cooperated with the United States and other nations to secure especially dangerous pathogens and enhance the Kenyan government's capability to prevent the sale, theft, diversion, or accidental release of chemical, biological or radiological weapons-related materials, technology, and expertise.

MALI

Overview: Following the March 2012 coup that toppled the elected government of President Amadou Toumani Touré, northern Mali – representing 10 percent of Mali's population and over half of its territory – was taken over by terrorist groups including al-Qa'ida in the Islamic Maghreb (AQIM), the Movement for Unity and Jihad in West Africa (MUJAO), and Ansar al-Dine (AAD). The interim Government of Mali requested international support to reunite the country and combat the terrorist threat. At year's end, the UN, the AU, and the Economic Community of West African States (ECOWAS) were working with the United States and European partners to prepare and conduct a Malian-led and ECOWAS-supported military action to recapture the north and combat terrorist groups.

Consistent with the legislative restriction on assistance to the government of a country whose duly elected head of government is deposed by military coup d'état, all U.S. assistance to the

Government of Mali, including military and security assistance, was terminated following the coup.

2012 Terrorist Incidents: During the year, AQIM, MUJAO, and AAD captured the entire northern half of Mali, including the towns of Timbuktu, Gao, and Kidal. AAD destroyed UNESCO World Heritage sites, including sacred Sufi shrines in Timbuktu, and enforced a severe form of Sharia law, cutting off the hand of an alleged cattle thief and stoning to death an unmarried couple with two children. Other terrorist incidents included:

- On April 5, seven Algerian diplomats were kidnapped by MUJAO from their post in Gao. At least four members of the group were being held at year's end; two of the hostages had been released, and one died in custody.
- On October 14, MUJAO kidnapped six African aid workers in Niger and transported them to Mali. MUJAO had allegedly been targeting an Italian anthropologist working for the NGO Doctors without Borders in the region. Five Nigerien nationals were released at the Mali-Niger border on November 3, but the sixth victim, a Chadian national, died from his wounds.
- On November 20, a French tourist was kidnapped by MUJAO in Diema, a town in northwestern Mali, as he traveled to Bamako.
- In addition to these kidnapping victims, at year's end MUJAO and AQIM held nine other people hostage in northern Mali from kidnapping operations conducted in previous years.

Legislation, Law Enforcement, and Border Security: Malian law enforcement arrested a number of alleged terrorists, both Malian and foreign, who were suspected of trying to join northern armed groups. Some were cases of mistaken identity, such as two al-Jazeera journalists arrested on December 1, who were later released. There were no successful prosecutions as a result of these arrests.

Countering Terrorist Finance: Mali is a member of the Inter-Governmental Action Group against Money Laundering in West Africa, a Financial Action Task Force-style regional body. Mali's Financial Intelligence Unit is the National Center for the Treatment of Financial Information (CENTIF). In 2012, the director of the CENTIF received training on asset freezing, while the magistrate assigned to the CENTIF received training on prosecution-related issues. CENTIF is authorized by law to freeze assets for a maximum of 48 hours while conducting an investigation. The 48-hour period can be extended, but only by a magistrate. The main impediments to improving the Malian law enforcement response to terrorist finance were a lack of coordination between CENTIF and the law enforcement community, as well as insufficient judicial capacity to transform CENTIF investigations into effective prosecutions.

Mali's capacity and will to freeze and confiscate assets remains unclear. Mali has yet to identify or freeze any assets under Malian jurisdiction of UN-designated terrorist individuals or entities. For further information on money laundering and financial crimes, we refer you to the *2013 International Narcotics Control Strategy Report (INCSR), Volume 2, Money Laundering and Financial Crimes*: http://www.state.gov/j/inl/rls/nrcrpt/index.htm.

Regional and International Cooperation: In the aftermath of the coup d'état, Mali was suspended from regional bodies such as ECOWAS and the AU, but was reinstated into the AU in October. Mali has been a member of the Combined Operational General Staff Committee

(CEMOC), based in Tamanrasset, Algeria, since CEMOC's creation in 2010. An AU/ECOWAS sponsored military training mission has been planned cooperatively with members of the Malian Armed Forces Chiefs of Staff.

Countering Radicalization and Violent Extremism: Malian officials and prominent religious leaders routinely condemned violent extremist ideology and terrorist acts. As a general matter, violent extremist ideologies have not found a receptive audience among Malians.

MAURITANIA

Overview: The Government of Mauritania continued to take a firm stance against terrorism. Regional events have caused President Mohamed Ould Abdel Aziz to shift the military's focus from offensive operations to border security and protection of the homeland. Al-Qa'ida in the Islamic Maghreb remained a threat. However, Mauritania applied effective measures to counter terrorist activity, enhancing initiatives launched in 2011.

During a national press conference on November 29, President Aziz confirmed the readiness of the armed forces to react to terrorists approaching Mauritanian territory and announced the construction of a new airbase at Limreye, in the heart of the desert some 500 miles east of Nouakchott. President Aziz has used his public addresses to explain Mauritania's past forays into northern Mali as a response to terrorist attacks on Mauritanian soil, which targeted Mauritanian citizens and their interests. President Aziz has excluded Mauritania's participation in an international military intervention in northern Mali, but has vowed to respond swiftly and strongly to any threat to the safety of Mauritanian citizens or foreign residents in Mauritania.

Under the framework of the Trans-Sahara Counterterrorism Partnership, U.S. training for specialized Mauritanian counterterrorism battalions continued. Mauritania also participated in the Department of State's Antiterrorism Assistance program, which strengthened Mauritania's counterterrorism capacity by providing training and equipment to the national police, gendarmerie, and civil aviation agency. Mauritania's enthusiastic reception of U.S. AFRICOM Commander General Carter Ham during his September 26-27 visit highlights the two countries' bilateral partnership.

Legislation, Law Enforcement, and Border Security: Mauritania continued to arrest, prosecute, and convict terrorists. The Mauritanian judiciary convicted four individuals for terrorism-related offenses in 2012.

- On March 10, Mauritania's state news agency confirmed the release of a gendarme who had been abducted by terrorists in December 2011 from his post in Adel Bagrou (1700 kilometers southeast of Nouakchott). President Aziz said that the armed forces also carried out raids on the terrorists involved in the kidnapping.
- On April 4, Mauritanian police took former al-Qa'ida member, Mauritanian Mahfoudh Ould Waled, also known as Abu Hafs, into custody upon his arrival at Nouakchott International Airport. Waled had returned to Mauritania from Iran, where he had been detained since 2002, after having fled Afghanistan. After questioning him, the Mauritanian authorities did not deem Waled a threat and released him on July 5.
- In May, an appeals court affirmed the convictions and sentences of the three terrorists responsible for the 2009 murder of an American citizen in Nouakchott. Though one of

the terrorists received the death penalty, the government had appealed the other two original sentences, which it considered too lenient, seeking 30 years for the defendant who had received a 12-year sentence and 15 years for the defendant previously sentenced to three years. On September 27, the authorities released one of the defendants, Mohamed Ould Ghadda, after he completed his three-year prison sentence.

- In November, local and international media reported that Mauritania's security services arrested a French national in Nema (1200 kilometers southeast of Nouakchott) suspected of attempting to engage in terrorist activity in Timbuktu.

Countering Terrorist Finance: Mauritania is a member of the Middle East and North Africa Financial Action Task Force, a Financial Action Task Force-style regional body, and has observer status with the Inter-Governmental Action Group against Money Laundering in West Africa. Mauritania's Financial Intelligence Unit, known by its French acronym CANIF, collaborated with the UN Office on Drugs and Crime on anti-money laundering/combating the financing of terrorism training. Although there is legislation regulating alternative remittances, Mauritania did not have the resources to monitor the sizable flow of funds through money and value transfer systems, most notably *hawala*, nor did the government consider it a priority. For further information on money laundering and financial crimes, we refer you to the *2013 International Narcotics Control Strategy Report (INCSR), Volume 2, Money Laundering and Financial Crimes*: http://www.state.gov/j/inl/rls/nrcrpt/index.htm.

Regional and International Cooperation: Mauritania continued its strong engagement with international and regional partners, taking a leadership role in multilateral fora, particularly the 5+5 Initiative, and facilitated greater cooperation on security issues through regional meetings in Nouakchott. On February 18, the Arab Maghreb Union, which consists of Mauritania, Algeria, Tunisia, Morocco, and Libya, selected Mauritania as co-president of the foreign affairs committee of the 5+5 Initiative focused on regional security challenges for countries in the Mediterranean (Mauritania, Algeria, Tunisia, Morocco, Libya, Italy, France, Spain, Portugal, and Malta). Mauritania's Defense Minister Ahmedou Ould Mohamed Radhi called for an end to paying ransoms for hostages at a 2011 meeting of 5+5 Defense Ministers. President Aziz attended the 5+5 October 4, 2012 conference for heads of state in Malta.

On January 23 and April 8, the Foreign Ministers of the field countries, known as the *pays du champ* (Mauritania, Algeria, Mali, and Niger), met in Nouakchott to discuss regional responses to the instability in Mali. On July 11, the chiefs of staff of the armed forces of these countries represented in the Committee of Joint Operational Staff gathered in Nouakchott to focus on the terrorist threat in northern Mali.

Countering Radicalization and Violent Extremism: The Government of Mauritania continued to collaborate with independent Muslim religious organizations to promote moderation and to counter violent extremism. The Ministry of Islamic Affairs and Traditional Education and the International Wasatiyya (Centrist) Forum co-sponsored a January conference on "Reformist Thought and Banishment of Violent Discourse." In March and April, the Ministry of Islamic Affairs and Traditional Education organized a series of training seminars for 170 imams across the country, in cooperation with the independent Union of Imams group. The training focused on Islam's role in society, the danger of violent Islamist extremism, and the unity of rite in a harmonious society.

On September 24, Arab Maghreb Union Ministers of Islamic Affairs opened a two-day meeting in Nouakchott to discuss the role of Sunni Islam in promoting tolerance and moderation. The conference's theme was the creation of a unified strategy to counter violent extremism and terrorism "perpetrated under the label of Islam." After a meeting with President Aziz on the margins of the event, Libyan Minister of Religious Affairs, Hamza Abul Fariss, declared that the five countries decided to create a new TV channel with the goal of presenting "the real moderate and tolerant image of Islam."

The government also continued to broadcast a state-sponsored Quranic radio station and sponsored regular TV programming on themes of moderation in Islam. On July 23, the government announced the recruitment of 300 moderate imams, bringing the total number to 800.

NIGER

Overview: Al-Qa'ida in the Islamic Maghreb (AQIM) and other terrorist organizations were able to operate within undergoverned spaces in Nigerien territory, in particular the border areas with Libya, Algeria, and Mali. Porous borders and the huge expanse of Niger that lacks a permanent government presence provided terrorist groups with an environment conducive to recruiting, contraband smuggling, and kidnapping. Arms from Libya, including heavy weapons, have been trafficked into and through Niger, despite the government's efforts to disarm mercenaries of the former regime of Muammar Qadhafi.

Historic tensions with Tuareg rebel groups, traditionally associated with cross-Sahara smuggling in northern Niger, contributed to the potential establishment of a breeding ground for future terrorists, as limited job opportunities for former rebels and returnees from Libya may provide recruits. Niger was fully engaged in preparations to participate in military intervention against terrorist groups in northern Mali under the aegis of the Economic Community of West African States (ECOWAS), of which it is a member. Niger also continued its counterterrorism cooperation with other regional partners and organizations.

The presence of the violent extremist group Boko Haram (BH) in northern Nigeria, just across Niger's southern border, posed a threat – BH members have been arrested inside Niger. The Government of Niger is committed to fighting AQIM and BH, but needs and welcomes external support and greater regional cooperation. The United States significantly increased its counterterrorism cooperation with Niger in 2012. U.S. Army personnel executed five separate training events with Nigerien Army forces in Tillia, Arlit, Dirkou, and Diffa.

Niger took delivery of base radio stations, personnel protective gear, vehicle fuel, and Global Positioning System devices. In addition, over 150 Nigerien law enforcement and security forces received five Antiterrorism Assistance training courses and other training opportunities. Topics included joint terrorism task force operations, forensics, preventing attacks on soft targets, Critical Response Team Operations, and respect for human rights. Regional Security Initiative and MANPADS funding provided equipment including 4x4 pickup trucks, motorcycles, computers, and other items.

2012 Terrorist Incidents: Incidents included:

- On August 7, Nigerien Armed Forces engaged in a firefight against members of the Movement for Unity and Jihad in West Africa (MUJAO) in the Tillabery region of Niger (near the Mali border).
- On October 14, MUJAO kidnapped six aid workers, five Nigeriens, and one Chadian from a guest house in the town of Dakoro, Maradi region. The Chadian was fatally wounded during the abduction. MUJAO took the Nigeriens to Gao, Mali, before releasing them on November 3.

Legislation, Law Enforcement, and Border Security: Diori Hamani International Airport in Niamey began biometric screening for passengers, using the Personal Identification Secure Comparison and Evaluation System (PISCES) border security system. In response to events in Mali, Niger increased its security forces along its borders with Mali, Algeria, and Libya. It selected over 500 troops to receive training in preparation for deployment as part of an ECOWAS intervention force in Mali.

The Counterterrorism Center in Niamey made several arrests of Boko Haram suspects on charges that included planning acts of terrorism, recruitment, and finance.

Countering Terrorist Finance: Niger is a member of the Inter-Governmental Action Group against Money Laundering in West Africa, a Financial Action Task Force-style regional body. Niger's financial intelligence unit, known by its French acronym, CENTIF, was fully operational with an active new chairman and a substantial increase in its budget. In 2012, CENTIF carried out a number of awareness-raising activities for reporting entities, but had yet to receive any suspicious transaction reports on the financing of terrorism. For further information on money laundering and financial crimes, we refer you to the *2013 International Narcotics Control Strategy Report (INCSR), Volume 2, Money Laundering and Financial Crimes*: http://www.state.gov/j/inl/rls/nrcrpt/index.htm.

Regional and International Cooperation: Niger continued to work with Mali, Algeria, and Mauritania through the Algerian-led counterterrorism center, the General Staff Joint Operations Committee (CEMOC) in Tamanrasset, Algeria. In May, Niger hosted a meeting of the Global Counterterrorism Forum Working Group on Border Security in the Sahel. In October, Niger signed a security agreement with Nigeria to include joint border patrols aimed at fighting BH. In August, the EU deployed a 50-person team to Niger to build capacity in fighting terrorism and other organized crime. Niger continued to permit French forces to be based in Niamey to conduct surveillance operations.

Countering Radicalization and Violent Extremism: Government-led initiatives to provide employment, especially to returnees from Libya, have sought to counter radicalization and violent extremism. In November, Niger held a conference to discuss strategic communication to combat terrorism. Niger did not have programs to reintegrate or rehabilitate former terrorists, but the Office of the National Mediator has spearheaded efforts for prison de-radicalization.

NIGERIA

Overview: The militant sect "People Committed to the Propagation of the Prophet's Teachings and Jihad," better known by its Hausa name Boko Haram (BH), conducted killings, bombings, kidnappings, and other attacks in Nigeria, resulting in numerous deaths, injuries, and the widespread destruction of property in 2012. The states where attacks occurred more frequently included Adamawa, Bauchi, Borno, Gombe, Kaduna, Kano, Kogi, Plateau, Taraba, and Yobe, as well as the Federal Capital Territory. No terrorist attacks occurred in the southern states of Nigeria. Suspected BH attackers killed Nigerian government and security officials, Muslim and Christian clerics, journalists, and civilians. Of particular concern to the United States is the emergence of the BH faction known as "Ansaru," which has close ties to AQIM and has prioritized targeting Westerners – including Americans – in Nigeria.

President Goodluck Jonathan appointed a new National Security Adviser (NSA) in June, with the mandate to improve the Nigerian government's coordination, communication, and cooperation on counterterrorism matters, both domestically and internationally. Most operations to counter BH were headed up by the military-led Joint Task Force, some members and units of which committed indiscriminate and extrajudicial use of force, including killings of civilians and BH suspects. The Nigerian government's efforts to address grievances among Northern populations, which include high unemployment and a dearth of basic services, continued to fail, as did the security forces' efforts to contain BH. The United States called on the Nigerian government to employ a comprehensive security strategy that is not predicated on the use of force, and that also addresses the economic and political exclusion of vulnerable communities in the north.

Nigerian-U.S. counterterrorism cooperation continued in 2012. In practice, the NSA retained the lead as coordinator of the Nigerian government's counterterrorism strategy. In November, the Nigerian government formally requested assistance from the United States to develop an intelligence fusion center that would be able to streamline coordination and information sharing on counterterrorism matters among key agencies, including the State Security Service (SSS), the intelligence agencies, the national police, and the military. An inaugural working group to develop Nigeria's intelligence fusion capability, composed of Embassy officials and staff of the Office of the National Security Adviser, met on December 15 to determine how the United States can best support this initiative.

On December 31, 2011, President Jonathan declared a state of emergency in 15 local government areas in Borno, Niger, Plateau, and Yobe states, which remained in effect throughout most of 2012. According to Nigerian government officials, the declaration of a state of emergency gives the government sweeping powers to search and arrest without warrants.

2012 Terrorist Incidents: Elements of BH increased the number and sophistication of attacks in 10 northern states and the Federal Capital Territory, with a notable increase in the lethality, capability, and coordination of attacks. Notable terrorist incidents committed by elements of BH, and factions claiming to be BH or affiliated with BH, included:

- On January 20, multiple near-simultaneous attacks in Kano were carried out on at least 12 targets including police stations, an immigration office, and the Kano residence of an Assistant Inspector General of Police. Over 150 persons were killed and hundreds wounded.
- On January 26, a German construction worker was kidnapped on the outskirts of Kano city. On June 1, he was killed by his captors in a raid on the house where he was being held.

- On March 8, an Italian citizen and a British citizen who were kidnapped in May 2010 in Kebbi state, were killed in Sokoto state by their captors during an attempted rescue by Nigerian and British special forces.
- In April, assailants attacked Theatre Hall at Bayero University, Kano, with improvised explosive devices (IEDs) and gunshots, killing nearly 20 persons.
- On April 26, vehicle-borne improvised explosive devices (VBIEDs) simultaneously exploded at the offices of *This Day* newspaper in Abuja and Kaduna, killing five persons and wounding many.
- On June 17, attacks on three churches in Kaduna state killed worshippers and instigated violence throughout the state. At least 10 people were killed and an additional 78 injured in the ensuing riots, as groups barricaded roads, burned mosques, and used machetes to attack and kill. In response, the Kaduna state government imposed a 24-hour curfew and deployed additional security forces; however, violence between Christians and Muslims continued for nearly one week.
- In July, the assassination of three traditional Muslim leaders was attempted in Borno, Yobe, and Kaduna states respectively. None of the targets was killed.
- On July 30, police stations and markets in Sokoto were attacked, resulting in the death of six persons.
- In July and August, churches were targeted in Bauchi, Kaduna, and Kogi states. The total killed in these attacks was 22 persons.
- On December 19, a French engineer was kidnapped in Katsina state, near the Niger border. Ansaru, considered a splinter faction of BH, claimed the kidnapping, and the victim's whereabouts remained unknown at year's end.

Legislation, Law Enforcement, and Border Security: The weakest aspect of the Prevention of Terrorism Law of 2011 is that it does not clearly delineate the lead agency to investigate suspected terrorist crimes.

The trial of six suspects accused of the Christmas Day 2011 bombing of a Catholic church at Madalla in Niger state began in September and was ongoing at year's end.

In February, a U.S. District Court sentenced Nigerian national Umar Abdulmutallab to life in prison for his unsuccessful attempt to detonate an explosive aboard a U.S.-flagged air carrier approaching Detroit, Michigan on December 25, 2009. Throughout the trial, the Nigerian government cooperated closely with DHS, the U.S. Federal Aviation Administration, and the International Civil Aviation Organization.

The Nigerian government actively cooperated with the United States and other international partners to prevent further acts of terrorism in Nigeria against U.S. citizens, citizens of third countries, and Nigerian citizens.

Countering Terrorist Finance: Nigeria is a member of the Inter-Governmental Action Group against Money Laundering in West Africa (GIABA), a Financial Action Task Force (FATF)-style regional body. Nigeria was publicly identified by the FATF in February 2010 for strategic anti-money laundering/combating the financing of terrorism deficiencies. In October 2011, Nigeria was named in the FATF Public Statement for its lack of progress in implementing its action plan. In 2012, Nigeria made significant progress in addressing its outstanding deficiencies, including through the adoption of amendments to its Money Laundering (Prevention) Act.

While Nigeria regularly froze the assets of individuals and entities designated under relevant UNSCRs, and others designated by the United States under U.S. domestic designation authorities only, delays sometimes occurred. All requests to freeze assets must first be sent to the National Security Adviser, who disseminates the information to relevant financial institutions and Nigerian government agencies. Consequently, delays of up to four weeks occasionally occurred before authorities would block assets. Nigeria did not monitor non-profit organizations to prevent misuse and terrorist financing.

For further information on money laundering and financial crimes, we refer you to the *2013 International Narcotics Control Strategy Report (INCSR), Volume 2, Money Laundering and Financial Crimes*: http://www.state.gov/j/inl/rls/nrcrpt/index.htm.

Regional and International Cooperation: At the June 7 Ministerial Plenary Meeting of the Global Counterterrorism Forum (GCTF), Nigeria announced it would partner with Switzerland to co-host a Sahel Working Group meeting on combating the financing of terrorism in early 2013. In January, the UN Counter-Terrorism Implementation Task Force launched three projects under the Integrated Assistance for Counter-Terrorism initiative to support Nigerian government efforts to combat terrorism. Nigeria is a lead member of the Economic Community of West African States and has committed ground forces and logistical support for a possible intervention force in Mali. Through its Office of the National Security Adviser, Nigeria has taken a lead role in initiating a multilateral dialogue between regional countries on how they can better coordinate their efforts to confront networks of terrorist groups that span international borders.

RWANDA

Overview: Rwanda worked to increase border security and cooperation with its neighbors in the East African Community, and signed new bilateral memorandums of understanding on police cooperation during the year. In early 2012, the Government of Rwanda, in tandem with the UN Organization Stabilization Mission in the Democratic Republic of the Congo (MONUSCO) and the Government of the Democratic Republic of Congo (DRC), worked to get the DRC-based Democratic Forces for the Liberation of Congo (FDLR), and other armed combatants, to demobilize and reintegrate into Rwandan society. In April, cooperative efforts between Rwanda and the DRC ended when a group of DRC soldiers rebelled and left the Armed Forces of the DRC to form the M23 rebel group, with the stated aim of overthrowing the government of the DRC. The Rwandan government, including Rwandan Defense Forces (RDF), provided assistance to M23 during the year, even though M23 leadership had been sanctioned by the U.S. Department of Treasury for its abuses in the eastern DRC and its leader was wanted by the International Criminal Court.

Counterterrorism training for border control officials, police, military, and security forces remained a priority, and relations with the United States on these issues remained strong.

2012 Terrorist Incidents: In 2012, there were several grenade and other attacks in Rwanda that the Rwandan government defined as terrorism, and the FDLR took responsibility for many of them. Grenade attacks consistently targeted busy markets or transit hubs in major urban areas, a pattern seen in Rwanda since 2009. Most attacks also coincided with high-profile Rwandan government events. Attacks that the Rwandan government classified as terrorist included:

- On January 3, a grenade attack killed two and wounded 16 in a Kigali market.
- On January 24, a grenade attack in Gitarama injured at least 14 people. Rwandan National Police (RNP) arrested two suspects
- On March 23, an explosion at Ruhengeri bus station killed one and injured five. There were no arrests.
- On March 30, two nearly-simultaneous grenade attacks in Kigali markets injured six. Four suspects were arrested by the RNP.
- On November 27, approximately 120 armed men reportedly crossed into Rwanda from the DRC to attack Rubavu province. The attack was repulsed by the RDF with no civilian casualties.

Legislation, Law Enforcement, and Border Security: On June 14, Rwanda promulgated a new penal code, which increased the Rwandan government's ability to combat terrorism, in accord with relevant international conventions. The law includes new penal provisions for terrorism aboard aircraft or at airports, attacks on internationally protected persons, weapons of mass destruction, and other matters. The new code also expressly forbids exportation of arms, ammunition, and related materials to an area of armed conflict or a country under an arms embargo imposed by the UNSC or by organizations of which Rwanda is a member.

The poor security situation in the eastern DRC put pressure on Rwanda's western borders.

Rwanda has been active in prosecutions of terrorist attacks. On January 13, judges convicted 21 defendants and acquitted eight in relation to several grenade attacks that took place in 2011 and earlier. Prosecutors in this case earlier dropped charges against more than 70 others. On December 6, the High Court in Musanze District convicted 11 of 12 defendants for threatening state security in relation to grenade attacks and other "terrorist acts" that occurred prior to 2012. On December 14, criminal trials started involving defendants charged in the 2012 grenade attacks.

Countering Terrorist Finance: Rwanda is not a member of a Financial Action Task Force-style regional body. Rwanda's new 2012 penal code prohibits money laundering and terrorist financing by individuals and entities. The Government of Rwanda continued efforts to implement its 2009 law on the "Prevention and Suppression of Money Laundering and Financing of Terrorism," which established the legislative framework to adhere to international money laundering standards. For further information on money laundering and financial crimes, we refer you to the *2013 International Narcotics Control Strategy Report (INCSR), Volume 2, Money Laundering and Financial Crimes*: http://www.state.gov/j/inl/rls/nrcrpt/index.htm.

Regional and International Cooperation: Rwanda is not a member of any regional organization or grouping that carried out counterterrorism activities, but hosted security and terrorism-focused conferences held under the auspices of regional organizations like the International Conference on the Great Lakes Region and the East Africa Police Chiefs Cooperation Organization, a sub-regional organization of Interpol.

Countering Radicalization and Violent Extremism: In January, the Government of Rwanda sponsored an Africa Center for Strategic Studies conference on "Preventing Youth Radicalization in East Africa" in Kigali. Until April, Rwanda worked with MONUSCO and the

DRC to encourage the FDLR and other armed combatants to demobilize and reintegrate into Rwandan society. After cooperation with the DRC ended, the Rwandan government continued demobilization and reintegration programs through the Rwandan Demobilization and Reintegration Commission (RDRC). Through November, a total of 1,576 civilian noncombatants who had been living in areas of the DRC controlled by the FDLR rebel armed group returned, according to the RDRC.

The Rwandan government also supported the Musanze Child Rehabilitation Center in Northern Province, which provided care and social reintegration preparation for 58 children who had previously served in armed groups in the DRC. As of September, 18 of the former child soldiers were reunited with their families.

SENEGAL

Overview: The Government of Senegal played an active role in countering terrorist financing in 2012. Senegal is a member of the West African Economic and Monetary Union (WAEMU). As of 2012, Senegal had an operational Financial Intelligence Unit (FIU) and anti-money laundering/combating the financing of terrorism (AML/CFT) legislation in place.

Legislation, Law Enforcement, and Border Security: Senegal has no comprehensive counterterrorism legislation. Senegalese legislation criminalizes illegal possession of a firearm. Possessing, bearing, transporting, importing, and the marketing of weapons and ammunition are subject to prior authorization from the Ministry of the Interior. In accordance with Economic Community of West African States (ECOWAS) recommendations, Senegal has established a national commission on light weapons to monitor arms trading carried out within the country and across its borders. Senegalese law provides that international treaties are supreme over domestic law. However, matters not expressly covered by international treaty are governed by domestic law.

Countering Terrorist Finance: Senegal is a member of the Inter-Governmental Action Group against Money Laundering in West Africa (GIABA), a Financial Action Task Force-style regional body. Senegal continued to work with its partners, GIABA, the West African Economic and Monetary Union (WAEMU), and ECOWAS to develop a comprehensive AML/CFT regime. At the regional level, Senegal implemented the AML/CFT framework of the common law passed by the member states of WAEMU; all member states are bound to enact and implement the legislation. Among the WAEMU countries, Senegal was the first to have the new AML/CFT legal framework in place. Senegal has established procedures for the freezing of an account and other assets of indicted, convicted, or designated terrorists and terrorist organizations. For further information on money laundering and financial crimes, we refer you to the *2013 International Narcotics Control Strategy Report (INCSR), Volume 2, Money Laundering and Financial Crimes*: http://www.state.gov/j/inl/rls/nrcrpt/index.htm.

Regional and International Cooperation: Senegal is a party to both international and regional conventions related to counterterrorism.

SOMALIA

Overview: Building upon the February 2011 offensive that began the liberation of Mogadishu from al-Shabaab, 2012 marked another year of progress for Somalia. The Transitional Federal Government (TFG) and its successor, the Federal Government of Somalia (elected indirectly in September) – with the assistance of the AU Mission in Somalia (AMISOM), led by Uganda and Burundi, as well as Ethiopian and allied Somali militia forces – secured areas neighboring Mogadishu and drove al-Shabaab from many cities and towns in south-central Somalia. Most notably, Kenyan forces gained primary control of the financial hub and port city of Kismayo on September 28.

Al-Shabaab continued to control large sections of rural areas in the middle and lower Juba regions, as well as Bay and Bakol regions, and augmented its presence in northern Somalia along the Golis Mountains and within Puntland's larger urban areas. Areas under al-Shabaab control provided a permissive environment for the group to train operatives, including foreign fighters, and plot attacks. The ability of Somali federal, local, and regional authorities to prevent and preempt al-Shabaab terrorist attacks remained limited.

International terrorists remained in Somalia and continued to mount operations within Somalia and in neighboring countries, particularly Kenya. Al-Shabaab suffered from internal leadership disputes while Ahmed Abdi aw-Mohamed struggled to maintain control over the group's factions. On September 23, Hisbul Islam (HI) announced its split from al-Shabaab; HI is a violent Islamist extremist movement headed by Sheikh Hassan Dahir Aweys, who joined al-Shabaab and became a "spiritual advisor" in December 2010.

The TFG, partnering with Somali regional state and administration leaders in Puntland, Galmudug, and Ahlu Sunnah Wal Jamaa, established permanent governmental institutions during the year, marking the end of an eight-year transitional period of governance. This included finalizing a provisional federal constitution, forming an 825-member National Constituent Assembly that ratified the provisional constitution, selecting a 275-member federal parliament, and holding speakership and presidential elections. On September 10, parliament elected Hassan Sheikh Mohamud as president of the Federal Republic of Somalia. Neither the TFG nor the newly-established Government of Somalia had effective control over some parts of the country outside Mogadishu. Regional administrations, including Somaliland in the northwest and Puntland in the northeast, provided essential governance functions in those areas.

2012 Terrorist Incidents: In 2012, al-Shabaab and other violent extremists conducted suicide attacks, remote-controlled roadside bombings, kidnappings, and assassinations of government officials, journalists, humanitarian workers, and civil society leaders throughout Somalia. Many killings were beheadings, stonings, or other horrific public events designed to instill fear and obedience in communities. Other al-Shabaab attacks targeted government and foreign convoys. For example, on December 14, al-Shabaab attacked an AMISOM convoy with a car bomb in Mogadishu, which an al-Shabaab spokesman claimed was an attempt to target individuals they believed were American.

Al-Shabaab also conducted several attacks against Puntland security forces and their outposts on the foothills of the Golis Mountains, which run along the Puntland-Somaliland border, to include skirmishes in December which left over 30 dead or wounded.

Examples of high-profile al-Shabaab incidents in 2012 included:

- On April 4, a bombing of the national theater in Mogadishu where the TFG Prime Minister and several other government officials were attending a ceremony killed eight, including the Somali Olympic Committee Chair Aden Yabarow Wiish and Somali Football Federation Chief Said Mohamed Nur "Mugambe."
- On April 10, al-Shabaab detonated an explosive device in a Baidoa food market killing 13 and wounding 40, almost all of whom were female traders, street vendors, and customers.
- In June, al-Shabaab decapitated at least 13 men and women it accused of collaborating against the group in Galgaduud and Hiraan regions.
- On September 12, President Hassan Sheikh Mohamud survived an attempted assassination during a press conference with Kenya's foreign minister. Several AMISOM and TFG soldiers were killed in the suicide attack.
- On September 20, multiple suicide bombings at a restaurant in Mogadishu killed at least 14 people, including three local reporters.

Legislation, Law Enforcement, and Border Security: The TFG (through August) and the Government of Somalia (from September on), along with regional governments, continued to pursue al-Shabaab suspects throughout the year. In partnership with AMISOM and neighbors, the government conducted a successful military campaign against al-Shabaab strongholds in southern and central Somalia, capturing al-Shabaab strongholds of Baidoa, Afgoye, Afmadow, Balad, Lanta Buuro, Merca, Miido, Wanla Weyn, and Jowhar. Their most significant victory was the September 28 capture of the port-city of Kismayo, which al-Shabaab had used as a primary source of revenue through extortion activities and charging of duties, in particular on the export of charcoal.

The Puntland regional government stepped up its security campaign against al-Shabaab encouraging citizens to report any actions they believed could lead to insecurity or may be linked to or assist al-Shabaab. On July 21, for example, Puntland security forces arrested 53 people suspected of links with either al-Shabaab or piracy. Puntland forces also engaged in a number of skirmishes with al-Shabaab militants along the outskirts of the Golis Mountains – al-Shabaab's hideout in northern Somalia – leaving at least nine dead on March 3, and 31 dead and wounded on December 5, according to Puntland government authorities and Somali media.

The TFG (through August), the Government of Somalia (from September on), and regional governments cooperated with U.S. law enforcement on numerous occasions, including investigations concerning suspected terrorists, kidnapping, and other acts of terrorism committed inside and outside Somalia.

Countering Terrorist Finance: Somalia is not a member of a Financial Action Task Force-style regional body. There are no known laws in Somalia that criminalize terrorist financing. Somalia does not have a formal banking sector, however there has been a reported increase in the establishment of "banks" throughout Somalia, which includes two unregulated commercial banks, one operating in Somaliland and the other in Mogadishu.

Somalia's central government does not have a system or mechanism for freezing terrorist assets. In 2012, no government entities were capable of tracking, seizing, or freezing illegal assets. There is no mechanism for distributing information from the government to financial institutions (principally remitters or *hawalas*). Many institutions operating in Somalia have international offices, however, and those that do adhere to minimum international standards, including freezes on terrorist entities' finances. Many money remittance companies based abroad, for example, use electronic anti-money laundering systems which flag names listed on the UN 1267/1989 and 1988 Sanctions Committees' consolidated list. Somalia does not have any mechanisms in place under which to share information related to terrorist financing with the United States or other countries. The Government of Somalia has committed to public financial management and was in the process of drafting new banking laws at year's end.

The Somali government called on regional governments to help stem the flow of terrorist financing, requesting that local governments trace, freeze, and seize al-Shabaab-related finances. The government also requested governments to assist in the enforcement of a long-standing national ban on charcoal exports, which have been used to finance al-Shabaab activities. This request resulted in the UNSC banning the import and export of Somali charcoal in UNSCR 2036 (2012).

For further information on money laundering and financial crimes, we refer you to the *2013 International Narcotics Control Strategy Report (INCSR), Volume 2, Money Laundering and Financial Crimes*: http://www.state.gov/j/inl/rls/nrcrpt/index.htm.

Regional And International Cooperation: In 2012, the Somali government worked with international and regional partners, including Kenya, Ethiopia, the AU, and the UN to degrade al-Shabaab as a domestic threat to stability and a terrorist threat abroad. Somalia is a member of the AU, the Intergovernmental Authority on Development, the League of Arab States, and the Organization of Islamic Cooperation.

Countering Radicalization and Violent Extremism: The Somali government has increasingly become more adept at proactively countering al-Shabaab's violent extremist messaging. Examples of successful counter-messaging included the Countering Violent Extremism programs on Radio Mogadishu and the state-owned TV station. In 2010, the TFG's Ministry of Information and Telecommunications began airing the Islamic Lecture Series (ILS) in Mogadishu, a program which has since expanded to include former al-Shabaab strongholds Baidoa, Beledweyne, Dhusamareb, and Abudwaq. ILS is a one-hour, call-in radio program designed to undercut al-Shabaab's efforts to acquire religious legitimacy for its violent extremist ideology.

SOUTH AFRICA

Overview: In 2012, South Africa and the United States had little formal counterterrorism cooperation. The South African State Security Agency (SSA) did not significantly engage with U.S. counterterrorism interlocutors.

SSA has used the government's ongoing effort to centralize all intelligence activities under the SSA's umbrella to implement new protocols and enforce old ones. In 2012, SSA began to aggressively enforce the requirement that any counterterrorism-related coordination be directly through SSA's Foreign Branch, which then determines which other entities within SSA or other parts of the South African government will be involved. As a result, U.S. officers working on counterterrorism issues have been largely prevented from engaging their counterparts, who have arrest authority in South Africa. This has also inhibited coordination and information exchanges between some South Africa government agencies and western interlocutors on counterterrorism issues.

Legislation, Law Enforcement, and Border Security: South Africa took steps this year to address document fraud and border security vulnerability. South Africa's Department of Home Affairs (DHA) introduced a new passport with additional security features aimed at eliminating forgery of passports by organized criminal networks. DHA also instituted a new electronic accounting system with protocols on passport issuance in an attempt to combat corruption.

In October, the government opened its testimony as the prosecution witness in a case involving Henry Okah, the leader for the Movement for Defense of the Niger Delta. Okah, a South African citizen since 2003, stood trial in the Gauteng South High Court for his role in the twin bombings during the October 2010 Independence Day Anniversary celebrations in Abuja, Nigeria, that killed and wounded scores of people. On January 21, 2013 Okah was found guilty on 13 counts of terrorism, and on March 26, was sentenced to 24 years in prison. This case is one of the first to be prosecuted under the 2004 Protection of Constitutional Democracy against Terrorism and Related Activities Act.

In 2012, the South African Revenue Service (SARS) built on its strong relationship with the U.S. Customs and Border Protection's (CBP) Container Security Initiative team in Durban. SARS worked with CBP to build capacity to meet the World Customs Organization Framework of Standards.

South Africa continued to participate in the Department of State's Antiterrorism Assistance program by attending courses on Maritime Interdiction, Explosive Ordinance and Forensics, Land Border Interdiction, Management of Special Events, Document Fraud, and Crime Scene Management. South African officials also participated directly with the International Law Enforcement Academy (ILEA) in Gaborone, Botswana. Courses at the ILEA focus on training of mid-level police managers in a wide range of law enforcement and police programs. Unfortunately, South African attendance at these courses was plagued by poor participation and it attendees were often unaffiliated with counterterrorism activities.

Countering Terrorist Finance: As a member of the Financial Action Task Force (FATF) and the Eastern and Southern Africa Anti-Money Laundering Group, a FATF-style regional body, South Africa largely complied with FATF standards for anti-money laundering and counterterrorist finance, and has a well-functioning Financial Intelligence Unit, the Financial Intelligence Centre (FIC). Those required to report to the FIC included banks, financial institutions, car dealers, attorneys, gold dealers, gambling establishments, real estate agents, foreign exchange dealers, securities traders, money lenders (including those who lend against shares, e.g., brokers), entities selling travelers checks, and Johannesburg stock exchange-registered people, and companies. South Africa's FIC is a member of the Egmont group.

Most major cities have a sizable community of those who use a multitude of locally owned money/value transfer (MVTs) services that tend to be poorly regulated, including *hawalas*. Analysts believe that given a sizable Somali community, and presence of al-Shabaab sympathizers in South Africa, *hawalas* and other MVTS are likely being exploited to transfer funds to violent extremists in East Africa.

For further information on money laundering and financial crimes, we refer you to the *2013 International Narcotics Control Strategy Report (INCSR), Volume 2, Money Laundering and Financial Crimes*: http://www.state.gov/j/inl/rls/nrcrpt/index.htm.

Regional and International Cooperation: South Africa is a founding member of the Global Counterterrorism Forum and sent representatives from its embassies to participate in working group meetings. South Africa finished its second two-year term as a non-permanent member of the UNSC (2011-201w) and played a leading role in the AU Peace and Security Council.

SOUTH SUDAN

Overview: South Sudan is the newest country in the world, one of its least developed, and is recovering from 22 years of civil war. In 2012, the Government of South Sudan suffered from multiple institutional weaknesses – including insufficient policing and intelligence gathering capabilities, capacity and professionalism deficits within the military, inadequate border controls, and deficient aviation security and screening at the country's main international airports in Juba, Malakal, and Rumbek. The government's ability to enact preventive measures and to conduct counterterrorism operations was extremely limited. The Lord's Resistance Army (LRA), led by Joseph Kony, a Specially Designated Global Terrorist under Executive Order 13224, remained a threat.

Legislation, Law Enforcement, and Border Security: Airport security improved slightly with the implementation of some International Civil Aviation Organization security standards. Juba International Airport accepts travel documents in the form of identity cards and passports that generally meet international standards. South Sudan has very limited monetary and human resource capacity to provide effective law enforcement and border security with respect to counterterrorism. Additionally, the border with Sudan is disputed in many locations.

Countering Terrorist Finance: South Sudan is not a member of a Financial Action Task Force-style regional body. In August, South Sudan passed anti-money laundering/combating the financing of terrorism legislation. The country's capabilities to implement or enforce the law remained limited. For further information on money laundering and financial crimes, we refer you to the *2013 International Narcotics Control Strategy Report (INCSR), Volume 2, Money Laundering and Financial Crimes*: http://www.state.gov/j/inl/rls/nrcrpt/index.htm.

Regional and International Cooperation: South Sudan is a member of the UN, the AU, the Intergovernmental Authority on Development, Interpol, and the Eastern Africa Police Chiefs Cooperation Organization, a sub-regional organization of Interpol. South Sudan participated in the AU Regional Task Force (AU-RTF), a joint military task force that includes Uganda, the Democratic Republic of Congo, and the Central African Republic. The AU-RTF is tasked with eliminating the LRA threat in the region, and is supported by the UN and AU.

TANZANIA

Overview: Since the bombing of the U.S. Embassy in July 1998, Tanzania has not experienced another major terrorist attack. Al-Shabaab attacks in Kenya, however, have served as a reminder that the threat in the region is still very real. According to Tanzania's interagency National Counterterrorism Center (NCTC), the June arrest of al-Qa'ida (AQ) and al-Shabaab associate,

Emrah Erdogan, in Dar es Salaam suggests that the organizations have elements and plans within the country's borders. The NCTC sees itself as a means of preventing terrorist attacks rather than responding to them. In September and October, intermittent political unrest in Zanzibar, combined with mounting religious tensions on the mainland, created an environment in which the NCTC was on heightened alert watching for potential terrorist attacks. These developments resulted in demonstrations, rioting, and the destruction of property on a localized scale, but the NCTC did not consider any of these actions terrorism-related.

The NCTC has identified the most historically radicalized areas of the country, and the police are therefore planning to install counterterrorism police units in these regions in order to better track and respond to violent extremism. The NCTC continued to work with local police to engage community elders and religious leaders in these regions to encourage dialogue as a means of addressing grievances rather than violence.

Legislation, Law Enforcement, and Border Security: Regulations for the 2002 Prevention of Terrorism Act were drafted in 2011 and published in August 2012 as the Prevention of Terrorism Regulations 2012. The regulations establish the police and the Financial Intelligence Unit (FIU) as the institutions that are to collect and respond to reports of terrorist activity. The regulations also formalized the process for deeming someone a suspected terrorist, freezing assets, and sharing information between government agencies. To improve border security, the United States provided the police with several patrol boats in Dar es Salaam, Zanzibar, Mwanza, and Tanga. The NCTC reported that its personnel were reviewing border control systems to determine areas of further need.

The most significant counterterrorism law enforcement action this year was the arrest of AQ and al-Shabaab associate Emrah Erdogan, a German citizen of Turkish origin. According to media reports, police received a tip from German authorities and arrested Erdogan on June 10 as he arrived at Dar es Salaam's international airport. Erdogan was wanted for suspected connections to al-Shabaab and for suspected involvement in bombings in Nairobi. Tanzania transferred Erdogan to Germany for trial. In addition to the Erdogan arrest, the Tanzanian government interdicted several youth allegedly heading to and returning from terrorist training facilities in Somalia and the Middle East.

Tanzania shares borders with eight countries and lacks sufficient resources to adequately patrol those borders. Officers manning border posts are often underequipped and undertrained. Some border posts do not have access to electricity, so computerized systems are not always an option. Among the points of entry that do use computerized systems, there is no single border management software that integrates the information available at all posts. Several Ministry of Home Affairs officials have commented that border posts need better inter-operability.

Countering Terrorist Finance: Tanzania is a member of the Eastern and Southern Africa Anti-Money Laundering Group, a Financial Action Task Force (FATF)-style regional body. Since October 2010, Tanzania has been publicly identified by the FATF as a jurisdiction with strategic anti-money laundering/combating the financing of terrorism deficiencies, for which it has developed an action plan with the FATF to address these weaknesses. In February 2012, Tanzania was named in the FATF Public Statement for its lack of progress in implementing its action plan. Since that time, however, Tanzania has made significant progress to address its outstanding deficiencies, including amending its Prevention of Terrorism Act in June 2012.

Tanzania's Financial Intelligence Unit (FIU) is responsible for combating money laundering and terrorist finance, and is seeking membership in the Egmont Group of Financial Intelligence Units. The Anti-Money Laundering Law dictates that the FIU has the responsibility to follow up on cases referred from other organizations rather than to seek out cases on its own. FIU staff attributed this increase in referrals to a series of training exercises they conducted with referring organizations throughout the year.

For further information on money laundering and financial crimes, we refer you to the *2013 International Narcotics Control Strategy Report (INCSR), Volume 2, Money Laundering and Financial Crimes*: http://www.state.gov/j/inl/rls/nrcrpt/index.htm.

Regional and International Cooperation: Tanzania is a member of the South African Development Community and the East African Community, both of which have regular working groups that address counterterrorism. Through the East African Police Chiefs' Cooperation Organization and South African Police Chiefs' Cooperation Organization, the NCTC maintained more frequent, informal contact with other police forces in the region.

UGANDA

Overview: Uganda remained a strong force for regional stability, coordination, and counterterrorism efforts in 2012. The Ugandan government cooperated with U.S. counterterrorism efforts, was a strong advocate of cross-border solutions to security issues, and showed increased political will to secure its borders and apprehend suspected terrorists. Resource limitations, porous borders, and corruption presented challenges, however. Uganda has been the backbone of the AU Mission in Somalia (AMISOM) and has played an active role in countering Lord's Resistance Army (LRA) efforts.

Legislation, Law Enforcement, and Border Security: With U.S. assistance, Uganda continued to expand its border control system to additional points of entry and upgraded it to capture biometric information. Although Uganda significantly improved its ability to investigate terrorist acts, additional training and resources are needed. A Constitutional Court challenge over jurisdiction, extradition, and treatment of the 12 individuals arrested for orchestrating the July 2010 bombings in Kampala indefinitely delayed the trial because the Court lacked a quorum.

Countering Terrorist Finance: Uganda is a member of the Eastern and Southern Africa Anti-Money Laundering Group, a Financial Action Task Force-style regional body, and does not have a financial intelligence unit. Uganda's financial sector remained vulnerable to money laundering, terrorist financing, and other illicit financial transactions; Uganda has not criminalized money laundering. Legal and law enforcement measures to combat terrorist financing, based on the Anti-Terrorist Act of 2002 and the Financial Institutions Act of 2004, are inadequate and do not meet international standards. Uganda lacked the capacity needed to effectively monitor and regulate alternative remittance services and wire transfer data.

The Anti-Terrorist Act inadequately criminalizes terrorist financing. Ugandan authorities have not used this Act to investigate any terrorist financing cases, and Uganda did not prosecute any terrorist financing cases in 2012. The Anti-Terrorist Act lists al-Qa'ida; the LRA; the Allied Democratic Forces, a violent extremist group based in eastern Democratic Republic of the Congo

(DRC); and one defunct Ugandan rebel group as terrorist organizations. The Act has no suspicious transaction reporting requirement, and can take up to 21 days to update.

The Bank of Uganda asks local banks to report suspicious transactions, but there is no clear implementation mechanism for enforcing this or investigating potentially suspicious activity. Uganda routinely distributed the UN lists of designated terrorists or terrorist entities to financial institutions through the Ministry of Foreign Affairs, the Ministry of Finance, and the Bank of Uganda. Uganda has the ability to monitor NGOs, but primarily uses this capability to monitor the activities of NGOs critical of the Ugandan government.

For further information on money laundering and financial crimes, we refer you to the *2013 International Narcotics Control Strategy Report (INCSR), Volume 2, Money Laundering and Financial Crimes*: http://www.state.gov/j/inl/rls/nrcrpt/index.htm.

Regional and International Cooperation: Uganda is an active member of the AU, the Inter-Governmental Authority on Development, the Community of Eastern and Southern Africa, the East African Community, and the International Conference on the Great Lakes Region (ICGLR). Uganda contributed troops to the AU Mission in Somalia and continued to lead regional efforts to end the threat presented by the LRA in coordination with the DRC and South Sudan under the African Union Regional Task Force framework. As Chair of the ICGLR, Uganda led efforts to mediate discussions between M23 rebels and the DRC government.

Countering Radicalization and Violent Extremism: After the July 2010 terrorist attacks, Ugandan police increased outreach to local youth considered at risk for radicalization and recruitment into violent extremist organizations. Uganda has offered amnesty to former LRA combatants and members of the ADF since 2000, but announced in May that future amnesty requests would only be considered on a case-by-case basis.

EAST ASIA AND PACIFIC

Various transnational terrorist organizations continued activities in the East Asia and Pacific region during the year, while the nature of the terrorist threats evolved. In January, Thai authorities arrested a Hizballah operative, who led Thai officials to a significant cache of explosives and bomb making materials. The following month, two Iranians were arrested in Bangkok after accidentally discharging explosives allegedly intended to target Israeli diplomats. A third Iranian was arrested while transiting Malaysia, and two others successfully fled Thailand. All of the Iranian operatives used Malaysia as the entry and exit points for the region as they travelled to and from Bangkok. While still vulnerable to terrorist activity, Malaysia achieved significant legal reforms in 2012 by repealing its Internal Security Act and moving its counterterrorism approach away from detention without trial to a criminal prosecution-based system.

In the Philippines, terrorist acts were generally limited to criminal activities designed to generate revenue for self-sustainment, such as kidnapping for ransom or extortion, but members of terrorist groups were suspected to have carried out several bombings against public and private facilities primarily in the central and western areas of Mindanao. The Government of the Philippines moved toward a peace agreement with the Moro Islamic Liberation Front (MILF) by signing a Framework Agreement on the Bangsamoro in October. A comprehensive peace agreement with the MILF has the potential to improve peace and security in Mindanao.

The shift from large-scale assaults to smaller-scale attacks on domestic targets continued in Indonesia with attacks on police, including the murder and possible torture of two officers who had been investigating an alleged terrorist training camp that was associated with Jemaah Anshorut Tauhid. Militants also attempted to assassinate a provincial governor with a pipe bomb in the midst of a large crowd. Jemaah Islamiya member Umar Patek – the principal bomb maker in the 2002 Bali bombings – was found guilty and sentenced to 20 years in prison. Indonesia continued its close multilateral cooperation in Southeast Asia, most notably as co-chair of the Global Counterterrorism Forum's (GCTF) Southeast Asia Working Group and as co-chair of the ASEAN Defense Ministers Meeting Experts' Working Group on Counterterrorism.

Australia maintained its position as a regional leader in the fight against terrorism and worked to strengthen the Asia-Pacific region's counterterrorism capacity through a range of bilateral and regional initiatives in organizations such as ASEAN, the ASEAN Regional Forum, and the Pacific Island Forum. Australia is also co-chair of the GCTF Southeast Asia Working Group. The Japanese government continued to participate in international counterterrorism efforts at multilateral, regional, and bilateral levels through the Seventh ASEAN-Japan Counterterrorism meeting and the Japan-China Counterterrorism Consultations. Australia, Indonesia, Japan, China, and New Zealand are founding members of the GCTF. The Government of the Philippines hosted the second GCTF Southeast Asia Working Group meeting in November, which focused on youth radicalization.

CHINA

Overview: China's cooperation with the United States on counterterrorism issues remained marginal with little reciprocity in information exchanges. China continued to expand cooperation with countries in the region and conducted joint counterterrorism training exercises with Indonesia, Kazakhstan, Kyrgyzstan, Pakistan, Russia, Tajikistan, and Thailand. China's domestic counterterrorism efforts remained primarily focused against the East Turkestan Islamic Movement (ETIM) in the Xinjiang Uighur Autonomous Region (XUAR) of northwest China. In public statements, government officials singled out the "Three Evils" of extremism, separatism, and terrorism in Xinjiang as the main terrorist threat to the nation and characterized Uighur discontent as terrorist activity. Human rights organizations continued to maintain that China used counterterrorism as a pretext to suppress Uighurs, a predominantly Muslim ethnic group that makes up a large percentage of the population of the XUAR.

2012 Terrorist Incidents: The Chinese government characterized two incidents in the XUAR as terrorist attacks. On February 28, nine violent extremists armed with knives attacked a crowd in Kashgar prefecture, reportedly killing 15 and injuring 16 pedestrians. Seven of the attackers were reportedly killed in the ensuing clash with police, and the alleged ringleader, a Uighur, was sentenced to death. On June 29, six Uighurs allegedly attempted to hijack a Chinese airliner en route from Hotan to Urumqi, and injured 10, reportedly using aluminum pipes from a dismantled pair of crutches. According to official Chinese media, three Uighurs were sentenced to death and one received life in prison after reportedly confessing to the crimes of organizing, leading, or participating in a terrorist group, hijacking, and attempting to detonate explosives on an aircraft.

Legislation, Law Enforcement, and Border Security: In March, China's National People's Congress amended the country's criminal procedure law to include measures to provide protection for witnesses, victims, or their close relatives whose personal safety is at risk because of their testimony in cases involving, among other things, crimes of terrorism. The new legislation, which came into effect January 2013, also includes controversial measures that strengthen Chinese authorities' ability to arrest and detain individuals suspected of "endangering state security or crimes of terrorism." This legislation includes a clause that allows for detention without notification of a suspect's relatives in terrorism-related cases where such notification may "impede the investigation." The Chinese typically did not provide public information on law enforcement actions in response to terrorist attacks. Two exceptions were domestic media reports of trial results for those accused of participating in the two attacks cited above.

Although China continues to stress the importance of counterterrorism cooperation, Chinese law enforcement agencies remained reluctant to conduct joint investigations with U.S. law enforcement agencies or provide assistance in cases involving suspected terrorists.

Countering Terrorist Finance: China is a member of the Financial Action Task Force (FATF) and the Asia/Pacific Group on Money Laundering (APG), a FATF-style regional body. In October 2011, the Chinese government established a legal framework and administrative authority for enforcing UN designations: the "Decision of the Standing Committee of the National People's Congress on Strengthening Counterterrorism Work" and the accompanying "Statement of Decision on Strengthening Counterterrorism Work." This authority provides the legal basis for the establishment of a national interagency terrorist asset freezing body that, if robustly implemented, should strengthen China's implementation of UNSCRs 1267/1989, 1988, and 1373.

Because the People's Bank of China, the Ministry of Public Security, and the Ministry of State Security are currently drafting implementing regulations for the Decision of the Standing Committee of the National People's Congress on Strengthening Counterterrorism Work and the accompanying Statement of Decision on Strengthening Counterterrorism Work, the impact of these new regulations remains to be seen. Although mandatory, Chinese courts still do not systematically pursue the confiscation of criminal proceeds, including terrorist assets. Regarding the monitoring of non-profit organizations, China has a deep and far-reaching system of oversight; however, there were no identifiable measures or requirements specifically for preventing terrorist finance abuses in this sector. For further information on money laundering and financial crimes, we refer you to the *2013 International Narcotics Control Strategy Report (INCSR), Volume 2, Money Laundering and Financial Crimes*: http://www.state.gov/j/inl/rls/nrcrpt/index.htm.

Regional and International Cooperation: Throughout the year, China publicly affirmed its commitment to working with international partners to counter terrorism. China continued to voice support for three UNSC committees – the 1267 Committee, the Counterterrorism Committee, and the 1540 Committee. China is a founding member of the Global Counterterrorism Forum and in June, supported the establishment of the International Center for Excellence for Countering Violent Extremism in Abu Dhabi. In January, China participated in the third APEC workshop on counterterrorism finance and the non-profit organization sector.

China cooperated with other nations on counterterrorism efforts through military exercises and assistance. In May, China hosted Thai marine forces in Guangdong province for joint counterterrorism drills (Blue Commando 2012). In July, Tajikistan hosted Shanghai Cooperation Organization members China, Kazakhstan, Kyrgyzstan, and Russia for counterterrorism exercises (Peace Mission 2012). Also in July, China and Indonesia held their second round of counterterrorism exercises in China (Sharp Knife 2012).

Hong Kong

Hong Kong continued its effective security and law enforcement partnership with the United States, including through the Hong Kong Customs and Excise Department's successful joint operation of the Container Security Initiative, and through participation in U.S.-sponsored capacity building training in counterterrorism-related topics, and through engagement with the U.S. military. In ratifying UN Conventions on terrorism, the People's Republic of China has specified that the treaties would also apply to the Hong Kong Special Administrative Region, which has subsequently implemented the Conventions through local ordinance. In July, Hong Kong further strengthened its UN Anti-Terrorism Measures Ordinance by replacing the term "funds" throughout, with the more comprehensive term "property," to cover terrorist assets of every kind. Counterterrorism, through policies on prevention, protection, and preparedness, remained an operational priority for the Hong Kong Police Force. The Police Security Wing coordinated potential terrorist threat information with relevant counterterrorism units. The Police Counterterrorist Response Unit provided a strong deterrent presence, assisting police districts with counterterrorist strategy implementation, and complementing the tactical and professional support of existing police specialist units, such as the Explosive Ordnance Disposal Bureau, Special Duties Unit, and the VIP Protection Unit.

Hong Kong is a member of the FATF, the APG, and the Egmont Group of Financial Intelligence Units. Terrorist financing is a criminal offense in Hong Kong, and financial institutions are required to continuously search for terrorist financing networks and screen accounts using designations lists made by the United States under relevant authorities, as well as the UN 1267 Sanctions Committee's consolidated lists. Filing suspicious transactions reports irrespective of transaction amounts is obligatory for financial institutions, but Hong Kong lacks mandatory reporting requirements for cross-border currency movements. In April, Hong Kong's Anti-Money Laundering and Counterterrorist Financing Ordinance went into effect mandating customer due diligence and record-keeping in the financial sector as well as imposing statutory supervision over money changers and remittance agents. For further information on money laundering and financial crimes, we refer you to the *2013 International Narcotics Control Strategy Report (INCSR), Volume 2, Money Laundering and Financial Crimes*: http://www.state.gov/j/inl/rls/nrcrpt/index.htm.

Macau

Macau's counterterrorism cooperation with the United States included information exchange as well as regular capacity building through the International Law Enforcement Academy (ILEA) and other international organizations. Under the Macau Public Security Police Force, the Police Intervention Tactical Unit (UTIP) is responsible for protecting important installations and dignitaries, and for conducting high-risk missions, such as deactivation of improvised explosive devices. UTIP's Special Operations Group conducts counterterrorism operations. Macau law enforcement officers attended U.S.-sponsored capacity building training at ILEA on cargo targeting and interdiction, and post blast investigations.

Macau is a member of APG and the Egmont Group of Financial Intelligence Units. Terrorist financing is a criminal offense in Macau, and banks and other financial institutions are required to continuously search for terrorist financing networks and screen accounts using U.S. designations lists, as well as the UN 1267/1989 and 1988 Committees' consolidated lists. Filing suspicious transactions reports irrespective of transaction amounts is obligatory, but Macau lacks mandatory reporting requirements for cross-border currency movements.

Macau's Financial Intelligence Office (FIO) signed a Memorandum of Understanding to cooperate formally with Fiji's Financial Intelligence Unit, making this the eleventh such agreement since the FIO's inception in 2006. Macau cooperated internationally in counterterrorism efforts through Interpol and other security-focused organizations.

INDONESIA

Overview: A decade after the 2002 Bali bombings, Indonesia continued its counterterrorism efforts and initiatives and cooperated with a range of partners, including the United States. Law enforcement authorities made a series of preemptive arrests in 2012, demonstrating enhanced investigative techniques and an increasing ability to disrupt terrorists' plans before they could carry out attacks. Despite the security challenges inherent in governing a nation composed of more than 17,000 islands, authorities were diligent in efforts to deny terrorists a safe haven. Police conducted raids at several locations, including in Poso, Central Sulawesi, where authorities began operations in October to disrupt an alleged terrorist training program associated with Jemaah Anshorut Tauhid.

In May, authorities arrested suspected terrorists based in Medan, North Sumatra, who had hacked into a multi-level marketing website and transferred funds to private accounts. This trend of terrorists seeking illicit funding through online crime is new to Indonesia. Limited weapons smuggling, often through the Philippines, posed an ongoing challenge. Authorities have expressed concern that, in some cases, explosive devices were of increasing sophistication.

Indonesia worked with international partners, including the United States, to deter and prevent terrorist attacks. Coordination among the various agencies responsible for preventing terrorism and prosecuting terrorists continued to pose challenges. Indonesia has sought to address this through better training for law enforcement, prosecutorial, and judicial officials, and by encouraging better information sharing between stakeholder agencies.

2012 Terrorist Incidents: Continuing a trend in recent years, terrorists targeted Indonesian law enforcement officials. Incidents included:

- In August, terrorists attacked police in the Central Java city of Surakarta (also known as Solo). On August 17, two police officers were shot by a passenger on a motorcycle. On August 18, a grenade was thrown at a police post, resulting in damage to the building. On August 30, a police officer was shot and killed by terrorists.
- On August 31, during a police raid, one law enforcement official was killed and one terrorist suspect was arrested. Two suspected terrorists were also killed during the

shootout. Both had been students at Al Mukmim Islamic boarding school in Solo, had links to regional terrorist groups, and had participated in terrorist training in the Philippines.

- In the fall, terrorists in Poso targeted civilians, police, and public officials in a series of violent attacks. Two police officers who had been investigating an alleged terrorist training camp in Poso were found murdered on October 16, bearing signs of torture.
- On October 18-22, bombs were placed near police facilities, a church, a market, a home, and a vacant lot in Poso. Three people were injured, though not all of the bombs detonated.
- On November 11, suspected Poso-trained militants tried to assassinate the Governor of South Sulawesi with pipe bombs during a public rally in Makassar. The bombs did not detonate, however.
- On November 15, a suspected terrorist tried to assassinate the Chief of Police in Poso at his home, but the shooter missed and the officer was uninjured.

Legislation, Law Enforcement, and Border Security: In 2012, a multi-agency drafting team under the guidance of Indonesia's Ministry of Law and Human Rights was revising Indonesia's 2003 antiterrorism law. New provisions being considered would strengthen the legislation to better facilitate the investigation and prosecution of terrorism cases by: addressing the material support of terrorism; better facilitating the use of intelligence information: extending the detention period that police may hold suspected terrorists before filing charges; and outlawing membership in, and training with, terrorist organizations.

Police arrested more than 150 people on charges of terrorism, and in the process of arrest, killed 10 suspects.

- In March, five suspected terrorists were killed on the resort island of Bali as police tried to arrest them. Authorities believed the group may have been planning an attack similar to the 2002 and 2005 attacks against tourist sites on Bali.
- In early May, police arrested 12 terrorists who were connected to the 2011 suicide bombing of a Christian church in Solo, Central Jakarta, and were involved in hacking a multi-level marketing website to fund terrorist activities, including a terrorist training camp in Poso, Central Sulawesi.
- In early September, police made a series of arrests after bomb making facilities were discovered at two separate locations in the greater Jakarta area. Nitroglycerine was found at one of the sites, a first-time discovery of this substance linked to bomb making in Indonesia.
- In late October, police arrested 11 suspected terrorists in a series of coordinated raids at four locations on the island of Java. A list of possible targets that included U.S. diplomatic facilities was among the items seized. Three suspected terrorists were killed in police operations in Central Sulawesi, and nine others were arrested in separate operations in Central and South Sulawesi.
- Raids following the attacks on Poso police resulted in the arrests of dozens of suspects. At least three suspected ring leaders were killed and authorities seized weapons, extremist publications, and explosive materials during the raids.

The Attorney General's Office received 42 terrorism cases to prosecute. As of early December, at least three cases were completed, 18 were under review, and 22 were in the trial stage. In

February, the Supreme Court rejected the appeal of Abu Bakar Ba'asyir to overturn his conviction on charges of terrorism and reinstated a 15-year sentence. This reversed an October 2011 decision wherein judges at the Jakarta High Court threw out the original 15-year sentence and issued a nine-year jail term based on lesser charges.

In mid-April, seven members of a radical group were found guilty of plotting to poison the water and food supplies at a police cafeteria in Jakarta and sentenced to jail terms ranging from three to five years. This case prompted authorities to express concern about terrorists obtaining chemical and biological agents for use in attacks.

On June 21, judges at the West Jakarta District Court announced a guilty verdict and 20-year jail sentence for Umar Patek. The trial lasted four months and featured testimony from victims and legal experts, including American witnesses. Patek was found guilty on all six counts for terrorist actions spanning more than a decade. He was the last remaining terrorist yet to be sentenced for the 2002 Bali bombings, for which he was the principal bomb maker.

Indonesia remained an important partner nation in the Department of State's Antiterrorism Assistance program, which provided enhanced training in investigative and tactical skills for Indonesian National Police officers, including elite units that regularly conducted major operations against terrorists in the region.

Countering Terrorist Finance: Indonesia belongs to the Asia/Pacific Group on Money Laundering, a Financial Action Task Force (FATF)-style regional body. In February 2012, FATF placed Indonesia on its Public Statement list because of Indonesia's failure to make sufficient progress in implementing its anti-money laundering/combating the financing of terrorism action plan. Indonesia faces possible FATF sanctions for failure to pass terrorist financing legislation. At year's end, revised terrorist financing legislation was pending before parliament.

Indonesia continued to lack a comprehensive law to implement UNSCRs 1267 and 1373, though the AML legislation provides for the freezing of terrorist assets linked to the UN List of designated terrorists and terrorist organizations. The Indonesian Financial Intelligence Unit routinely shared designated terrorists and terrorist entities with banks nationally through the Central Bank of Indonesia, but this had little effect since Indonesian authorities have not used existing regulations to freeze assets under UNSCR 1267. For example, Indonesia made little to no progress in freezing assets of JAT and three of its members after they were placed on the UNSCR 1267 list in March and April. Prosecutors and police need additional training to be able to convincingly follow and explain the money trail in a court of law. Judges also need training on money laundering and financial crimes. Corruption, particularly within the police ranks, also impeded effective investigations and prosecutions. Charitable and religious institutions remained largely unregulated, although the Indonesian government was looking at creating an administrative process to monitor non-profit organizations.

For further information on money laundering and financial crimes, we refer you to the *2013 International Narcotics Control Strategy Report (INCSR), Volume 2, Money Laundering and Financial Crimes*: http://www.state.gov/j/inl/rls/nrcrpt/index.htm.

Regional and International Cooperation: A founding member of the Global Counterterrorism Forum (GCTF), Indonesia and Australia co-hosted the GCTF's inaugural South East Asia

Capacity Building Working Group meeting in Semarang, Indonesia on March 6-7. Indonesian officials regularly participated in GCTF events throughout the year. On March 20, the Indonesian House of Representatives formally ratified the ASEAN Convention on Counterterrorism.

Countering Radicalization and Violent Extremism: The Government of Indonesia broadened its efforts to counter radicalization and violent extremism. The Vice President's office convened an interagency taskforce charged with creating a blueprint for counterterrorism that includes initiatives to counter violent extremism. In concert with other government agencies, the National Counter Terrorism Agency (BNPT) developed plans for a media campaign to counter extremist narratives. BNPT identified schools, universities, and religious institutions as targets for outreach efforts. BNPT enlisted repentant terrorists to publicly denounce violence at book launches and other public venues. For example, on June 20, BNPT organized a launching of the book *The Cloud of Jihad* authored by Khairul Ghazali, a repentant violent extremist currently serving a five-year jail term. BNPT invited members of extremist groups to the event with the aim to open dialogue among groups that hold divergent beliefs. The Ministry of Religious Affairs held a symposium in September called "The Strategic Role of Religious Education in the Development of a Culture of Peace."

BNPT also established a Terrorism Prevention Communication Forum in 15 of Indonesia's 34 provinces as a means to better coordinate counterterrorism efforts at the local level, and plans are underway to expand the program. Recognizing that campuses are sometimes recruiting grounds for violent extremists, BNPT co-sponsored a religious education curriculum workshop in Solo as an effort to undercut radical messages being spread on some university campuses. Plans were underway to open a rehabilitation and de-radicalization center for imprisoned terrorists in Sentul, one hour south of Jakarta. This facility, where terrorist prisoners would serve the latter part of their jail terms, would help prepare convicted terrorists for successful and non-violent reintegration back into society after their release. However, reforming the Indonesian corrections sector remained a daunting challenge, and the government had no comprehensive or standardized system in place to handle terrorist prisoners.

NGOs complemented government efforts with civil society members, academics, and victims of terrorism engaged in outreach and programs, primarily to students at educational institutions in communities identified as most vulnerable to violent extremism.

DEMOCRATIC PEOPLE'S REPUBLIC OF KOREA (NORTH KOREA)

Overview: The Democratic People's Republic of Korea (DPRK) is not known to have sponsored any terrorist acts since the bombing of a Korean Airlines flight in 1987. On October 11, 2008, the United States rescinded the designation of the DPRK as a state sponsor of terrorism in accordance with criteria set forth in U.S. law, including a certification that the DPRK had not provided any support for international terrorism during the preceding six-month period and the provision by the DPRK of assurances that it would not support acts of international terrorism in the future.

Four Japanese Red Army members who participated in a 1970 jet hijacking continued to live in the DPRK. The Japanese government continued to seek a full accounting of the fate of 12 Japanese nationals believed to have been abducted by DPRK state entities in the 1970s and

1980s. Despite two rounds of DPRK-Japan bilateral talks in the latter half of 2012, the DPRK had not yet fulfilled its commitment to re-open its investigation into the abductions.

Legislation, Law Enforcement, and Border Security: In May, the United States re-certified North Korea as "not cooperating fully" with U.S. counterterrorism efforts under Section 40A of the Arms Export and Control Act, as amended. In making this annual determination, the Department of State reviewed the DPRK's overall level of cooperation with U.S. efforts to combat terrorism, taking into account U.S. counterterrorism objectives with the DPRK and a realistic assessment of DPRK capabilities.

Countering Terrorist Finance: The DPRK is not a member of the Financial Action Task Force (FATF) or the Asia-Pacific Group (APG) on Money Laundering, a FATF-style regional body. Throughout the year, the FATF reiterated its concern about the DPRK's failure to address "significant deficiencies" in its anti-money laundering/combating the financing of terrorism (AML/CFT) regime. In 2012, DPRK officials engaged the FATF and the APG to discuss technical issues. While the FATF welcomed such engagement and noted that it remained open to "assisting the DPRK to address its AML/CFT deficiencies," the DPRK appeared to have made little meaningful progress in strengthening its AML/CFT infrastructure. In an October public statement, FATF renewed its call on members to "apply effective countermeasures to protect their financial sectors" from the "on-going and substantial money laundering and terrorist financing...risks" posed by the DPRK. For further information on money laundering and financial crimes, we refer you to the *2013 International Narcotics Control Strategy Report (INCSR), Volume 2, Money Laundering and Financial Crimes*: http://www.state.gov/j/inl/rls/nrcrpt/index.htm.

REPUBLIC OF KOREA (SOUTH KOREA)

Overview: While the Republic of Korea has no active counterterrorism cases, it continued to take terrorism seriously and cooperated with U.S. counterterrorism efforts. Information sharing through formal and informal channels has been strong and responses to requests for information positive. The 18th Republic of Korea National Assembly session expired on May 28, without passing the Counter-Terror Prevention Act bill. First proposed in late 2001 shortly after September 11 by the 16th National Assembly, the bill has faced consistent opposition from civic groups and the National Human Rights Committee.

Legislation, Law Enforcement, and Border Security: The Republic of Korea has met the requirements for information sharing under the Visa Waiver Program. In January, the Republic of Korea began collecting the biometric data of foreign nationals aged 17 and over at ports of entry. Through the Preventing and Combating Serious Crime agreement, U.S. law enforcement will be able to use this biometric data to identify terrorists and criminals and share relevant information.

Countering Terrorist Finance: The Republic of Korea is a member of the Financial Action Task Force (FATF) and the Asia/Pacific Group on Money Laundering, a FATF-style regional body. In February, the National Assembly approved an amendment to the Financial Transaction Reports Act imposing stricter penalties on financial institutions that violate reporting requirements, which the Financial Intelligence Unit (FIU) had submitted in December 2010. On June 13, 2012, the FIU submitted a separate bill amending the Financial Transaction Reports Act to abolish the suspicious transaction report threshold. The bill was submitted to the National Assembly in November. To meet the global standard, the FIU revised the Enforcement Decree of the Prohibition of Financing for Offenses of Public Intimidation Act in September. The Republic of Korea actively cooperated with authorized investigations involving or initiated by international organizations, and shared the records or related information with foreign authorities. In this regard, the FIU has signed Memoranda of Understanding for cooperation with 48 foreign authorities and added the U.S. Financial Crime Enforcement Network (FINCEN) into its global network on June 20. For further information on money laundering and financial crimes, we refer you to the *2013 International Narcotics Control Strategy Report (INCSR), Volume 2, Money Laundering and Financial Crimes*: http://www.state.gov/j/inl/rls/nrcrpt/index.htm.

Regional and International Cooperation: South Korea is a member of the UN, APEC, ASEAN+3, East Asia Summit, Asia-Europe Meeting, Asia Cooperation Dialogue, Forum for East Asia-Latin America Cooperation, OECD, G-20, and the Conference on Interaction and Confidence-Building Measures in Asia. It is also a partner country of the OSCE and NATO.

On March 26-27, the Republic of Korea hosted the 2012 Nuclear Security Summit in Seoul; combating nuclear terrorism was a significant conference component. In September in Seoul, the South Korean government hosted the ASEAN Regional Forum (ARF) Seminar on Confidence Building Measures in Cyberspace, under the endorsement of the ARF Counter-Terrorism and Transnational Crime Inter-Sessional Meeting.

The Republic of Korea government continued to help developing countries build law enforcement capacities through bilateral and regional channels such as the ASEAN+3 Ministerial Meetings on Transnational Crimes. In 2012, the Republic of Korean government organized 21 training courses covering topics such as forensic science investigation, crime prevention, and cyber crime investigation, and invited 342 government officers from developing countries to participate.

In 2012, the Korean government held bilateral consultations on counterterrorism with Japan, China, Russia, Brazil, Mexico, and India.

In February, the Korean National Police Agency partnered with the International Tactical Officers Training Association to co-host the 2012 Evolution Counterterrorism Conference, with a dual theme of "Command and Leadership" and "Counterterrorism Operations."

MALAYSIA

Overview: Malaysia's counterterrorism cooperation with the United States has continued to improve in recent years, and it was an important counterterrorism partner in 2012. Malaysia has not suffered a serious incident of terrorism for several years, but was vulnerable to terrorist activity and continued to be used as a transit and planning site for terrorists. Weak border controls persisted in the area contiguous with Thailand in northern Malaysia, and there were gaps in maritime security in the tri-border area of the southern Philippines, Indonesia, and the Malaysian state of Sabah. The repeal of the decades-old Internal Security Act and its replacement by the new Security Offenses (Special Measures) Act, along with several amendments to existing laws, moved Malaysia's counterterrorism approach away from detention without trial to a criminal prosecution-based system. The Royal Malaysia Police (RMP) cooperated closely with the international community on counterterrorism efforts, and RMP and other law enforcement officers participated in capacity building training programs.

Legislation, Law Enforcement, and Border Security: In April, the parliament repealed Malaysia's Internal Security Act (ISA), under which Malaysia had for decades routinely detained suspected terrorists without formal judicial proceedings for renewable two-year terms. Three separate declarations of emergency were also repealed on November 24, 2011, which led to the expiration of the Emergency Ordinance in May 2012. In place of the ISA, the parliament passed the Security Offenses (Special Measures) Act (SOSMA) which took effect on July 31, along with amendments to the Penal Code, Criminal Procedure Code, and Evidence Act. Under the SOSMA, once an arrest has been made, the next-of-kin must be notified immediately and the accused must have access to a lawyer within 24 hours. A high-ranking police officer can extend the detention period to 28 days, at which time the accused must be charged or released. The law also states that a person cannot be charged for his political beliefs or activities. The repeal of the decades-old ISA and its replacement by the SOSMA, along with several amendments to existing laws, was a positive development, moving Malaysia's counterterrorism approach toward a criminal prosecution-based system.

There were no reported arrests under the ISA in 2012. In October, Lebanon arrested two Malaysians believed to be suicide bombers with suspected al-Qa'ida links. In February, Malaysian police detained Iranian Masoud Sedaghatzadeh, who had allegedly fled to Malaysia from Thailand after a group of Iranians in Bangkok accidentally detonated bombs allegedly intended to target Israeli interests. Sedaghatzadeh was captured when he attempted to depart Malaysia for Iran from the Kuala Lumpur International Airport. A Malaysian court ordered his extradition to Thailand but Sedaghatzadeh reportedly was appealing the order; at year's end he remained in Malaysian custody pending appeal.

Malaysia has very liberal visa requirements generally, and does not require an entry visa for citizens of many countries. As part of its visa and immigration controls, Malaysia continued to implement a biometrics system introduced in June 2011 that records the fingerprints of the right and left hand index fingers at all ports of entry. The National Foreigners Enforcement and Registration System reportedly was linked to the police's existing Biometric Fingerprint Identification System. The system has had problems, but the police reported that the new biometric system was successful overall. The country also continued an effort to register foreign workers, many of whom were undocumented, and to regularize their status or facilitate their return to their countries of origin. The effort involved the biometric registration of over two million foreign workers and undocumented immigrants.

Malaysia continued to participate in the Department of State's Antiterrorism Assistance program. The program began to transition in 2012 from its focus on cyber investigations and cyber security to a focus on border security. Installation of the eighth and final maritime surveillance radar was completed in 2012. Located on the northeastern coast of Sabah, these radars provided additional maritime domain awareness capability for the Malaysian Joint Forces Command. At Malaysian government request, the United States conducted a three-day counterterrorism workshop for Malaysian police and prosecutors entitled "Preventing Acts of Terrorism Through Proactive Policing and Prosecution," which focused on best practices for investigating and successfully prosecuting conspiracy and material support cases under Malaysia's new law.

Countering Terrorist Finance: Malaysia is a member of the Asia/Pacific Group on Money Laundering, a Financial Action Task Force-style regional body. Malaysia's Money Service Business Act of 2011 (MSBA), which took effect on December 1, 2011, was used for prosecution for the first time on August 10 when a company was charged with operating as a money-changer without a license. The MSBA represents an improved legislative framework that criminalized terrorist financing and strengthened the safeguards of the money services industry (the remittance, money-changing, and wholesale currencies businesses) against abuses. Compliance with the MSBA is monitored closely by Bank Negara Malaysia. Malaysia did not prosecute any counterterrorist finance crimes in 2012.

In September, Malaysia's Compliance Officers' Networking Group organized the fourth International Conference on Financial Crime and Terrorist Financing, a two-day event. The event was attended by more than 300 people, including speakers from the U.S. Department of Treasury, the U.S. Department of State, Homeland Security Investigations, and the FBI. For further information on money laundering and financial crimes, we refer you to the *2013 International Narcotics Control Strategy Report (INCSR), Volume 2, Money Laundering and Financial Crimes:* http://www.state.gov/j/inl/rls/nrcrpt/2012/database/index.htm.

Regional and International Cooperation: Malaysia actively participated in ASEAN and the APEC forum. Malaysian law enforcement officials routinely met with regional counterparts to discuss counterterrorism issues at meetings such as the Heads of Asian Coast Guard Agencies Meeting in New Delhi in October, and the ASEAN Senior Officials Meeting on Transnational Crime in Bangkok in September. The Malaysian Maritime Enforcement Agency hosted boarding officer training and a Maritime Law Enforcement Commanders' Forum, funded by the Department of State's Export Control and Related Border Security program, to improve maritime law enforcement collaboration among Gulf of Thailand littoral nations.

Malaysia's Southeast Asia Regional Center for Counterterrorism (SEARCCT) hosted five seminars and training events with regional participation, including: a three-day Sub-Regional Seminar on International Joint Investigations for Southeast Asian States jointly organized by SEARCCT and the UN Counter-Terrorism Committee Executive Directorate with support from the government of New Zealand; a five-day Regional Aviation Security Seminar in collaboration with the New Zealand and UK High Commissions; and a four-day seminar on "The Dynamics of Youth and Terrorism," attended by 39 participants.

Countering Radicalization and Violent Extremism: Malaysia facilitated talks between the Philippine government and the Moro Islamic Liberation Front that resulted in the October signing of a historic peace framework agreement, an effort which some Malaysian officials have said was partly intended to reduce the potential for radicalization in a region of the Philippines that borders Malaysia.

The RMP and the Department of Islamic Development operated a disengagement program for terrorist suspects who were held under the ISA in Malaysia's Kamunting Prison. The program involved religious and social counseling and vocational training. It employed psychologists, religious scholars, police officers, and family members. A committee evaluated detainees' progress toward eligibility for release from prison. The committee's reports were reviewed by a panel from the detention center and also by the Home Ministry. Upon release, former inmates were visited by parole officers and continued to face restrictions on their activities, including curfews and limits on their travel and contacts. While the government portrayed the disengagement program as highly successful, it lacked demonstrable metrics for its effectiveness. As this program was directed primarily at ISA detainees, it was unclear what will become of the program in the wake of the ISA's mid-2012 repeal.

PHILIPPINES

Overview: The Philippines maintained its strong counterterrorism cooperation with the United States. The ability of terrorist groups, including the Abu Sayyaf Group (ASG), Jemaah Islamiya (JI), and the Communist People's Party/New People's Army (CPP/NPA), to conduct terrorist activities inside the Philippines remained constrained. Terrorist groups' acts were generally limited to criminal activities designed to generate revenue for self-sustainment, such as kidnapping for ransom or extortion. Nonetheless, members of these groups were suspected to have carried out bombings against government, public, and private facilities, primarily in the central and western areas of Mindanao; others were linked to extortion operations in other parts of the country.

The Government of the Philippines continued to implement its 2011–2016 Internal Peace and Security Plan that calls for the transition of internal security functions from the Armed Forces of the Philippines (AFP) to the Philippine National Police (PNP). The increasing role of the police in maintaining internal security in conflict-affected areas will permit the AFP to shift its focus to enhancing the country's maritime security and territorial defense capabilities.

On October 15, the peace panels of the government and the Moro Islamic Liberation Front signed the Framework Agreement on the Bangsamoro, which lays out a roadmap to a comprehensive peace agreement and calls for the creation of the Bangsamoro entity to replace the Autonomous Region in Muslim Mindanao. A comprehensive peace agreement has the potential to improve peace and security in Mindanao.

2012 Terrorist Incidents: High-profile terrorist incidents included:

- On May 31, an improvised explosive device (IED) detonated in front of the residence of Isabela City Mayor Santos-Akbar, wounding two civilians.
- On July 26, nine soldiers were killed and 12 wounded when the AFP clashed with militants in Sumisip on the island of Basilan. Five militants were reportedly killed in the incident.
- On August 16, a bomb destroyed a city bus in Zamboanga City, injuring at least seven. A second bomb exploded an hour later in front of a nearby mosque. No one was injured in the second blast.
- On September 1, 48 civilians were injured when a grenade exploded during a village fiesta in Paquibato District outside of Davao City. The NPA later issued an apology for the attack, claiming the grenade was thrown at an AFP detachment but bounced off some netting and landed inside an adjacent basketball gym where a circus was being held.
- On October 11, an IED exploded near the entrance of Maxandrea Hotel in downtown Cagayan de Oro City, killing two civilians after police arrived to investigate suspicious activity reported in the area. A second IED was found in a street adjacent to the hotel, but was safely detonated.

Legislation, Law Enforcement, and Border Security: The Philippines coordinated with U.S. law enforcement authorities, especially regarding U.S. fugitives and suspected terrorists. An under-resourced and understaffed law enforcement and justice system coupled with widespread official corruption, however, resulted in limited domestic investigations, unexecuted arrest warrants, few prosecutions, and lengthy trials of cases.

A petition filed in 2010 by the Philippine Department of Justice with the Regional Trial Court in Basilan for the proscription of the ASG as a terrorist group and 202 identified associates as terrorists, was pending action at year's end.

- On February 2, the AFP launched an operation on Jolo Island that reportedly killed ASG commander Umbra Jumdail (aka Dr. Abu) and 14 other ASG members.
- On May 23, Philippine National Police Officer Arnold Mayo was charged with murder. Witnesses reportedly identified him as planting a bomb that exploded inside a commuter bus on a major highway in Makati City and killed five passengers in January 2011.
- On June 21, Alawie Pasihul was arrested in Zamboanga City on suspicion of being part of an ASG group that kidnapped American citizens Martin and Gracia Burnham and Guillermo Sobero in May 2001. (Fourteen other ASG members were convicted in 2007 and sentenced to life imprisonment for their participation in the kidnapping that resulted in the deaths of Sobero, Martin Burnham, and Philippine nurse Ediborah Yap.)
- In September, due to a technical issue, a regional trial court in Manila dismissed the extradition case against an ASG leader wanted in the United States to stand trial on criminal hostage-taking charges in the 1993 kidnapping of U.S. national Charles Walton.
- On December 14, Mohammad Noor Fikrie bin Abdul Kahar, a suspected Malaysian JI member, was killed in Davao by police after he threatened to detonate an explosive device in his backpack.

The Philippines continued to improve the security of its passports. Beginning in 2007, the Philippines started to issue machine readable passports. Three million such passports remained in circulation at year's end, the last of which will expire in 2013. In August 2009, the Philippines started to produce "e-passports" containing a biometric chip. Six million Philippine passports in circulation are e-passports, accounting for 65 percent of all valid passports, according to the Philippines Passport Office.

The Philippines remained an important partner nation in the Department of State's Antiterrorism Assistance program, which provided tactical and investigative training to support the transition in the southern Philippines from military to civilian counterterrorism authority.

Countering Terrorist Finance: The Philippines is a member of the Asia/Pacific Group on Money Laundering (APG), a Financial Action Task Force (FATF)-style regional body. Republic Act No. 10168, the Terrorism Financing Prevention and Suppression Act of 2012, was signed into law June 18 and took effect July 5. The law made terrorist financing a stand-alone crime in line with APG/FATF recommendations and specifically authorizes the Anti-Money Laundering Council to issue an ex parte order to freeze without delay property/funds related to the financing of terrorism or acts of terrorism, including the property/funds of individuals and entities on the UNSCs 1267/1989 and 1988 consolidated lists.

Republic Act No. 10167, which amended the Anti-Money Laundering Act of 2001, was signed into law June 18 and took effect July 6. It allows the Anti-Money Laundering Council to inquire into bank accounts based on an ex parte application, without the depositor's knowledge for a limited period of time, and allows additional courts other than the Court of Appeals to issue asset freeze orders.

There is no single supervisory authority responsible for entities in the non-profit sector; coordination is insufficient. Monitoring is weak due to insufficient coordination and resources of non-profit organization regulatory bodies.

For further information on money laundering and financial crimes, we refer you to the 2013 International Narcotics Control Strategy Report (INCSR), Volume 2, Money Laundering and Financial Crimes: http://www.state.gov/j/inl/rls/nrcrpt/index.htm.

Regional and International Cooperation: The Philippines participated in the ASEAN Defense Ministers' Meeting Plus (ADMM-Plus) and supported the ADMM-Plus Experts' Working Group on Counterterrorism that met in Washington in April. Through U.S.-sponsored counterterrorism training, the PNP developed contacts with law enforcement agencies in Indonesia and Malaysia.

Countering Radicalization and Violent Extremism: The Philippine government continued its counter-radicalization program: Payapa at Masaganang Pamayanan or PAMANA (Resilient Communities in Conflict Affected Communities). In November, the Philippines hosted the second meeting of the Global Counterterrorism Forum Southeast Asia Working Group, which focused on youth radicalization. Experts from around the region and world gathered to share best practices and experiences in countering youth radicalization.

SINGAPORE

Overview: In 2012, Singapore's bilateral and multilateral engagement on counterterrorism intelligence and law enforcement cooperation was inconsistent and marked by a transactional mindset that impeded the development of broad, deep, and predictable agency-to-agency relationships. While some agencies have had success from time to time, Singapore appeared to provide selective cooperation dependent upon the issue.

As of December, Singapore had detained 16 terrorist suspects. Detainees included members of Jemaah Islamiya (JI), who had plotted to carry out attacks in Singapore in the past, and members of the Moro Islamic Liberation Front. Two persons with links to terrorist groups were newly detained in 2012. In 2012, Singapore released 23 persons on Restriction Orders (RO) and one on Suspension Direction (SD). Detainees released on ROs and SDs were monitored by the Singapore authorities and required to report to authorities on a regular basis.

Legislation, Law Enforcement, and Border Security: Singapore used its Internal Security Act (ISA) to arrest and detain suspected terrorists without trial. The ISA authorizes the Minister for Home Affairs (MHA), with the consent of the president, to order detention without judicial review if it is determined that a person poses a threat to national security. The initial detention may be for up to two years, and the MHA may renew the detention for an unlimited number of additional periods up to two years at a time with the president's consent.

Singapore's 2012 law enforcement actions included:

- In February, Singapore released a member of JI, Jumari bin Kamdi, who was detained under the ISA in January 2011. According to an MHA press release, he was cooperative with investigators, and it was assessed that he no longer posed a security threat that required further detention.
- In February, Singapore detained JI member Abd Rahim Abdul Rahman. He attended terrorist training in Afghanistan with al-Qa'ida (AQ) in 1999 and 2000. Rahman was arrested in Malaysia in February 2012 and deported to Singapore.
- In May, Singapore detained JI member Husaini Ismail. He was arrested in Indonesia in June 2009 for immigration violations and deported to Singapore after his release in May. He attended terrorist training in Afghanistan with AQ in 1999 and 2000. According to the MHA, both he and Rahman were actively involved in reconnoitering several potential local and foreign targets in Singapore for the purpose of a terrorist attack.

Countering Terrorist Finance: Singapore is a member of the Financial Action Task Force (FATF) and the Asia/Pacific Group on Money Laundering, a FATF-style regional body. There were no assets frozen or confiscated for terrorist finance-related crimes. For further information on money laundering and financial crimes we refer you to the *2013 International Narcotics Control Strategy Report (INCSR)*, *Volume 2, Money Laundering and Financial Crimes*: http://www.state.gov/j/inl/rls/nrcrpt/2012/.

Regional and International Cooperation: In August, the Republic of Singapore Navy participated in the annual Southeast Asia Cooperation Against Terrorism exercise, together with the U.S. Navy and the navies of Brunei, Indonesia, the Philippines, and Thailand. Singapore was an active participant in ASEAN and is a member of the Proliferation Security Initiative.

Countering Radicalization and Violent Extremism: Singapore maintained a de-radicalization program that focused on countering detainees' extremist ideology. Singapore enlists the support of religious teachers and scholars to study JI's ideology, develops teachings to counter the group's spread within Singapore's Muslim community, and provides counseling to detainees. Religious counseling for detainees continues after release. Among those individuals released from detention, there were no reported cases of recidivism.

THAILAND

Overview: Counterterrorism cooperation with Thailand remained strong. Thailand engaged with the United States on investigations into Hizballah and Iranian activities after incidents involving both occurred in January and February. On January 12, Thai police detained a Hizballah operative on immigration charges as he was attempting to depart Thailand from Suvarnabhumi International Airport. He led police to nearly 10,000 pounds of urea-based fertilizer and 10 gallons of liquid ammonium nitrate in a commercial building about 20 miles south of Bangkok. It was unclear if the materials were intended to be used to carry out terrorist attacks in Thailand – possibly against Israeli tourists – or if they were to be transported to another country. The Hizballah operative was awaiting trial at year's end.

On February 14, Thai police arrested two Iranian men after they accidentally set off explosives that were allegedly intended to target Israeli diplomats. A third Iranian was arrested in Malaysia and was awaiting extradition to Thailand at year's end. Two other Iranians successfully fled Thailand. All the operatives traveled in and out of Bangkok through Malaysia; two of them may have traveled from Malaysia to Thailand through the land border at least once. The bombs were similar to bombs targeting Israeli diplomats in Georgia and India during that same week.

There was no direct evidence of operational linkages between the southern Thai insurgent groups and international terrorist networks.

Legislation, Law Enforcement, and Border Security: The porous nature of Thailand's southern border with Malaysia remained an issue of concern. At the same time, cross-border law enforcement cooperation, based on long association between Thai and Malaysian police officers, remained strong. With support from the United States, Thailand continued to use the Personal Identification Secure Comparison and Evaluation System (PISCES) border security system at five airports and four land border stations until June. In June, the Thai government replaced PISCES with the Personal Identification and Blacklist Immigration Control System (PIBICS) – an information capture and query system designed for the Thai Immigration Bureau – at eight points of entry, except Suvarnabhumi International Airport in Bangkok, for a three month trial evaluation. Thailand continued to participate in the Department of State's Antiterrorism Assistance program.

Countering Terrorist Finance: Thailand is a member of the Asia/Pacific Group on Money Laundering, a Financial Action Task Force (FATF)-style regional body. Thailand's 2010-2015 National Strategy for Combating Money Laundering and the Financing of Terrorism was developed by the Anti-Money Laundering Office (AMLO), Thailand's official Financial Intelligence Unit. The strategy called for the legislative enactment of key counterterrorist finance measures by October 31, 2012; however, widespread flooding and political transitions delayed the passage of legislation.

In 2010, the Thai government expressed high-level political commitment to addressing deficiencies that the FATF identified in Thailand's anti-money laundering/combating the financing of terrorism regime, and reported taking multiple steps to address FATF recommendations. Thailand's failure to pass the amended Anti-Money Laundering Act and the draft bill of Anti-Financing of Terrorist prompted the FATF, in February 2012, to downgrade Thailand to its 'blacklist' of countries, raising concern about financial transactions in Thailand. Since then, Thailand has passed the legislation and will be considered by the FATF for removal from the blacklist from its enhanced monitoring process in June 2013, pending a successful completion of the on-site visit.

The AMLO's 2010-2015 National Strategy for Combating Money Laundering and the Financing of Terrorism specifically calls for enhanced measures to provide for greater transparency and oversight of non-profit organizations by December 2014. More specifically, the 2010-2015 National Strategy calls for implementation of appropriate licensing procedures, supervision, monitoring, and oversight in line with international standards. This includes ensuring that information on the operations of each non-profit organization is publicly available. The Bank of Thailand does not have regulations that give it explicit authorization to control charitable donations; however, the Financial Institutions Business Act and the Electronic Payment Services Business Decree require all financial institutions and non-bank service providers to adopt both know-your-customer rules and customer due diligence procedures for all clients, and must meet the Anti-Money Laundering Act's reporting requirements, which would include transactions deriving from charitable donations.

For further information on money laundering and financial crimes, we refer you to the *2013 International Narcotics Control Strategy Report (INCSR), Volume 2, Money Laundering and Financial Crimes*: http://www.state.gov/j/inl/rls/nrcrpt/index.htm.

Regional and International Cooperation: Thailand participated in international counterterrorism efforts, including through APEC, ASEAN, the ASEAN Regional Forum, the Asia-Europe Meeting, and the Bay of Bengal Initiative for Multi-Sectoral, Technical, and Economic Cooperation. Thailand, along with the U.S. Pacific Command, co-hosted 11 countries for the annual Pacific Area Security Sector Working Group.

Countering Radicalization and Violent Extremism: A range of Thai government agencies, including the Southern Border Provincial Administration Center and the Internal Security Operations Command, continued to organize outreach programs to ethnic Malay-Muslims to counter radicalization and violent extremism. A small group of international NGOs also reached out to communities in the southern provinces to provide services and to identify the underlying causes of the area's violence.

EUROPE

Various terrorist groups continued to plot against European targets and interests in 2012, and the year was marked by several high-profile attacks. European security services continued their effective efforts to counter terrorism through close cooperation among countries and with the United States, and through the use of the sophisticated technical capabilities available to most partner states. Nonetheless, in March, before he was killed by police, "lone wolf" violent extremist gunman Mohammed Merah killed seven persons, including three children, in Toulouse and Mantauban, France before he was killed by police.

In July, a terrorist attack carried out on a passenger bus in Bulgaria killed five Israelis and a Bulgarian citizen. During the same month Cypriot authorities arrested an individual suspected of plotting a similar attack in that country. On February 5, 2013, Bulgarian Deputy Prime Minister Tsvetan Tsevtanov, publically linked Hizballah to the Burgas bombing. On March 21, 2013, a Cyprus court found a Hizballah operative guilty of charges stemming from his surveillance activities of Israeli tourist targets.

A wide range of violent extremist ideologies remained a threat: anarchists in Greece continued to launch low-level attacks against government offices, private businesses, and symbols of the state, and long-active radical ethno-nationalist groups like the Kurdistan Workers' Party (PKK) in Turkey continued their campaigns of violence. Of these groups, the deadliest was the PKK. According to the NATO Centre of Excellence-Defence Against Terrorism in Ankara, there were 226 terrorist incidents reported through November.

Transatlantic cooperation on counterterrorism, including the sharing of intelligence and judicial information, capacity building in non-European countries, extradition of terrorist suspects, and efforts to counter violent extremism remained excellent, though differing perspectives on issues like data privacy and long-term detention sometimes complicated efforts. A number of European countries signed or ratified agreements with the United States on preventing and combating serious crime. The EU and a number of European countries continued to play leading roles in the Global Counterterrorism Forum (GCTF).

Counterterrorism cooperation with the Russian Federation continued bilaterally and in various multilateral fora, including the GCTF. The activities of two joint counterterrorism working groups supported these efforts, one led by diplomatic counterparts under the auspices of the Bilateral Presidential Commission, and the other bringing together law enforcement and intelligence professionals of the two countries.

Prosecutions of suspected terrorists continued apace, with significant trials and/or convictions taking place in several countries. In Norway, violent nationalist extremist Anders Breivik was convicted of murder in August for his 2011 attacks on government offices and a political party youth camp that killed a total of 77 people. A German court sentenced to life imprisonment Arid Uka, who was responsible for shooting U.S. airmen at Frankfurt Airport in 2011.

AUSTRIA

Overview: Austria maintained its diligence in its counterterrorism efforts and U.S.-Austrian law enforcement cooperation was generally strong. Austria's Agency for State Protection and Counterterrorism (BVT), the key counterterrorism agency within the Ministry of the Interior, noted that while the number of violent extremists has been growing in Austria, their overall number remained small, and it did not see a climate fostering terrorist attacks within Austria. The pace of approving and implementing counterterrorism legislation was often slowed by concerns over data privacy protections. Counterterrorism efforts were further complicated by a general public perception that Austria is safe from terrorism. The BVT said the threat from transnational violent extremism remained a concern, and estimated the number of radicalized individuals among second- and third-generation Muslim immigrants and among converts to Islam in the country at approximately 500. The BVT remained concerned by individuals who seek training in terrorist camps abroad.

Legislation, Law Enforcement, and Border Security: Parliament approved the bilateral U.S.-Austrian Preventing and Combating Serious Crime agreement, and it came into force in May. As of year's end, the agreement had not been implemented.

Austria implemented a 2006 EU counterterrorism directive on data retention on April 1. In an effort to accommodate widespread public skepticism of the directive, the Austrian parliament's justice committee heard concerns over the directive in November. Intelligence and law enforcement officials also responded to public concerns about the use of expanded legislative tools enacted in 2011 to monitor terrorism.

In July, an Austrian court sentenced an Austrian citizen to three years in prison for membership in a terrorist organization. The accused had planned a trip to Somalia in 2009 to receive terrorist training from al-Shabaab.

Countering Terrorist Finance: Austria is an active member of the Financial Action Task Force (FATF). The Austrian Financial Market Authority (FMA) regularly updates a regulation issued January 1, 2012, which mandates banks and insurance companies to apply additional special due diligence in doing business with designated countries. The FMA regulation currently includes 21 jurisdictions. This regulation implements Austria's new anti-money laundering/combating the financing of terrorism (AML/CFT) regime requiring banks to exercise enhanced customer due diligence, and is based on the Austrian Banking Act, the Insurance Supervision Act, and FATF statements on jurisdictions with AML/CFT deficiencies. For further information on money laundering and financial crimes, we refer you to the *2013 International Narcotics Control Strategy Report (INCSR), Volume 2, Money Laundering and Financial Crimes*: http://www.state.gov/j/inl/rls/nrcrpt/index.htm.

Regional and International Cooperation: Austria maintains security partnerships with several countries in the region and the Ministry of the Interior has counterterrorism liaison officers in a number of Austria's embassies in southeastern Europe. Austria participated in various regional security platforms, including the OSCE, the Central European Initiative, and the Salzburg Forum. In November, Austria announced it planned to intensify cooperation with source-countries of illegal migration in a preventive effort against terrorism and human trafficking.

Austrian Finance Ministry officials conducted customs administration training courses for Afghan and other customs officials at an OSCE training facility in Dushanbe.

Countering Radicalization and Violent Extremism: The State Secretary for Integration visited the United States and Canada in August to meet with relevant officials, and to learn about best practices from successful integration projects in both countries. The Ministry of Interior's "National Action Plan for Integration" seeks to address social, cultural, and economic issues affecting immigrants and is headed by the State Secretary. The State Secretary also initiated the "Dialogue Forum Islam" to institutionalize communication with Austria's Muslim community. Establishment of a program focused on countering violent extremism and countering Islamophobia was under consideration at the end of 2012.

AZERBAIJAN

Overview: Azerbaijan actively opposed terrorist organizations seeking to move people, money, and material through the Caucasus. The country continued to strengthen its counterterrorism efforts and had some success in both reducing the presence of terrorist facilitators and hampering their activities.

Legislation, Law Enforcement, and Border Security: On January 19, Azerbaijan's Ministry of National Security announced that it had arrested two Azerbaijani citizens, and was pursuing a third Azerbaijani citizen living in Iran, for planning to assassinate two foreign rabbis teaching at a Jewish school in Baku. Authorities presented evidence, including seized weapons and cash, connecting Iranian intelligence services to these individuals and the terrorist plot.

In March, Azerbaijani security services reported the arrest of 22 individuals, all Azerbaijani citizens, accused of working with Iran's Islamic Revolutionary Guard Corps to carry out terrorist attacks against Western embassies and other groups with Western ties.

On April 6, security services conducted a raid on a suspected violent extremist group in Ganja, resulting in a standoff in which one militant and one law enforcement officer were killed. The raid was part of a sweep throughout the country that resulted in the arrest of 17 individuals and the confiscation of assault rifles, ammunition, hand grenades, remote controlled explosives, and communication equipment, among other items.

In May, Azerbaijan's security service reported it had arrested 40 terrorist suspects and thwarted planned terrorist attacks during the May Eurovision Song Contest held in Baku. Planned targets during the event included major hotels frequented by foreigners as well as the song contest venue.

Countering Terrorist Finance: Azerbaijan is a member of Moneyval, the Committee of Experts on the Evaluation of Anti-Money Laundering Measures and the Financing of Terrorism, a Financial Action Task Force (FATF)-style regional body. In order to bring Azerbaijan's legislative framework into conformity with international standards and requirements, including those of the EU and FATF, a significant number of legislative acts – four codes, 15 laws, and six presidential decrees covering more than 100 articles – have been amended but the Financial Monitoring Service (FMS), Azerbaijan's Financial Intelligence Unit, since 2009. Azerbaijan continued to work with Moneyval to address the full range of anti-money laundering/combating the financing of terrorism (AML/CFT) issues identified in its Mutual Evaluation Report. The U.S. government, primarily USAID and Treasury, has been one of the leading partners of the FMS since its formation in 2009, working with it along with the Prosecutors office and others to provide technical assistance and training to upgrade enforcement capabilities, which included four distinct training sessions on AML/CTF issues in FY 2012.

The Government of Azerbaijan has legislation in place that permits the freezing of assets without delay, and has presented a draft law to Parliament that proposes additional measures to streamline and simplify the confiscation and release of frozen assets. UN lists are updated and submitted to reporting institutions. For further information on money laundering and financial crimes, we refer you to the *2013 International Narcotics Control Strategy Report (INCSR), Volume 2, Money Laundering and Financial Crimes*: http://www.state.gov/j/inl/rls/nrcrpt/index.htm.

Regional and International Cooperation: In 2012, Azerbaijan began a two-year term as a non-permanent member of the UNSC, supporting various terrorism-related UNSCRs. In May, Azerbaijan held the presidency of the UNSC, which focused on strengthening international cooperation in the implementation of counterterrorism obligations. Azerbaijan also participated in the Istanbul Process and supported counterterrorism confidence building measures referred to in the June 14 Heart of Asia Ministerial Conference Declaration. Azerbaijan also took part in working group meetings of Caspian Sea littoral states to coordinate law enforcement efforts aimed at countering terrorism as well as smuggling, narcotics trafficking, and organized crime on the Caspian.

Countering Radicalization and Violent Extremism: The Government of Azerbaijan restricts religious activity, including television broadcasts and the sale of religious literature at metro stations. Only imams trained and licensed in Azerbaijan were permitted to give religious sermons and to lead Muslim religious ceremonies. Critics claimed that by driving the practice of religion underground, these governmental policies could ultimately contribute to the growth of violent extremism. We refer you to the Department of State's *Annual Report to Congress on International Religious Freedom* (http://www.state.gov/j/drl/irf/rpt/index.htm) for further information.

BELGIUM

Overview: Belgian authorities continued to maintain an effective counterterrorism apparatus overseen by the Ministries of Interior and Justice. The primary actors in this apparatus are the Belgian Federal Police, State Security Service, Office of the Federal Prosecutor, and the inter-ministerial Coordination Unit for Threat Analysis. In addition, the Belgian Financial Intelligence Unit oversees an efficient and comprehensive inter-agency effort to prevent terrorist financing. Belgium continued to investigate, arrest, and prosecute terrorist suspects and worked closely with U.S. authorities on counterterrorism matters. A series of public reports and statements by the Belgian Civilian Intelligence Service (BCIS) highlighted the increased threat posed by violent extremism in Belgium. The small but vocal violent extremist group Sharia4Belgium, which disbanded in September but whose members continued to be active, was cited by BCIS as a movement of particular concern.

2012 Terrorist Incidents: On March 12, a Sunni Muslim Moroccan immigrant broke into a Shia mosque in Brussels, threatened worshippers with an axe, poured gasoline on the premises, and set fire to the mosque. The imam of the mosque, Abdallah Dadou, died of smoke inhalation. The alleged perpetrator told police he attacked the mosque in retaliation against Shia-led repression of Sunnis in Syria. On June 8, Brahim Bahrir, a 34-year-old French violent extremist, stabbed and seriously wounded two Belgian police officers in a subway station in the Brussels neighborhood of Molenbeek. He was subsequently arrested. He traveled from Paris to Brussels that morning with the intent of retaliating against Belgian authorities for their handling of a June 1 incident in which a niqab-wearing woman got into a violent altercation with police officers in Molenbeek.

Legislation, Law Enforcement, and Border Security: The Belgian government has been moving slowly to implement the U.S.-Belgium Preventing and Combating Serious Crime Agreement, signed in 2011. The agreement was approved by the cabinet in December 2012, and at year's end was pending review by the Council of State before being presented to Parliament.

The Belgian order to extradite convicted terrorist Nizar Trabelsi to the United States, signed in 2011, was held up pending an appeal by Trabelsi's lawyers before the European Court of Human Rights. Trabelsi, a Tunisian national, was arrested in Belgium on September 13, 2001 and later convicted for plotting an attack on the Belgian Air Force base at Kleine Brogel, where U.S. military personnel are stationed. He remains in Belgian custody.

Other Belgian judicial actions included:

- On February 10 and May 3, in two separate decisions, Antwerp-based judges sentenced the spokesman of the violent extremist movement Sharia4Belgium, Fouad Belkacem (alias Abu Imran), of incitement to violence and hatred for video clips in which he threatened various political figures and called on Belgian Muslims to reject democracy. On June 7, he was arrested as a result of statements he made in the wake of the June 1 altercation between police and a *niqab*-clad woman in Brussels that led to violent demonstrations. In the statements he called for Muslims to defend their honor and resort to violence, if necessary. On November 29 an Antwerp court sentenced him to six months imprisonment for these statements.

- On June 25, six members of the so-called Ayachi cell were sentenced for recruiting militants to fight in Iraq and Afghanistan in the mid-2000s. Their sentences ranged from three to 11 years. Their case was under appeal at year's end.
- On October 10, police arrested seven members of a cell suspected of recruiting violent extremists to fight in Somalia.
- On December 5, a Belgian court sentenced Hassan Hamdaoui, the figure at the center of the so-called Hamdaoui cell of 14 suspected terrorists arrested in November 2010, to five years imprisonment for attempting to participate in terrorist activities. The other 13 were acquitted for lack of evidence. Hamdaoui, a Belgian citizen of Moroccan origin, was accused of planning terrorist attacks in Belgium and seeking to fight in Chechnya.

Countering Terrorist Finance: Belgium is a member of the Financial Action Task Force. Belgium's banking industry is medium sized, with assets of over $1.5 trillion dollars in 2011. According to Belgium's Financial Intelligence Unit, the Cellule de Traitement des Informations Financieres (CTIF), most of the criminal proceeds laundered in Belgium are derived from foreign criminal activity. Belgium generally has very little public corruption that contributes to money laundering and none known related to terrorist financing. According to the 2011 CTIF annual report, contraband smuggling represented 10.1 percent of all cases, while terrorist financing represented only 1.63 percent.

In 2012, there were credible reports in the Belgian media of possible ties between Hizballah and individuals under investigation in Belgium for money laundering, drug trafficking, and other activities involving the Port of Antwerp and the Antwerp diamond trade. These investigations were ongoing at year's end.

For further information on money laundering and financial crimes, we refer you to the *2013 International Narcotics Control Strategy Report (INCSR), Volume 2, Money Laundering and Financial Crimes*: http://www.state.gov/j/inl/rls/nrcrpt/index.htm.

Regional and International Cooperation: Belgium participated in EU, UN, and Council of Europe counterterrorism efforts. In addition, Belgium joined the advisory board of the UN Counter-Terrorism Center in 2012. As an EU member state, Belgium has contributed trainers and capacity-building expertise to EU counterterrorism assistance programs in Sahel countries, including the Collège Sahélien de Sécurité; and the Belgian Federal Police have provided training to counterparts in the Maghreb.

Countering Radicalization and Violent Extremism: The Coordination Unit for Threat Analysis and other Belgian governmental partners took further steps to develop the "Action Plan Radicalism." One of the goals of the Action Plan is to develop measures to limit the impact of violent extremist messaging. The Ministry of Interior continued to coordinate Belgium's effort to develop a government-wide strategy to counter radicalization and violent extremism.

BOSNIA AND HERZEGOVINA

Overview: Bosnia and Herzegovina (BiH) increased its counterterrorism capacity in 2012 and remained a cooperative partner on international counterterrorism issues. BiH's Joint Terrorism Task Force continued to work toward improving coordination between its many security and police agencies to better counter potential terrorist threats and to better respond to acts of terrorism. However, the task force faced budgetary challenges and a fragmented security and law enforcement sector that made coordination among different agencies difficult. External violent Islamic extremist ideological influences and the presence of regional nationalist violent extremist groups found in the former Yugoslavia represented sources of potential terrorist threats in BiH.

Legislation, Law Enforcement, and Border Security: Following the October 28, 2011 attack on the U.S. Embassy in Sarajevo, the Ministry of Security established a working group to evaluate methods to improve the coordination of police and security agencies charged with responding to terrorist incidents. To date, the working group has yielded no concrete results. The challenge in coordination stems primarily from overlapping jurisdictions, particularly in Sarajevo, where at least three distinct police forces have a role in responding to terrorist incidents: the State Investigative and Protective Agency (SIPA) – BiH's state-level police authority, Sarajevo cantonal police, and Federation entity police. In addition, the state-level Directorate for the Coordination of Police Bodies (DCPB) is charged with the protection of diplomatic and certain other public facilities. While state-level laws give DCPB the authority to coordinate the responses of all state-level police agencies, this organization remained underfunded and under-supported by government authorities. In practice, SIPA generally takes a lead role in responding to attacks and the Prosecutor's Office has the authority to investigate and prosecute acts of terrorism. The Ministry of Security consulted with state, entity, district, and cantonal police and security agencies to evaluate whether an improved legal framework could be established to enhance security cooperation to counter terrorism.

Bosnia's Joint Terrorism Task Force, led by BiH's Chief Prosecutor, began operations in January 2011. It includes members from BiH's state law enforcement agencies and Brcko District Police. The BiH Ministry of Security funds the Joint Task Force, which operates out of SIPA Headquarters. The Task Force remained in the formative stages, nearly two years after its establishment. The Ministry of Security continued to work toward implementing its 2010-2013 strategy on preventing and combating terrorism, which was adopted in 2010.

To help improve the tracking of entries into Bosnia, the BiH Border Police (BP) installed a new computerized database/software system to support immigration and passenger information collection. The new system, in place since March 2012, links all 55 border crossings and all four airports (Sarajevo, Tuzla, Mostar, and Banja Luka) via the State Police Information Network, a network developed and donated by the U.S. Department of Justice's International Criminal Investigative Training Assistance Program. The new system provides the BP with immediate access to other supporting databases, including the Agency for Identification Documents, Registers, and Data Exchange, the Ministry of Security, the Foreigner Affairs Service, and Interpol, to run appropriate checks and cross-checks.

BiH saw several terrorism-related prosecutions in 2012. These included:

- On September 6, the Court of Bosnia and Herzegovina (Court of BiH) Appellate Chamber upheld the November 11, 2011 first instance ruling that found Rijad Rustempasic, Abdulah Handzic, and Edis Velic guilty of planning to carry out a terrorist attack and sentenced them to terms ranging from three to four-and-a-half years.
- On November 20, the Court of BiH issued a first-instance ruling that found Zijad Dervisevic, Amel Sefer, and Sasa Bonic guilty of charges of terrorism and illegal

possession of weapons. They were sentenced to eight, seven, and six years imprisonment, respectively.

- On December 6, the Court of BiH found Mevlid Jasarevic, a Serbian citizen, guilty of terrorism for his October 28, 2011 shooting attack targeting the U.S. Embassy in Sarajevo. He was sentenced to 18 years imprisonment, the longest terrorism-related sentence ever handed down in Bosnia. Two other defendants, Emrah Fojnica and Munib Ahmetspahic, were found not guilty of supporting the attack and for being members of a terrorist organization responsible for the attack.
- The trial of Haris Causevic and five other defendants accused of carrying out the terrorist bombing of the Bugojno police station on June 27, 2010, that killed one police officer and injured six others, began on March 22, 2011 and remained ongoing at year's end.

BiH continued its participation in the Department of State's Antiterrorism Assistance program.

Countering Terrorist Finance: BiH is a member of Moneyval, the Committee of Experts on the Evaluation of Anti-Money Laundering Measures and the Financing of Terrorism, a Financial Action Task Force-style regional body. For further information on money laundering and financial crimes, we refer you to the *2013 International Narcotics Control Strategy Report (INCSR), Volume 2, Money Laundering and Financial Crimes*: http://www.state.gov/j/inl/rls/nrcrpt/index.htm.

Regional and International Cooperation: BiH's criminal code and related legal framework is harmonized with UN and EU standards related to combating terrorism. BiH law enforcement agencies regularly interacted with their U.S. and European counterparts on counterterrorism investigations. Regional cooperation at the professional law enforcement level with Croatia and Serbia is improving.

Countering Radicalization and Violent Extremism: The main religious communities in Bosnia and Herzegovina – Muslim, Serbian Orthodox, Catholic, and Jewish – worked together, through the Interreligious Council, to promote tolerance and to confront violent extremism within their ranks. As part of their efforts, they conducted mutual exchange programs of young theologians from three major theological educational institutions (Muslim, Serbian Orthodox, and Roman Catholic) and offered workshops for high school students to promote inter-religious dialogue and tolerance.

BULGARIA

Overview: With the assistance of the United States, the EU, and NATO, Bulgaria actively worked to develop improved counterterrorism measures. According to Bulgaria's lead agency for counterterrorism, the State Agency for National Security, Bulgaria is a potentially attractive target for terrorists based on its strong cooperation with its partners, as well as Bulgaria's large population of refugees, particularly from Syria and Iran. Bulgaria's creation of a Crisis Management Unit within the Ministry of Foreign Affairs was developed in 2012 to strengthen Bulgaria's response to a terrorist attack, among other crises.

2012 Terrorist Incidents: On July 18, a terrorist attack was carried out on a passenger bus transporting Israeli tourists at the Burgas Airport. The bus was carrying 42 Israelis who had arrived on a flight from Tel Aviv. The explosion killed five Israelis, as well as a Bulgarian citizen, and injured 32 Israelis. While no organization publicly claimed responsibility for the attack, the plot bears the hallmark of Hizballah. On February 5, 2013, following a lengthy investigation, the Bulgarian government publically implicated Hizballah in the Burgas bombing.

Legislation, Law Enforcement, and Border Security: A revision to Bulgaria's penal code (enacted in 1968) has been drafted, which includes strengthened and improved definitions for terrorism and organized crime, but it had not been enacted by year's end.

Countering Terrorist Finance: Bulgaria is a member of Moneyval, the Committee of Experts on the Evaluation of Anti-Money Laundering Measures and the Financing of Terrorism, a Financial Action Task Force-style regional body. For further information on money laundering and financial crimes, we refer you to the *2013 International Narcotics Control Strategy Report (INCSR), Volume 2, Money Laundering and Financial Crimes*: http://www.state.gov/j/inl/rls/nrcrpt/index.htm.

Regional and International Cooperation: Bulgaria participated in several bilateral and multilateral fora regarding security and assistance, including the Global Initiative to Combat Nuclear Terrorism, the Proliferation Security Initiative, and the Nuclear Smuggling Outreach Initiative.

CYPRUS

Overview: Despite limited resources, Cyprus took a clear stand against terrorism, particularly with its arrest, investigation, and prosecution of a Lebanese Hizballah suspect. The Republic of Cyprus government was responsive to efforts to block and freeze terrorist assets, sought to implement Financial Action Task Force (FATF) recommendations, and made significant efforts to conform to EU counterterrorism directives. The Government of Cyprus viewed counterterrorism as a foreign policy priority and partnered with other governments, bilaterally and multilaterally, to fight terrorism. Cyprus' counterterrorism partnership with the United States included regular, routine protection for transiting U.S. military personnel, aircraft and naval vessels throughout 2012, and participation in the Department of State's Antiterrorism Assistance and Regional Security Initiative programs, which strengthened the government's capacity to counter terrorism.

Since 1974, Cyprus has been divided *de facto* into the Republic of Cyprus-controlled area, composed of the southern two-thirds of the island, and a northern third, administered by the Turkish Cypriots; the Republic of Cyprus does not exercise effective control over the area administered by the Turkish Cypriots. In 1983, the Turkish Cypriots declared the northern part an independent "Turkish Republic of Northern Cyprus" (TRNC). The United States does not recognize the "TRNC," nor does any country other than Turkey. The UN Peacekeeping Force in Cyprus patrols the buffer zone separating the two sides, but people, narcotics, and other illicit goods routinely cross uncontrolled.

The division of the island has obstructed counterterrorism cooperation between the two communities' law enforcement authorities, and between Cyprus and Turkey. In the Turkish Cypriot-administered area, issues of status and recognition inevitably restricted the ability of authorities to cooperate on counterterrorism with international organizations and countries other than Turkey. Turkish Cypriots cannot sign treaties, UN conventions, or other international agreements; and lacked the legal and institutional framework necessary to counter money laundering and terrorist financing effectively. Within these limitations, however, Turkish Cypriots cooperated in pursuing specific counterterrorism objectives.

Legislation, Law Enforcement, and Border Security: The Cypriot government remained committed to conforming to all European Council guidelines for countering terrorism. The Cypriot government invoked its Counter Terrorism Act of 2010 for the first time with the case of a suspected Hizballah operative detained by the Cypriot authorities in July for allegedly helping plan an attack against Israeli tourists in Cyprus. The prosecution subsequently dropped the terrorism-related charges, in part since Hizballah is not currently listed within the EU as a terrorist organization, to pursue conviction under the penal code for eight other charges, including: conspiracy, consent to commit a criminal offense, and participation in a criminal organization. On March 21, 2013, a Cyprus court found the Hizballah operative guilty of charges stemming from his surveillance activities of Israeli tourist targets.

In 2012, Cyprus' National Counterterrorism Coordinator led an ongoing interagency process to develop a new National Counterterrorism Strategy for Cyprus. The strategy is reportedly based on the four EU counterterrorism pillars of "Prevent, Protect, Pursue, and Respond." Security measures were put in place for the protection of western interests and soft targets, especially during Cyprus's Presidency of the Council of the EU.

Authorities issued a number of search warrants in response to suspected terrorist activity but found no evidence of terrorism. Although there were anecdotal reports of a low-level Kurdistan Workers' Party (PKK) presence, there was no noticeable activity in 2012. Cyprus maintained it was fulfilling all responsibilities with respect to the EU designation of the PKK as a terrorist organization.

Cypriot Police created and put into practice a screening watchlist mechanism. The Police's Counterterrorism Office is watchlisting, among others, all the persons subject to travel bans and asset freezing sanctions by UNSCRs and EU decisions concerning terrorism.

Countering Terrorist Finance: Cyprus is a member of Moneyval, the Committee of Experts on the Evaluation of Anti-Money Laundering Measures and the Financing of Terrorism, a Financial Action Task Force-style regional body, and its Financial Intelligence Unit is a member of the Egmont Group. The United States and Cyprus cooperated closely on anti-money laundering/ combating the financing of terrorism. Cypriot authorities have taken legislative steps to counter and suppress such activities. The Cypriot Anti-Money Laundering Authority implemented new UNSCR 1267/1989 and 1988 listings immediately and informally tracked suspect names listed under U.S. E.O.s. The Cypriot government maintained a "Prevention and Suppression of Money-Laundering Activities Law" that contained provisions on tracing and confiscating assets. For further information on money laundering and financial crimes, we refer you to the *2013 International Narcotics Control Strategy Report (INCSR), Volume 2, Money Laundering and Financial Crimes*: http://www.state.gov/j/inl/rls/nrcrpt/index.htm.

Regional and International Cooperation: Cyprus participated in counterterrorism initiatives by regional and multilateral organizations, including the UN, the OSCE, and the Global Initiative to Combat Nuclear Terrorism. During the Cypriot presidency of the Council of the EU, from July to December 2012, Cyprus chaired the Working Party on International Aspects of Terrorism (COTER) and the Terrorism Working Party (TWP).

The Cyprus COTER chair focused discussions on cooperation in capacity building, intelligence and threat analysis briefings; developments in the Global Counterterrorism Forum; and promotion of human rights while countering terrorism. Other priorities of Cyprus' presidency included exchanging views on international developments, such as the outcome of the Third Review of the UN Global Counter-Terrorism Strategy, and the prospect of creating a single UN Counterterrorism Coordinator position. Progress was made towards finalizing the EU Counterterrorism Action Plan for the Horn of Africa and Yemen. As COTER chair, Cyprus also participated in EU political dialogues held under the European External Action Service Chairmanship, including: individual counterterrorism dialogues with Russia, the United States, and the UN; and the counterterrorist finance dialogue with the United States.

Cyprus' Presidency Program for the TWP led to approval by the EU Council of Ministers of updated EU implementation plans and documents in a number of areas, including protection of soft targets, countering violent extremism, and aviation security. Cyprus' TWP Chair organized an EU conference in Nicosia on October 31, to raise awareness about the importance of protecting aviation from terrorist attacks, and to strengthen cooperation between all public and private services to collectively address this risk. The Cypriot Police's Counterterrorism Office also participated in the EU Police Working Group on Terrorism.

Countering Radicalization and Violent Extremism: One of the initiatives of Cyprus' EU presidency in the TWP was revising the EU implementation plan for its Radicalization and Recruitment Action Plan and assessing implementation by each member state. Cypriot Police (CNP) started to implement the different measures of the Action Plan, and also focused on educating police officers about violent extremism. The Counterterrorism Office participated as a partner to the Community Policing and the Prevention of Radicalization (COPPRA) project that was initiated by the Belgian presidency of the European Council; the COPPRA training manuals were fully incorporated into the training programs on violent extremism that were created and implemented by the CNP's Counterterrorism Office.

The CNP Counterterrorism Office provided training programs to prison staff to identify violent extremism in prisons. Under the Radicalization and Awareness Network, the European Commission also provided special training programs and seminars to social workers, health care officials, and other service providers.

DENMARK

Overview: The Kingdom of Denmark (Denmark, Greenland, and the Faroe Islands) has developed both short-term and long-term counterterrorism strategies and continued to cooperate closely with the United States on potential terrorist threats. Denmark remained a target of terrorist groups, including al-Qa'ida, due to cartoons depicting the prophet Mohammed published in September 2005 and reprinted in 2008. In May, the Danish government released the *Government Report on Counter-Terrorism Efforts*, which concluded, "The Danish police and justice system carry out law enforcement measures against attempts to commit terrorism, and the legislation in this area is continuously evaluated. In addition, Denmark maintains a counterterrorism emergency and response capability that can be activated in the event of a crisis.

Prevention constitutes a key element of the Government's approach, which is why the Government, through an inter-ministerial approach, regularly develops and implements initiatives aimed at reducing radicalization."

Legislation, Law Enforcement, and Border Security: Significant law enforcement actions against terrorists and terrorist groups in 2012, including arrests and prosecutions, follow:

- On January 10, Copenhagen City Court sentenced ROJ-TV and its parent company Mesopotamia Broadcast A/S METV under Article 1114E of the Fight Against Terrorism Act for promoting the Kurdistan Workers' Party (PKK) and spreading propaganda in programs that incite terrorism during the period February 2008 to September 2010. Each was sentenced to pay fines of $450,000. In its ruling, the court emphasized that ROJ-TV received funding from the PKK. The court sent to the Danish Radio and Television Council (Council) the question of whether the station's license should be revoked. In September, the Council ordered ROJ-TV to cease broadcasting for two months for failure to maintain archives of programs.
- On April 27, police arrested three men in Copenhagen on suspicion of plotting a terrorist attack against Danish soldiers returning from Afghanistan. The men, a 22-year-old citizen of Jordan, a 23-year-old Turkish man, and a 21-year-old Danish national from Egypt, were arrested in possession of illegal automatic weapons and ammunition at two separate sites in Copenhagen. The individuals were ultimately charged with weapons possession, and, in November, each received a sentence of three-and-a-half years in prison.
- On May 3, the Danish Supreme Court upheld the sentence of Mohamed Geele to nine years in prison to be followed by expulsion from Denmark. Geele was convicted of attempted commission of an act of terrorism, attempted murder, and aggravated assault of a police officer. The conviction resulted from Geele's January 1, 2010 attack with an axe on cartoonist Kurt Westergaard, one of the creators of the Mohammed cartoons.
- On May 28, Danish officials arrested a 23-year-old Danish national originally from Somalia, and his brother, age 18, and charged them with receiving terrorism training.
- On June 4, a Danish court sentenced four men, one Tunisian national and three Swedish citizens of Middle Eastern origin, each to 12 years in prison for planning a gun attack in 2010 intended to kill as many people as possible at *Jyllands-Posten*, a major Danish newspaper that previously published cartoons depicting the prophet Mohammed. The court also ordered the men to be expelled from Denmark after serving their sentences and to pay the trial costs. The men were arrested in Denmark in December 2010 after they arrived from Sweden, before the planned attack.

Countering Terrorist Finance: Denmark is one of the 36 member nations of the Financial Action Task Force. For further information on money laundering and financial crimes, we refer you to the *2013 International Narcotics Control Strategy Report (INCSR), Volume 2, Money Laundering and Financial Crimes*: http://www.state.gov/j/inl/rls/nrcrpt/index.htm.

Regional and International Cooperation: Denmark held the rotating Presidency of the Council of the EU from January 1 – June 30 and had, as one of its four priorities, "A Safe Europe," an initiative "to enhance European police cooperation in the fight against human trafficking, terrorism, and economic crime." One of the key accomplishments during the Danish EU Presidency was achieving European Council support for the creation of a European Passenger Name Record system to ensure law enforcement has the most current tools in the fight against terrorism and other serious crime. Denmark is a founding member of the Global Counterterrorism Forum and is an active member of the UN, NATO, and the OSCE, as well as Interpol, Europol, Middle Europe Conference, the Bern Club, and the EU Counterterrorism Group.

Denmark continued its capacity building engagement in Afghanistan, particularly with Afghan police forces, and also with anti-piracy operations in the Horn of Africa. Denmark has actively supported activities in East Africa and the Horn of Africa, including technical assistance to the Ethiopian Financial Intelligence Center and other African financial bodies. Denmark supported the First Annual Convention of Counterterrorism Practitioners in Eastern Africa and the Horn, held in Addis Ababa, Ethiopia in May, and published a report titled *ISSP-CGCC Joint Baseline Study on Anti-Money Laundering and Countering the Financing of Terrorism in the Intergovernmental Authority on Development (IGAD) in Eastern Africa Subregion.*

Countering Radicalization and Violent Extremism: Counter-radicalization programs were first implemented in 2009, empowering local governments to implement initiatives aimed at building tolerance, supporting democracy, and undertaking targeted interventions with radicalized persons. In 2012, the national plan retained the targeted interventions, administered through the Danish Security and Intelligence Service (PET), and local governments implemented their own individual programs. Denmark continued to base its local counter-radicalization programs on a previously existing, nationwide crime-prevention program of cooperation between schools, social services, and police.

Danish communications efforts to mitigate or counter terrorist propaganda were in the nascent stages. The Ministry of Social Affairs and Integration funded small grants to two immigrant-focused community groups to train employees on how to post positive messages on the groups' websites and how to counter violent extremist postings.

PET is establishing "Dialogue Forum" as a series of meetings attended by approximately 50 people twice a year in three major Danish cities (Copenhagen, Aarhus, and Vejle). The meetings will afford invited members of the Muslim community the opportunity to meet and discuss issues with PET officials.

The Danish government is continuing two projects previously funded by the EU: "De-radicalization – Targeted Intervention," to create mentoring programs and exit interviews for those desiring to leave terrorist organizations; and "De-radicalization – Back on Track" with the aim of developing methods for helping inmates affiliated with terrorist organizations re-integrate into society after serving a prison sentence. Mentoring programs are continuing at the local level; PET now funds and implements exit interviews. The inmate program continued to be funded through the EU and administered by the Ministry of Social Affairs and Integration; 12 mentors have been trained, but mentoring of selected prison inmates was just beginning at year's end.

FRANCE

Overview: The United States and France maintained a strong relationship in the fight against terrorism in 2012. U.S. government agencies worked closely with their French counterparts for the exchange and evaluation of terrorist-related information, and partnered in fostering closer regional and international cooperation. France's security apparatus and legislation afford broad powers to security services for the prevention of terrorist attacks. France was subjected to lone wolf attacks in March in Toulouse and Mantauban. The French government was concerned about the possibility of attacks against its interests inside and outside of Syria, Mali, and Mali's neighbors. Also, instability in Mali and the Sahel heightened French concerns about the ability of terrorists to operate in and recruit from northern Africa.

2012 Terrorist Incidents:
- On March 11 and 15, Mohamed Merah, killed three French soldiers and critically injured another, in Montauban and Toulouse.
- On March 19, Merah killed a teacher and three children at a private Jewish school in Toulouse. Merah was killed by police on March 22, after a 32-hour siege at his apartment.
- On March 21, a package bomb exploded outside the Indonesian Embassy in Paris. The building sustained damage, but no injuries were reported. French militant Frederic C. Jean Salvi, who has been on Indonesia's wanted list since 2010 for allegedly planning a car bombing with other members of a terrorist cell, was suspected by Indonesia's anti-terrorism agency of having carried out the attack.
- On September 19, an individual threw a Molotov cocktail into a kosher supermarket in Sarcelles, injuring one person. An investigation into the attack led to the October 6 dismantling of a suspected Islamic terrorist cell located in several French cities.

Legislation, Law Enforcement, and Border Security: On December 12, the French government adopted new counterterrorism legislation. The new law allows authorities to prosecute French citizens who return to the country after having committed an act of terrorism abroad, or after training in terrorist camps (notably in the Afghanistan-Pakistan region) with the intention of returning to France to commit terrorist attacks.

France works diligently to maintain strong border security and implements national and EU border security legislation. On June 29, Marseille-Provence airport implemented the Automated Fast Track Crossing at External Borders (PARAFE) system, which, combined with biometric authentication technology, simplifies border crossing and results in an average crossing time of 20 seconds. Paris' Charles de Gaulle and Orly airports use the PARAFE system. In 2012, French customs actively participated in the National Targeting Center (NTC) activities. The NTC, located in Washington, DC, allows for real-time information sharing as it relates to passenger and cargo targeting. On December 20, the French government adopted new legislation that increases the length of time illegal immigrants may be detained for not having a residency permit to 16 hours. The law responds to criticism that the previous length of detention, four hours, mandated by the French Supreme Court, allowed criminal networks to traffic immigrants to another country before police could complete their checks.

On March 19, following the attacks by Mohamed Merah, France raised its *Vigipirate* national security alert system to scarlet (the highest) for the first time since the creation of the system. The alert notified the public "of a risk of major attacks, simultaneous or otherwise, using non-conventional means and causing major devastation; preparing appropriate means of rescues and response, measures that are highly disruptive to public life are authorized." The alert was lowered back to level red ("high chance of threat") on March 24.

On May 4, a French court sentenced Algerian-born particle physicist, Adlene Hicheur, 35, to five years in prison for "criminal association with the intent to prepare terrorist acts." While Hicheur studied and was employed in France, he exchanged 35 emails, some of them encrypted, with a representative of al-Qa'ida in the Islamic Maghreb (AQIM) in Algeria in 2009.

The following high profile arrests took place in 2012:

- On January 25, French Police arrested Basque Fatherland and Liberty (ETA) member Ernesto Prat Urzainqui, one of Spain's most wanted terrorists.
- On March 19, the brother of violent extremist Mohamed Merah, Abdelkader Merah, was arrested, and on March 25 was charged with criminal conspiracy for planning terrorist acts, and of complicity in murder and gang robbery.
- On March 30, police conducted raids targeting suspected terrorists in Toulouse, Nantes, Le Mans, Lyon, Nice, and in the Paris region, arresting 17. On April 3, 13 of the suspects were placed under formal investigation, one remained in pre-trial detention, and four were released. Several of the suspects were accused of planning the kidnapping of Albert Levy, a Jewish magistrate from Lyon.
- On April 4, police conducted raids targeting suspected terrorists in Marseille, Roubaix, Trappes, Carpentras, Valence, and Pau, arresting 10. The suspects reportedly visited websites that expressed violent extremist views, and some were suspected of traveling to Afghanistan and Pakistan to train in terrorist camps.
- On May 27, the military leader of ETA, Oroitz Gurruchaga Gorgorza, and his deputy, Xabier Aramburu, were arrested in the southwestern French village of Cuana following a joint operation conducted by the French Internal Security Service, the Spanish Civil Guard, and the Spanish intelligence services.
- On October 6, police conducted raids targeting suspected terrorists in Cannes, Strasbourg, and the Paris suburb of Torcy, killing one suspect and arresting 12 others. Five of the 12 suspects were released on October 10 without charges.
- On October 27, French authorities, as the result of a joint investigation by the Spanish Civil Guard and French police, arrested ETA members Izaskun Lesaka Arguelles and Joseba Iturbide Ochoteco. Lesaka was one of the three members of ETA's leadership (ETA's "Holy Trinity," as they are referred to in press). Lesaka read many of the group's communiqués in televised statements.
- On December 17, French intelligence services arrested three individuals suspected of violent extremism in the neighborhoods of Bon-Voyage and les Moulins in Nice. The three men were accused of training in terrorist training camps in Jakarta, Indonesia.

Other actions in 2012 included:
- On April 2, violent Islamic extremist Ali Belhadad (Algerian), and Imam Almany Baradji (Malian), were deported from France. The Ministry of Interior also announced that Imam Saad Nasser Alchatry (Saudi Arabian) would not be allowed back into France; while Imam Yusuf Yuksel (Turkish) and violent extremist Malek Drine (Tunisian) would also be deported at a later date. According to the Ministry, the imams made anti-Semitic statements in their sermons and called for Muslims to reject Western values.
- On November 21, Paris' Sentence Enforcement Court granted parole to Georges Ibrahim Abdullah, on the condition that he immediately be deported to Lebanon. Abdallah, the convicted terrorist and Lebanese national sentenced to life in prison for his involvement in the 1982 murders of a U.S. military attaché and an Israeli diplomat in Paris, and the

attempted murder of a U.S. consul in Strasbourg, is one of Europe's longest serving prisoners. The French government immediately appealed the decision. The appellate court was scheduled to consider the appeal in early 2013.

Countering Terrorist Finance: France is a member of the Financial Action Task Force (FATF) and underwent a mutual evaluation in February 2011. France belongs to the following FATF-related bodies: Cooperating and Supporting Nation to the Caribbean Financial Action Task Force, Observer to the Financial Action Task Force of South America, Observer to the Asia Pacific Group, Observer to the Eurasia Group, Observer to the Middle East and North Africa Financial Task Force, member of the Egmont Group, and member of the Anti-Money Laundering Liaison Committee of the Franc Zone. The FATF also designated France as a member of Moneyval, the Committee of Experts on the Evaluation of Anti-Money Laundering Measures and the Financing of Terrorism, for a period of two years beginning in the fall of 2012. The Government of France began implementing FATF's April 2012 recommendations to detect, prevent, and suppress the financing of terrorism and terrorist acts.

- On January 31, five people were arrested in the Paris region by the sub-Directorate of the Anti-Terrorism unit of the Ministry of Interior for channeling funds through restaurants to the Kurdistan Workers' Party (PKK).
- On February 16, Taoufik Boussedra, a member of the Cherifi group, was deported to Tunisia for financing al-Qa'ida (AQ). Boussedra was one of eight men convicted of financing terrorism in January 2011. The other seven men received from 15 years imprisonment to a one-year suspended sentence. The men were found to be funneling funds through shops they opened in several Paris suburbs.
- On June 29, Nabil Amdouni, a 34-year-old Tunisian citizen, was arrested in Toulon and placed under formal investigation for allegedly funding AQIM.
- On July 15, the Ministry of Economy and Finance froze the assets of "Emily K" who actively supported the violent extremist organization, Forsane Alizza.
- On October 6 and 7, three members of the PKK in Europe were arrested outside of Paris and Mayenne for trying to provide 1.2 million euros (US $1.56 million) in arms to the Iraqi wing of the PKK.
- During the last week of October, the Ministry of Economy and Finance froze the assets of Imam Mohamed Hammami, and expelled him to Tunisia, for calling for a "violent jihad" and violence against women during his sermons at the Omar Mosque in Paris. The funds of the Association of Faith and Practice, which Hammami chaired, were also frozen.
- On November 28, 15 people were charged with illegally financing the Revolutionary People's Liberation Front (DHKP-C), a Turkish revolutionary organization designated as a terrorist organization by the EU and United States, and banned in Turkey. The individuals are accused of channeling money made through the sale of a Turkish magazine to the DHKP-C through the Anatolia's Cultural and Solidarity Association in Paris. Prosecutors are seeking jail terms of up to eight years.
- On December 17, 10 people went on trial in Paris for allegedly raising 300,000 euros (approximately US $395,000) for the Islamic Movement of Uzbekistan, which the UN lists as associated with AQ. The trial is occurring four years after the suspects, most of whom are of Turkish origin, were arrested in France, Germany, and the Netherlands.

For further information on money laundering and financial crimes, we refer you to the *2013 International Narcotics Control Strategy Report (INCSR), Volume 2, Money Laundering and Financial Crimes*: http://www.state.gov/j/inl/rls/nrcrpt/index.htm.

Regional and International Cooperation: France is a founding member of the Global Counterterrorism Forum. France is actively engaged with the UN Counterterrorism Committee (CTC) and also played a strong role on the UNSCR 1267/1989 and 1988 Sanctions Committees. France participated in the drafting of the European Council's Counterterrorism Strategy action plan. France helped create and implement NATO's new Strategic Concept and the Lisbon Summit Declaration, both of which include major counterterrorism measures for member states. Through the OSCE, France engaged in new measures to counter transnational threats, including terrorism. The French government undertook joint counterterrorism operations with countries including the UK, Belgium, Germany, Italy, and Spain.

France also plays an active role in efforts to support counterterrorism capacity building in other countries both bilaterally and within the EU.

Countering Radicalization and Violent Extremism: The French government does not have a program in place that specifically addresses countering violent extremism, but considers its integration programs for all French citizens and residents a major tool in countering radicalization and violent extremism in France. Many of these programs target disenfranchised communities and new immigrants. For example, the Ministry of Education works to instill "universal values" in all French pupils, regardless of ethnic origin or country of birth. Ministry regulations mandate that all French public schools teach civic education, and that all students attend school until age 16. The government also offers adult vocational training for older immigrants and/or minorities who never attended French schools. The Ministry of Interior plays a significant role in countering radicalization by targeting areas, neighborhoods, and regions with high criminality and juvenile delinquency rates.

The Ministry of Justice implements rehabilitation and reintegration programs for former criminals. To help curb radicalization, the penitentiary system announced in 2012 that it would increase the number of Muslim chaplains in French prisons in 2013 to 166 (from 151) to help curb radicalization. In 2012, there were an estimated 200 violent Islamist extremists in the French prison system, 60 to 70 of whom were strongly suspected of belonging to a terrorist network. The majority of these prisoners were located in prisons in northern France, the Paris region, and Marseille.

GEORGIA

Overview: In 2012, Georgia continued its close cooperation with U.S. government agencies on a wide-range of counterterrorism-related issues. Specifically, the U.S. Embassy's Regional Security, Defense Threat Reduction Agency, Export Control and Border Security, Department of Justice Resident Legal Advisor, and International Narcotics and Law Enforcement officers all provided significant training and equipment to relevant agencies in the Georgian government. The Georgian government's lack of control of the occupied territories of Abkhazia and South Ossetia limited its ability to counter terrorism in these regions and to secure its border with Russia.

2012 Terrorist Incidents: The year was marked by the discovery of an improvised explosive device (IED) attached to the car of a locally employed staff member of the Israeli Embassy in Tbilisi on February 13. No injuries were reported, and the Ministry of Internal Affairs was able to successfully neutralize the IED. The discovery of the IED coincided with similar incidents, on the same day, in which Israeli diplomats were targeted in Thailand and India. These attacks were linked to Iran's Revolutionary Guards Qods Force.

In August, an armed confrontation with suspected violent Islamist extremists from Chechnya occurred in the Lopota Gorge region of Georgia. The Georgian government initially did not classify the confrontation as a terrorist incident, but in November, the newly-elected government reopened an investigation into the events surrounding the attack.

Legislation, Law Enforcement, and Border Security: Georgia amended legislation on technological terrorism and cyber terrorism. The United States, Georgia, and Armenia participated in cross-border exercises that successfully demonstrated the Governments of Georgia and Armenia's internal, bilateral, and international notification and response procedures in the detection and interdiction of illicit trans-border movements of weapons of mass destruction materials.

In early 2012, Georgia arrested and convicted two individuals in two separate instances attempting to place IEDs in the Samegrelo region of Georgia. The bombings allegedly originated in Abkhazia, and the bombers were apprehended before they could detonate the IEDs.

Countering Terrorist Finance: Georgia is a member of Moneyval, the Committee of Experts on the Evaluation of Anti-Money Laundering Measures and the Financing of Terrorism, and saw improved scores in 2012. Georgia amended its criminal code in 2012, adding two articles. The first classifies the financing of actions that pose a danger to the navigation of an aircraft as terrorist financing, and the other classifies and defines the financing of an action that leads to an explosion as terrorist financing.

In January, the Permanent National Interagency Antiterrorist Commission (PNIAC) was established. The PNIAC, which is chaired by the Minister of Justice, significantly expedites the court order process for freezing assets of individuals or entities on the UNSCR 1267/1989 and 1988 consolidated lists. If an entity or individual is on any of the lists, the PNIAC passes the names to the National Bank for dissemination to privately registered banks in Georgia.

For further information on money laundering and financial crimes, we refer you to the *2013 International Narcotics Control Strategy Report (INCSR), Volume 2, Money Laundering and Financial Crimes*: http://www.state.gov/j/inl/rls/nrcrpt/index.htm.

Regional and International Cooperation: On the regional level, Georgia is an active member of the Organization of Black Sea Economic Cooperation and the GUAM (Georgia, Ukraine, Azerbaijan, and Moldova) Organization for Democracy and Economic Development. Bilaterally, Georgia concluded a counterterrorism and law enforcement cooperation agreement with Hungary and Turkey in 2012, bringing the number of bilateral counterterrorism and law enforcement agreements Georgia has signed to 21. Georgia is in the process of concluding these bilateral agreements with every European country.

GERMANY

Overview: The threat from violent extremism remained elevated in 2012. Germany investigated, arrested, and prosecuted numerous terrorist suspects and disrupted terrorist-related groups within its borders with connections to al-Qa'ida (AQ) and other violent Islamist extremist, Kurdish nationalist, and Nazi terrorist organizations.

2012 Terrorist Incidents: Authorities are investigating a suspected attempted terrorist attack after a bomb was discovered in a gym bag December 10 at the Bonn train station. It apparently did not explode because of poor workmanship.

Legislation, Law Enforcement, and Border Security: In January, the Federal Cabinet decided to create a central database of violent neo-Nazis and those who call for the use of violence. The database became operational in late September. In June, Interior Minister Friedrich banned the Solingen-based violent extremist group Millatu Ibrahim. In November, Germany launched its Joint Terrorism and Defense Center. Modeled after existing centers against violent extremism and right-wing radicalism, the new center addresses politically motivated crime.

Arrests and prosecutions:

- In February, Arid Uka was sentenced to life in prison for shooting U.S. airmen at Frankfurt Airport in 2011.
- In February, a Düsseldorf court sentenced Sadi Naci Ö. to six years and Ünalkaplan D. to four years in prison for membership in the Turkish terrorist group Revolutionary People's Freedom Party/Front.
- In March, the trial against Afghan-born German citizen Ahmad Wali Sidiqi began in Koblenz. German authorities had arrested him at Ramstein airbase upon his release from U.S. custody in April 2011. Sidiqi allegedly received instructions from Sheik Younis to carry out attacks in Europe.
- In May, a German engineer who was kidnapped in northern Nigeria was killed. Al-Qa'ida in the Islamic Maghreb had demanded in March that Germany free convicted terrorist supporter Filiz Gelowicz in exchange for the engineer.
- In May, the trial against an AQ terror cell began in Düsseldorf. The defendants were accused of conspiring to set off explosives in crowded areas.
- In October, a judge sentenced Murat K. to six years in prison and more than US $12,000 in damages for a knife attack against two police officers during a demonstration.
- In November, charges were filed against alleged National Socialist Underground (NSU) member Beate Zschäpe and four accomplices. The NSU terror cell is suspected of murdering nine people with immigrant backgrounds for racist/xenophobic reasons and one policewoman between 2000 and 2007.
- In December, a Berlin court sentenced German national Thomas U. (a.k.a. Hamsa al-Majaari) to four years and three months imprisonment for membership in the German Taliban mujahedin, training to commit terrorist acts, and uploading violent extremist propaganda to the internet.

Countering Terrorist Finance: Germany is a member of the Financial Action Task Force (FATF), and an observer to the Eurasian Group on Combating Money Laundering and Terrorist Financing, the Asia/Pacific Group on Money Laundering, and the Financial Action Task Force of South America against Money Laundering, all FATF-style regional bodies. Germany's Financial Intelligence Unit is a member of the Egmont Group. German agencies filed 12,868 suspicious transaction reports in 2011 (2012 figures were not available), designating 194 for suspected terrorist financing. Germany remained a strong advocate of the UNSCR 1267/1989 and 1988 Taliban and AQ sanctions regimes.

In April, Filiz Gelowicz, wife of Fritz Gelowicz – who is serving time for planning attacks against U.S. interests in Germany in 2007 – was released from prison. She had been convicted of financially supporting the German Taliban Mujahedin and the Islamic Jihad Union. In March, a trial began against Ömer C., who is charged with membership in the Islamic Movement of Uzbekistan (IMU), and Turgay C., who is charged with providing US $52,000 to the IMU.

For further information on money laundering and financial crimes, we refer you to the *2013 International Narcotics Control Strategy Report (INCSR), Volume 2, Money Laundering and Financial Crimes*: http://www.state.gov/j/inl/rls/nrcrpt/index.htm.

Regional and International Cooperation: Germany is a founding member of the Global Counterterrorism Forum and continued to participate in various multilateral counterterrorism initiatives.

Countering Radicalization and Violent Extremism: Germany has numerous programs to counter violent extremism, at the state and federal levels. In North-Rhine Westphalia alone, there is the "Ibrahim Meets Abraham" community relations initiative; the Information and Education Center against Right-Wing Extremism; the former National-Socialistic Center Vogelsang, which is now used for cultural and civic education; the "No Racism in Schools" and "Prevention of Extremism in Sports" efforts; as well as city programs. Dortmund has a "Prevention of Extremism in the City of Dortmund" program. The German Soccer Federation awards a prize to organizations and persons who use their positions to work for freedom, tolerance, and humanity; and against intolerance, racism, and hatred. Other cities, such as Cologne, host street soccer tournaments to bring together NGOs and at-risk youths. In Berlin, the Violence Prevention Network runs a training program that serves – both during and after detention – ideologically motivated perpetrators.

In January, the Federal Ministry of the Interior established a radicalization help center for parents and friends of violent Islamist extremists. The Interior Ministry started a promotion campaign that included posting simulated missing person notices for fictitious violent extremists who have cut off contact with their friends and families; the notices feature contact information for the radicalization help center. Four Muslim organizations were offended by the campaign and have discontinued their cooperation with the Interior Ministry's Security Partnership Initiative (SPI), in protest against the Countering Violent Extremism poster project. The Muslim organizations complained that the posters linked Islam to violence. The Interior Ministry plans to continue the SPI.

Germany continued its HATIF (the Arabic word for telephone) program to assist violent Islamist extremists with reintegration. The Interior Ministry also continued a project, first launched in 2001, to stop radicalization among young right-wing offenders. The Ministry expanded the program in 2007 to function in eight states. In 2012, the Interior Ministry also continued a project in three states to counter radicalization of young delinquents influenced by violent extremist ideology.

GREECE

Overview: In 2012, Greece continued to experience small-scale attacks like targeted arson and improvised explosive device detonation by domestic anarchist groups. Generally, such attacks did not aim to inflict bodily harm but rather sought to make a political statement. Many members of the two most active domestic terrorist groups, Revolutionary Struggle and Conspiracy of Fire Nuclei, have been imprisoned since 2011. Overall, Greek government cooperation with the United States on counterterrorism and the physical security of American interests in Greece was strong.

2012 Terrorist Incidents: On February 25, a group under the name "February 12 Movement" claimed responsibility for a failed bomb attack at the Egaleo subway station where an improvised incendiary device (IID) was placed inside an Athens subway car. The device was placed next to a seat and consisted of a plastic container with flammable liquid, a small quantity of an explosive substance, a timer, wires, and batteries. The bomb did not explode, most likely due to faulty construction.

Greece's two largest cities, Athens and Thessaloniki, experienced frequent, relatively small-scale anarchist attacks that used inexpensive and unsophisticated incendiary devices against the properties of political figures, party offices, private bank ATMs, ministries and tax offices, and privately-owned vehicles.

One incident was reported against U.S. interests. On June 27, a group calling itself "Deviant Behaviors for the Proliferation of Revolutionary Terrorism – International Revolutionary Front" claimed responsibility for an attack in which a van full of IIDs was driven through the front of the Microsoft headquarters building in an Athens suburb. The IIDs were subsequently detonated, causing a high intensity explosion. No casualties or injuries were reported.

Legislation, Law Enforcement, and Border Security: Seven members of Revolutionary Struggle were released from pretrial detention in October 2011 (due to a Greek law that allows a maximum of 18 months of imprisonment without trial proceedings beginning). The Greek Counterterrorism Unit was not informed by the local police precinct that two of the lead members failed to show up for their required check-in (also October 2011) at the precinct until July 2012. Police have not been able to locate the two, and Greek authorities had not prosecuted the case by year's end.

The trial of 17 suspected members of Conspiracy of Fire Nuclei, which began in 2011, was repeatedly postponed due to work stoppages by judges and judicial postponements in 2012.

The porous nature of Greece's borders is of concern. While Greek border authorities try to stem the flow of illegal migration, its ability to control large-scale illegal migration via its land and sea borders with Turkey is limited. The recent political upheavals in North Africa and the Middle East have intensified illegal migration to and through Greece via the Greece-Turkey border and the Greek Aegean islands.

DHS/ICE provided training to Hellenic National Police and Coast Guard in Athens, Crete, Patras, and Thessaloniki to advance knowledge of border security agents. The U.S. National Counterterrorism Center facilitated a multi-day tabletop exercise in Athens in an effort to prepare Hellenic Police Forces for a large-scale terrorist incident. Participation on the part of the Greek government was broad-based and comprehensive.

Countering Terrorist Finance: Greece is a member of the Financial Action Task Force. The Foreign Ministry's Sanctions Monitoring Unit is tasked with ensuring that Greece meets its commitments to enforce international sanctions, including terrorism-related sanctions. The Financial Intelligence unit inspected 3,586 suspicious transactions in 2012, but did not discover evidence of terrorist financing in Greece. For further information on money laundering and financial crimes, we refer you to the *2013 International Narcotics Control Strategy Report (INCSR), Volume 2, Money Laundering and Financial Crimes*: http://www.state.gov/j/inl/rls/nrcrpt/index.htm.

Regional and International Cooperation: Greece is a member of the UN Counter-Terrorism Committee. Overall, Greece engaged constructively on counterterrorism initiatives in international fora. Greece regularly participated in regional information exchange and seminars through such bodies as the EU, the OSCE, the Southeast European Law Enforcement Center for Combating Trans-Border Crime, and the Organization of Black Sea Economic Cooperation.

IRELAND

Overview: The United States and Ireland collaborated closely on counterterrorism, law enforcement, and information-sharing. An Garda Siochana (Irish Police at both the national and local level) has comprehensive law enforcement, immigration, investigative, and counterterrorism responsibilities, and continued to work closely with American counterparts. In 2012, as was the case in 2010 and 2011, there were incidents by dissident republican groups in Ireland, generally targeting other republican factions and often involving criminal activity. Some violent actions committed in neighboring Northern Ireland by members of dissident groups were traced back to support provided by persons living in Ireland. The immediate targets of violence were law enforcement personnel and the security structures of Northern Ireland in an attempt to disrupt the ongoing post-peace process community rehabilitation efforts. Irish authorities handle these legacy issues stemming from "The Troubles," and are actively involved in dealing with transnational terrorism issues.

2012 Terrorist Incidents: The list below details terrorism-related incidents reported in the public domain. As of December 31, 96 viable improvised explosive devices (IEDs) were disarmed and analyzed by Ireland's Army bomb disposal teams. Incidents included:

- On January 5, five pipe bombs were found in County Clare. Army bomb disposal teams secured the devices.
- On February 16, Garda recovered a handgun and three IEDs. The items were found in County Kildare during ongoing investigations into the activities of dissident republicans.
- On May 1, Garda and Army bomb disposal experts neutralized a live 45-pound IED found in Phoenix Park near the residences of the U.S. Ambassador and the Irish President. The location of the IED was only one mile from Garda headquarters.
- On June 23, Garda discovered eight pipe bombs in a housing estate in Limerick City.

- On August 11, a device wrapped in plastic was discovered in Limerick. An army explosive ordnance disposal unit carried out a controlled explosion to destroy the device.
- On August 21, Army bomb disposal teams dealt with four separate incidents in Dublin, two of which involved viable explosive devices.
- On September 3, RIRA leader Alan Ryan was killed in north Dublin.
- On September 17, a petrol bomb did considerable structural damage to Sinn Fein Irish Member of Parliament Aengus O Snodaigh's constituency office in Dublin. No one was injured.
- On October 5, Garda uncovered what they believe to be a pipe bomb-making facility in north Dublin. Garda later arrested the man suspected of directing the facility.
- On November 1, David Black, a prison officer from Northern Ireland, was murdered on his way to work; an investigation is underway. A Dublin-based alliance of dissident republican splinter groups claimed responsibility for his murder.
- On December 4, Eamon Kelly, an alleged criminal gang leader and dissident republican, was shot in north Dublin.

Legislation, Law Enforcement, and Border Security: On November 9, the Irish government approved the drafting of the Criminal Justice (Terrorist Offences) (Amendment) Bill 2012. This bill, if enacted, would amend the Criminal Justice (Terrorist Offences) Act 2005 and create three new offences of: (1) public provocation to commit a terrorist offence, (2) recruitment for terrorism, and (3) training for terrorism.

A series of investigations into historical cases from "The Troubles" related to the Smithwick Tribunal were ongoing at year's end. The Smithwick Tribunal, begun in 2006, is reviewing the events surrounding the murders of Chief Superintendent Harry Breen and Superintendent Robert Buchanan of the Royal Ulster Constabulary, the predecessor to the present day Police Services of Northern Ireland. Public hearings for the tribunal began in July 2011.

The Irish government has a good track record in responding positively and thoroughly to U.S. requests for cooperation on all law enforcement issues.

2012 arrests related to terrorist activity included:

- On February 7, Garda arrested two men as part of an ongoing investigation into dissident republican activity.
- On June 11, Garda arrested two men for dissident republican activity.
- On July 3, Garda arrested a man and seized a gun during an investigation into dissident republican paramilitary activity.
- On September 15, three men were charged by the Special Criminal Court in Dublin with membership in the RIRA. They were among 17 people who were detained during Operation Ambience, a Garda investigation into a paramilitary display that transpired at the funeral of RIRA boss Alan Ryan.
- On September 27, police in Dublin investigating dissident republican activities arrested two men after surveillance equipment was found in a hotel room overlooking a Garda station.

2012 prosecutions related to terrorist activity included:

- On January 24, an individual was sentenced to life imprisonment by the Special Criminal Court in Dublin for the 2008 murder of a man in County Donegal. The murder was linked to the dissident republican group, Oglaigh na hEireann.
- On February 24, two men were found guilty of possessing explosive substances by an Irish court following a 2010 Garda raid on a suspected dissident republican bomb-making facility in Dundalk.
- On March 31, a man was sentenced to four years imprisonment after he admitted to a 2010 charge of gun and ammunition possessing.

Countering Terrorist Finance: Ireland is a member of the Financial Action Task Force (FATF). The Criminal Justice (Money Laundering and Terrorist Financing) Bill of 2010 enacted the EU's third money-laundering directive into Irish law, giving effect to several FATF recommendations. The act consolidated Ireland's existing Anti-Money Laundering/ Counterterrorist Finance Laws and increased the obligations on a wide range of individuals and organizations to disclose information related to money laundering and terrorist financing.

Ireland implements all EU Council Regulations on financial sanctions against listed terrorists and related directives. The government continues to amend its primary 2010 legislation to strengthen it and implement FATF recommendations.

Law enforcement authorities monitor non-profit organizations for breaches of criminal law, but the Charities Act has yet to be fully implemented. Ireland is on the regular follow-up FATF list and is not yet eligible to be placed on the biennial review list. For further information on money laundering and financial crimes, we refer you to the *2013 International Narcotics Control Strategy Report (INCSR), Volume 2, Money Laundering and Financial Crimes*: http://www.state.gov/j/inl/rls/nrcrpt/index.htm.

Regional and International Cooperation: Ireland is a member of all relevant regional and international bodies to combat terrorism. This includes the Council of Europe, the OECD, the OSCE, and NATO's Partnership for Peace. Ireland has held the Chairmanship of the OSCE for the duration of the 2012 calendar year and hosted the 19th OSCE Ministerial Council in Dublin on December 6-7.

U.S. government officials worked with the Irish government on security efforts surrounding the 2012 Olympics in London.

In addition to counterterrorism capacity building in foreign states, it is important to mention the counterterrorism efforts in a regional context with Northern Ireland. The Irish Defense Forces provided a robust explosive ordnance disposal capability to the civil authority, routinely deploying to investigate and disarm ordnance around the country. The 2nd Eastern Brigade, which is responsible for the Dublin area and a significant portion of the territory along the border with Northern Ireland, responded to over 100 reports of explosive devices in 2012.

Countering Radicalization and Violent Extremism: The Government of Ireland continued its significant efforts to assist in the integration process of minority groups in Ireland. These measures included providing social benefits, language training, and the proactive advocacy work of an ombudsman's office.

ITALY

Overview: Italy aggressively investigated and prosecuted terrorist suspects, dismantled terrorist-related cells within its borders, and maintained high-level professional cooperation with international partners in all areas. Terrorist activity by domestic anarchists and other violent extremists remained a threat.

2012 Terrorist Incidents:
- On January 16, three explosive devices exploded outside the Naples office of the national tax agency. No information was available about the attackers.
- On May 7, two men shot and wounded Roberto Adinolfi, chief executive officer of a nuclear engineering company, Ansaldo, in Genoa. The Informal Anarchist Federation claimed responsibility for the attack on May 11. On September 13, police arrested two members of the group accused of being the attackers.
- On May 12, two Molotov cocktails were thrown against the entrance of the Livorno office of the national tax agency. On July 10, Livorno prosecutors announced that nine anarchists were under investigation for the episode.
- On August 30, three broadcasting repeaters were set afire near Parma by a group of anarchists who demanded the release from a Swiss prison of a Swiss environmentalist arrested in Italy in 1991.

Legislation, Law Enforcement, and Border Security: The Italian government continued to make use of reinforced counterterrorism legislation enacted in 2005 that facilitates detention of suspects, mandates arrest for crimes involving terrorism, and expedites procedures for expelling persons suspected of terrorist activities.

The Italian Civil Aviation Authority (CAA) and Ministry of Interior continued improvements to aviation security. In May, the CAA and the Transportation Security Administration signed an Annex to a Memorandum of Cooperation setting the framework for future collaboration. The CAA purchased additional Advanced Image Technology units (otherwise known as body scanners) for use at the Rome and Milan international airports.

Law enforcement actions included:

- On February 6, former Guantanamo detainee Riadh Ben Mohamed Nasri was cleared of charges of international terrorism by a Milan appeals court. Nasri, who was detained for eight years at the Guantanamo Bay detention facility and was subsequently confined for two years and two months in an Italian jail, had been accused of supporting a terrorist group that recruited volunteers who had joined insurgents abroad between 1997 and 2001. In January 2011, an Italian court had sentenced Nasri to six years of imprisonment.
- On February 21, police arrested nine alleged members of Turkish Hizballah (unrelated to the similarly-named Hizballah that operates in Lebanon) who were accused of abetting illegal immigration and assisting fake asylum seekers in Terni.
- On March 15, authorities arrested Mohamed Jarmoune, a Moroccan national who had lived in Italy for 16 years, on suspicion of providing online training in arms and explosives to supporters in Brescia and planning a violent attack against a synagogue in Milan.

- On March 27, Venice prosecutors ordered the arrest of five members of the Kurdistan Workers' Party (PKK) accused of extortion. They allegedly had forced several Turkish nationals to regularly pay up to US $6,783 as contribution for the operations of the PKK.
- On June 13, police arrested eight members of the Informal Anarchist Federation (IAF), a network that claimed responsibility for letter bombs sent to: the director of a center for migrants in Gradisca d'Isonzo; Bocconi University in Milan; a Deutsche Bank office in Frankfurt; an office of the national tax agency in Rome; and the Greek ambassador in Paris. The group reportedly cooperated with the Swiss and Spanish anarchists, Marco Camenisch and Gabriel Pombo de Silva.
- On September 11, the Cassation Court confirmed the May 24 ruling of a Milan appeals court that had sentenced11 members of the Red Brigades to prison terms between 14 months and 11 years and six months for two attacks against offices of political parties and for a conspiracy against a senator and a senior labor expert. Another defendant was acquitted.
- On September 13, Genoa police arrested Nicola Gai and Alfredo Cospito, members of IAF, accused of the May 7 terrorist attack against Roberto Adinolfi.
- On September 25, the Ministry of Interior announced the arrest and expulsion of two Libyans suspected of violent extremist proselytism and planning a violent attack. The two were injured during the conflict in Libya and had traveled to Rome for medical treatment.
- On October 4, Italy extradited an al-Qa'ida (AQ) member to the United States who is charged with conspiracy to murder U.S. nationals, conspiracy to bomb a government facility, conspiracy to provide material support to a foreign terrorist organization, and use of firearms and explosives. He travelled from Saudi Arabia to Afghanistan in 2001, where he attended AQ training camps and later fought in tribal areas of Pakistan against U.S. and Coalition Forces.

Countering Terrorist Finance: Italy worked closely with the United States on anti-money laundering and information sharing, and cooperated with other foreign governments as an active member of the Financial Action Task Force and the Egmont Group. Italy also participated in the UNSCR 1267/1989 and 1988 designation process, both as a sponsoring and co-sponsoring nation. As of October, the Italian Guardia di Finanza and Anti-Mafia Investigative Unit had carried out more than 500 money-laundering investigations and seized more than 120 million euros (US $162,800,000) in laundered money. In 2012, the Italian Treasury's Financial Information Unit upgraded its technology resources and training it provides to financial entities to improve the rate and quality of suspicious transaction reports. For further information on money laundering and financial crimes, we refer you to the *2013 International Narcotics Control Strategy Report (INCSR), Volume 2, Money Laundering and Financial Crimes*: http://www.state.gov/j/inl/rls/nrcrpt/index.htm.

Regional and International Cooperation: Italy is a founding member of the Global Counterterrorism Forum. Italy also supported counterterrorism efforts through the G-8 Roma-Lyon Group (including capacity building through the Counterterrorism Action Group), the OSCE, NATO, the UN, and the EU.

Countering Radicalization and Violent Extremism The Ministry of Justice Penitentiary Police continued financing an NGO-administered counter-radicalization program to place imams in the three prisons where Muslims convicted of terrorism were incarcerated. To counter potential radicalization, the Ministry of Interior conducted training in September for more than 1,000 law enforcement officers in Milan, Turin, and Venice on how to engage more effectively with immigrant communities.

KOSOVO

Overview: The Government of Kosovo continued to cooperate with the United States on counterterrorism-related issues in 2012, with progress made along numerous fronts. The security and political situation in northern Kosovo continued to limit the government's ability to exercise its authority in that region, where the NATO Kosovo Force (KFOR) and the EU Rule of Law Mission (EULEX) are responsible for maintaining a safe and secure environment and strengthening the rule of law, including at the borders. While Kosovo and neighboring Serbia did not directly cooperate on counterterrorism issues, both governments worked to implement an Integrated Border Management (IBM) plan with joint checkpoints in December.

Legislation, Law Enforcement, and Border Security: The Kosovo Assembly approved a new criminal code (CC) and criminal procedure code (CPC) in December, both of which came into force on January 1, 2013. The new laws preserve the UN model on counterterrorism criminal legislation, which was also the basis of the previous code. The CC raises the punishment for terrorism-related crimes, and provides a greater range of criminal offenses to charge against putative terrorists, such as weapons offenses or intrusion into computer systems. In addition, the new CC permits the prosecution of terrorists even if a planned terrorist act is not executed. The new CPC grants Kosovo authorities a greater flexibility to investigate criminal acts in the planning stages to prevent crimes and terrorist acts. Furthermore, the CPC has an integrated confiscation process to ensure that assets related to the execution of criminal acts, both funds and weapons, are confiscated. Evidence from other countries will also be able to be used more easily in Kosovo courts, thus allowing the conduct of international counterterrorism investigations in Kosovo.

U.S. training programs, supplemented by donations of equipment through the Export and Border-Related Security Program, continued to improve the ability of the Kosovo Customs Authority and the Kosovo Border Police to control Kosovo's borders and detect and interdict weapons and other contraband at border crossing points.

In December, the Government of Kosovo began implementing the IBM agreement reached in February with Serbia and brokered by the EU. Kosovo and Serbia opened four jointly managed crossing points by the end of 2012, with support from EULEX officials. The IBM agreement stipulates that Kosovo and Serbia will establish mechanisms for exchanging information and other data from the areas which are or may be of relevance to, the prevention, detection, and investigation of criminal activities. Implementation of the agreement is anticipated to strengthen Kosovo's border security.

Despite implementation of the IBM agreement and the establishment of the four jointly administered crossing points, much of the traffic into northern Kosovo uses bypass roads that circumvent the official checkpoints. KFOR and EULEX are limited in their ability to shut down the illegal crossings into Kosovo, which allow traffic and goods to avoid Kosovo border and customs controls. As a consequence, the border remains porous and trafficking of goods and people is widespread.

In December, the Supreme Court of Kosovo upheld the guilty verdict of Amir Sopa, who was sentenced in 2011 to 10 years' imprisonment on two charges of terrorism. Sopa was found guilty of firing a rocket-propelled grenade at the office of the District Court of Pristina in 2003 and sending death threats to the former mayor of Pristina on behalf of the Albanian National Army, a violent extremist organization.

Also in December, the Government of Kosovo extradited Shukri Aliu to Macedonia, where he was in pretrial detention on terrorism-related charges at year's end. (Aliu was born in Kosovo and also holds Macedonian citizenship.) In 2011, Macedonia convicted Aliu in absentia of aggravated theft, but he is also believed to have been involved in other criminal acts in Macedonia and to have ties to terrorist organizations.

Countering Terrorist Finance: Kosovo is not a member of a Financial Action Task Force-style regional body. In December, the Kosovo Assembly considered revisions to the Law on the Prevention of Money Laundering and Terrorist Financing, which would strengthen legislation passed in 2010. The amendments, if passed, would help Kosovo fully implement international anti-money laundering and counterterrorist finance standards, create enforcement mechanisms for the examination of reporting entities, and more narrowly define terrorist financing.

In order to prevent money laundering, terrorist financing, and fraud, the Central Bank of Kosovo (CBK) would benefit greatly from obtaining a code from the Society for Worldwide Interbank Financial Telecommunication (SWIFT). This code would facilitate the CBK's monitoring of cross-border banking operations and adherence to international oversight requirements. Without this SWIFT code, Kosovo's access to information about the nature of cross-border financial transactions is limited, and thus Kosovo is seriously hampered in its efforts to prevent terrorist financing, money laundering, and other types of fraud and corruption. The Central Bank of Kosovo has sought to join the SWIFT system since 2004.

For further information on money laundering and financial crimes, we refer you to the *2013 International Narcotics Control Strategy Report (INCSR), Volume 2, Money Laundering and Financial Crimes*: http://www.state.gov/j/inl/rls/nrcrpt/index.htm.

THE NETHERLANDS

Overview: The Netherlands continued to respond effectively to the global terrorist threat in the areas of border and transportation security, terrorist financing, and bilateral counterterrorism cooperation. Cooperation with U.S. law enforcement remained excellent. In its December quarterly terrorism threat analysis, the Dutch National Coordinator for Counterterrorism and Security (NCTV) maintained the national threat level at "limited," meaning chances of an attack in the Netherlands or against Dutch interests were relatively small but could not be ruled out entirely. The threat against the Netherlands is mainly from violent Islamist extremists, though the attention of the fragmented and leaderless network is mostly focused on overseas conflict areas. Individuals traveling to those areas to fight are the main focus for Dutch authorities, but domestic lone wolves also appeared on the radar. Resilience by the Dutch population to terrorism continued to be high and there was a trend towards less radicalization and alienation.

In 2012, the NCTV completed its two year internal reorganization process; national security, counterterrorism, and cyber security are now under the NCTV umbrella.

Legislation, Law Enforcement, and Border Security: In 2011, the government published the first comprehensive assessment of Dutch counterterrorist measures over the past decade. The study, which had been commissioned to the Nijmegen Radboud University, concluded that post-9/11 Dutch counterterrorism policy was solid and reliable and the measures taken were not contrary to the European Convention on Human Rights.

The Dutch police were reorganized into a new national police service, scheduled to become operational in 2013. The multi-year, country-wide reorganization effort is expected to improve investigation and public order capabilities.

The Netherlands continued to improve its border security. Cameras were installed at the border, primarily focused on illegal immigration and organized crime, and the government established an interagency coordination center to share this information and provide for a more effective and efficient response. Dutch ports of entry have biographic and biometric screening capabilities.

The Netherlands remained strongly committed to effective cooperation with the United States on border security. The Port of Rotterdam was the first European port to participate in the Container Security Initiative. The Netherlands had high-level discussions with the United States through the annual Agreed Steps program, and exchanged information on security measures for airports, ports, and critical infrastructure. In addition, agreements have been made on dealing with forged documents. In February, the Netherlands signed a Letter of Intent with the United States on cyber-security cooperation and in November, the Netherlands and the United States signed an agreement on cooperation in science and technology concerning homeland and civil security matters.

Significant law enforcement actions included:

- On July 3, the Dutch Supreme Court directed the re-trial of two members of the Hofstad Group, an identified terrorist organization, due to insufficient evidence. In 2010, both men were sentenced to 15 months in prison.
- On September 20, Samir Azzouz was arrested in prison for attempting to recruit fellow inmates and planning an attack. He was imprisoned in 2008, and was serving a nine-year sentence for a terrorist plot.
- On October 18, Mahamud Said Omar of Somalia was convicted by a court in Minneapolis, Minnesota, for sending money and recruiting fighters from the United States to Somalia. Omar was arrested in the Netherlands in 2009 and extradited to the United States in 2011. Dutch authorities and witnesses contributed significantly to the success of the investigation and prosecution. No sentencing date was set as of year's end.
- On December 3, police arrested 55 people at an alleged meeting of the Kurdistan Workers' Party (PKK), which is listed as a terrorist organization by both the Netherlands and the EU. Those arrested came from Turkey, France, Germany, Syria, Switzerland, Sweden, and the Netherlands. Authorities viewed this as a training meeting and nine suspects will face trial. The others were released, with a handful handed over to immigration.
- In 2011, at the request of U.S. authorities, the Dutch police arrested Dutch terrorist suspect Sabir Ali Khan at Schiphol airport. Khan was suspected of fighting against ISAF troops in Afghanistan. The district court of Rotterdam declared Khan's extradition to the

United States admissible, which was upheld by the Supreme Court in April. After an independent investigation into Khan's mental health delayed the process, the Justice Minister decided December 20 to approve the extradition. Khan has appealed the decision to the European Court of Human Rights.

- In 2011, an Iraqi national was released while awaiting trial by the Rotterdam district court, pending the investigation. He was suspected by the General Intelligence Service of intending to travel to Syria to join al-Qa'ida. While awaiting continuation of his trial, the man traveled abroad. His whereabouts were unknown at year's end.

Countering Terrorist Finance: The Netherlands has been a member of the Financial Action Task Force (FATF) since 1990, and is one of the cooperating and supporting nations of the Caribbean Financial Action Task Force. The European Commission sets many rules for countering terrorist finance in directives that EU member states (including the Netherlands) implement themselves. Dutch officials cooperated with the United States in designating terrorist organizations and interdicting and freezing their assets.

The Cabinet has submitted to the Council of State, the government's highest advisory body, a proposal to amend current legislation on economic crimes, including changing sentences for terrorist financing. This legislation is in line with FATF recommendations and EU directives. The Netherlands is working to resolve legal issues that affect it when challenged at court, and is enhancing its due process rules.

For further information on money laundering and financial crimes, we refer you to the *2013 International Narcotics Control Strategy Report (INCSR), Volume 2, Money Laundering and Financial Crimes*: http://www.state.gov/j/inl/rls/nrcrpt/index.htm.

Regional and International Cooperation: The Netherlands is a founding member of the Global Counterterrorism Forum (GCTF) and contributed to the creation of Hedayah, the International Center of Excellence for Countering Violent Extremism. The Dutch are also planning to contribute to the curriculum development of the International Institute for Justice and the Rule of Law, to be established in Tunisia. The Netherlands contributed to the counterterrorism work of the UN Office on Drugs and Crime.

The Netherlands continued to chair the Global Initiative to Combat Nuclear Terrorism's Nuclear Detection Working Group. In November, the Netherlands hosted a table top exercise to improve cooperation in preventing a nuclear or radiological terrorist event. This exercise was in preparation of the March 2014 Nuclear Security Summit to be held in The Hague. In 2011, the International Centre for Counterterrorism – an independent body established in The Hague in 2010 – and the Interregional Crime and Justice Research Institute organized an international conference on prison radicalization, rehabilitation, and reintegration of violent extremist offenders, which contributed to the adoption in 2012 of a document on rehabilitation and reintegration at the Global Counterterrorism Forum ministerial meeting in Istanbul. The Dutch also cooperate on EU and OSCE counterterrorism efforts.

The Netherlands was a strong voice on Lebanese Hizballah; the Dutch Foreign Minister publicly highlighted the dangers the group posed and called on the EU to designate it as a terrorist organization.

The Netherlands is implementing counterterrorism capacity building projects in Pakistan, Yemen, Morocco, Algeria, Kenya, and Indonesia.

Countering Radicalization and Violent Extremism: The resilience of the Dutch population to violent extremism is high. Radical efforts by political and religious leaders seemed to have little effect on immigrant communities or on the general population as a whole. After completing the *2007-2011 Action Plan: Polarization and Radicalization*, the Netherlands has shifted from a broad, general, catch-all effort to a more narrowly focused, more localized approach.

Countering violent extremism is locally organized, instead of relying on national programs. There have been no major communication efforts or public awareness campaigns, because of this emphasis on specific locales. There is a view that national campaigns on violent extremism may actually promote or attract extremism.

The national government serves in advisory and capacity-building roles. Local partners are expected to build upon the knowledge and experiences generated in the past. National support of the local approach is focused on identifying high-priority areas that are of interest to or might host radicalized individuals, and developing specific plans and approaches. The NCTV develops tools and training and offers them to local police departments, social workers, and other stakeholders, both directly and through an online database.

Another focus for countering violent extremism is on lone actors and persons who travel to combat zones. Systems are being built by local governments around these individuals. The NCTV invests in information systems that combine reports and red flags from different parties in order to distill signals about potential actions by violent extremists and to develop a tailored approach. There are a handful of programs, administered to individuals, which focus on disengagement and rehabilitation.

The Netherlands participates in the European Policy Planners Network on Countering Polarization and Radicalization, which is occasionally attended by the United States.

NORWAY

Overview: Although the Norwegian Police Security Service considers violent Islamist extremism the biggest threat to Norway, the July 2011 attacks in Oslo and Utoya, conducted by a Norwegian violent extremist, have heavily influenced the Government of Norway's approach to countering terrorism. The report of the independent July 22 commission that was formed to evaluate Norway's handling of the attacks was issued in August and detailed a number of preparedness and response failings. Partially in response to this, authorities have continued focusing on new terrorism prosecutions, expanding efforts to counter violent extremism, strengthening cyber security measures, and proposing legislative changes to penalize individual terrorists (those not affiliated with groups). The government is also focusing on efforts to criminalize terrorist training, to criminalize the possession of certain materials that may be used by terrorists, and to increase surveillance tools for the Police Security Service. In the wake of these attacks, the government has also continued to increase security measures at government buildings and security for government officials.

Legislation, Law Enforcement, and Border Security: The government is currently in the process of crafting legislation to strengthen its counterterrorism laws. Following a lengthy public discussion period, the Ministry of Justice is writing new legislation that will be presented to Parliament for approval in 2013. The law is expected to include provisions to close the "lone wolf" loophole (which requires proof of a large conspiracy for a terrorist conviction) and to criminalize the receipt of terrorist training.

Norway is a party to EU border control data sharing arrangements. Norwegian immigration authorities obtained biometric equipment for the fingerprinting of arrivals from outside the Schengen area, though they have not yet implemented this program. Immigration to Norway is facilitated and regulated by the Norwegian Directorate of Immigration (UDI), which processes all applications for asylum, visas, family immigration, work and study permits, citizenship, permanent residence, and travel documents. In 2012, UDI took steps to improve border control with the introduction of a new Norwegian permanent residency permit card. Introduced as a part of the Schengen Agreement, the new card is tied to fingerprint and facial biometrics, has numerous security features, is required to be renewed regularly, and the bearer is charged approximately US $50 for replacing a lost or stolen card.

Anders Behring Breivik was found guilty of murder and assault as a result of his 2011 attacks in Oslo and on the island of Utoya. The trial began in April 2012 and concluded in August. The court found him competent to stand trial, sane at the time of the acts, and gave him the maximum possible sentence of 21 years. This sentence can be reviewed by a court and extended by up to five years at a time, as many times as the government seeks court review and applies for extension.

An Iraqi citizen, Mullah Krekar (aka Najmuddin Faraj Ahmad), the founder of Ansar al-Islam, continued to reside in Norway on a long-term residence permit. In March, a trial court convicted Krekar of issuing threats and inciting terrorism, and sentenced him to six years in prison. Krekar appealed, and in December an appeals court affirmed his convictions for issuing threats and intimidating witnesses, but reversed his conviction for "inciting terrorism." The appeals court reduced his sentence to two years and 10 months in prison.

On September 20, a court of appeals upheld terrorist charges against Mikael Davud and Shawan Bujak. They and a third Norwegian long-term resident, David Jakobsen, were charged with plotting an attack on a Danish newspaper that published cartoons depicting the Prophet Muhammed. The court of appeals increased Davud's sentence from six to seven years, and reduced Bujak's from four years to three-and-a-half years. The appeals court overturned Jacobsen's conviction on terrorist charges but confirmed his conviction for purchasing bomb ingredients. Davud and Bujak have indicated that they will appeal to the Supreme Court; that hearing date was pending at year's end. These were the first terrorism convictions in Norway's courts.

Countering Terrorist Finance: Norway is a member of the Financial Action Task Force (FATF) and held the FATF presidency in 2012. The Government of Norway adopted and incorporated FATF standards and recommendations, including the special recommendations on terrorist financing, into Norwegian law. For further information on money laundering and financial crimes, we refer you to the *2013 International Narcotics Control Strategy Report*

(INCSR), Volume 2, Money Laundering and Financial Crimes:
http://www.state.gov/j/inl/rls/nrcrpt/index.htm.

Regional and International Cooperation: Norway continued its support for the UN Counter-Terrorism Implementation Task Force (CTITF) with a contribution of US $446,000 to a project designed to facilitate counterterrorism technical assistance in two pilot countries (Nigeria and Burkina Faso), and a contribution of US $80,300 to a CTITF project on implementing the regional counterterrorism strategy for Central Asia. Norway has also provided US $80,300 to a joint project led by the UN's Counter-Terrorism Executive Directorate and the Center on Global Counterterrorism Cooperation to promote regional counterterrorism cooperation in South Asia. Furthermore, Norway has provided US $375,000 to the University of Pretoria's Institute for Strategic Studies to build counterterrorism capacity in the police and judiciary systems of African countries. Norway remains a member of the EU's Radicalization Awareness Network, an umbrella network of practitioners and local actors involved in countering violent extremism that is designed to enable the members to share and discuss best practices in spotting and addressing radicalization and recruitment leading to acts of terrorism.

Countering Radicalization and Violent Extremism: The Norwegian government continues to implement its plan to counter radicalization and violent extremism. The plan covers 2010 to 2013 and focuses on four priority areas: increased knowledge and information; strengthened government cooperation; strengthened dialogue and involvement; and support for vulnerable and disadvantaged people.

On November 8, the Police Security Services and the Oslo Police announced a plan to address radicalization in Oslo. The plan will be modeled on previous initiatives to de-radicalize members of violent right-wing extremist groups.

RUSSIA

Overview: Terrorist attacks stemming from instability in the North Caucasus continued to be committed in Russia. Separatists and violent Islamist extremists calling for a pan-Islamic caliphate within the Caucasus constituted the main terrorist threats. Separatism, inter-ethnic rivalry, revenge, banditry, and violent Islamist extremist ideology were the primary motivating factors for terrorism-related violence in 2012. Violence similar to that observed in the North Caucasus has also occurred in other areas of Russia, as seen most notably in July with the bombing in Tatarstan. Russia continued its efforts to arrest and disrupt militants.

Under the framework of the U.S.-Russia Bilateral Presidential Commission (BPC), the U.S. and Russian Chairmen of the Counterterrorism Working Group (CTWG) met in February 2012 to discuss U.S.-Russian counterterrorism cooperation. The Chairmen discussed cooperation in the Global Counterterrorism Forum (GCTF), countering violent extremism, countering terrorist threats to the tourism industry, terrorist designations, and preparations for the Sochi Olympics. Additional BPC activity in counterterrorism included several joint military exercises that dealt explicitly with terrorism-related scenarios, collaboration on nuclear and transportation security, and joint programs on financial monitoring.

Russia also continued to participate in the yearly Four-Party Counterterrorism Working Group, which includes the Federal Security Service (FSB), the Foreign Intelligence Service (SVR), the

Federal Bureau of Investigation (FBI), and the Central Intelligence Agency (CIA). Operational and intelligence information regarding terrorism-related threats was shared among these four agencies, with senior leaders meeting in Moscow and in Washington. FBI-FSB relationships at the working level showed improvement during the year.

2012 Terrorist Incidents: The North Caucasus region remained Russia's primary area of terrorist activity. Separatists seeking an Islamic caliphate within the Caucasus reportedly claimed responsibility for bombings, shootings, kidnappings, and extortion in Dagestan, Kabardino-Balkaria, Ingushetia, North Ossetia, and Chechnya. Federal and local security organizations conducted counterterrorism operations throughout the Caucasus, including raids, roadblocks, and larger-scale military-style operations in rural areas. Media and eyewitness reports suggested that separatism is not the only factor driving violence in the Caucasus, and that motives such as inter-ethnic rivalry, business arguments, and revenge were factors involved.

In 2012, almost half of terrorist attacks targeted law enforcement, security services, and emergency responders, using increasingly sophisticated tactics. For example, in a May 3 attack, a suicide bomber exploded a vehicle near a police station in Makhachkala, Dagestan. When the Emergency Ministry and police units arrived, a second bomb exploded in a nearby vehicle. About 100 people were injured. Thirty-seven police officers were injured and seven died. Two rescuers were also injured. In 2012, Dagestani authorities approved the creation of ethnic-based internal security units and have agreed to host additional federal police and regular army units to combat terrorism.

Across Russia, the press reported 659 killed and 490 wounded in 182 terrorist attacks in 2012. Of the casualty totals for Russia, 325 of those killed and 365 of those injured were security personnel. Official terrorism statistics are similar to those found in open press. In December, Viktor Orlov, the head of the National Counterterrorism Committee, said over 260 acts of terrorism were committed in Russia in 2012. Additionally, Alesksandr Bortnikov, Director of the Federal Security Service, announced that the special services prevented 92 terrorist-related crimes in 2012. In October, President Putin spoke about Russia's fight against terrorism saying that within Russia during the past several months, 479 militants were detained, and 313 terrorists who refused to surrender were killed, including 43 leaders.

Legislation, Law Enforcement, and Border Security: The National Antiterrorism Coordinating Committee, organized in 2006, is the main government body coordinating the Russian government's response to the terrorist threat.

The Russian Federation uses a machine-readable passport for foreign travel, and citizens have the option of purchasing a more expensive biometric passport. The biometric passports contain robust security features and are gaining in popularity. The latest version of the Russian passport is valid for 10 years. Among Russian applicants for American visas this year, the majority used the new Russian biometric passport.

Cooperative efforts are also underway on a project to identify high-risk shipping containers entering Russia. The goal of the project is to consolidate efforts of U.S.-based field offices with Russian law enforcement in a cooperative effort to share law enforcement intelligence and ultimately interdict contraband that could be used in terrorist acts. The primary focus is the interdiction of smuggling in weapons of mass destruction, dual use materials, small arms, narcotics, bulk cash, and human trafficking.

Russia was also in the process of implementing a major program to introduce paperless entrance and clearance systems for cargo. This system, currently operational in one port of entry (Kashirsky), implements automated risk management and cargo selectivity procedures. The Russian Federation is expanding this system nationally.

Cooperative relationships continued to develop between the heads of the State Border Guard Service of the FSB and the U.S. Border Patrol. Similarly the U.S. Coast Guard enjoyed a close working relationship with the Coast Guard of the FSB Border Guard Service.

Significant law enforcement actions against terrorists and terrorist groups included:

- On May 17, a court in Vladikavkaz sentenced two men for the 2010 suicide bombing that killed 19 and injured 230 people at a market.
- On November 28, a man was convicted of plotting a terrorist attack on Red Square on New Year's Eve 2010. Four of his associates were previously convicted, and six more were standing trial at year's end.
- On December 10, four Russian men from the Caucasus Emirate were sentenced to 15 to18 years in prison for plotting a 2011 bombing of the high-speed Sapsan train running between Moscow and St. Petersburg.

Countering Terrorist Finance: Russia is a member of the Financial Action Task Force (FATF). It is also a leading member, chair, and primary funding source of the Eurasian Group on Combating Money Laundering and Financing of Terrorism (EAG), a FATF-style regional body. Through the EAG, Russia provided technical assistance and other resources towards improving legislative and regulatory frameworks and operational capabilities. Russia is also a member of the Egmont Group, as well as the Asia/Pacific Group on Money Laundering and Moneyval, the Council of Europe Committee of Experts on the Evaluation of Anti-Money Laundering Measures and the Financing of Terrorism, both FATF-style regional bodies.

Russian banks must report suspicious transactions to the Financial Monitoring Federal Service (Rosfinmonitoring), a Financial Intelligence Unit whose head reports directly to the President (in 2011 Rosfinmonitoring reported to the Prime Minister). The Central Bank and the markets regulator (the Financial Markets Federal Service) can access these transaction reports after requesting them from Rosfinmonitoring. In the first quarter of 2012, Rosfinmonitoring seized US $334 in alleged terrorist funds, a reduction from US $16,805 during the same quarter in 2011.

In July 2012, the Duma adopted a new law, N 121-FZ, intended to increase scrutiny and oversight of non-commercial organizations that receive foreign funding. Provisions in this law require Rosfinmonitoring to report to the relevant non-profit registration body if an organization is found to be non-compliant with Russian Anti-Money Laundering/Combating the Financing of Terrorism (AML/CFT) regulations. This new legislation also amends Russia's AML/CFT law by requiring monitoring of any foreign donations over 200,000 rubles (approximately US $6,000).

For further information on money laundering and financial crimes, we refer you to the *2013 International Narcotics Control Strategy Report (INCSR), Volume 2, Money Laundering and Financial Crimes*: http://www.state.gov/j/inl/rls/nrcrpt/index.htm.

Regional and International Cooperation: Russia is a founding member of the GCTF and is an active member of the NATO-Russia Council Counterterrorism Working Group. Russia continued to work with other regional and multilateral groups to address terrorism, including counterterrorism groups in the EU, the Global Initiative to Combat Nuclear Terrorism(GICNT), the G-8 Counterterrorism Action Group, the Shanghai Cooperation Organization, the Collective Security Treaty Organization, the OSCE, and engaged actively with the "Istanbul Process" working group on combating terrorism in Afghanistan, as well as chairing the Istanbul Process counter-narcotics working group.

In September, Russia's FSB hosted the "Guardian-2012" demonstration and detection-related exercise. Held under the auspices of the GICNT, the event brought together representatives of approximately 45 of its member states and international organizations. In addition to plenary and panel discussions, the event featured a day-long demonstration of Russian technology and procedures to detect and prevent illicit trafficking in nuclear materials. Russia is also a member of the G-8 Global Partnership Against the Spread of Weapons and Materials of Mass Destruction (GP), and will chair the initiative in 2013. The underlying goal of the GP is to fund programs and activities that combat WMD terrorism.

Within ASEAN, Russia was important in advancing the Southeast Asia Nuclear Weapons Free Zone, and is actively advocating progress towards a Middle East Weapons of Mass Destruction Free Zone. In addition to the annual Collective Security Treaty Organization (CSTO) exercise, Russia also participated in CSTO exercises in Kazakhstan simulating a domestic terrorism situation.

The Russian security services have begun to implement a security plan to protect the 2014 Sochi Olympic Games. In October, the Sochi Olympic Organizing Committee held the first briefing for the diplomatic community, and in November held the first session of the Sponsor Security Working Group for the marketing partners of the 2014 Winter Games, which is a smaller multilateral working group that will meet quarterly and continue through the Olympics.

In October, the Russian Federation hosted a high-level gathering of law enforcement and intelligence professionals from many countries. In May, the U.S. Deputy Director of National Intelligence attended a Security Council forum in St. Petersburg, where he discussed cooperation in counterterrorism with senior leaders.

Countering Radicalization and Violent Extremism: The Government of Russia has adopted an overarching plan for the socio-economic development of the North Caucasus through 2025. In December, North Caucasus Presidential Envoy Alexander Khloponin stated that 90 percent of the funding for a 13-year, US $80.9 billion development program will come from private industry, with Rosneft cited as an early contributor. As outlined, the program will improve economic opportunity in the region. In partnership with Russian universities, the government also plans to establish new programs to improve vocational training and education in the region.

SERBIA

Overview: The Government of Serbia sustained its efforts to counter international terrorism in 2012. Serbian and U.S. law enforcement and intelligence agencies collaborated against potential terrorist threats. Serbia's two main specialized police organizations, the Special Anti-Terrorist Unit and the Counter-Terrorist Unit, both operated as counterterrorism tactical response units. Serbia accepted and welcomed U.S.-funded counterterrorism training. Harmonization of law enforcement protocols with EU standards remained a priority for the Serbian government.

Legislation, Law Enforcement, and Border Security: Transnational terrorism concerns within Serbia were similar to those in other Balkan states, all of which are collectively located on the historic transit route between the Middle East and Western Europe. Serbian authorities are sensitive to and vigilant against any efforts by violent extremists to establish a presence in or transit the country. The Serbian government continued to participate in the UN Office on Drugs and Crime regional program to promote the rule of law and human security in Southeast Europe, which primarily focuses on increasing member states' counterterrorism capacities.

In line with proposed amendments to the Criminal Code (which were approved by the Government of Serbia in early December and submitted to the National Assembly, and are expected to be passed by the National Assembly by the end of the calendar year), criminal legislation would be harmonized with the 2005 Council of Europe (COE) Convention on the Prevention of Terrorism (ratified in 2009) and the EU Council Framework Decision on Combating Terrorism (2002/475/JHA) of June 13, 2002 (amended in 2008). The existing criminal offense of terrorism would also be expanded to include five new offenses: public instigation of terrorist acts, recruitment and training for terrorist acts, use of deadly devices, damage and destruction of a nuclear facility, and terrorist conspiracy.

The United States provided counterterrorism training and assistance to Serbia through a number of agencies and programs.

Countering Terrorist Finance: Serbia is a member of Moneyval, the COE Committee of Experts on the Evaluation of Anti-Money Laundering Measures and the Financing of Terrorism, a Financial Task Force regional-style body. Although the National Assembly did not adopt any new terrorism-related legislation, Serbia's Administration for the Prevention of Money Laundering (APML) developed a draft law on restrictions on property disposal, with the aim of preventing terrorist financing. The draft law is intended to rectify existing shortcomings in implementing UNSC resolutions. The law had not been approved by year's end.

In December, Moneyval adopted a Progress Report on improvements in Serbia's anti-money laundering/combating the financing of terrorism system.

As part of Serbia's efforts to meet EU standards and advance its EU accession effort, several conferences and workshops connected to the Project against Money Laundering and Terrorist Financing in Serbia (MOLI-Serbia Project) took place in Serbia. MOLI-Serbia, which is co-sponsored and funded by the EU and the COE, principally benefits APML, and once it is fully implemented, Serbia will have a more robust legislative and operational capacity to counter money laundering and terrorist finance systems in accordance with EU and international standards.

According to the Prosecutor's Office for Organized Crime, Serbian police did not arrest anyone involved in terrorist finance activities, nor were any cases related to the financing of terrorism prosecuted in 2012. For further information on money laundering and financial crimes, we refer you to the *2013 International Narcotics Control Strategy Report (INCSR), Volume 2, Money Laundering and Financial Crimes*: http://www.state.gov/j/inl/rls/nrcrpt/index.htm.

Regional and International Cooperation: Serbia supports the UN Global Counter-Terrorism Strategy. In October, members of special police units from 14 Southeast European countries completed a counterterrorism exercise at the Special Anti-Terrorism base near Belgrade. The exercise was carried out as part of an international counterterrorism seminar, which featured lectures by two U.S. instructors from the Federal Bureau of Investigation Hostage Rescue Team.

The Office of Defense Cooperation provided approximately US $128,000 worth of counterterrorism-related training for 17 representatives of the Ministry of Defense (MOD), Ministry of Interior, the Security Information Agency, and the National Assembly at the George C. Marshall Center and at the National Defense University (NDU). Two MOD graduates of the NDU's International Counterterrorism Fellows (ICTF) Program attended an NDU Alumni Seminar in April. This close and continuing collaboration supports individual ICTF graduates as they move up to more senior levels of responsibility with the goal of increasing their effectiveness in joint counterterrorism efforts. Two MOD lieutenant colonels completed the International Intelligence Fellows Program (IIFP) at the National Defense Intelligence College (Defense Intelligence Agency) in late April. The theme of the IIFP this year was "Intelligence Support to Combating Terrorism."

SPAIN

Overview: Spain continued to confront the threat posed by the domestic terrorist group Basque Fatherland and Liberty (ETA), as well as the transnational threat from al-Qa'ida (AQ) and its affiliates. With sustained focused international cooperation, in particular with France, Spain enjoyed such success in countering ETA that the weakened terrorist group announced in October 2011 a "definitive cessation of armed activity," re-confirmed by ETA in a July 9, 2012 communiqué.

Europol's annual terrorism report on the EU, released in April and supported by Spanish security services, indicated however, that "ETA continues recruiting members and collecting information about new objectives," despite having announced the cessation of violence. According to the report, "ETA has not announced either the turning over of the weapons or the dissolution of the terrorist organization. The experience obtained from previous ceasefires indicates that ETA returns to its activity because it does not achieve its political objectives." According to the report, ETA appears to have ceased its practice of extortion of local businesses, although there are reports of "personal visits, door to door" looking for "voluntary" contributions.

Spain also focused on the continued kidnapping threat presented by al-Qa'ida in the Islamic Maghreb (AQIM) and increased its cooperation with Algeria, Mali, and Mauritania to combat and contain the group. Spain cooperated closely with the United States to counter terrorism and was a cooperative partner in joint investigations and information sharing.

2012 Terrorist Incidents: No terrorist attacks occurred in Spain in 2012. Nonetheless, two Spanish citizens working with NGO Doctors without Borders kidnapped by al-Shabaab terrorist in Kenya in 2011 remained in captivity at year's end, and the Spanish government was working with local authorities to ensure their safe release. Two Spaniards and an Italian who were kidnapped in Algeria in 2011 by the Movement for Unity and Jihad in West Africa, an organization closely linked to AQIM, were released on July 18, 2012.

Legislation, Law Enforcement, and Border Security: Spain continued to focus on improved security and the detection of false documents at its borders in 2012. Spain participated in the U.S. Immigration Advisory Program, which maintained staff at Madrid-Barajas International Airport. The program allowed coordination between Customs and Border Protection officers, airline security personnel, and police regarding high risk passengers traveling to the United States. Spain continued to roll out an automated system to read EU passports with biometric data. Explosive trace detection equipment was also deployed at Spain's five largest airports at passenger checkpoints. Spanish Airports and Civil Guard participated in an EU-coordinated Liquids and Gels (LAGs) pilot program to test LAGs explosive detection equipment and work toward the development of implementation metrics. Spain continued to utilize a network of radar stations, known as the Integrated External Surveillance System, along its maritime borders. Spain maintained its participation in the Megaports and Container Security Initiatives. In September, the Civil Guard began integrating Europol information in its fight against terrorism and organized crime. Previously, only the Spanish National Police had access to the Europol data.

As of December, Spanish security forces had arrested a total of five people accused of terrorist ties in 2012:

- On June 26, Spanish National Police in the North African Spanish enclave of Melilla arrested Spanish citizens Rachid Abdellah Mohamed and Nabil Mohamed Chaib, leaders of a violent extremist cell with international connections dedicated to recruiting young Muslims for training in Afghanistan and Pakistan.
- On August 2, in cooperation with international security services, Spanish National Police arrested three suspected AQ activists, Eldar Magomedov, alias "Muslim Dost;" Muhamed Ankari Adamov, a Russian citizen of Chechen origin; and Turkish facilitator Cengiz Yalzin in the largest operation against violent Islamist extremism in Spain in recent years.

In cooperation with international partners, security services also arrested 25 alleged ETA members or associates, including 16 in France and six in other countries. Key raids included:

- On June 28 in London, British Security Forces arrested ETA members Antonio Troitiño Arranz and Ignacio Lerín Sánchez, two of Spain's most wanted terrorists. Troitiño, alias "Antxon," was responsible for 22 murders and had direct connections with ETA's current leadership.
- On July 4, a joint investigation between the Spanish Civil Guard and the French Information Services led to the arrest of Juan María Múgica Dorronsoro, the fourth member of an ETA cell that attempted to assassinate former President José María Aznar in 2001.

- Additional information on arrests of ETA members in 2012 can be found in the report on France in this chapter.

Spanish security forces and Spain's judicial system continued investigations into allegations of ETA training camps in Venezuela and ETA links to Colombian Revolutionary Armed Forces of Columbia (FARC) terrorists. In June, the Colombia Prosecutor General's office reported that Colombia had evidence that ETA members trained FARC personnel on the use of sticky bombs to attack former Minister of Justice Fernando Londoño. On October 27, Consuelo Ordóñez, the spokesperson for ETA victims association COVITE, met with Venezuelan retired military official Milton Revilla, who passed her information on links between ETA and the FARC. Spanish National Court prosecutors have asked the investigating judge to demand all documents related to Revilla's information from the Venezuelan justice system.

Countering Terrorist Finance: A longtime member of the Financial Action Task Force, Spain continued to demonstrate leadership in the area of anti-money laundering/combating the financing of terrorism. Spain enacted its current law on Preventing Money Laundering and the Financing of Terrorism in 2010; the law entered into force immediately. However, implementation of regulations will not be approved until 2013. The regulations will greatly enhance authorities' capacity to counter terrorist financing by placing greater requirements, with stiffer penalties for non-compliance, on financial institutions and other businesses, and by strengthening monitoring and oversight. The government diligently implemented relevant UNSCRs and had the legal authority to impose autonomous designations. For further information on money laundering and financial crimes, we refer you to the *2013 International Narcotics Control Strategy Report (INCSR), Volume 2, Money Laundering and Financial Crimes*: http://www.state.gov/j/inl/rls/nrcrpt/index.htm.

Regional and International Cooperation: Spain is a founding member of the Global Counterterrorism Forum (GCTF), and on July 9-10, hosted the "High Level Conference of Victims of Terrorism." Spain has worked to advance a number of counterterrorism initiatives through the EU, including work with the G-6 and the United States on cyber-crime and countering online radicalization. Spain continued its leadership role in the Global Initiative to Combat Nuclear Terrorism and served as Coordinator of its Implementation and Assessment Group, a working group of technical experts. On May 24, the Spanish National Police and the Civil Guard were awarded the "Outstanding Achievement in the Prevention of Terrorism" Award from the Terrorism Commission of the International Association of Chiefs of Police for their successes against ETA and international terrorist threats.

Spain signed numerous bilateral agreements on police and security force cooperation, including agreements signed January 31 with Serbia, February 18 with Morocco and Jordan, March 3 with Bosnia and Herzegovina, October 21 with Mexico, and October 24 with Croatia. On December 3, Spain issued a joint declaration with Israel to increase bilateral cooperation against organized crime and terrorism. In July, Spain joined Belgium, Italy, Austria, and France in capacity building work in the Sahel to train judges, military personnel, and police officers in the fight against AQ and associated groups, creating specialized groups with participation from Mali, Mauritania, and Nigeria. Seven million euros (US $9,240,000) was obligated to the joint effort, which deployed two retired French police officers to Bamako, Mali and Nouakchott, Mauritania; a Spanish Civil Guard trainer is deployed to Niger.

Countering Radicalization and Violent Extremism: Spain participated in several international meetings focused on countering violent extremism. On July 9-10, Spain hosted a GCTF high-level conference on Victims of Terrorism; attended the December 14 GCTF Ministerial meeting in Abu Dhabi; and committed to send experts to participate in Hedayah, the newly established International Center of Excellence on Countering Violent Extremism. Spain's inter-ministerial CVE working group emphasized the prevention of radicalization and sought to counter radical propaganda both online and in other arenas. In addition to promoting international cooperation on these issues, Spanish efforts to counter radicalization were tied closely to the fight against illegal immigration and the integration of existing immigrant communities. The Spanish government sought the support of civil society and the general public in rejecting violence. In fulfillment of applicable laws, Spanish prisons employed rehabilitation programs designed to achieve the reintegration of inmates into society.

SWEDEN

Overview: Violent Islamist extremists in Sweden and abroad have increasingly looked to Sweden as a target for attacks. Perceived insults to Islam and Sweden's military presence in Afghanistan have, as previously, been used as motives. Individuals within violent extremist groups in Sweden have continued to have contacts with foreign terrorist networks. The contacts include financial and logistical support as well as the recruitment of individuals to travel to conflict areas to attend terrorism-related training and combat. In previous years, Somalia and Pakistan were well established destinations for travelers from Sweden, but in the past year, Yemen and Syria became increasingly popular. Authorities estimated that at least 10 individuals left Sweden for Syria and some of these individuals are frequently using social media to circulate photos and recruitment videos that clearly are targeting a Swedish audience. The travelers who remain abroad and keep in touch with actors in Sweden, as well as returnees who stay in contact with foreign terrorist networks, continued to pose a potential threat to Sweden according to Swedish authorities.

The National Threat Advisory level in Sweden has remained "elevated" since it was first raised in October 2010, due to sustained terrorist-related activities with a connection to Sweden.

On February 14, the government released an updated version of its national counterterrorism strategy. This is the first revision Sweden has done since the original strategy was announced in 2008.

A Swedish citizen who was kidnapped by al-Qa'ida in the Islamic Maghreb (AQIM), together with two other Westerners when visiting Mali in November 2011, remained in AQIM's custody at year's end.

Legislation, Law Enforcement, and Border Security: On November 28, the Swedish Parliament approved the government's bill on changing the current legislation to allow the Swedish Security Service and the National Bureau of Investigation to order specific signal intelligence from the Swedish Radio Defense Establishment. The required legislative changes were scheduled to come into effect on January 1, 2013.

Resolution and continuation of cases from 2010 and 2011:

- Swedish citizen Paul Mardirossian, who was arrested in Panama City in April 2011 for allegedly having agreed to provide weapons to the Revolutionary Armed Forces of Colombia in exchange for cocaine, pled guilty in U.S. court to charges for conspiracy to engage in narco-terrorism, conspiracy to provide material support to a foreign terrorist organization, attempting to provide material support to a foreign terrorist organization, and money laundering.
- The three men who were arrested and charged for "preparation to murdering" Swedish cartoonist Lars Vilks in September 2011, were acquitted of the attempted murder charges by the district court, which was affirmed on appeal. In the end, the court fined all three for being in possession of knives in public.
- A pre-investigation related to the December 11, 2010 suicide bombing carried out by Taimour Abdulwahab in Stockholm was still being conducted in 2012 by the prosecutor for national security cases. Authorities were investigating whether the perpetrator acted alone.
- On June 4, the four men from Sweden who were arrested in Copenhagen in December 2010 for planning a terrorist attack on Danish newspaper *Jyllands-Posten*, were each sentenced to 12 years in prison.
- On August 27, the case in Glasgow, where Nasserdine Menni, among other things, was tried for providing funds to Taimour Abdulwahab in 2010, was concluded and Menni was sentenced to seven years in prison for terrorist financing.

Countering Terrorist Finance: Sweden has been a member of the Financial Action Task Force (FATF) since 1990, but is not a member of any of the regional FATF-style bodies. Sweden provided its latest Mutual Evaluation Report to the FATF in October. For further information on money laundering and financial crimes, we refer you to the *2013 International Narcotics Control Strategy Report (INCSR), Volume 2, Money Laundering and Financial Crimes*: http://www.state.gov/j/inl/rls/nrcrpt/index.htm.

Regional and International Cooperation: Sweden continued to contribute to counterterrorism capacity-building projects through its development aid work carried out by the Swedish International Development Agency, and also via funding to the UN Office on Drugs and Crime-Terrorism Prevention Branch and the OSCE. Sweden also supported the EU's work with capacity-building projects in prioritized countries and regions such as Pakistan, Yemen, the Horn of Africa, Maghreb, and the Sahel. Sweden provided trainers to the EU's Training Mission to assist with the training of Somalia's Transitional Federal Government security forces. Sweden was the largest donor to the UN's Counter-Terrorism International Task Force (CTITF), with special focus on the CTITF workgroup that works on strengthening human rights in counterterrorism work.

Countering Radicalization and Violent Extremism: On March 22, the Government of Sweden hosted a conference on Sweden's national action plan to safeguard democracy against violence-promoting extremism. Since the Swedish government announced its first action plan to counter violent extremism in December 2011, several projects have been initiated as part of the implementation process. An expert group has been established and will conduct a study on how work to prevent violent extremism can be carried out more efficiently. Funds have been distributed to organizations that provide individuals with assistance in leaving violent extremist organizations. The National Media Council is conducting a study on how youth are using the internet and how they are influenced by what they read. The Swedish National Defense College was drafting a report on foreign fighters that will include suggestions on preventive measures.

Under the auspices of the EU's Community Policing Preventing Radicalization and Terrorism (COPPRA) project, the Swedish National Police continued to work to increase knowledge to detect radicalization and added sessions on the topic on the curricula for National Police Academy students. The education material from COPPRA that was translated into Swedish has been used during training sessions to educate police officers who now will "train the trainers" for a wider distribution throughout Sweden.

TURKEY

Overview: Turkey is a long-standing counterterrorism partner of the United States. It co-chairs the Global Counterterrorism Forum (GCTF) with the United States, and received U.S. assistance to address the terrorist threat posed by the Kurdistan Workers' Party (PKK) in 2012.

The limited definition of terrorism under Turkish law, restricted to activities targeting the Turkish state and its citizens, represented an impediment to effective action by Turkey against global terrorist networks. For example, although Turkish police temporarily detained several al-Qa'ida (AQ)-affiliated operatives attempting to transit through Turkey illegally in 2012, Turkish authorities chose to deport these individuals to their countries of origin quickly rather than pursue domestic legal action against them, at least in part because of the lack of appropriate legal tools.

In 2012, Turkey faced a significant internal terrorist threat and has taken strong action in response. Most prominent among terrorist groups in Turkey is the PKK. Composed primarily of ethnic Kurds with a nationalist agenda, the PKK operates from areas in southeastern Turkey and northern Iraq and targets mainly Turkish security forces. Other prominent terrorist groups in Turkey include the Revolutionary People's Liberation Party/Front (DHKP-C), a militant Marxist-Leninist group with anti-U.S. and anti-NATO views that seeks the violent overthrow of the Turkish state, and Turkish Hizballah (unrelated to the similarly-named Hizballah that operates in Lebanon). Public sources also highlighted detentions of Islamic Jihad Union members as well as supporters of AQ and other groups. The Turkish Workers' and Peasants' Liberation Army, though largely inactive, was also considered a potential threat by the Turkish government.

2012 Terrorist Incidents: The PKK continued to demonstrate its nation-wide reach. Typical tactics, techniques, and procedures included ambushes of military patrols in the countryside, improvised explosive devices (IEDs) along known military or police routes, and bombings of both security and civilian targets in urban areas. According to the NATO Centre of Excellence-Defence Against Terrorism in Ankara, there were 226 terrorist incidents reported through November. The following 12 attacks garnered particular attention and condemnation:

- On March 1, an explosion near the ruling party's headquarters in Istanbul wounded at least 16 people, most of them policemen traveling by bus. No claim of responsibility was issued.
- On March 5, a small bomb exploded near the Turkish Prime Ministry building in Ankara about an hour before a cabinet meeting was scheduled; one person was injured.

- On May 25, a policeman was killed and 18 others wounded in a suicide bombing outside a police station in the central Turkish province of Kayseri.
- On August 4, clashes between Kurdish rebels and the Turkish military near the Iraqi border left 22 people dead, according to reports quoting the area's governor. Turkish media reported the rebels launched simultaneous attacks on Turkish border posts, causing casualties in the village of Gecimli in Hakkari province.
- On August 9, a vehicle belonging to the Turkish Navy was bombed in Foca, a small coastal resort north-west of Izmir; two navy personnel were killed and another was injured.
- On August 20, a remote-controlled car bomb exploded outside a police station in Gaziantep, close to the border with Syria. At least nine people were killed and 69 were injured, most of them police officers. Security officials suspected the PKK was behind the attack, although the group later denied this.
- On September 2, around 100 suspected PKK fighters simultaneously attacked four government and security buildings in the small town of Beytüşşebap, near the Syrian border, killing at least 10 soldiers and three of the attackers; seven soldiers were injured.
- On September 11, a policeman was killed and several injured in a suicide bombing at a police station in the Sultangazi district of Istanbul. The DHKP-C claimed responsibility.
- On September 16, a roadside bombing in Turkey's southeastern Bingol Province killed eight soldiers and injured nine others, less than a day after four officers were killed in an attack near the borders with Iran and Iraq.
- On September 18, PKK militants killed 10 soldiers and wounded at least 60 when they fired rockets at a military convoy traveling between the provinces of Bingol and Mus in eastern Turkey.
- On September 25, an IED hidden in a car exploded as an Army patrol was passing by in the eastern Turkish city of Tunceli, killing six soldiers and a civilian. Several others were injured in the blast, which authorities blamed on the PKK.
- On December 11, one police officer was killed and two civilians were injured in an attack in the Gaziosmanpasa district of Istanbul.

Legislation, Law Enforcement, and Border Security: The Council of Europe Convention on Prevention of Terrorism entered into force for Turkey on July 1, 2012. Also, Turkey deposited the instrument of ratification for the International Convention for the Suppression of Acts of Nuclear Terrorism on September 24.

As a result of ongoing military operations targeting PKK forces, 494 insurgents were killed, 21 injured, and 44 arrested, while 155 surrendered themselves to the authorities during the first 10 months of the year. Counterterrorism law enforcement efforts in Turkey remained focused on the domestic threat posed by several terrorist groups, including the PKK. Turkey's methodology and legislation are geared towards confronting this internal threat.

Efforts to counter international terrorism are hampered by legislation that defines terrorism narrowly as a crime targeting the Turkish state or Turkish citizens. This definition of terrorism posed concerns for operational and legal cooperation. Several AQ-affiliated operatives were temporarily detained by Turkish National Police (TNP) authorities while transiting Turkey, but were deported to their countries of origin as expeditiously as possible. Also, criminal procedure secrecy rules prevent TNP authorities from sharing investigative information once a prosecutor is assigned to the case.

In the aftermath of the 2011 TNP arrest of 16 people involved in an AQ cell who were likely targeting the U.S. Embassy in Ankara among other locations, U.S. Embassy officials have been denied any additional information regarding the conduct of the case.

Article 157 of the Turkish Criminal Procedure Code states: "Unless provided otherwise by the code and under the requirement to not harm the defense rights, procedural interactions during the investigation phase shall be kept a secret." This language has been interpreted by Turkish prosecutors and police to require an investigation to remain secret once a prosecutor becomes involved in a criminal case. After the investigation, the evidence and files are transferred from the prosecutor to the court where they are also sealed. Only parties to a case may access court-held evidence. This legal interpretation has resulted in limited information sharing on criminal cases between U.S. and Turkish law enforcement officials.

The TNP received training in counterterrorism skills through the Department of State's Antiterrorism Assistance (ATA) program. The TNP has highly developed counterterrorism capabilities in a number of areas and is planning to expand its law enforcement training for other countries in the region.

Countering Terrorist Finance: Turkey is a member of the Financial Action Task Force (FATF) and an observer of the Eurasian Group on Combating Money Laundering and Terrorism Financing, a FATF-style regional group. In February 2010, the FATF publicly identified Turkey for its strategic deficiencies in its counterterrorist financing regime. At that time, Turkey had provided a high-level political commitment to address these deficiencies by December 2010. Due to Turkey's continued lack of progress in adequately criminalizing terrorist financing and establishing a legal framework to freeze terrorist assets, the FATF downgraded Turkey to its Public Statement in June 2011. In October 2012, FATF issued a Public Statement noting that, "Given Turkey's continued lack of progress in these two areas, as a counter-measure, the FATF has decided to suspend Turkey's membership on February 22, 2013 unless the following conditions are met before that date: (1) Turkey adopts legislation to adequately remedy deficiencies in its terrorist financing offence; and (2) Turkey establishes an adequate legal framework for identifying and freezing terrorist assets consistent with the FATF Recommendations."

According to the Turkish Banks Act, Nr: 4389, only banks and special financial establishments are authorized to carry out banking activities, including money remittance or transfers. Informal banking networks are not allowed to operate in Turkey. A duly issued license is required for all kinds of banking activities. As alternative remittance services are illegal in Turkey, there is no regulatory agency that covers their activities.

The nonprofit sector is not audited on a regular basis for counterterrorist finance vulnerabilities and does not receive adequate AML/CFT outreach or guidance from the Turkish government. The General Director of Foundations issues licenses for charitable foundations and oversees them, but there are a limited number of auditors to cover the more than 70,000 institutions.

For further information on money laundering and financial crimes, we refer you to the *2013 International Narcotics Control Strategy Report (INCSR), Volume 2, Money Laundering and Financial Crimes*: http://www.state.gov/j/inl/rls/nrcrpt/index.htm.

Regional and International Cooperation: Turkey is a founding member of the GCTF and is co-chair along with the United States. Foreign Minister Davutoğlu co-chaired the second GCTF Ministerial meeting in Istanbul in June, and the third GCTF Ministerial in Abu Dhabi in December. As co-chair, Turkey has provided extensive secretariat support. Turkey also participates actively in the OSCE. Turkey has taken part in expert meetings on the prevention of violent extremism and radicalization that lead to terrorism (VERLT) organized by the OSCE/Office of Democratic Institutions and Human Rights and the OSCE Secretariat, including through the participation of the Permanent Representative of Turkey to the OSCE, as moderator of one session of the October 23-24 meeting on "Youth Engagement to counter VERLT."

The TNP also created a new multilateral training organization, the International Association of Police Academies, to increase sharing of policing research and best practices in the field of police education. The TNP offers 18 counterterrorism-related training programs at its Anti-Terrorism Academy that are designed primarily for law enforcement officers from Central Asian countries.

Countering Radicalization and Violent Extremism: The Government of Turkey has two significant programs in place to counter radicalization and violent extremism. The first, administered by the TNP, is a broad-based outreach program to affected communities, similar to anti-gang activities in the United States. Police work to reach vulnerable populations (before terrorists do) to alter the prevailing group dynamics and to prevent recruitment. Police use social science research to undertake social projects, activities with parents, and in-service training for officers and teachers. Programs prepare trainers, psychologists, coaches, and religious leaders to intervene to undermine radical messages and prevent recruitment. The second program, administered by the Turkish government's Religious Affairs Office (Diyanet), works to undercut violent extremist messaging. In Turkey, all Sunni imams are employees of the Diyanet. In support of its message of traditional religious values, more than 66,000 Diyanet imams throughout Turkey conducted individualized outreach to their congregations. Diyanet similarly worked with religious associations among the Turkish diaspora, assisting them to establish umbrella organizations and providing them access to instruction. Diyanet supported in-service training for religious leaders and lay-workers via a network of 19 centers throughout Turkey.

UNITED KINGDOM

Overview: In 2012, the UK continued to play a leading role in countering international terrorism. The UK government implemented its updated counterterrorism strategy, CONTEST, which was released in 2011. This update of CONTEST, the first under the coalition government, set out the UK's strategic framework for countering the terrorist threat at home and abroad for 2011-2015. The foreword to the updated strategy by UK Home Secretary Theresa May states, "Greater effort will be focused on responding to the ideological challenge and the threat from those who promote it; we will also work harder to prevent people from being drawn into terrorism and ensure that they are given appropriate advice and support. CONTEST's alignment with the U.S. National Strategy for Counterterrorism will help facilitate continued close counterterrorism cooperation between the United States and the UK."

The Queen's Diamond Jubilee and the London 2012 Olympics ensured the world's attention was on the UK for much of the year and as a result, British security services mobilized forces and resources to successfully host both events. There were terrorist threats against UK interests in 2012, although extensive and collaborative work led to the disruption of known threats. In the lead up and throughout the summer, the UK services conducted arrests and worked to remove violent extremists and obstructionists from the streets.

On October 24, the British Security Service downgraded the threat to Great Britain from dissident Irish republicans from "substantial" to "moderate." The decrease shows the authorities regard an attack on London and other British cities from such groups as possible, but not likely. Previously it was deemed a strong possibility. The threat level in Northern Ireland has not changed. It remained "severe" with an attack still highly likely. On its website, MI5 said: "The threat level for Northern Ireland-related terrorism is separate from that for international terrorism. It is also set separately for Northern Ireland and Great Britain."

Legislation, Law Enforcement, and Border Security: In October 2011, the UK government published a Green Paper proposing legislation to protect sensitive information from public disclosure in judicial proceedings. The impetus for the Green Paper stems from the civil case brought by former Guantanamo detainee Binyam Mohammed, in which a UK court ruled in 2009 that U.S. intelligence cited in that case must be released into the public domain, over the objections of both the U.S. and UK governments. The Justice and Security bill was introduced to the House of Commons on November 28, 2012. At year's end it remained in the legislative process.

The Crime and Courts Bill creating the National Crime Agency was introduced on May 10, 2012 in the House of Lords.

A Draft Communications Data Bill proposed by Home Secretary May would require additional data collection and retention of user activity by internet service providers and mobile phone services, recording contact information for each user's webmail, voice calls, social media, internet gaming, and mobile phone contacts and store them for 12 months. Retention of email and telephone contact data for this time is already required.

2012 law enforcement actions included:

- In January, Ryan Lavery, 27, of Ballymote Park, Downpatrick was arrested and accused of possessing or collecting documents that could have been of use to terrorists in Northern Ireland. Police said his computer had photos of vehicles coming in and out of the Ballykinler Army Base, County Down, Northern Ireland. Mr. Lavery also possessed a list of vehicle registration numbers.
- April marked the first time a convicted UK terrorist entered into an agreement with the Crown Prosecution Service to give evidence in a trial against other alleged terrorists. Saajid Badat testified during the trial of Adis Medunjanin, a Bosnian-born U.S. citizen, who denied involvement in a suicide bomb plot on the New York subway in 2009. Zarein Ahmedzay and Najibullah Zazi were both jailed in 2010 after admitting their part in the foiled plot. The trial revealed details of young Western Muslims travelling to South Asia to receive training from al-Qa'ida.
- On April 24, five men, aged between 21 and 35, were arrested on suspicion of the commission, preparation, or instigation of acts of terrorism. They were arrested at

separate addresses in Luton under the Terrorism Act 2000 by unarmed Metropolitan Police officers assisted by Bedfordshire Police in an intelligence-led operation.

- On May 1, seven people were arrested on suspicion of funding overseas terrorism with money linked to smuggling of the stimulant khat. Six men and a woman were arrested in London, Coventry, and Cardiff in early morning raids by counterterrorism officers. The arrests were part of an international probe into alleged terrorist fundraising and money-laundering.

- On May 15, more than 100 Cheltenham residents attended a meeting called by police after two local men were arrested on suspicion of terrorism offenses. The pair, aged 52 and 31, was initially held under the Explosive Substances Act after suspicious items were found in a garage. In a sign of a strong community-oriented policing program, representatives from the police, the fire service, and the Cheltenham Borough Council answered questions to reassure residents. The arrests came after police found suspicious items in a garage in Buttermere Close in the Up Hatherley area of the town. About 100 houses were evacuated but residents were allowed to return to their homes following controlled explosions carried out by a bomb disposal team.

- On June 28, two men were arrested in London on suspicion of terrorist offenses. The men, aged 18 and 32, were held under the Terrorism Act 2000 on suspicion of the commission, preparation, or instigation of acts of terrorism. Officers searched both of the addresses where the suspects lived.

- On June 29, Minh Quang Pham, who was wanted in the United States for terrorism-related offenses, was arrested in the UK, and was remanded in custody. An indictment released by the U.S. Department of Justice accused Pham of providing material support to al-Qa'ida in the Arabian Peninsula and receiving military-style training while he was in Yemen.

- On June 30, following a routine traffic stop of a vehicle near Sheffield, South Yorkshire, three men from the West Midlands were arrested and charged with terrorist offenses after police found guns, knives, machetes, and a home-made explosive device. Jewel Uddin, 26, Omar Mohammed Khan, 27, and Mohammed Hasseen, 23, all from Sparkhill, Birmingham, appeared at Westminster Magistrates' Court accused of preparing for an act or acts of terrorism with the intention of committing such acts. They were accused of manufacturing an improvised explosive device, as well as acquiring firearms and other weapons, and vehicles connected with their alleged plans to attack the anti-Islamic group, English Defense League, who had held a rally in Dewsbury, West Yorkshire, earlier that day.

- On September 30, four men stabbed a visiting General from India, Lieutenant General Kuldeep Singh Brar. Lieutenant General Brar, who survived the stabbing, led the 1984 raid on Sikhism's holiest shrine. The stabbing is being treated as an attack by violent extremists and there have been at least 11 follow-up arrests in connection with the case.

- On October 4, a brother and sister from Birmingham were arrested under the Terrorism Act, and were freed on police bail. West Midlands Police said the pair, aged 23 and 18, was suspected of possessing documents likely to be of use to someone committing or preparing an act of terrorism. They were arrested at an address in the Small Heath district. Police added the arrests had been pre-planned and not made in response to any threat to public safety. Computers and other electronic devices were seized for forensic examination.

- On October 5, Abu Hamza al Masri, Babar Ahmad, Syed Talha Ahsan, Adel Abdul Bary, and Khaled al-Fawwaz were extradited to the United States to face terrorism charges.

Their extradition was upheld following a court decision that stated the prisoners did not show "new and compelling" reasons to stay in the UK. Their appeal came after the European Court of Human Rights backed successive UK courts in ruling for extradition.

- On October 10, two people were arrested at Heathrow Airport on suspicion of committing terrorist offenses. Police said the man and woman were being questioned as part of an investigation into travel to Syria in support of alleged terrorist activity.

Countering Terrorist Finance: The UK has a wide range of anti-money laundering/combating the financing of terrorism (AML/CFT) laws. It is a member of Financial Action Task Force (FATF) and an active participant in FATF-style regional bodies to meet evolving AML/CFT threats. For further information on money laundering and financial crimes, we refer you to the *2013 International Narcotics Control Strategy Report (INCSR), Volume 2, Money Laundering and Financial Crimes*: http://www.state.gov/j/inl/rls/nrcrpt/index.htm.

Regional and International Cooperation: The UK is a leader in all regional and international fora that it belongs to. It cooperates with other nations and international organizations on counterterrorism, including in the UN and UNSC, EU, NATO, Council of Europe, G-8, the International Atomic Energy Agency, the IMF, World Bank, the Global Initiative to Combat Nuclear Terrorism, and Interpol. The UK is a founding member of the Global Counterterrorism Forum and co-chairs its Countering Violent Extremism Working Group.

Countering Radicalization and Violent Extremism: In 2007, the UK launched its *Prevent* strategy to counter radicalization. *Prevent* is part of the government's overall CONTEST counterterrorism strategy. In 2011, *Prevent* was revised to correct several perceived problems. There had been complaints from members of Muslim organizations that UK government interaction with their communities was focused solely on security concerns. As a result, the UK divided the responsibilities for various strands of *Prevent* among different government organizations. The Department of Communities and Local Government took over responsibility for "integration" work, designed to ensure that Muslim communities were receiving all the government services to which they were entitled and that immigrants were given assistance to integrate into British society. The Home Office will focus on countering the ideology of violent extremism, including the identification of at-risk youth and their placement in de-radicalization pre-programs. The revised strategy calls for a much more focused effort to target those most at risk of radicalization. Finally, the government has decided that organizations that hold "extremist views," even those that are non-violent, will not be eligible to receive government funding or participate in *Prevent* programs.

MIDDLE EAST AND NORTH AFRICA

The Near East region continued to experience significant levels of terrorist activity in 2012, further complicated by ongoing regional instability across portions of North Africa and the Levant. Al-Qa'ida was not a part of the popular uprisings that led to democratic transitions across the Middle East and North Africa, but violent extremists looked for opportunities to exploit the political transitions underway.

In Libya, the security vacuum in the aftermath of the 2011 revolution provided more opportunities for terrorists to operate. This vacuum, combined with the weakness of Libya's nascent security institutions, allowed violent extremists to act, as we saw too clearly on September 11 in Benghazi, when J. Christopher Stevens, the U.S. Ambassador to Libya, and three staff members, died during attacks on U.S. facilities.

Al-Qa'ida in Iraq (AQI) – even with diminished leadership and capabilities – continued to conduct attacks across Iraq, while Shia militants largely ceased attacks but continued to threaten U.S. targets in Iraq. AQI also took advantage of a significantly depleted security situation in Syria. Operating under its alias, al-Nusrah Front, the group sought to portray itself as part of the legitimate Syrian opposition and attempted to hijack Syria's struggle for democracy. The United States designated al-Nusra as an alias of AQI in December 2012.

Al-Qa'ida in the Islamic Maghreb (AQIM) has also taken advantage of the instability in the region, particularly in Libya and Mali. Kidnapping for ransom operations continued to yield significant sums for AQIM, and it conducted attacks against members of state security services within the Trans-Sahara region.

In the spring of 2012, a Yemeni military offensive, with the help of armed residents, regained government control over territory in the south, which AQAP had seized and occupied in 2011. Although weakened, AQAP was not eliminated as a threat. AQAP increasingly turned to asymmetric tactics to target Yemeni government officials, pro-government tribal militias known as Popular Committees, and their leaders, soldiers, civilians, and U.S. embassy personnel.

In 2012, there was a clear resurgence of Iran's state sponsorship of terrorism, through the Islamic Revolutionary Guard Corps-Qods Force (IRGC-QF), its Ministry of Intelligence and Security, and Tehran's ally Hizballah, who remained a significant threat to the stability of Lebanon and the broader region. Attacks in Europe, Africa, the Middle East, South Asia, and the Far East were linked to the IRGC-QF or Hizballah. In fact, Hizballah's terrorist activity has reached a tempo unseen since the 1990s with attacks plotted in Southeast Asia, Europe, and Africa.

Despite these persistent threats, governments across the region improved their own counterterrorism capabilities, effectively disrupting the activities of a number of terrorists. The Iraqi government displayed increased capability and efficacy in pursuing multiple Sunni violent extremist groups. Though AQIM's presence and activity in the Sahel and parts of the Maghreb remains worrisome, the group's isolation in Algeria grew as Algeria increased its already substantial efforts to target it. And in 2012, Yemeni forces were successful in reducing the physical territory that AQAP had previously gained in Yemen as the result of political turmoil.

In Gaza, a sharp increase in the number of rocket attacks launched by Hamas and other Gaza-based terrorist groups led Israel to launch Operation Pillar of Defense in November 2012. During the course of the eight-day operation, Israeli forces targeted more than 1,500 terrorist sites. Since the Egypt-brokered November 21 ceasefire, the United States has engaged with our Egyptian and Israeli counterparts to strengthen and sustain the peace, in keeping with the President's pledge to Prime Minister Netanyahu to intensify efforts to help Israel address its security needs, especially the issue of the smuggling of weapons and explosives into Gaza. For instance, with U.S. encouragement, Egypt has increased its focus on border security and weapons interdictions. Israel has reciprocated by easing some of its economic sanctions on Gaza. The end result was a period of calm in Gaza. The United States is also in close contact with Egypt and Israel on enhancing security in the Sinai, where an August 5 terrorist attack against an Egyptian military outpost killed 16 soldiers.

Algeria, Egypt, Jordan, Morocco, Qatar, Saudi Arabia, and the United Arab Emirates played an active role in the newly formed Global Counterterrorism Forum (GCTF). At the December 2012 GCTF ministerial meeting, the Algiers Memorandum on Good Practices on Preventing and Denying the Benefits of Kidnapping for Ransom by Terrorists was adopted, and the UAE Foreign Minister announced the opening of *Hedayah* – the International Center of Excellence on Countering Violent Extremism in Abu Dhabi. At the June 2012 GCTF ministerial, Tunisia announced that it would host the International Institute for Justice and the Rule of Law, to provide interested governments the necessary training to strengthen criminal justice and other rule of law institutions to counter terrorism.

ALGERIA

Overview: Al-Qa'ida in the Islamic Maghreb (AQIM) remained a significant security threat to Algeria in 2012. AQIM operated primarily in the mountainous areas east of Algiers and in the expansive desert regions near Algeria's southern border. The deteriorating security situation in neighboring northern Mali, the proliferation of weapons smuggled out of Libya, and the emergence of the Mali-based Movement for Unity and Jihad in West Africa (MUJAO), which targeted Algeria on several occasions, all contributed to the terrorist threat to Algeria. Within Algeria, AQIM remained the most active terrorist threat. The group's Algeria-based contingent remains dedicated to the overthrow of the Algerian government. AQIM continued its historical targeting practices, largely attacking Algerian security forces. It frequently attacked local government targets and westerners in the Sahel, but as of year's end, had not conducted an attack outside the region. Over the past year, Algerian security forces further isolated AQIM in the north and decreased the number of successful terrorist attacks, sustaining pressure on the group's Algeria-based leadership and capturing a number of key terrorists.

Algeria has a long history of fighting terrorism, and continued its aggressive campaign against AQIM. In recent years, Algeria's sustained military, security, and policing efforts undercut AQIM's capabilities in northern Algeria, and largely limited the group's operations to more rural areas. This contrasted with AQIM's Sahel-based battalions, which historically served as support nodes for Algeria-based AQIM, but have increasingly taken advantage of chaos and rebellion to expand their areas of control and assert autonomy of action. Algerian officials frequently cited links between AQIM and narco-traffickers in the Sahel, and view terrorism as fundamentally linked to the criminal enterprises that fund the terrorist groups.

2012 Terrorist Incidents: Despite Algeria's counterterrorism efforts, AQIM continued to execute suicide attacks, attacks using improvised explosive devices (IEDs), and ambushes in areas outside Algiers. In total, Algeria's National Gendarmerie reported at least 175 terrorist acts in 2012. The majority of these attacks occurred in the northern Kabylie region.

As in years past, Algeria experienced a spike in terrorist incidents during Ramadan. In 2012, however, AQIM's yearly Ramadan offensive was significantly reduced, and was publically described as the least violent Ramadan in the past decade.

- On March 3, a vehicle-borne IED was used to attack the military base in the southern city of Tamanrasset. Twenty-three people were injured in the attack. The Mali-based group MUJAO claimed responsibility for that attack.
- On June 27, a vehicle-borne improvised explosive device (VBIED) was detonated at the gate of the Gendarmerie headquarters in the town of Ouargla, located approximately 50 miles northwest of Hassi Messaoud, situated within Algeria's oilfield area. The attack was significant due to its proximity to oil operations and because it took place in a military exclusion zone. The device detonated at the gate of the base, killing the occupant of the vehicle and one Gendarme.

Although much lower profile than the kidnappings of westerners by AQIM in neighboring Mali, kidnappings of Algerian citizens continued to occur within the country's borders. In October, the Algerian National Gendarmerie noted that 15 kidnappings had occurred in the northern Kabylie region throughout the year.

Legislation, Law Enforcement, and Border Security: Algerian security forces, primarily gendarmerie under the Ministry of National Defense, continued to conduct periodic sweep operations in the Kabylie region southeast of the capital to capture groups of AQIM fighters. Algerian law enforcement has been effective in protecting diplomatic missions and strengthening security assets when necessary. Regionally, Algeria has participated in discussions on the creation of the International Institute for Justice and the Rule of Law.

Algerian security forces made a number of key arrests in 2012. In August, Algerian press reported that three members of AQIM were arrested in Ghardaya at a security checkpoint. These individuals included Necib Tayeb (alias Abu Ishaq Essoufi), reportedly the head of AQIM's Legal Committee, and a member of AQIM's "council of notables." Local press reported that the three were traveling to neighboring northern Mali to meet with AQIM leaders. In December, press reported that Mohamed Abu Salah, the second in command to AQIM head Abdelmalek Droukdel, was arrested by Algeria near the town of Bouira. Abu Salah was reportedly in charge of AQIM communication and propaganda efforts, and his arrest would represent a significant set-back for AQIM. In total, press reported that Algerian gendarmes arrested over 300 individuals on terrorist charges, although it is difficult to confirm the accuracy of this number.

The Department of State's Antiterrorism Assistance (ATA) program provided a strong framework for improving the capabilities of Algerian institutions that fight terrorism and crime. In 2012, Algerian law-enforcement personnel participated in a variety of ATA courses designed to enhance investigative capacity, strengthen border security, and build response capacity to critical incidents. The majority of these courses combined students from different ministries in an effort to promote inter-ministerial cooperation and coordination in law enforcement.

Countering Terrorist Finance: Algeria works actively to counter terrorist financing. The Government of Algeria maintains – and advocates that others also maintain – a strict "no concessions" policy with regard to individuals or groups holding its citizens hostage and played a leadership role in the Global Counterterrorism Forum's (GCTF's) efforts to raise awareness among governments to prevent the payment of ransoms to terrorist organizations. Algeria is a member of the Middle East and North Africa Financial Action Task Force (MENAFATF), a Financial Action Task Force (FATF)-style regional body. Since October 2011, Algeria has been publicly identified by the FATF as a jurisdiction with strategic anti-money laundering/combating the financing of terrorism (AML/CFT) deficiencies. To address those deficiencies, it has developed an action plan with the FATF.

As part of its broader efforts to combat terrorist financing and comply with the FATF recommendations, and after a review of its 2005 AML/CFT legislation, Algeria adopted a new law in 2012 on the prevention of money laundering and terrorist financing. The 2012 law entered into force on December 14, and requires banks and other financial institutions to improve tracking and record keeping. The law also strengthens the obligations of financial regulators to monitor and ensure that banks and financial institutions cooperate with law enforcement authorities on investigations and prosecutions. Finally, the law authorizes judges to freeze or seize funds belonging to terrorist organizations. This legislation addresses prior concerns that Algeria had no specific legislation to freeze terrorist assets, although Algeria maintained that its ratification of international terrorist financing conventions gave it the authority to do so. Algeria worked throughout 2012 to improve its Financial Intelligence Unit's analytical and resource capacity, strengthen its authority, and increase its resources.

Algeria has a cash-based economy and a vast informal sector that poses challenges to monitoring and regulating money and value transfer services. Although the Algerian government, particularly the Central Bank, has mechanisms in place to control and collect data on wire transfers – and although Algeria requires the collection of wire transfer data – it is unclear whether legal requirements were consistently enforced. The Algerian government monitors NGO activities and financing. A 2012 law on associations included new provisions to limit foreign funding to local NGOs. The Central Bank is responsible for disseminating information about UN lists of designated terrorists or terrorist entities to financial institutions.

For further information on money laundering and financial crimes, we refer you to the *2013 International Narcotics Control Strategy Report (INCSR), Volume 2, Money Laundering and Financial Crimes*: http://www.state.gov/j/inl/rls/nrcrpt/index.htm.

Regional and International Cooperation: Algeria is a founding member of the GCTF and co-chairs the group's Sahel Working Group, in which capacity it championed the development of the Algiers Memorandum on Good Practices on Preventing and Denying the Benefits of Kidnapping for Ransom by Terrorists.

Regional counterterrorism cooperation remained challenging, particularly in the wake of the conflicts in neighboring northern Mali and Libya. Algeria is actively combating AQIM within its borders, but its long-standing policy of non-intervention has limited its involvement in neighboring northern Mali, where several AQIM battalions collaborated with the tribal and violent Islamist extremists that seized the northern half of Mali in spring 2012. Algeria has dramatically increased border security and reportedly sent thousands of additional security forces to reinforce the border and reduce weapons smuggling. Nonetheless, the long, porous borders remain a persistent security challenge.

In September 2010, Algeria in collaboration with southern neighbors Mali, Mauritania, and Niger, formed the Comite d' État-Major Opérationnel Conjoint (CEMOC). While the role of the CEMOC military command center (based in the southern Algerian city of Tamanrasset) in regional security has been limited, conferences among the CEMOC Joint Chiefs of Staff have resulted in additional coordination with regard to border security strategies.

Countering Radicalization and Violent Extremism: Algeria's 2006 Charter for Peace and National Reconciliation offered amnesty to former terrorists who laid down their weapons and disavowed violence. Perpetrators of particularly egregious acts, such as rape and bombings, were excluded from this amnesty. The program was controversial but succeeded in demobilizing a number of former militants.

Beginning in 2010, the Algerian government expanded its efforts at countering violent extremism by enlisting religious scholars and former terrorists to speak on its Radio Quran radio station, attempting to dissuade terrorists still fighting the government. The Algerian government appoints, trains, and pays the salaries of imams. The penal code outlines strict punishments, including fines and prison sentences, for anyone other than a government-designated imam who preaches in a mosque. The Algerian government monitors mosques for possible security-related offenses and prohibits the use of mosques as public meeting places outside of regular prayer hours. The government has the authority to pre-screen and approve sermons before they are delivered during Friday prayers, but more often it provides preapproved sermon topics prior to Friday prayers. In practice, each province and county employed religious officials to review sermon content.

The Ministry of Religious Affairs' educational commission is responsible for establishing policies for hiring teachers at Quranic schools and ensuring that all imams are well-qualified and follow governmental guidelines aimed at stemming violent extremism. Algerian imams have organized talks with Islamist militants and others susceptible to violent extremist ideologies, to challenge fatwas used to justify violence. The Ministry of Youth and Sports has implemented new policies aimed at creating alternative and constructive activities for disadvantaged youth, including expanding English-language programs, sports, and access to technical facilities at the thousands of Youth Centers they manage around the country. The government also continued to collaborate with the Muslim Scouts to manage programs on civic engagement, volunteerism, and leadership throughout the country.

BAHRAIN

Overview: Following a year of political and social unrest, Bahrain continued to develop its counterterrorism capacities while trying to address its citizens' demands for political reform. Bahrain contributed manpower to international counterterrorism operations, participated in international technical training, realigned internal responsibilities, and continued to invest in border control and security. Bahraini-U.S. counterterrorism cooperation remained strong, especially on the investigations of several suspected domestic terrorist incidents.

2012 Terrorist Incidents:
- In April, two improvised explosive devices (IEDs) detonated in the Diraz neighborhood, injuring four security officers.
- On August 22, according to Chief of Public Security Major General Tariq al-Hassan, a terrorist explosion threatened the lives of two men working security jobs in Sitra, causing burns and injuries. Preliminary information revealed that the explosion was caused by a locally made, remote controlled IED.
- On October 20, an IED exploded in Al-Ekr, causing the death of a police officer.

- On November 5, six homemade pipe bombs exploded, killing two expatriate workers and injuring a third individual.
- On November 7, a car caught fire after coming into contact with an explosive device left on the ground near the Atlas Hotel in Gudaibiya. No casualties were reported.
- On November 28, the Ministry of Interior reported that a homemade bomb exploded in a garbage bin in Adliya. No casualties were reported.

Legislation, Law Enforcement, and Border Security: The Bahrain National Security Agency established an agreement with the Ministry of Interior (MOI), giving the MOI authority to conduct arrest and detention operations of designated targets. The agreement, while signed in 2011, was enacted in 2012.

In June, police raided what they determined was a bomb-making facility. Follow-up investigations were conducted with the participation of forensic experts from London's Metropolitan Police.

In the case of the "Qatar Cell," uncovered in 2011 with the cooperation of the Qatari Security Authority, the MOI revealed that it found a terrorist cell targeting vital facilities and prominent figures. The Higher Criminal Court sentenced six defendants to 15 years imprisonment, and acquitted two other defendants. At year's end the case was with the Higher Appellate Court of Bahrain, who has adjourned it until February 2013, for the defense argument.

Bahrain continued to participate in the Department of State's Antiterrorism Assistance program, which focused on enhancing border security, investigations, and critical incident management capacity for law enforcement and first responders.

Countering Terrorist Finance: Bahrain is a member of the Middle East and North Africa Financial Action Task Force, a Financial Action Task Force-style regional body. In 2012, there were no public prosecutions of terrorist finance cases. Ministry of Interior officials from the Financial Intelligence Unit attended a U.S.-sponsored conference in Virginia in April and a Central Bank of Bahrain compliance official attended training in October. For further information on money laundering and financial crimes, we refer you to the *2013 International Narcotics Control Strategy Report (INCSR), Volume 2, Money Laundering and Financial Crimes*: http://www.state.gov/j/inl/rls/nrcrpt/index.htm.

Regional and International Cooperation: Bahrain worked closely and cooperatively with international partners throughout the region. Since formally endorsing the Global Initiative to Combat Nuclear Terrorism in March 2008, Bahrain has proactively worked to expand air, sea, and causeway border control points. On December 30, the Cabinet endorsed a collective security agreement of the six Gulf Cooperation Council member states. The agreement outlines mutual responsibilities to preserve security and stability in the region. One of its goals is to help combat transnational and organized crime and terrorism through information exchanges and coordination. Before implementation, the agreement must be ratified by each member state.

Regional and International Cooperation: The Government of Bahrain's efforts to counter radicalization and violent extremism were spearheaded by the Ministry of Justice and Islamic Affairs (MOJIA), which organized regular workshops for clerics and speakers from both the Sunni and Shia sects. One specific course addressed the definition of fanaticism, the adverse effects of fanaticism, and ways to guard against fanatic thought. The MOJIA also undertook an annual review of schools' Islamic Studies curricula to evaluate interpretations of religious texts.

EGYPT

Overview: Egyptian security services faced an evolving political, legal, and security environment in which they continued to combat terrorism and violent extremism. In June, Egypt elected a President, replacing the military council that had ruled the country since February 2011. In August, an attack on an Egyptian military installation near Rafah resulted in the deaths of 16 Egyptian soldiers and the hijacking of military vehicles, which were then used in an attempt to attack targets in Israel. This attack brought the problem of lawlessness in the Sinai to the forefront of President Morsy's security agenda. While the National Security Sector, which replaced the State Security Investigations Service in 2011, has struggled to fully understand and effectively combat terrorist threats, it has had some successes, such as the October raid and arrest of al-Qa'ida (AQ) aspirants in Cairo's Nasr City neighborhood. In addition, following the September 11 breach of the U.S. Embassy compound in Cairo, the Ministry of Interior ordered improvements to security measures around the Embassy.

Egypt's Northern Sinai region remained a transit route for smuggling arms and explosives into Gaza, as well as a base and transit point for Palestinian violent extremists. The smuggling of humans, weapons, cash, and other contraband through the Sinai into Israel and Gaza supported criminal networks with possible ties to terrorist groups in the region, although media accounts of Egyptian action to collapse smuggling tunnels increased later in the year. The smuggling of weapons from Libya to and through Egypt has increased since the overthrow of the Qadhafi regime. The security forces interdicted some of these arms. While it remained opposed to violent extremism, the Egyptian government largely focused its efforts on protecting official installations, restoring basic security, and ensuring a peaceful political transition.

2012 Terrorist Incidents: Nearly all of the reported terrorist incidents involved attacks on security forces – Egyptian, Israeli, or international – guarding or monitoring the Sinai, its state infrastructure, and its border with Gaza and Israel. These incidents included:

- On April 5, a rocket attack was fired from Sinai on Eilat, Israel.
- On June 16, two rockets were fired from Sinai on Israel.
- On June 18, a cross-border improvised explosive device attack targeted workers constructing the Israeli security fence along the Gaza-Sinai border. The Mujahidin Shura Council claimed responsibility.
- On July 22, there was a cross-border shooting at a bus of Israeli soldiers.
- On August 5, an attack near Rafah resulted in the death of 16 Egyptian soldiers. Attackers hijacked two Egyptian military vehicles and unsuccessfully attempted to cross the border and assault the Israeli side of the Kerem Shalom border crossing.
- On August 15, Ansar Bayt al-Maqdis (Partisans of the Holy Sanctuary) claimed responsibility for two rockets fired at Eilat, Israel.
- On September 21, an attack on an Israeli checkpoint resulted in the death of one Israeli Defense Force soldier; Ansar Bayt al-Maqdis claimed responsibility.
- On November 3, suspected violent Islamist extremists killed three Egyptian policemen in El-Arish in the northern Sinai.

111

Legislation, Law Enforcement, and Border Security: Egypt's Emergency Law, in effect since 1981, expired on May 31, 2012. State emergency courts continued to adjudicate those arrested for Emergency Law violations that occurred prior to its annulment. Officially, after that date, terrorism suspects were supposed to be investigated by civilian prosecutors for trial in regular civilian courts. In some cases, involving attacks on military personnel and facilities, however, military prosecutors and courts continued to function and assert jurisdiction.

Egypt continued its incremental efforts to improve border security with U.S. assistance and maintained its strengthened airport and port security measures and security for the Suez Canal, though the country's political transition and change in government delayed further progress. Egyptian border officials maintained a watch list for suspected violent extremists.

The United States provided technical assistance to Egypt to ensure the peaceful and legal movement of people and goods through the Rafah border crossing with Israel. To combat Sinai-Gaza frontier smuggling, installation was completed for Omniview scanners at the Peace Bridge on the Suez Canal at El Qantara. In addition, five Egyptian officers travelled to the United States in September to visit U.S. Customs and Border Protection (CBP), the Department of Homeland Security (DHS) headquarters, and the U.S. Port of Entry along the U.S.-Mexico border in California. CBP worked with Egyptian Customs Authority in Alexandria, Egypt to identify its customs-specific training needs.

On October 24, Egyptian security services raided a Cairo apartment in the Nasr City neighborhood and arrested a number of Egyptians, Libyans, and Tunisians associated with AQ aspirants in Egypt. On October 30, they arrested Sheikh Adel Shehato, an Egyptian Islamic Jihad official who is accused of founding and financing the Nasr City cell. The Egyptian security services subsequently arrested group leader Muhammad Jamal al Kashef. Authorities seized weapons, some of which may have been smuggled from Libya, and claimed that the cell planned attacks on Egyptian and international targets in the country. These actions appeared to indicate an increase in security officials' willingness to enforce existing laws.

The Department of State's Antiterrorism Assistance program provided training and equipment grants designed to meet needs and objectives specific to Egypt amid the country's evolving political landscape.

Countering Terrorist Finance: Egypt is a member of the Middle East and North Africa Financial Action Task Force, a Financial Action Task Force (FATF)-style regional body. Egypt's terrorist finance regulations were in line with relevant UNSCRs, though compliance with FATF international standards remained lacking. Egypt regularly informed its own financial institutions of any individuals or entities that are designated by the UN 1267/1989 and 1988 sanctions committees. Egypt's Code of Criminal Procedures and Penal Code adequately provides for the freezing, seizure, and confiscation of terrorism-related assets. With regard to implementation of UNSCRs 1267/1989 and 1988, however, the Egyptian notification process falls short of the requirements of FATF standards, particularly the use of measures and procedures for competent authorities to be able to freeze or seize terrorist-identified assets without delay. In Egypt, implementation requires a series of steps for actions by the relevant agencies and entities throughout the Egyptian government. Authorities have explained that according to current procedures, the Ministry of Foreign Affairs receives the UN lists and sends such lists to the Egyptian Money Laundering Combating Unit, which then directs concerned agencies to take the required actions. There are no specific procedures related to the un-freezing of assets. Moreover, delays in Egypt's judicial process could cause unnecessary delays and defeat the rationale for taking expedited freezing action in relation to individuals and legal persons designated on the UN lists.

For further information on money laundering and financial crimes, we refer you to the *2013 International Narcotics Control Strategy Report (INCSR), Volume 2, Money Laundering and Financial Crimes*: http://www.state.gov/j/inl/rls/nrcrpt/index.htm.

Regional and International Cooperation: Egypt is a founding member of the Global Counterterrorism Forum and, together with the United States, co-chaired its Rule of Law and Justice Committee. Egypt participated in the Arab League's Counterterrorism Committee, and the Egyptian Customs Authority's Alexandria training center served as the location for counterterrorism capacity building for other regional governments.

Countering Radicalization and Violent Extremism: The Ministry of Awqaf (Endowments) is legally responsible for issuing guidance to imams throughout Egypt, including how to avoid extremism in sermons. Al-Azhar University maintained a program to train imams who promote moderate Islam, interfaith cooperation, and human rights.

IRAQ

Overview: Iraqi security forces made progress combating al-Qa'ida in Iraq (AQI) and other Sunni insurgent organizations in 2012. While there has been clear and measurable success against AQI over the years, the group still remains a dangerous threat to the Iraqi people. In 2012, there were no significant attacks on U.S. interests or U.S. fatalities. The Iraqi government succeeded in securing multiple large public religious gatherings and government events – most notably the Arab League Summit in late March and P5+1 talks in May in Baghdad – but terrorist bombings and other attacks continued to occur.

The Government of Iraq concentrated its counterterrorism efforts against AQI and other Sunni-affiliated terrorist organizations. AQI remained capable of large-scale coordinated attacks and conducted numerous high-profile suicide and car bombings on government and civilian targets, aiming to increase tensions among Iraqi sectarian groups and ethnic minorities, and undercut public perceptions of the government's capacity to provide security. Jaysh Rijal al-Tariqah al-Naqshabandiyah (JRTN), a Sunni nationalist insurgent group with links to the former Baath Party, also continued attacks during the year. JRTN largely targeted Iraqi and U.S. interests in northern Iraq. Shia militant groups Kata'ib Hizballah, Asa'ib Ahl Haqq, and the Sadrist Promised Day Brigades adhered to the cease-fire they declared in the latter half of 2011 and early 2012. Some former Shia militant leaders began engaging in the political process and competing for political influence.

Terrorist tactics and weapons remained largely unchanged from 2011, as AQI and other terrorists relied predominantly on suicide bombings and car and roadside bombs and to a lesser extent on gunmen using assault rifles or silenced weapons to assassinate government and security officials. Iraq-U.S. counterterrorism cooperation remained strong, particularly in training, advisory, and intelligence-sharing programs.

The Iraqi Security Forces proved capable of working together to find, arrest, and charge terrorism suspects. In November, the Iraqi Police, Federal Police, and Iraqi Army – at times working together – arrested over 350 people on terrorism charges and seized several weapon and rocket caches, as part of a major counterterrorism operation. Iraq's Counterterrorism Services (CTS) also conducted approximately 1,600 terrorism related arrests in 2012.

2012 Terrorist Incidents: Terrorist groups conducted numerous attacks throughout the country. The deadliest attacks involved suicide bombings that targeted security forces, government buildings, and religious gatherings:

- On January 5, car bombs in Shia areas in Baghdad's Sadr City and Kadhimiyah District killed at least 25 civilians and wounded nearly 70. A suicide bomber also targeted Shia pilgrims celebrating Arbaeen near the city of Nassiriya, killing at least 40 people and wounding over 70.
- On February 23, a series of coordinated car bombs, improvised explosive devices (IEDs), and shootings orchestrated by AQI killed at least 55 people and wounded over 200 in Baghdad and 11 other cities.
- On March 20, over 30 car bombings, later claimed by AQI, killed at least 50 people and wounded over 200 in over 12 cities, including Baghdad.
- On April 19, over 20 roadside bombs and IEDs killed at least 36 people and wounded approximately 150 in Kirkuk City, Baghdad, and four other cities.
- On June 13, roadside and car bombs in 10 different cities, including Baghdad, killed over 60 people and wounded another 153. The casualties were predominantly Shia pilgrims.
- On July 23, a series of highly coordinated attacks targeting mostly Shia using car bombs, checkpoint ambushes, and assaults on a military base and police officers' homes, killed at least 107 people and wounded another 268 people throughout the country.
- On August 16, a wave of shootings and IEDs killed more than 80 people and wounded over 270 in Baghdad and Kirkuk City, as well as Salah-ad-din, Anbar, Wasit, and Diyala provinces during the month of Ramadan.
- On September 9, coordinated car bombings in a dozen Iraqi cities killed at least 100 people and wounded another 285, following news that an Iraqi court had sentenced Vice President Tareq al-Hashemi to death. September was also the deadliest month in Iraq in over two years with approximately 365 people killed and another 683 wounded.
- On December 17, a wave of bombings hit neighborhoods in the disputed areas and other parts of Iraq killing 25 people and wounding dozens. The bombs targeted civilians of Shabak ethnicity in al-Mouafaqiyah, a village north of Mosul, and Turkomen neighborhoods in the city of Tuz Khormato.

Legislation, Law Enforcement, and Border Security: The Government of Iraq took several steps to improve border security. Iraq, with U.S. support, continued to install, repair, and improve inspection equipment at ports of entry. The government also expanded the number of ports of entry with biometric data capture, but continued to face challenges linking border security systems together. Iraq is also incorporating non-intrusive inspection equipment at its land border crossings to scan for contraband, is improving roads along the borders, and received three littoral patrol ships in March.

Iraq's major counterterrorism organizations made progress in investigating cases and arresting terrorists, but continued to suffer from a lack of interagency coordination and inadequate cooperation between investigators, prosecutors, and the judiciary. While the Federal Intelligence and Investigations Agency (FIIA) arrested a significant number of terrorist suspects in 2012, Iraqi federal law enforcement and intelligence entities continued to struggle with intelligence analysis and targeting efforts relating to terrorist organizations and often resorted to rounding up locals to elicit intelligence information. The Major Crimes Task Force (MCTF), a collaborative task force involving U.S. federal law enforcement officers and FIIA investigators, targeted counterterrorism, organized crime, and government corruption cases from 2005 through late 2011. In 2012, the MCTF functioned as an Iraqi-only investigative element focusing on terrorist groups. However, like many other law enforcement entities, the MCTF operated independent of other Iraqi agencies working terrorism matters to include the Counterterrorism Organized Crime General Directorate.

Iraq continued to face significant challenges investigating and moving criminal cases from arrest to trial due to resource limitations, inadequate training, poor interagency coordination, and at times, limited political will. Prosecution of sectarian crimes carries a significant political risk. Separately, many among Iraq's Sunni community believed that the government used terrorism laws to unfairly target the Sunni population. Iraqi law enforcement officials, with U.S. training support, continued to improve investigative skills such as forensic evidence collection.

In 2011, the Central Criminal Court of Iraq (CCCI) convicted a former Iraqi Army sergeant and suspected AQI member of the murder of two U.S. soldiers in 2007 and sentenced him to life in prison. In the spring of 2012, however, the Federal Court of Cassation (FCC) overturned this decision on appeal and dismissed the charges. Even though substantial evidence was presented, the FCC determined that critical forensic evidence was of limited reliability and probative value. The U.S. government requested that the FCC correct and reverse this decision, but this request was formally denied on October 8. Subsequent to the spring 2012 FCC decision dismissing the charges in the above case, a companion case against the same defendant before the CCCI for other soldiers wounded in the attack resulted in the dismissal of similar terrorism charges on similar evidentiary grounds. On October 21, the CCCI convicted a suspected Shia Jaysh al-Mahdi member on terrorism charges stemming from an attack that killed one U.S. soldier and wounded three others, and sentenced him to 15 years in prison. It is anticipated that this case will be subject to review on appeal by the FCC.

On November 16, citing a lack of a legal basis to continue holding him, Iraq also released Lebanese Hizballah member Ali Musa Daqduq, who was accused of involvement in a 2007 attack that killed five U.S. soldiers. The CCCI had dismissed the charges against Daqduq in May citing insufficient reliable evidence, a decision that was upheld on appeal in June by the FCC.

Judicial security continued to be a challenge. Judges investigating and adjudicating terrorism cases continued to face threats to their personal safety and that of their families:

- In April, terrorists targeted the Chief Judge of Karkh Appellate Court (Najim Abdallah Ahamd al-Mashhadani) with a vehicle-born improvised explosive device at an intersection about 50 meters from the judge's vehicle.
- In June, terrorists again targeted Judge Najim, this time by a suicide bomber on a bicycle. The explosion killed one bystander.

- In October, terrorists assassinated Dr. Talib Al Shraa' of the Iraqi Ministry of Justice (MOJ). Dr. Talib was MOJ's liaison to the National Center for State Courts, a U.S.-partner assisting the MOJ in its strategic planning and budgeting.

At year's end, the Security and Defense Committee of the Council of Representatives was still working on draft legislation to codify the mission and authorities of the CTS. This effort has remained stalled since 2009.

Iraq remained an important partner nation in the Department of State's Antiterrorism Assistance program, which focused on helping the Government of Iraq build capacity in law enforcement investigations, critical incident management, and border security.

Countering Terrorist Finance: In 2012, the Iraqi government underwent its first-ever mutual evaluation to review compliance with international anti-money laundering/combating the financing of terrorism (AML/CFT) standards by the Middle East and North Africa Financial Action Task Force (MENAFATF), a Financial Action Task Force-style regional body. This important step affirmed Iraq's commitment to interrupt terrorist finance domestically. Although Iraq's Mutual Evaluation Report found the country to be non-compliant in most areas, the engagement of the Iraqi government, including at the MENAFATF plenary in November, served as an indicator of Iraq's commitment to address the AML/CFT challenges it faces. The United States provided subject matter expertise to assist Iraq in preparing for the mutual evaluation, post-evaluation follow-up, and in drafting a new AML/CFT statute.

The Prime Minister has approved the formation of a committee, or task force, to coordinate cases involving asset recovery, including the recovery of assets illegally taken outside of Iraq by members of the former regime, and tracing funds used to support terrorism. The committee will include representatives from the Ministry of Interior Economic Crimes Section, the Federal Investigation Information, and the Commission of Integrity. The Prime Minister's legal advisor announced the formation of the task force the week of October 21.

The Acting Governor of the Central Bank has agreed to move the Iraqi Financial Intelligence Unit (formerly the Money Laundering Reporting Office, now referred to as the Anti-Money Laundering Unit, or AMLU) into a secure space with dependable utilities, to facilitate the work of the unit.

For further information on money laundering and financial crimes, we refer you to the *2013 International Narcotics Control Strategy Report (INCSR), Volume 2, Money Laundering and Financial Crimes*: http://www.state.gov/j/inl/rls/nrcrpt/index.htm.

Regional and International Cooperation: Iraq is increasingly engaging with its neighbors through the Arab League. Iraq hosted the Arab League Summit in March of this year. Iraq, Turkey, and the United States continued a trilateral security dialogue as part of ongoing efforts to counter the Kurdistan Workers' Party.

The U.S.-supported NATO Transition Cell in Iraq assisted over 70 Iraqi officials in receiving NATO training abroad on various topics, including counterterrorism. CTS also partnered with Jordan, sending nearly 40 of its soldiers to the Jordanian Counterterrorism Academy for training. In April, CTS sent observers to a U.S.-Jordanian joint counterterrorism exercise.

Countering Radicalization and Violent Extremism: Iraqi leaders routinely denounced terrorism and countered terrorist propaganda in public statements. The Iraqi government took steps to bring certain violent violent extremist groups into the political process, and made limited attempts to foster broader reconciliation between sectarian groups.

ISRAEL, THE WEST BANK, AND GAZA

Overview: Israel continued to be a stalwart counterterrorism partner in 2012. It faced continued terrorist threats from Hamas, the Popular Resistance Committees, and Palestinian Islamic Jihad (PIJ), particularly from Gaza but also from the West Bank; and from Hizballah in Lebanon. Fourteen Israelis were killed as a result of terrorist attacks in 2012. Gaza-based Palestinian terrorist organizations continued rocket and mortar attacks into Israeli territory, and multiple terrorist attacks were launched along the Gaza security fence as well as the Israel-Egypt border. Gaza also remained a base of operations for several violent Islamist extremist splinter groups. The Government of Israel responded to these threats with operations directed at terrorist leaders, infrastructure, and activities such as rocket launching, most notably in Operation Pillar of Defense during the November 14-21 Gaza conflict.

A Hamas and PIJ-linked terrorist cell based in the West Bank also carried out a bombing on a Tel Aviv city bus, the first such attack in years, and Israel faced a wave of plots and attacks against its interests abroad that Israeli officials linked to Iran and Hizballah. Arms smuggling continued from Iran through Egypt into Gaza to Palestinian terrorist organizations. Israeli officials also continued to be concerned about the smuggling of weapons from Libya via Sudan into Gaza.

Israel was hit by a record volume of rocket fire from Gaza in 2012. The rocket attacks demonstrated technological advancements, and Gaza militants for the first time used longer-range rockets to target major Israeli population centers in the greater Tel Aviv and Jerusalem areas. Israeli experts maintained that militants successfully smuggled long-range rockets from the Sinai Peninsula through tunnels into Gaza, and subsequently began producing rockets in Gaza. Israeli counterterrorism officials said Gaza militants made significant quantitative and qualitative advances in capabilities in the four years since Operation Cast Lead. Before Cast Lead, Israeli officials estimated that Gaza militants had 1,000 rockets with ranges up to 25 kilometers (km); at the start of Pillar of Defense, stockpiles had increased to approximately 6,000, with ranges up to 80 km. During this period, Gaza militants also developed the ability to employ dual-use materials smuggled into Gaza to manufacture the M-75 rocket, which was used twice for longer-range strikes against Israel during Pillar of Defense. The Israeli government continued to hold Hamas, as the dominant organization in effective control of Gaza, responsible for the attacks emanating from Gaza, and Israeli officials pointed to these attacks as proof that Hamas has not abandoned terrorism. In the aftermath of the Gaza escalation, Israel is seeking enhanced cooperation with regional partners and the international community to effectively counter arms smuggling in the region.

On the Northern Border, Israeli security officials remained concerned about the terrorist threat posed to Israel from Hizballah and its Iranian patron, arguing that Iran, primarily through the efforts of the Islamic Revolutionary Guard Corps-Qods Force, continued to transfer arms to Hizballah in Lebanon. Also, in light of the unrest in Syria, Israeli officials were concerned about proliferation of conventional and non-conventional weapons from Syria to terrorist organizations. Israeli politicians and security officials pointed to Hizballah's efforts to rebuild and re-arm following the 2006 Lebanon War as evidence that the group remained a threat to Israel. According to the Government of Israel, Hizballah has stockpiled 50,000 missiles in Lebanon, some of which are capable of striking anywhere in Israel, including population centers.

A series of terrorist attacks and foiled plots against Israeli interests abroad that began in 2011 continued in 2012. Though most of these plots were disrupted, a July 18 suicide attack against Israeli tourists in Burgas, Bulgaria, killed five Israeli citizens and one Bulgarian and injured dozens, and a February 13 attack in New Delhi injured the wife of an Israeli Ministry of Defense employee. Terrorist plots were also uncovered against Israeli targets in Thailand, Azerbaijan, and Cyprus, and an attack was foiled in Georgia. Israeli officials publicly linked many of these plots and attacks to Hizballah and its Iranian sponsors. [On February 5, 2013, the Bulgarian government publically implicated Hizballah in the July 2012 Burgas bombing that killed five Israelis and one Bulgarian citizen, and injured 32 others. On March 21, 2013, a Cyprus court found a Hizballah operative guilty of charges stemming from his surveillance activities, carried out in 2012, of Israeli tourist targets, while Thailand was prosecuting a Hizballah member for his role in helping plan a possible terrorist attack in that country.]

2012 Terrorist Incidents: Incidents included rocket and mortar fire from Gaza, a bus bombing, attacks along the Gaza security fence, and cross-border attacks from Egypt's Sinai Peninsula. Rocket and mortar fire emanating from Gaza was the most prevalent form of attack by Palestinian terrorist organizations. Israel experienced major escalations in rocket attacks in March, June, October, and November. According to figures released by the Israel Security Agency (ISA), as of the end of November, a total of 2,331 rockets were fired from Gaza at Israel in the course of 2012, up from the previous peak of approximately 2,000 in 2008. In addition, 224 mortar shells were launched toward Israel. Following attacks from Gaza, Israeli forces targeted sites used by terrorists to launch indirect-fire attacks against Israeli civilians and security forces. In addition, Israel faced terrorist threats abroad, including attacks that were carried out in Bulgaria and India, and at least five plots or attempted attacks in other countries. Please see the country reports for Azerbaijan, Bulgaria, Cyprus, Georgia, India, Kenya, and Thailand in this chapter for information on attacks against Israeli citizens.

Between November 14 and 21, some 1,814 rockets and mortars were launched from Gaza toward Israel. The bulk of incoming fire targeted communities in the South, but some longer-range rockets were fired from Gaza at Tel Aviv and the Jerusalem area for the first time. Although most of these landed in open areas or were intercepted, one rocket struck a residential building in the Tel Aviv suburb Rishon Lezion, causing extensive damage. The Iron Dome missile defense system intercepted 421 rockets during the operation, successfully engaging approximately 85 percent of rockets targeted for interception.

Despite Iron Dome and other civil defense efforts, incoming rocket and mortar fire resulted in the deaths of six Israelis and significant property damage. On November 15, three people were killed in a direct rocket hit on an apartment building in Kiryat Malachi. On November 20, an Israeli soldier and an Israeli civilian were killed by mortar fire in the Eshkol Regional Council. On November 22, an Israel Defense Forces (IDF) reserve officer died of wounds suffered in a November 21 rocket attack from Gaza.

On November 21, a bomb exploded in a city bus in central Tel Aviv, near the headquarters of the Ministry of Defense, wounding 26 Israeli civilians. Hamas spokesman Sami Abu Zuhiri praised the bombing. In December, the ISA announced that it arrested the perpetrators of the attack, who it said were members of a Ramallah-area-based terrorist cell consisting of Hamas and PIJ-affiliated operatives. According to the ISA, the cell was led by Ahmed Salah Ahmed Musa, a Hamas operative who was responsible for intelligence collection, production of the improvised explosive device (IED), and recruiting the individual who planted the IED and remotely activated it. Muhammad Abed Al Jfar Nasser Mfarja, an Israeli citizen, was recruited to Hamas by Musa, and planted the IED on the bus. The ISA described Fuad Rabach Sucry Azai as a PIJ operative who provided Musa with a handgun and ammunition and attempted to provide him with an M-16 rifle. Prior to the attack, Musa requested the assistance of another Hamas operative, Muhammad Mahpod Said Damara, who reportedly admitted the possession of a rifle that was to be used during the attack. On December 19, the Tel Aviv District Advocate filed an indictment in the Tel Aviv District Court against Mfarja; indictments against the remaining operatives were expected to follow.

Incidents along the Gaza security fence included:
- On May 1, IDF soldiers came under fire near the security fence in central Gaza; two armored vehicles were damaged.
- On June 1, an Israeli soldier was killed when a terrorist attempting to enter Israel from southern Gaza opened fire on IDF soldiers.
- On October 23, an IDF officer was injured in an IED attack on the Gaza border. Israel subsequently uncovered additional explosive devices near the security fence, and on November 9, an "explosive tunnel" on the Gaza border detonated during an operational activity by the IDF.
- On November 10, an anti-tank missile was fired at an IDF patrol along the security fence in northern Gaza, injuring four Israeli soldiers.

Incidents on the Israel-Egypt border included:
- In February, an IDF team found an explosive device with a remote trigger along the portion of the Israel-Egypt border known as the Philadelphi Corridor.
- In a June 18 cross-border attack from Egypt, militants detonated a roadside bomb and fired anti-tank rockets and live ammunition at two Israeli vehicles. An Israeli civilian working on the Israel-Egypt border fence was killed, and two others were wounded.
- On August 5, terrorists identified by the IDF as a global terrorist cell operating in the Sinai stormed an Egyptian military post near Rafah, killing 16 Egyptian soldiers and border guards and capturing an armored personnel carrier (APC) and a truck filled with explosives. The truck exploded at the Israel-Egypt border, and the APC entered Israeli territory near Kerem Shalom with four attackers inside, where it was targeted by the Israel Air Force. The attack came shortly after a mortar barrage from Gaza pounded the Kerem Shalom border crossing in Israel, and rockets were fired at adjacent towns.

Hizballah-linked incidents included:
- According to the ISA, in early June, Hizballah smuggled 20 kilograms of C-4 explosive and an IED detonation system into Israel from Lebanon, using a network of narcotics dealers. Weapons were also seized as part of a joint ISA-Israel National Police operation

that exposed the scheme. Twelve suspects were detained and questioned, and charges were filed against eight.

- On October 6, the IAF shot down an unmanned aerial vehicle (UAV) that entered Israeli airspace, and the IDF posted a video clip of the interception online. According to press, Hizballah leader Hassan Nasrallah, in televised remarks on October 11, acknowledged that the group had sent the drone, and claimed its parts were manufactured in Iran and assembled by Hizballah in Lebanon.

Legislation, Law Enforcement, and Border Security: On December 2, the Cabinet declared the following entities to be terrorist organizations, pursuant to Article 8 of the 1948 Prevention of Terrorism Ordinance. Israeli counterterrorism officials indicated that each of these entities was already subject to counterterrorism sanctions prior to this decision, which was intended to reinforce existing measures and enhance enforcement.

- The al-Qods Force of the Revolutionary Guards;
- The Change and Reform List or al-Atzlach v'al-Tajair;
- The Charity Coalition (Atlaf Alchayir);
- The Iranian (or) Palestinian Humanity Support and Coordination Staff, the Popular Committee for Support of the Palestinian People, and the Iranian Popular Committee for Support of the Palestinian Intifada;
- The al-Qods Institution and al-Qods International Institution;
- The Palestinian and Lebanese Families Welfare Trust;
- The Popular Resistance Committees and its military arm, the Saladin Brigade;
- The IHH ("Insan Haklary ve Hurriyetleri"), Vakfi International Humanitarian Relief Organization, "Internationale Humanitere Hilfsorganisation."

On the law enforcement front, the ISA and Israel National Police (INP) continued to cooperate with U.S. law enforcement agencies on cases involving U.S. citizens killed in terrorist attacks, as well as other counterterrorism initiatives of mutual interest.

Countering Terrorist Finance: Israel had active observer status in Moneyval, the Council of Europe's Select Committee of Experts on the Evaluation of Anti-Money-laundering Measures, a Financial Action Task Force-style regional body. The Israeli Financial Intelligence Unit, known as the Israeli Money-Laundering and Terror Finance Prohibition Authority, is a member of the Egmont Group. Israel's counterterrorist finance regime continued to be enhanced through enforcement operations and the inclusion of new groups under national terrorist finance laws; the well-regulated Israeli banking industry worked to address suspected terrorist activity. Financing of Hamas through charitable organizations remained a concern for Israeli authorities, as did the funding of Hizballah through charities and criminal organizations. For further information on money laundering and financial crimes, we refer you to the *2013 International Narcotics Control Strategy Report (INCSR), Volume 2, Money Laundering and Financial Crimes*: http://www.state.gov/j/inl/rls/nrcrpt/index.htm.

Regional and International Cooperation: Israel continued its counterterrorism cooperation with a range of regional and international institutions, including the UN, the OAS, and the OSCE. Israel conducted strategic dialogues that included counterterrorism discussions with the United States, Canada, Russia, the UK, France, Germany Italy, and the EU. Israel continued to cooperate with the OAS Inter-American Committee against Terrorism to assist Latin American states with counterterrorism efforts. Israel also deepened its cooperation with the UN Counter-Terrorism Implementation Task Force. As a member of the Conference on Interaction and Confidence Building Measures in Asia, Israel continued to explore ways to enhance cooperation on counterterrorism with Central Asian states. Israel also engaged with the EU on transportation and aviation security efforts and sought to deepen its counterterrorism cooperation with NATO.

Countering Radicalization and Violent Extremism: Attacks by extremist Israeli settlers against Palestinian residents, property, and places of worship in the West Bank continued, and several were condemned by senior Israeli officials as acts of terrorism. Following the evacuation of the Migron outpost and subsequent desecration of the Latrun Monastery in September, Minister of Internal Security Aharonovitch, according to local media, announced the establishment of a new police unit to counter settler violence and called for a "zero tolerance policy against terror, the desecration of religious institutions, attacks on symbols of governance, and attacks commonly known as 'price tag.'"

West Bank and Gaza

The Palestinian Authority (PA) continued its counterterrorism efforts in the West Bank. Hamas, PIJ, and the Popular Front for the Liberation of Palestine (PFLP) remained present in the West Bank, although the improved capacity of Palestinian Authority Security Forces (PASF) constrained those organizations' ability to carry out attacks. The IDF continued arresting members of terrorist organizations operating in the West Bank. Gaza continued to be administered by Hamas; and Hamas, PIJ and Popular Resistance Committees (PRC) launched attacks against Israel from Gaza.

Palestinian militants initiated attacks against Israelis inside the West Bank and Israel. Attacks by extremist Israeli settlers against Palestinian residents, property, and places of worship in the West Bank continued and were largely unprosecuted, according to UN and NGO sources. The ISA reported a total of more than 750 of what it defined as terrorist attacks originating in the West Bank against Israeli citizens from January through November. Of these, more than 700 involved firebombs; but the attacks also included shootings, stabbings, grenade and IED incidents, and rock throwing. According to Israeli authorities, despite continued violence, for the first time since 1973, an entire year passed without an Israeli fatality from a terrorist attack in the West Bank.

The primary PASF services operating in the West Bank were the Palestinian Civil Police, the National Security Force (NSF), the Preventive Security Organization, the General Intelligence Service, the Presidential Guard, the Military Intelligence Service, and the Civil Defense. Based on available payroll numbers, PASF forces in the West Bank numbered approximately 29,000. Much of the PASF were under the Interior Minister's operational control and followed the Prime Minister's guidance, while others reported directly to the PA president. Israeli authorities, among others, noted continuing improvements in the capacity and performance of PASF as a leading contributor to the improved security environment in the West Bank and a dramatic reduction in terrorist incidents in and emanating from the West Bank over the past six years. The United States continued to assist the PA's counterterrorism efforts through capacity building programs for PA security forces, which included training, equipping, and provision of infrastructure to PASF personnel in the West Bank. U.S.-funded training of PASF also took place in Jordan at the

Jordan International Police Training Center, and at the Prince Hussein Bin Abdullah II Academy of Civil Protection in Jordan.

Hamas continued to consolidate its control over Gaza, eliminating or marginalizing potential rivals. Hamas and other armed groups in Gaza smuggled weapons, cash, and other contraband into Gaza through an extensive network of tunnels from Egypt. Gaza remained a base of operations for several violent extremist splinter groups, such as Tawhid wa Jihad and the Mujahedin Shura Council; and clan-based criminal groups that engaged in or facilitated terrorist attacks.

During the year, PA President Mahmoud Abbas and PA Prime Minister Salam Fayyad consistently reiterated their commitment to nonviolence and recognition of the State of Israel. They continued to support a security program involving disarmament of fugitive militants, arresting members of terrorist organizations, and gradually dismantling armed groups in the West Bank.

In August, six Palestinians were wounded after a fire bomb was thrown at their vehicle near the West Bank settlement of Bayt Ayin, and two Israeli settlers, both minors, were arrested by Israeli authorities in connection with the crime. Israeli Vice Premier Moshe Ya'alon described the incident as a hate crime and a terrorist act. In July, UN officials and several local NGOs issued a statement noting that Israeli settler violence against Palestinians had risen sharply, by nearly 150 percent since 2009. More than 90 percent of the complaints filed against settlers in recent years have not been addressed, according to the UN. In 2011, Israeli Defense Minister Ehud Barak labeled settler acts as having "the characteristic of homegrown terror;" several months earlier, IDF Head of Central Command Avi Mizrahi labeled attacks against Palestinians and their property in the West Bank as "terror" and ordered the administrative deportation of a dozen Israeli settlers from the West Bank settlement of Yitzhar. In 2012, four mosques in the West Bank, and five churches in the West Bank and Jerusalem were vandalized in apparent "price tag" attacks carried out by Israeli settlers in retribution for Israeli government actions they perceived as against their interests.

There were multiple acts of violence conducted by different sub-state actors in the West Bank, both Palestinian and Israeli, and Gaza-based militants attacked Israel. Attacks included:

- In March, a 19-year-old female IDF soldier was stabbed while riding the Jerusalem light rail in a suspected terrorist attack.
- On March 31, four Palestinians were hospitalized after they were attacked by Israeli settlers near the Mikhmas junction outside Ramallah.
- On June 19, settlers reportedly set fire to the main mosque in the West Bank village of Jabaa in Ramallah governorate.
- On August 22, 17 year-old Palestinian Jamal Julani was beaten into an unconscious state by a group of Israeli teenagers reportedly yelling racist slurs in Zion Square in Jerusalem. Israeli vice premier Moshe Ya'alon condemned the incident as a terrorist attack.
- On September 4, pro-settler vandals thought to be participating in a "price tag attack" set fire to the entrance door of the Latrun Monastery outside of Jerusalem, spray-painting the names of West Bank outposts and "Jesus is a monkey."

The PASF detained terrorists in the West Bank and PA authorities tried some detainees in civilian and military courts. Despite factional reconciliation talks between Hamas and Fatah, PASF personnel continued to detain Hamas elements in operations often protested by Hamas officials.

- In February, after the PASF arrested several high profile Hamas members in the West Bank, Hamas released a statement demanding that Fatah stop its "irresponsible" acts.
- In May, according to press reports, Israel's Shin Bet published a report saying that it had intercepted and broken up three militant cells in Hebron City.
- In June, Hamas spokesman Sami Abu Zuhri denounced what he called an "arrest campaign" against Hamas activists in Halhoul and Hebron. Hamas media sites reported that PASF personnel summoned nearly two dozen Hamas members for interrogation.
- In September, PASF discovered and seized an underground bunker used by Hamas members in the northern West Bank village of Urif reportedly being prepared as a place to hide a kidnapped IDF soldier or Israeli settler.
- In late September, Hamas officials issued a statement saying that the PASF had arrested its supporters who reportedly participated in "violent riots" against the PA during protests against economic conditions in the West Bank. In total, Hamas claimed that the PASF arrested 184 of its members in September.
- In October, the PASF confiscated documents and weapons belonging to Hamas in a residential area of Nablus.
- On December 3, West Bank Hamas official Rafat Nasif said publicly that the PASF continued its political arrests "despite the talk about reconciliation."

No progress was made in apprehending, prosecuting, or bringing to justice the perpetrators of the October 2003 attack on a U.S. embassy convoy in Gaza that killed three U.S. government contractors and critically injured a fourth.

The primary limitation on PA counterterrorism efforts in Gaza remained Hamas' continued control of the area and the resulting inability of PASF to operate there. Limitations on PA counterterrorism efforts in the West Bank included restrictions on the movement and activities of PASF in and through areas of the West Bank for which the Israeli government retained responsibility for security under the terms of Oslo-era agreements. The limited capacity of the PA's civilian criminal justice system also hampered PA counterterrorism efforts.

The PA continued to lack modern forensic capability. In late 2012, the Canadian International Development Agency, through the UN Office on Drugs and Crime, began project activity on a multi-year project to initiate forensic criminal capacity within Palestinian law enforcement.

U.S. efforts to train and equip the PASF have provided them with new tools to enforce law and order and counter terrorism. U.S.-trained NSF special battalions have been instrumental in ongoing PASF law and order and anti-terror efforts since 2008, and security campaigns designed to root out terrorist and criminal elements across the West Bank have been widely praised for improving security and returning normalcy to major West Bank urban areas. In January and February 2012, the PASF successfully conducted their first operations since 1997 in the Israeli controlled H2 section of downtown Hebron City, and arrested several dozen suspected criminals. U.S-trained PASF maintained public order in 2012 during Palestinian demonstrations surrounding the anniversary of Israeli Independence known as "Nakba Day."

The PA continued to increase its capacity to combat illicit finance. Terrorist financing is not specifically addressed in current law, but the PA is drafting appropriate legislation and can prosecute terrorism-related offenses, such as financing, under current laws. The Palestinian Financial Intelligence Unit, known as the Financial Follow-up Unit, added additional staff and continued building its technical capacity while conducting outreach to other parts of the PA on anti-money laundering/countering terrorist finance. The PA, an observer to the Middle East and North Africa Financial Action Task Force, submitted its application for membership and was given an action plan for attaining membership. The banking sector in Gaza continued to repel Hamas attempts to influence and tax the sector. The PA Interior and Awqaf and Religious Affairs Ministries monitored the charitable sector for signs of abuse by terrorist organizations.

According to the PA's Palestinian Broadcasting Company's code of conduct, no programming is allowed that encourages "violence against any person or institution on the basis of race, religion, political beliefs, or sex." The PA continued its efforts to monitor and control the content of Friday sermons delivered in over 1,800 West Bank mosques to ensure that they do not endorse or incite violence. The PA's ability to enforce these guidelines varies depending upon its location, and it has limited authority to control the context of sermons in Israeli-controlled Area C.

JORDAN

Overview: In 2012, Jordan remained a steadfast partner in counterterrorism. In addition to its diplomatic and political assistance to the Israel-Palestinian peace process, Jordan assisted the Palestinian Authority's continued development of state institutions through law enforcement training programs at the Jordan International Police Training Center (JIPTC). JIPTC-trained forces continued to earn the respect of regional actors for their success in maintaining security in the West Bank.

The Jordanian government further developed its counterterrorism capabilities and improved its capacity. At the same time, the political reform process in Jordan initiated an open discussion of the country's security institutions, and Jordan wrestled with the challenge of making its security organizations more transparent while maintaining their effectiveness. Security institutions have stepped up vigilance as Jordan faced the threat of spillover violence from the conflict in Syria.

Legislation, Law Enforcement, and Border Security: Jordan remained committed to securing its borders and denying safe haven to terrorists within the country for attacks against its neighbors. Jordan completed the first phase of the Jordan Border Security Program (JBSP) – a sophisticated package of sensors and barriers to help improve situational awareness and prevent illicit infiltration into Jordan or unauthorized transit out of the country. The JBSP is located along the country's northern border with Syria, an area that has historically been vulnerable to unmitigated cross-border transit.

Jordan remained an important partner nation in the Department of State's Antiterrorism Assistance program, which also supported an expansion of the capacity of the JIPTC to provide tactical skills training courses for up to 40 ATA partner nations.

Although they faced steady domestic demonstrations throughout the country, Jordanian security services remained alert and acted quickly to counter potential terrorist threats.

124

The State Security Court (SSC) is Jordan's primary judicial body for addressing national security threats. The SSC remained the topic of intense public discussion and parliamentary debate because SSC proceedings are not open to the general public and many civil society organizations consider the SSC's jurisdiction too broad and their procedures opaque. The Government of Jordan announced that it intends to amend the SSC law to ensure that the law is consonant with the constitutional amendments passed in September 2011; however, even if the parliament passes a law restricting the court's jurisdiction, the court would retain authority over issues regarding terrorism. Several significant cases were adjudicated during the course of the year, including:

- In June, the Court of Cassation endorsed a State Security Court decision sentencing Salafi jihadist theorist, Isam Muhammad al-Utaybi, also known as Abu-Muhammad al-Maqdisi, to five years in prison. The SSC charged al-Maqdisi with plotting unsanctioned acts that would subject the kingdom to hostile acts, undermining Jordan's relations with another country, and recruiting persons inside the kingdom to join armed terrorist groups and organizations.
- In November, the State Security Court heard evidence in the trial of the members of the *takfiri* terrorist group linked to the ideology of the al-Qa'ida organization, composed of 11 members under the name "Operation of the Second 9/11," a reference to the November date of attacks at Amman hotels in 2005. Jordanian security officials successfully foiled the terrorist plan that targeted commercial malls and diplomatic missions.

Regional and transnational terrorist groups, as well as local violent extremists, have demonstrated the willingness and ability to mount attacks in Jordan. In late October, Jordan's General Intelligence Department uncovered and foiled a major terrorist plot that targeted several shopping centers and cafes in Amman known to be frequented by diplomats and Westerners, as well as the U.S. Embassy. The highly sophisticated plot, orchestrated by members of al-Qa'ida in Iraq, who had recently operated in Syria, was designed to take place in several phases; first targeting commercial locations to draw the attention of security forces, and culminating in a complex attack on the U.S. Embassy involving vehicle-borne improvised explosive devices, suicide bombers, and mortars. The plot was disrupted prior to the group moving to the operational phase. Jordanian authorities arrested all 11 members (all Jordanian citizens) believed to be involved.

Countering Terrorist Finance: Jordan is a member of the Middle East and North Africa Financial Action Task Force, a Financial Action Task Force-style regional body; its Financial Intelligence Unit joined the Egmont Group in 2012. Jordan actively volunteered to host training events, and hosted a number of anti-money laundering/combating the financing of terrorism activities. For further information on money laundering and financial crimes, we refer you to the *2013 International Narcotics Control Strategy Report (INCSR), Volume 2, Money Laundering and Financial Crimes*: http://www.state.gov/j/inl/rls/nrcrpt/index.htm.

Regional and International Cooperation: Jordan is a founding member of the Global Counterterrorism Forum.

Countering Radicalization and Violent Extremism: Jordan has sought to confront and weaken the violent ideology that underpins al-Qa'ida and other radical organizations. Jordanian prisons have a religiously based de-radicalization program that seeks to re-engage violent extremist inmates into the peaceful mainstream of their faith. Based upon the individual needs of the inmate, this program can include basic literacy classes, employment counseling, and theological instruction.

The Royal Aal al-Bayt Institute for Islamic Thought, under the patronage of Prince Ghazi bin Mohammad, is Jordan's most important center promoting religious tolerance and coexistence. This institute continued its sponsorship of a series of ecumenical events promoting interfaith dialogue.

KUWAIT

Overview: Kuwait lacked legal provisions that deal specifically with terrorism and terrorist financing, although the government maintained its efforts to counter terrorism and violent extremism, notably through other legal statutes and official statements. There were no significant attacks attributed to terrorists or terrorist organizations in 2012.

The risk of terrorist attacks in Kuwait remained high. As in previous years, the Kuwaiti Armed Forces, National Guard, and Ministry of Interior conducted a number of exercises aimed at responding to terrorist attacks, including joint exercises with regional and international partners.

Legislation, Law Enforcement, and Border Security: The Government of Kuwait lacks a clear legal framework for prosecuting terrorism-related crimes, often having to resort to other legal statutes to try suspected terrorists, which hampered enforcement efforts.

The government extended the application of the biometric fingerprinting system to include all land and sea entry points. The Interior Ministry announced plans to start operation of the advanced computer tomography x-ray monitor system at Kuwait International Airport to boost airport security authorities' ability to detect contraband items, including explosives and metals, without the need for human inspection, thus reducing the chance for human error. However, the project announced by the government to install retina scanning capabilities at ports of entry had not been implemented by year's end.

After the full implementation and distribution of smart civil ID cards to Kuwaiti citizens, the Public Authority for Civil Information started issuing the new smart ID cards to expatriates. With electronic chips that save large volumes of data, including photographs and fingerprints, the new ID cards are meant to enable holders to travel freely within the Gulf Cooperation Council (GCC) countries. Holders of the cards can also use them for electronic signature.

On May 28, Kuwait's Court of Appeals commuted the death sentences of three defendants (two Iranians and a Kuwaiti), convicted of belonging to an Iranian espionage cell, to life in prison. The court also upheld the life imprisonment sentence for the fourth defendant (a stateless man) and the acquittal of two other Iranians, but overturned the life sentence imposed by a lower court against a Syrian defendant and acquitted him. The cell's seven members (four Iranians, a Kuwaiti, a Syrian, and a stateless man) were apprehended in May 2010 on charges of espionage, terrorist plotting, and vandalism. The Court of Appeal's verdicts are not final, and are expected to be challenged at the Court of Cassation (Supreme Court equivalent), whose rulings are final.

Countering Terrorist Finance: Kuwait is a member of the Middle East North Africa Financial Action Task Force, a Financial Action Task Force-style regional body. Of particular note, Kuwait lacked comprehensive legislation that criminalizes terrorist financing. In June 2012, Kuwait was publicly identified by the FATF as a jurisdiction with strategic anti-money laundering/combating the financing of terrorism deficiencies, for which it has developed an action plan with the FATF to address these weaknesses.

Kuwait had a comprehensive confiscation, freezing, and seizing framework that applies to all offenses under Kuwaiti criminal legislation. The lack of specific legislation related to terrorist finance precluded immediate freezes, although cases prosecuted under other elements of the criminal code were able to initiate freezing and confiscation of assets. Kuwait lacked an effective monitoring framework for transfers outside of the formal sector, and lacked explicit laws and regulations requiring due diligence on customer data.

The Ministry of Social Affairs and Labor and Ministry of Foreign Affairs continued monitoring and supervising charities, including enforcing the ban on cash donations, except during Ramadan; implementing an enhanced receipt system for Ramadan cash donations; and coordinating closely with the Ministry of Islamic Affairs to monitor and prosecute fraudulent charities. The monitoring of foundations was not as comprehensive as it was for charities.

Despite these obstacles, competent authorities continued efforts to combat financial crimes. The Central Bank of Kuwait engaged the International Monetary Fund in a 12-month technical assistance program aimed at addressing weaknesses in Kuwait's anti-money laundering/terrorist finance regime, and reached out to other partners as well.

For further information on money laundering and financial crimes, we refer you to the *2013 International Narcotics Control Strategy Report (INCSR), Volume 2, Money Laundering and Financial Crimes*: http://www.state.gov/j/inl/rls/nrcrpt/index.htm.

Regional and International Cooperation: On December 25, GCC heads of state signed a collective security agreement to enable member states to respond quickly to, and take appropriate preventive measures to confront potential security threats. The pact stipulates full cooperation between the six member states and delineates mutual responsibilities to preserve collective security and stability. It also promotes security coordination and information exchanges to help combat transnational and organized crime and terrorism. To be implemented, the 45-article treaty must be approved by the GCC countries' parliaments and *Shura* councils.

LEBANON

Overview: The Government of Lebanon – led by a centrist President and Prime Minister, but with a cabinet dominated by the pro-Syrian regime and the Hizballah-aligned March 8 coalition – continued to make selective progress in building its counterterrorism capacity and cooperation with U.S. counterterrorism efforts. Lebanese authorities continued efforts to disrupt suspected terrorist cells before they could act; arrested suspected al-Qa'ida (AQ)-affiliated militants and Palestinian violent extremists; and uncovered several weapons caches of varying sizes. The Lebanese Armed Forces (LAF), in particular, were credited with capturing wanted terrorist fugitives and containing sectarian violence. The Internal Security Force (ISF) continued to improve as a law enforcement organization and has become a viable counterbalance to armed militias and violent extremist groups. As the ISF improved its capabilities and aggressively pursued terrorism and corruption cases, its leadership has become a bigger target for those who seek to destabilize the country.

Lebanese authorities have not apprehended the four members of Hizballah, indicted in 2011 by the Special Tribunal for Lebanon for the murder of former Lebanese Prime Minister Rafik Hariri and 22 other individuals.

Hizballah, with deep roots among Lebanon's Shia community and significant backing from the Iranian government, remained the most dangerous and prominent terrorist group in Lebanon. Several other terrorist organizations remained active in Lebanon. Hamas, the Popular Front for the Liberation of Palestine, the Popular Front for the Liberation of Palestine General Command (PFLP-GC), Asbat al-Ansar, Fatah al-Islam, Fatah al-Intifada, Jund al-Sham, the Ziyad al-Jarrah Battalions, Palestinian Islamic Jihad, and several other splinter groups all operated within Lebanon's borders, though primarily out of Lebanon's 12 Palestinian refugee camps. The LAF did not maintain a daily presence in the camps, but it occasionally conducted operations in the camps to counter terrorist threats. In November, the UN Interim Forces in Lebanon reported that there has been no progress in efforts to dismantle military bases maintained by the PFLP-GC and Fatah al-Intifada, which are primarily located along the Lebanese-Syrian border. Several of these groups, including Hizballah, have become embroiled in the civil war in Syria. Hizballah has directly trained Syrian government personnel inside Syria, has facilitated the training of Syrian forces by Iran's Islamic Revolutionary Guard Corps-Qods Force, and played a substantial role in efforts to expel Syrian opposition forces from areas within Syria. The media also reported that unidentified numbers of Lebanese Sunnis have joined the battle in Syria on behalf of Syrian opposition groups, which includes a number of various Free Syrian Army units, and possibly disparate violent extremist groups.

Over the course of the year, reports surfaced of weapons smuggling into Syria (arming regime and anti-regime forces) from Lebanon and vice versa, and from Syria and Iran to Hizballah and other militant groups in Lebanon.

2012 Terrorist Incidents: On October 19, a car bomb in downtown Beirut killed three individuals, including Brigadier General Wissam al-Hasan, head of the Information Branch of the ISF, the organization's intelligence arm. The ISF is leading the investigation into Hasan's assassination, but so far no suspects have been officially identified. Other major incidents of terrorism included:

- On April 4, Samir Geagea, leader of the Lebanese Forces party, survived an assassination attempt.
- On July 5, Boutros Harb, a Member of Parliament and former Minister, was the target of a failed assassination attempt.
- On August 15, the Miqdad clan, a large Shia criminal network, abducted 23 Syrian and Turkish citizens in Lebanon, claiming retaliation for the abduction of one of their family members in Syria. Nearly three weeks later, the LAF conducted a successful military operation in Hizballah-controlled south Beirut to free the hostages.
- In October, media reports revealed that three members of Fatah al-Islam escaped from Roumieh prison where they had been held since 2007. Lebanese authorities launched an investigation into the incident.

- On October 3, an explosion at a Hizballah munitions cache killed three militants in the town of Nabi Sheet.
- On October 6, Hizballah launched an unmanned aerial vehicle into Israel, which was shot down by the Israel Defense Forces over southern Israel.

Legislation, Law Enforcement, and Border Security: On May 12, the Directorate of General Security (DGS) arrested Shadi al-Mawlawi, a Sunni leader in the city of Tripoli, for his alleged ties to terrorist organizations. According to press reports, Lebanese authorities also arrested and interrogated Hamza Mahmoud Tarabay and a Qatari citizen, Abdulaziz al-Atiyeh. After al-Mawlawi's arrest, sectarian clashes broke out in Tripoli and other parts of Lebanon, killing several and wounding nearly a hundred. On May 22, al-Mawlawi was later released and al-Atiyeh was extradited to his home country.

On August 9, the ISF arrested Michel Samaha, former Information Minister and Member of Parliament, for allegedly smuggling explosives in his car from Syria, as part of a conspiracy to assassinate outspoken opponents of the Asad regime and their Lebanese supporters. Though Mr. Samaha later confessed to the charges against him, his case was pending a final resolution at year's end. On December 17, the United States designated Samaha as a Specially Designated Global Terrorist under Executive Order 13224 and as a Specially Designated National under Executive Order 13441.

Lebanese authorities maintained that amnesty for Lebanese involved in acts of violence during the 1975-90 civil wars prevented terrorism prosecutions of concern to the United States.

Corruption remained a factor influencing all aspects of society, including law enforcement.

Lebanon did not have biometric systems in place at points of entry into the country. Lebanese passports were machine readable, and the government was considering the adoption of biometric passports. The DGS, under the Ministry of Interior (MOI), controls immigration and passport services and uses an electronic database to collect biographic data for travelers at all points of entry. The Lebanese government maintained bilateral agreements for information sharing with Syria.

Lebanon has a Megaports and Container Security Initiative program, and participated in Export Control and Related Border Security programs. Lebanon also continued to participate in the Department of State's Antiterrorism Assistance program, which focused on enhancing Lebanese law enforcement capacity for border security, investigations, and leadership and management. Lebanon has also received nearly US $37 million in State Department assistance to develop the capacities of the ISF.

Countering Terrorist Finance: Lebanon is a member of the Middle East and North Africa Financial Action Task Force, a Financial Action Task Force-style regional body. The Special Investigation Commission (SIC), Lebanon's financial intelligence unit, is an independent legal entity empowered to investigate suspicious financial transactions and freeze assets. The SIC is a member of the Egmont Group. Of the 136 suspicious transaction reports received by the SIC between January and October 2012, it referred 29 cases to the Office of the Prosecutor General. During the same period, the ISF received requests to investigate 16 money laundering and 26 terrorist finance cases, mostly from Interpol, and it has launched investigations into each allegation. The SIC refers requests for designation or asset freezes regarding Hizballah and affiliated groups to the Ministry of Foreign Affairs, but the Lebanese government does not require banks to freeze these assets, because it does not consider Hizballah a terrorist organization. However, Banque du Liban, Lebanon's Central Bank, issued Basic Circular 126, on April 5, 2012, requiring banks and financial institutions to abide by regulations implemented by their correspondent banks, including banks with U.S. correspondents.

Three laws intended to strengthen Lebanon's anti-money laundering/combating the financing of terrorism regime were passed by the Council of Ministers on March 14, and were awaiting Parliament's approval at year's end. These include:

- Amendments to the existing money-laundering Law 318/2001 adding offenses to the existing law, imposing financial penalties on obliged entities for reporting violations, and requiring lawyers and accountants to report suspicious transactions
- New legislation imposing requirements for declaring cross-border transportation of cash
- New legislation on the Exchange of Tax Information, which would authorize the Ministry of Finance to join bilateral and multilateral agreements to exchange information related to tax evasion and tax fraud.

In principle, the MOI is responsible for monitoring the finances and management of all registered NGOs, but it was inconsistent in applying these controls, particularly in cases involving groups such as Hizballah. By law, all NGOs are obliged to submit a yearly financial statement to the MOI. The Lebanese banking sector conducts due diligence on NGOs with bank accounts, monitors their transactions, and reports suspicious transactions to the SIC, which scrutinizes NGOs utilizing the Lebanese banking system.

Exchange houses were allegedly used to facilitate money laundering, including by Hizballah. Financial institutions are required to keep records of transactions for five years.

For further information on money laundering and financial crimes, we refer you to the *2013 International Narcotics Control Strategy Report (INCSR), Volume 2, Money Laundering and Financial Crimes*: http://www.state.gov/j/inl/rls/nrcrpt/index.htm.

Regional and International Cooperation: Lebanon continued to voice its commitment to fulfilling relevant UNSCRs, including 1559, 1680, and 1701. Lebanon is a member of the Organization of Islamic Cooperation and is party to its Convention on Combating International Terrorism.

Countering Radicalization and Violent Extremism: Lebanon worked with donor countries and international organizations to provide development assistance in Palestinian refugee camps and to provide economic and social opportunities to counter violent extremism in the camps. The LAF continued to expand its public relations campaigns to bolster its presence and status as the sole protector of Lebanon's sovereignty and independence, particularly in southern Lebanon. There were no programs to rehabilitate and/or reintegrate terrorists into mainstream society.

LIBYA

Overview: In 2012, Libya was marked by grave insecurity, most apparent in the September 11 terrorist attack that resulted in the death of Ambassador J. Christopher Stevens and three staff members. The prevalence of loose weapons, the continued ability of extra-governmental militias to act with impunity, the country's porous borders, and the lack of government capacity to apply the rule of law outside of Tripoli contributed to this insecurity.

Despite these challenges, on July 7, the Transitional National Council peacefully transferred power to a new, democratically elected parliament, the General National Congress. Prime Minister Ali Zeidan and his cabinet have prioritized efforts to strengthen and centralize national security institutions, integrate and disarm armed militias, and confront criminal and terrorist groups that have taken advantage of the security vacuum. This government has recognized that continued instability threatens Libya's democratic transition and economic future.

The United States remains committed to Libya's democratic transition and focused on Libya's insecurity and the need to support Libya's government in its efforts to address it. The State Department and USAID have provided funding to implementers who support Libya's emerging civil society, advised Libya's new political leaders, and empowered minority communities as they seek to understand and participate in the democratic transition, particularly the drafting of a constitution that denounces violence and ensures the rights of all Libyans.

2012 Terrorist Incidents: The list of incidents below highlights some of the most significant terrorist attacks of the year. Violence was particularly prevalent in the East and in Bani Walid, one of the last strongholds of Qadhafi loyalists.

- On February 6, gunmen allegedly killed five refugees in a Tripoli camp.
- On May 22, assailants launched a rocket-propelled grenade at the International Committee of the Red Cross (ICRC)'s building in Benghazi. The violent Islamist extremist group Brigades of Captive Omar Abdul Rahman claimed responsibility for the attack. The ICRC evacuated Benghazi in mid-July.
- On June 4, approximately 200 armed fighters from the al-Awfea Brigade surrounded the international airport in Tripoli. The gunmen drove armed trucks onto the tarmac and surrounded several planes, which forced the airport to cancel all flights. The armed men were demanding the release of one of their military leaders who was being held by Tripoli's security forces.
- On June 6, violent extremists attacked the U.S. facilities in Benghazi with an improvised explosive device (IED). The group claimed that the attack was in retaliation for the assassination of Abu-Yahya al-Libi, the second highest ranking leader of al-Qa'ida.
- On June 11, a convoy carrying the British Ambassador to Libya was attacked in Benghazi.
- On June 12, assailants attacked the ICRC office in Misrata, wounding one.
- In August, there was a series of attacks against security personnel and facilities, including the bombing of the Benghazi military intelligence offices on August 1, a car bombing near the Tripoli military police offices on August 4, and the explosion of three car bombs near the Interior Ministry and other security buildings in Tripoli on August 19, killing at least two. Libyan security officials arrested 32 members of an organized network loyal to Qadhafi.
- On August 10, Army General Hadiya al-Feitouri was assassinated in Benghazi.

- On August 20, a car belonging to an Egyptian diplomat was blown up near his home in Benghazi.
- On September 11, terrorists attacked the U.S. facilities in Benghazi, which resulted in the death of Ambassador J. Christopher Stevens and three staff members.
- On October 13, the Benghazi police chief survived an assassination attempt.
- On November 21, Benghazi security chief Faraj al-Drissi was assassinated.
- On December 16 and 20, eight people were killed when violent extremists attacked Benghazi police stations.
- On December 31, attackers threw an IED at a Coptic church in the city of Dafniya. The explosion resulted in the death of two Egyptian men and wounded two others.
- On December 31, an IED exploded outside the headquarters of the public prosecutor in Benghazi. No one was killed or injured, but the explosion caused damage to the building.

Legislation, Law Enforcement, and Border Security: Following the September 11 attacks on U.S. facilities in Benghazi, senior Libyan authorities assured their U.S. counterparts that security was their top priority. In light of this and many other security incidents throughout the year, Prime Minister Ali Zeidan and his cabinet (seated on November 14) focused on bolstering the security sector in Libya and extending the reach of governmental security institutions beyond Tripoli. Significant challenges remained, however, and although the new Libyan authorities intended to make immediate improvements to the security situation, particularly in the east, they were unable to do so as security and justice sector institutions had been severely weakened following 42 years of mismanagement under Qadhafi, and eight months of violent conflict.

While the Transitional National Council did not feel it had the mandate to make lasting legislation, the General National Congress and Prime Minister Zeidan have been more aggressively confronting the security situation in Libya. Yet any legislation seeking to limit the power of heavily-armed, extra-governmental militias has been difficult to enforce, and Libyan judges did not hear criminal cases for fear it could lead to revenge attacks against them. Police and military personnel and facilities were the frequent targets of attacks by pro-Qadhafi and violent Islamist extremist groups, who fiercely resisted any efforts by the government to exert its authority. Many members of the militias that continue to undermine the authority of the army and police refused to join these institutions because they claimed Qadhafi-era officials continued to occupy their ranks.

The proliferation of weapons from Libya across the country's borders was of concern. The EU developed plans to provide significant border security assistance to the Libyan authorities, and throughout 2012, the United States worked with the Government of Libya to develop a complementary border security assistance package of its own. A delegation of Libyan officials from the Ministry of Defense and Customs Authority visited the United States in mid-September, during which they expressed interest in U.S. border security best practices, and American border security technology. Nevertheless, implementation of these programs has been slow, and the Libyan authorities lacked the basic training and equipment necessary to monitor their vast land and maritime borders, and to control the flow of people and goods through their airports. Violent extremists continued to exploit these weaknesses, which threatened to destabilize the Middle East and North Africa region.

The United States will cooperate with the EU and other international donors to provide further, complementary assistance in this vein, and the Libyan authorities have indicated that they will intensify cooperation with their neighbors, especially Algeria and Tunisia, to exert better control over their shared borders.

The United States has also provided assistance to help Libya professionalize its security sector institutions, as well as stem the proliferation of conventional weapons, and secure and destroy its chemical weapons stockpiles.

Countering Terrorist Finance: Libya is a member of the Middle East and North Africa Financial Action Task Force, a Financial Action Task Force-style regional body. However, Libya has yet to undergo a mutual evaluation. (Libya's mutual evaluation assessment was scheduled for March 2011, but was cancelled due to security concerns.) After the fall of the Qadhafi regime, there was little information or reliable data on the scope of Libya's anti-money laundering/counterterrorist regime. For further information on money laundering and financial crimes, we refer you to the *2013 International Narcotics Control Strategy Report (INCSR), Volume 2, Money Laundering and Financial Crimes*: http://www.state.gov/j/inl/rls/nrcrpt/index.htm.

Regional and International Cooperation: The United States has prioritized assistance to Libya's security and justice sectors since the end of the 2011 revolution. Libyan President Mohamed al Magariaf participated in the 67th UNGA in the wake of the September attacks on the U.S. facilities in Benghazi, and vowed to work with the international community, especially the United States, to address weaknesses in its security and justice sectors. On December 17, Libya's international partners met in London, during which the Libyan delegation articulated its security sector assistance priorities, and the international community agreed to coordinate assistance through the UN Support Mission in Libya.

Countering Radicalization and Violent Extremism: In 2012, member states of the AU, of which Libya is a member, signed a joint venture to create the African Center for Studies and Research on Terrorism (ACSRT). ACSRT's broad goals include assisting AU member states to develop strategies for preventing and countering terrorism.

MOROCCO

Overview: Morocco's counterterrorism efforts are comprehensive. In 2012, the Moroccan government continued its broad counterterrorism strategy of vigilant security measures, regional and international cooperation, and counter-radicalization policies. The terrorist threat in Morocco continued to stem largely from the existence of numerous small, independent violent extremist cells. Those groups and individuals, referred to collectively as adherents of so-called *Salafiyya Jihadiyya* ideology, remained isolated from one another, small in size, and limited in both capabilities and international connections. Morocco and the United States continued robust counterterrorism collaboration, and both countries committed to deepening this relationship during the September bilateral Strategic Dialogue in Washington, DC.

Toward the end of the year, authorities disrupted multiple groups with ties to international networks that included al-Qa'ida in the Islamic Maghreb (AQIM). AQIM expanded its efforts to recruit Moroccans for combat in other countries and called for attacks on U.S. ambassadors in Morocco and in the region. There were reports of Moroccans attempting to join or receive training from AQIM and other violent extremists in Mali, and the government was concerned about the return of these individuals to Morocco. The government was also concerned about veteran violent Moroccan extremists returning from Iraq, Afghanistan, and Libya to conduct terrorist attacks at home, and about Moroccans radicalized during their stays in Western Europe.

Legislation, Law Enforcement, and Border Security: The Government of Morocco made public commitments that the struggle against terrorism would not be used to deprive individuals of their rights and emphasized adherence to human-rights standards and the increased transparency of law enforcement procedures as part of its approach. Morocco convicted dozens of individuals, including the highlighted cases below:

- In February, the Salé Court of Appeals sentenced 27 men to prison terms of one to six years for planning terrorist attacks. The group, arrested in January 2011, had stockpiled weapons in Western Sahara and was planning suicide and car-bomb attacks against Moroccan and foreign security forces, according to the Ministry of Interior.
- In March, an appeals court upheld the death sentence for Adil el-Atmani, the primary perpetrator of the 2011 Marrakech bombing.
- In April, five men received sentences of one to five years under the terrorism law. The cell, dismantled in October 2011, had reportedly communicated with elements of al-Qa'ida through the internet, had links to el-Atmani, and planned to carry out attacks against tourist sites and western targets.

Morocco aggressively targeted and dismantled terrorist cells within the country by leveraging intelligence collection, police work, and collaboration with regional and international partners. Morocco's counterterrorism efforts led to the following disruptions of alleged terrorist cells:

- In May, authorities arrested 15 members of the Mujahedin Movement in Morocco, a terrorist cell with connections to the May 2003 Casablanca bombers and AQIM, according to the Ministry of Interior. The group reportedly had automatic weapons and ammunition hidden in several cities in Morocco.
- In October, the arrest of two men espousing violent extremist ideology in Salé led to the disruption of a nine member cell, according to the Ministry of Interior. The group reportedly was building a training camp in the Rif Mountains with the goal of attacking government targets in Morocco.
- In November, authorities arrested eight members of Ansar al-Sharia in the Islamic Maghreb for allegedly planning to attack public buildings, the security services, and tourist sites, according to the Minister of Interior. The group, which had created a *Facebook* page in September, stated that its primary goals were to "restore Sharia to its true place in society, warn against secularism, and work for the restoration of the caliphate." Hassan el-Younsi, who started the page, was reportedly arrested in October.
- In November, security services dismantled a 27-member cell including a Malian national, which allegedly recruited Moroccan youths for combat in Mali and the Sahel region. The cell consisted of individuals from Nador, Casablanca, Guersif, Laayoune, Kalaat Essraghna, Beni Mellal, and Berkane. The group reportedly sent at least 20 individuals to join the Movement for Unity and Jihad in West Africa and AQIM. Members were formally charged in December with forming a criminal gang, preparing to carry out acts of terrorism, jeopardizing public order, failure to report acts of terrorism, financing terrorism, persuading others to commit a terrorist crime, membership of a banned religious group, and holding meetings without permission.

- In December, authorities dismantled a six-member cell in Fez, which was reportedly recruiting individuals to join AQIM. The cell allegedly also planned to send some members to AQIM training camps, who would then return to carry out attacks in Morocco.
- In December, authorities arrested six individuals in Marrakech for allegedly planning to carry out terrorist attacks within the country.

Morocco continued to participate in the Department of State's Antiterrorism Assistance program, which helped enhance Moroccan counterterrorism capabilities by providing training in cyber forensics, crime scene forensics, and executive leadership to both the national police and gendarmes.

Countering Terrorist Finance: Morocco is a member of the Middle East and North Africa Financial Action Task Force, a Financial Action Task Force (FATF)-style regional body, and its Financial Intelligence Unit is a member of the Egmont Group. Since February 2010, Morocco has been publicly identified by the FATF as a jurisdiction with strategic anti-money laundering/combating the financing of terrorism deficiencies. To address those deficiencies, it developed an action plan with the FATF. Morocco continued to implement provisions created in 2011, including the extension of judicial authority to prosecute money laundering crimes committed within the country and abroad, and the expansion of the list of people and organizations obliged to report on suspicious financial activities. Following the adoption of the 2011 legislation, the FATF determined that Morocco has not criminalized terrorist financing in line with the international standard, and has called upon Morocco to do so as soon as possible. For further information on money laundering and financial crimes, we refer you to the *2013 International Narcotics Control Strategy Report (INCSR), Volume 2, Money Laundering and Financial Crimes*: http://www.state.gov/j/inl/rls/nrcrpt/index.htm.

Regional and International Cooperation: Morocco maintained cooperative relationships with European and African partners by sharing information, conducting joint operations, and participating in military, security, and civilian capacity-building events. Morocco is a founding member of the Global Counterterrorism Forum (GCTF) and hosted the GCTF Rule of Law Working Group meeting in February, which produced the Rabat Memorandum on Good Practices for Effective Counterterrorism Practice in the Criminal Justice Sector. Morocco also hosted a GCTF Workshop on Transnational Security Challenges in the South Atlantic in October. Morocco is a member of the Global Initiative to Counter Nuclear Terrorism (GICNT) and hosted a GICNT Implementation and Assessment Group meeting in February.

Morocco is a Mediterranean Dialogue partner of the EU's Barcelona Process and a major non-NATO ally. Morocco participates in multilateral peacekeeping operations on the continent as well as in training exercises such as maritime-focused Phoenix Express, the Flintlock regional security cooperation exercise, and special operations exercises. These engagements, coupled with Morocco's initiative to modernize its force through Foreign Military Sales, have significantly enhanced border security and improved capabilities to counter illicit traffic and terrorism. Morocco currently holds the rotating presidency of the 5+5 Defense Initiative, which brings together five European and five North African countries to address security issues in the Western Mediterranean. Morocco has also been active in the efforts of the Economic Community of West African States to address the conflict in Northern Mali. These are important steps, yet the lack of consistent cooperation among countries in the region remains a potential weakness that terrorist groups such as AQIM may exploit. Specifically, while Morocco and Algeria are members of the Trans-Sahara Counterterrorism Partnership and the GCTF, the level of bilateral counterterrorism cooperation did not improve. Algeria and Morocco's political disagreement over the Western Sahara remains an impediment to more profound counterterrorism cooperation.

Countering Radicalization and Violent Extremism: Morocco has a three-pillar strategy for countering violent extremism (CVE). First, the government takes a law-and-order approach to CVE, working closely with the United States and other international and regional partners to strengthen its security and counterterrorism capabilities. Second, Morocco has accelerated its rollout of education and employment initiatives for youth and expanded the legal rights and political empowerment of women. Finally, to counter what the government perceives as the dangerous importation of violent Islamist extremist ideologies, it has developed a national strategy to confirm and further institutionalize Morocco's widespread adherence to the Maliki school of Islam. The United States works closely with the government and key Moroccan civil-society organizations to support and complement related, existing programs. The Department of State's Bureau of International Narcotics and Law Enforcement funds a program to improve the overall management of Morocco's corrections system that seeks, among other objectives, to alleviate potential radicalism and recruitment of prisoners to terrorist ideology. In Morocco, disaffected and marginalized youth in urban and peri-urban environments have been identified as vulnerable to radicalization by and recruitment into violent extremist groups.

Every year during the month of Ramadan, the King hosts a series of religious lectures, inviting Muslim speakers from around the world to promote peaceful interpretations of Islam. In the past decade, and particularly since the Casablanca (2003) and Madrid (2004) terrorist bombings, Morocco has focused on countering youth radicalization; upgrading places of worship; modernizing the teaching of Islam; and strengthening the Ministry of Endowments and Islamic Affairs (MEIA). The MEIA has developed an educational curriculum for Morocco's nearly 50,000 imams to to counter violent extremism and advance tolerance, which is inherent in the Maliki school of Sunni Islam, the dominant form of Islam in the country. To counter the radicalization of Moroccans living abroad, the Moroccan Council of Ulema for Europe and the Minister Delegate for Moroccans Living Abroad also undertook similar programs to promote religious moderation among Moroccan expatriate communities in Europe.

OMAN

Overview: Oman is an important regional counterterrorism partner and was actively involved in working to prevent terrorists from conducting attacks within Oman, and using the country for safe haven or transport of weapons and materiel support. In 2012, several suspected terrorists, identified by the Government of Oman as members of al-Qa'ida in the Arabian Peninsula, illegally entered southern Oman from Yemen. The Government of Oman reported this event in its national press, stressing that security of the country was its foremost concern. The Omani government actively sought training and equipment from the United States and commercial entities, as well as those from other countries to support its efforts to control its land and maritime borders. Oman used U.S. security assistance to enhance nighttime operational capabilities on its maritime and land borders.

Legislation, Law Enforcement, and Border Security: In 2012, the Royal Oman Police (ROP) procured night vision equipment for the ROP-Coast Guard for use in patrolling its coastline and territorial waters. In addition, the Department of State's Export Control and Related Border Security (EXBS) training included a legal and regulatory advisor from the Monterey Institute, who consulted with the Omani government and private sector on the best route for Oman to take to adopt comprehensive strategic trade controls in accordance with international standards. EXBS also trained Omani Customs and Airport Security Officials on identifying contraband hidden in air cargo and identifying smugglers of contraband. The EXBS program trained members of the Royal Army of Oman on the tracking and apprehension of persons illegally crossing Omani borders, and the inspection of suspect vehicles. Oman also continued its participation in the Department of State's Antiterrorism Assistance program which provided training on vital infrastructure security, examination of terrorist crime scenes, terrorist investigations, and the interdiction of terrorist activities.

Countering Terrorist Finance: Oman is a member of the Middle East and North Africa Financial Action Task Force, a Financial Action Task Force-style regional body. In July 2010, Royal Decree number 79/2010 enacted new comprehensive legislation on Anti-Money Laundering/Combating the Financing of Terrorism (AML/CFT). The AML/CFT legislation consolidated Oman's previous AML/CFT laws, created a national committee for AML/CFT, and codified Oman's "safe harbor" and mutual legal assistance regulations. The law designated the Royal Oman Police Financial Intelligence Unit (FIU) as the responsible entity for enforcing AML/CFT laws and regulations. Oman has since put forward considerable funding and effort towards increasing the capabilities of its FIU, a member of the Egmont Group. The FIU recognizes its lack of capacity in forensic analysis, and increasingly sought U.S. assistance to increase the FIU's capacity to investigate and prosecute financial crimes, including terrorist finance.

The Government of Oman, led by the efforts of the Central Bank of Oman, has continued to exercise caution and a high degree of oversight in its commercial banking sector. In December 2012, Oman formally introduced Islamic banking services into the financial system through Royal Decree 69/2012, which added a provision to allow Islamic Banking services to be offered under existing banking law. *Hawalas* are not permitted in the financial service sector, and Omani authorities have acted on two occasions to shutter attempted *hawala* operations. For further information on money laundering and financial crimes, we refer you to the *2013 International Narcotics Control Strategy Report (INCSR), Volume 2, Money Laundering and Financial Crimes*: http://www.state.gov/j/inl/rls/nrcrpt/index.htm.

QATAR

Overview: In 2012, Qatar did not experience any terrorist attacks or any political changes that would affect the Government of Qatar's ability to combat terrorism. During the year, the Middle East and North Africa Financial Action Task Force (MENAFATF), a Financial Action Task Force-style regional body, removed Qatar from its regular follow-up process after the Task Force determined that Qatar had improved its anti-money laundering/combating the financing of terrorism regime and was either "Compliant or Largely Compliant" with all of the Task Force's recommendations. Still, Qatar's monitoring of private individuals' and charitable associations' contributions to foreign entities remained inconsistent. The Government of Qatar also maintained public ties to Hamas political leaders.

Legislation, Law Enforcement, and Border Security: Qatar did not pass any new terrorism legislation or make significant changes to border security procedures. There were no significant arrests or prosecutions in terrorist cases, or incidents requiring response, including terrorism affecting U.S. citizens or facilities in 2012.

Countering Terrorist Finance: Qatar is a member of the MENAFATF. In 2012, in addition to regular outreach to financial institutions, Qatar's Financial Intelligence Unit, a member of the Egmont Group, launched a multi-year strategy to promote greater transparency in financial transactions including issuing guidelines obligating reporting on suspicious transactions. Qatar's Combating Money Laundering and Terrorist Financing Law of 2010 requires Qatar's Public Prosecutor to freeze the funds of terrorist organizations designated by the UNSC, and the government has begun to distribute lists of UN-designated terrorist entities and individuals to financial institutions. Implementation, however, remained inconsistent. For further information on money laundering and financial crimes, we refer you to the *2013 International Narcotics Control Strategy Report (INCSR), Volume 2, Money Laundering and Financial Crimes*: http://www.state.gov/j/inl/rls/nrcrpt/index.htm.

Regional and International Cooperation: Qatar is a member of the Global Counterterrorism Forum, the Arab League, and the Gulf Cooperation Council. The Qatari government did not participate in any notable counterterrorism activities with those organizations in 2012, however.

Countering Radicalization and Violent Extremism: The Doha International Center for Interfaith Dialogue (a semi-public institute established by executive decree in 2007) organized a lecture series in 2012, with the Faculty of Islamic Studies at the Qatar Foundation, to help Qatari teachers "equip students with the skills and understanding to interact and communicate effectively and respectfully with other cultures." The Government of Qatar also contracted a Doha-based private institute to study best practices in countering narratives used by terrorist groups to recruit members. The first of three research papers, published in February 2012, focused on EU engagement programs to reduce violent conflict.

SAUDI ARABIA

Overview: During 2012, the Government of Saudi Arabia continued its long-term counterterrorism strategy to track and halt the activities of terrorists and terrorist financiers, dismantle the physical presence of al-Qa'ida, and impede the ability of militants to operate from or within the Kingdom. As part of this strategy, Saudi authorities also continued public trials of individuals suspected of engaging in or supporting terrorism. In August, Saudi authorities announced they had discovered and partially rounded up two separate terrorist cells (one in Riyadh and the other in Jeddah) affiliated with al-Qa'ida in the Arabian Peninsula (AQAP). AQAP continued to be the Kingdom's primary terrorist threat, and efforts to counter this threat were hampered by the ongoing instability in Yemen. Throughout the year, AQAP noticeably stepped up its efforts to inspire sympathizers throughout Saudi Arabia in an effort to compensate for difficulties in carrying out cross-border attacks. Saudi Arabia continued to maintain a robust counterterrorism relationship with the United States and supported enhanced bilateral cooperation to ensure the safety of U.S. citizens within Saudi territories and beyond.

2012 Terrorist Incidents: Beyond the two disrupted terrorist cells in August, there were at least two incidents involving suspected terrorists along the Saudi-Yemeni border. On October 14,

Saudi security forces in Jizan province killed two Yemeni nationals who attempted to pass a checkpoint with explosives and four suicide vests for use in "imminent attacks against vital targets," according to an official statement. On November 5, 11 former prisoners, who recently had been released after having served their sentences for terrorism-related offenses, attacked and killed two Saudi border guards who attempted to stop the former prisoners from crossing into Yemen near Sharurah in Najran province. The group, composed of 10 Saudis and one Yemeni, was subsequently arrested.

Legislation, Law Enforcement, and Border Security: Saudi Arabia continued its efforts to track, arrest, and prosecute terrorists within the Kingdom. The Ministry of Interior continued to improve border security measures, including the ongoing installation of biometric scanners at entry points throughout the Kingdom; aerial reconnaissance drones to patrol remote areas; thermal imaging systems; and motion detectors and electronic-sensor fencing along the borders with Iraq, Yemen, and Jordan.

Neighborhood police units engaged and worked directly with community members, encouraging citizens to provide tips and information about potential terrorist activity. The Saudi government offered rewards for information on suspected terrorists, and there were multiple announcements throughout the year of arrests of AQAP militants and supporters.

As part of the Saudi government's move to bring to trial groups and individuals suspected of terrorism, judicial actions included:

- On April 4, the Specialized Criminal Court began the public trial of a group dubbed the "Cell of 55" (composed of 54 Saudis and one Yemeni), which was allegedly responsible for the 2004 attack on the U.S. Consulate in Jeddah. The trial was ongoing at year's end.
- The trial of 11 Saudis linked to the May 2004 attack on a refinery in Yanbu, in which two American citizens were killed, continued during the year.
- On June 26, the Specialized Criminal Court sentenced one member of the 11-person "Khafji cell" to 15 years in prison followed by a 15-year travel ban; the man was found guilty of supporting terrorism through money laundering and other crimes, such as possessing unlicensed fire arms.

Countering Terrorist Finance: Saudi Arabia is a member of the Middle East and North Africa Financial Action Task Force, a Financial Action Task Force (FATF)-style regional body. Bulk cash smuggling from individual donors and charities has reportedly provided financing to violent extremist and terrorist groups over the past 25 years. With the advent of tighter bank regulations, funds are reportedly collected and illicitly transferred in cash, often via pilgrims performing Hajj or Umrah. The Saudi government has attempted to consolidate charitable campaigns under Ministry of Interior supervision. The Saudi Arabian Financial Intelligence Unit, or SAFIU, is a member of the Egmont Group. The Saudi government continued to provide special training programs for bankers, prosecutors, judges, customs officers, and other officials from government departments and agencies as part of its efforts to maintain financial controls designed to counter terrorist financing. Despite serious and effective efforts to counter the funding of terrorism originating from within its borders, entities in Saudi Arabia continue to serve as an important source of cash flowing to violent Sunni extremist groups. Saudi officials acknowledged difficulty in following the money trail with regard to illicit finance due to the preference for cash transactions in the country. For further information on money laundering and financial crimes, we refer you to the *2013 International Narcotics Control Strategy Report (INCSR), Volume 2, Money Laundering and Financial Crimes*: http://www.state.gov/j/inl/rls/nrcrpt/index.htm.

Regional and International Cooperation: Saudi Arabia cooperated regionally and internationally on counterterrorism issues. It is a founding member of the Global Counterterrorism Forum, and has been a member of the Global Initiative to Combat Nuclear Terrorism and the Proliferation Security Initiative since 2008. Saudi Arabia is also a member of the Gulf Cooperation Council (GCC), which itself is a member of the FATF. Saudi government officials issued statements encouraging enhanced cooperation among GCC and Arab League states on counterterrorism issues, and the Saudi government hosted international counterterrorism conferences on subjects ranging from combating violent extremist ideology to countering terrorist financing.

Throughout the year, Saudi security professionals regularly participated in joint programs around the world, including in Europe and the United States. In addition to Saudi Arabia's bilateral cooperation with the United States, Saudi security officials also worked with other international counterparts to conduct missions and exchange information. Throughout the year, Saudi Arabia concluded security-related bilateral agreements (including counterterrorism and anti-money laundering cooperation) with a number of countries, including Albania, Belarus, Bermuda, Comoros, Indonesia, Malta, the Netherlands, Poland, San Marino, and Singapore. In November, Saudi Arabia, along with the other five GCC member states, concluded a GCC-wide security agreement including counterterrorism cooperation. In April, the Kingdom ratified the Arab Agreement on Anti-Money Laundering and Counterterrorism Financing. In June, Saudi Arabia extradited Indian national Abu Jundal (also known as Zabiuddin Sayed Zakiuddin Ansari) to India to stand trial for his alleged involvement in the 2008 terrorist attacks in Mumbai.

Countering Radicalization and Violent Extremism: The Saudi government focused on: increasing public awareness campaigns; and conducting outreach, counter-radicalization, and rehabilitation programs. Some of these efforts involved seminars that refuted violent Islamist extremist interpretation and ideology. Public awareness campaigns aimed to raise awareness among Saudi citizens about the dangers of violent extremism and terrorism. Methods used included advertisements and programs on television, in schools and mosques, and at sporting events. The government also issued statements condemning terrorists and denouncing terrorist attacks across the world, including the September attack against the U.S. consulate in Benghazi, Libya.

The Ministry of Interior continued to operate its flagship de-radicalization program (the Sakina Campaign for Dialogue), as well as its extensive prison rehabilitation program to reduce recidivism among former inmates. The Ministry of Islamic Affairs continued to re-educate imams, prohibiting them from incitement to violence, and monitored mosques and religious education. The Saudi government also continued its ongoing program to modernize the educational curriculum, including textbooks used in religious training. We refer you to the Department of State's *Annual Report to Congress on International Religious Freedom* (http://www.state.gov/j/drl/rls/irf/) for further information.

TUNISIA

Overview: Tunisian security forces continued to deal with new threats from inside and outside the country, attacks on facilities, a dearth of resources, an inefficient and often ambiguous command and control structure, and a poor public image. Amid these challenges, Tunisia faced numerous security threats and clearly identifiable terrorist activities, while also taking action against individuals and cells. The most significant attacks were the September 14 events at the U.S. Embassy and the American Cooperative School of Tunis, which highlighted to the Government of Tunisia and Tunisian citizens the extent of the internal threats to security and stability. Tunisia also saw an increase in religiously motivated acts of vandalism and harassment, generally carried out by violent Salafist extremists.

With the ouster of Ben Ali's regime, Tunisia experienced a rise in political Islam and the emergence of hard-line Salafists, who reject Western values, seek the reestablishment of an Islamist Caliphate, and contend the Islamist Nahda Party is too accommodating to the West. Salafists repeatedly disrupted social order in 2012. As incidents of religious intolerance increased in Tunisia, the government at times vacillated in responding to excesses by Tunisia's Salafist movement. Both President Marzouki and Prime Minister Jebali denounced certain incidents and appealed for religious tolerance. The most notable examples included:

- On January 5, after a crowd shouted anti-Semitic slogans during the airport arrival of Hamas leader Ismail Haniyeh, the Nahda party publicly condemned the anti-Jewish statements.
- On April 5, the Tunisian Court of the First Instance formally accepted a complaint filed by Jewish Community President Roger Bismuth against a preacher who called for Tunisian youth to wage war against Jews. In response to the complaint, the government launched an investigation of the incident.
- On April 11, President Marzouki visited the El Ghriba synagogue in Djerba to commemorate the 10-year anniversary of the al-Qa'ida (AQ) attack there that killed 21 people. In the ceremony, Marzouki reiterated that Tunisian Jews were equal citizens under the law and the government was committed to the security of the 2,600 year-old community. Marzouki called the terrorist attack "cowardly," and expressed sympathy for the families of the victims who died.
- On April 14, President Marzouki visited the Russian Orthodox Church in Tunis, responding to the church's call for protection and displaying the Government of Tunisia's support for religious freedom. The visit followed the arrest of the individual who covered the church's crosses on March 30, and culminated in a series of actions taken to halt incidents of vandalism and intimidation against the church.

2012 Terrorist Incidents: The list of incidents below highlights some of the most significant terrorism-related events that took place during the year. There was a marked increase in the number of incidents fueled by violent extremism.

- On February 1, Tunisian security forces exchanged gunfire with suspected weapons smugglers near the town of Bir Ali Ben Khalifa in the governorate of Sfax. In the exchange, Tunisian forces killed two gunmen and arrested a third after the gunmen wounded a National Guard officer and three soldiers.
- On February 23, 200 Salafists confronted police in Jendouba with sticks, swords, and Molotov cocktails, setting fire to a police station.

- On May 19, bars were vandalized and an alcohol storehouse set on fire in Sidi Bouzid. The Justice Minister responded that the period of tolerance for violent extremist activities was over and that "all red lines have been crossed," but no clear enforcement actions followed.

- On May 26, between 200 and 500 Salafists clashed with police in Jendouba, who used tear gas and shotguns to break up the disturbance. Prime Minister Jebali warned that the law would be upheld, but was vague about what actions his government would take.

- From June 10-12, Salafists stormed an art exhibit in the Tunis suburb of La Marsa, sparking a wave of violence around the capital. The Tunisian government temporarily imposed a curfew and increased security. Interior Minister Laarayedh accused the instigators of having connections with AQ.

- From June 12-13, violent extremists torched three regional offices of the General Union of Tunisian Labor in Tunis, Jendouba, and Ben Guerdane.

- On June 21, Tunisian military aircraft, after taking fire, engaged suspected weapons smugglers near the Libyan border, destroying three vehicles.

- On September 14, a mob of 2,000-3,000, including individuals affiliated with the militant organization Ansar al-Sharia, attacked and attempted to destroy the U.S. Embassy and the American Cooperative School of Tunis, looting the school and causing extensive damage to both facilities. The authorities arrested more than 120 individuals suspected of being part of the attacks.

- On November 1, Tunisian police foiled a hostage-for-ransom plot involving four Tunisians, one of them a police officer, who allegedly planned to kidnap young Jewish people living in Zarzis.

- On December 10, four gunmen attacked a National Guard unit near Feriana, in Kasserine governorate, killing one Guardsman. Officials suspected an armed group of 40 men to be hiding in the Mt. Chaambi region.

Legislation, Law Enforcement, and Border Security: Human rights groups maintained that the Ben Ali regime used Tunisia's counterterrorism law to repress dissent and imprison political opponents and religious leaders on trumped-up charges. Because of this focus on political opposition, the Ministry of Interior's capabilities were depleted after the revolution, and the two subsequent transition governments were at times hesitant to arrest and prosecute suspected terrorists. The Government of Tunisia has recognized that some of these capabilities must be resurrected to address other security priorities, including civil unrest.

The Government of Tunisia arrested more than 120 individuals for their alleged involvement in the September 14 attacks on the U.S. Embassy and American Cooperative School of Tunis, but has shared little information with U.S. officials. There have been no trials or convictions, and some suspects have been released on bail or subject to small fines. Other arrests and prosecutions included:

- On February 13, in a follow-up operation to the February 1 attacks, Tunisian authorities announced the arrests of 12 suspects belonging to a terrorist cell with links to AQ. The group possessed 32 Kalashnikov automatic rifles, 2,500 bullets, and over US $60,000, which were confiscated by authorities. Tunisian Minister of the Interior Ali Laarayedh stated that interrogations of the suspects showed they "were stockpiling arms to be used when the time was ripe to impose an Islamic Emirate on Tunisia." Most of the suspects had a record of terrorist involvement and had been released from Tunisian prisons during the presidential amnesty granted after the 2011 revolution. Eight additional members of the group reportedly remained at large and in Libya.

- On April 30, the Tunisian army apprehended six Salafists near Sejnane and seized Kalashnikov rifles, ammunition, and unspecified documents.
- In mid-May, Tunisian authorities detained and ultimately deported two radical Moroccan theologians, Hassan Kattani and Omar El Hadouchi, who were implicated in the May 16, 2003 Casablanca bombings.
- On August 4, Tunisian security forces arrested a group in possession of firearms and grenades near Sfax.
- On October 24, the government sentenced Slim ben Belgacem ben Mohamed Gantri (alias Abou Ayoub) to one year in jail for his role in the June 10-12 clashes in La Marsa under Articles 50 and 51 of Decree No. 115, which stipulate punishment for any act or speech that leads to violence or hatred, or threatens stability and peace.
- On December 6, authorities arrested two Salafists in Fernana, near the Algerian border, and charged them with possession of illegal firearms, stun guns, other explosives, maps, military uniforms, and narcotics.
- On December 11, border police arrested three Salafists caught with automatic weapons, explosives, and illegal drugs near Jendouba, in western Tunisia.
- On December 12, Tunisian authorities arrested 11 violent extremists believed to be involved in a December 10 gun battle that took the life of a National Guardsman and wounded four others. Neither the number of people arrested nor their possible link to the December 10 event were confirmed by the MOI.
- On December 15, Tunisian officials announced they had uncovered and dismantled a terrorist cell in western Tunisia that had been recruiting violent extremists to serve in strongholds controlled by al-Qa'ida in the Islamic Maghreb (AQIM). Several AQIM members were killed. They also announced that another seven had been arrested and indicted before the Tunis Court of First Instance on December 13.
- On December 21, Interior Minister Laarayedh announced that security forces had dismantled a terrorist cell called the "Militia of Uqba Ibn Nafaa in Tunisia," affiliated with AQIM. The authorities captured 16 members and pursued another 18. Firearms, military fatigues, and plans were confiscated.

The fall of the Ben Ali regime resulted in the release or repatriation of individuals implicated in violent extremism. Of particular concern, two convicted terrorists, Seif Allah Ben Hassine (alias Abou Iyedh) and Tarek Maaroufi, returned to Tunisia in 2012. The two men are co-founders of the Tunisian Combatant Group. Ben Hassine was among those granted presidential amnesty after the collapse of the Ben Ali regime and is the political leader of the violent Salafist movement, Ansar al-Sharia. He was implicated as the mastermind behind the September 14 attack on the U.S. Embassy and at year's end, remained at large. On March 24, Maaroufi returned to Tunisia after serving nine years in a Belgian prison on terrorism charges; his Belgian citizenship has since been revoked. Maaroufi is a well known terrorist who took part in the planning and execution of the assassination of Afghan Northern Alliance Leader Ahmad Shah Mehsud on September 9, 2001. In addition, cleric Slim ben Belgacem ben Mohamed Gantri (alias Abou Ayoub) emerged as an influential leader in the Tunisian Salafist movement.

Border security remained a priority as Tunisian authorities sought to collaborate with their Libyan and Algerian counterparts in stemming the flow of weapons being smuggled across their common borders. Several members of the Tunisian security services were killed in the line of duty combating suspected terrorists and militants from AQIM and other AQ-affiliated groups. A state of emergency first imposed following the January 2011 revolution remained in effect throughout 2012.

In 2012, Ministry of Justice, Ministry of Interior, and Ministry of Finance (from the Customs Service) officials participated in U.S.-organized regional workshops on how to combat bioterrorism, kidnapping for ransom, and border infiltrations. The latter workshop was conducted by the Global Counterterrorism Sahel Capacity-Building Working Group. Tunisia continues to cooperate with the International Atomic Energy Agency and the Department of Energy's National Nuclear Security Administration and Sandia Laboratories in the safe use of radioactive materials.

Tunisia continued to participate in the Department of State's Antiterrorism Assistance (ATA) program with Tunisian security professionals receiving ATA training in 2012 in the areas of border security, investigations, and critical incident management. In September, Tunisia signed a Letter of Agreement with the United States, to initiate a multi-year multimillion dollar bilateral assistance program on security sector reform. On December 24, Tunisia and Algeria signed a security pact to coordinate action in the fight against terrorism, human trafficking, and illegal immigration; the pact called for the creation of joint border patrols.

Countering Terrorist Finance: Tunisia is a member of the Middle East and North Africa Financial Action Task Force, a Financial Action Task Force-style regional body. Since Tunisia has strict currency controls, it is likely that remittance systems such as *hawala* are prevalent. Trade-based money laundering is also a concern. Throughout the region, invoice manipulation and customs fraud were often involved in *hawala* counter-valuation. Tunisia's Financial Intelligence Unit, the Tunisian Financial Analysis Commission (CTAF), is headed by the governor of the Central Bank and includes representation from the Ministry of Finance, Customs General Directorate, National Post Office, Council of Financial Markets, Insurance General Committee, Ministry of Interior, and "an expert specialized in the fight against financial infringements." However, these interagency representatives are not analysts, and CTAF lacks analytical capacity due to both insufficient analytical staff and not enough training for the staff already in place. The Tunisian penal code provides for the seizure of assets and property tied to narcotics trafficking and terrorist activities. For further information on money laundering and financial crimes, we refer you to the *2013 International Narcotics Control Strategy Report (INCSR), Volume 2, Money Laundering and Financial Crimes*: http://www.state.gov/j/inl/rls/nrcrpt/index.htm.

Regional and International Cooperation: The Tunisian government has increased its cooperation with the United States on other law enforcement matters and at the second ministerial meeting of the Global Counterterrorism Forum (GCTF) in Istanbul in June 2012, offered to host the GCTF-inspired International Institute for Justice and the Rule of Law, which will provide a platform for the delivery of training to criminal justice officials in Tunisia and the wider region to prevent and respond to terrorist and related threats within a rule of law framework.

The principal focus of the Tunisian government's counterterrorism efforts continued to be securing its borders, especially in light of instability and armed conflict in neighboring Libya and the presence of violent extremists based in Algeria and Libya crossing clandestinely into

Tunisia. Tunisian authorities intensified their coordination with Libyan and Algerian counterparts, and during a November trip to Algiers, Prime Minister Jebali reiterated that Tunisia and Algeria were committed to cross-border cooperation to stem illegal arms and drug trafficking, contraband smuggling, illegal immigration, and infiltration of armed gangs. On December 3, Prime Minister Jebali and Algerian Prime Minister Selial signed a joint statement vowing to fight terrorism, organized crime, and drug trafficking. On December 24, Algerian Interior Minister Dahou Ould Kablia announced that Algeria and Tunisia had signed an agreement to strengthen border security coordination to include the creation of joint patrols to combat terrorism, human trafficking, smuggling, and illegal migration. The signing followed two days of meetings between Kablia and Tunisian Prime Minister Jebali and Interior Minister Laraayedh.

At various times, the Government of Tunisia closed border crossings with Libya and supported the Algerian authorities' decision to close part of its border with Tunisia in an effort to prevent militias, militants, and armed bandits from entering Tunisia. The Tunisian and Algerian security forces launched joint operations in December to root out an AQIM cell in western Tunisia.

Countering Radicalization and Violent Extremism: In addition to expressions of solidarity with Tunisia's minority religious groups, the Tunisian government instructed the Ministry of Religious Affairs to undertake mosque educational programs designed to promote peaceful coexistence and religious tolerance.

UNITED ARAB EMIRATES

Overview: The United Arab Emirates (UAE) government continued to build its counterterrorism capacity and strengthened international counterterrorism cooperation. Over the course of the year, the UAE government improved border security measures and renewed efforts to combat terrorist financing. The United States and UAE governments were in negotiations to establish a pre-clearance facility at the Abu Dhabi International Airport. Prominent officials and religious leaders continued to publicly criticize violent extremist ideology.

Legislation, Law Enforcement, and Border Security: The UAE participated in the Megaports and Container Security Initiatives (CSI). The CSI, which became operational at Port Rashid and Jebel Ali Port in the Emirate of Dubai in 2005, has two U.S. Customs and Border Protection (CBP) officers co-located with the Dubai Customs Intelligence Unit at Port Rashid. On average, CSI reviewed approximately 250 bills of lading each week, resulting in about 25 non-intrusive inspections per month of U.S.- bound containers; examinations were conducted jointly with Dubai Customs officers, who shared information on transshipments from high risk areas, including those originating in Iran.

In 2012, the UAE implemented the use of retina scanning devices at international airport arrival terminals. The risk analysis or targeting practice, i.e., who is subjected to the scans, remained unclear.

In 2010, Immigration and Customs Enforcement (ICE) signed two Memoranda of Cooperation (MOCs) to support the respective training academies of the UAE Ministry of Interior's (federal) Immigration Authority and the Abu Dhabi (emirate) Customs Authority (ADCA) and enhance capacity building of its police and customs authorities. The aforementioned MOCs remain in effect. In 2012, five retired ICE and CBP personnel were under direct contract of the UAE Ministry of Interior while six were under direct contract of the ADCA. All served the respective academies as subject-matter experts, course developers, and instructors. The two academies trained approximately 700 immigration and customs personnel in 2012.

A critical factor that poses a challenge to the effectiveness of the UAE's law enforcement, border security, and judicial system is the country's lack of human capacity. Emiratis compose only 11 percent of the country's total population, making it structurally difficult to develop the country's human resources to counter the full range of terrorist activities. Despite this, the UAE government remains vigilant in its overall counterterrorism pursuits.

Countering Terrorist Finance: The UAE is a member of the Middle East and North Africa Financial Action Task Force, a Financial Action Task Force-style regional body, and chairs the Training and Typologies Working Group. It is a major international banking and trading center. Its Financial Intelligence Unit (FIU), the Anti-Money Laundering and Suspicious Cases Unit in the UAE Central Bank, is a member of the Egmont Group. The UAE continued efforts to strengthen its institutional capabilities to combat terrorist financing, but challenges remained with its enforcement of local and international law. The UAE's last mutual evaluation report in 2008 recommended it amend the federal anti-money laundering (AML) law and increase dedicated resources available to the Central Bank's Financial Intelligence Unit.

The Central Bank continued to conduct AML training both locally and regionally, and was expanding its cooperation with FIUs worldwide to bolster its ability to counter terrorist finance. Exploitation of money transmitters by illicit actors, which included licensed exchange houses, *hawalas*, and trading firms acting as money transmitters, remained a significant concern. This vulnerability was compounded by the voluntary registration regime for *hawalas* and their lack of enforceable Anti-Money Laundering/Combating the Financing of Terrorism of terrorism obligations. Regional *hawalas* and associated trading companies in various expatriate communities, most notably Somalis, have established clearinghouses, the vast majority of which are not registered with the UAE government. There are some indications that trade-based money laundering occurs in the UAE and that such activity might support terrorist groups in Afghanistan, Pakistan, and Somalia. The UAE Central Bank provides direct oversight to the Foreign Exchange and Remittance Group, the UAE's exchange house industry group, but its capacity and willingness to effectively monitor the sector remained unclear. Currently Emirati authorities are not capable of supervising the vast number of *hawalas* in the country or enforcing *hawala* compliance. Continuing from previous years, the United States and the UAE worked together to strengthen efforts to counter terrorist finance, including cross-border Bulk Cash Smuggling (BCS) and money laundering, with training, collaborative engagement with the local financial community, and other bilateral government cooperation.

In September, the U.S. Federal Bureau of Investigation (FBI) Legal Attaché established a sub-office at the U.S. Consulate in Dubai to assist with Counterterrorism/Terrorist Financing Matters and provide a viable means to enhance cooperation between the FBI and UAE. Additionally, the FBI provided training courses to Gulf Cooperation Council (GCC) law enforcement counterparts.

In March, ICE and CBP provided BCS and AML training to UAE Customs and Law Enforcement officials in Dubai. The training consisted of academic and practical exercises concentrating on land-border interdiction and investigation of smuggled currency.

Regarding routine distribution of UN lists of designated terrorists or terrorist entities to financial institutions, the UAE's communication with the local financial community is largely driven by follow-up on suspicious transactions reports and close bilateral cooperation with partner governments. However, most if not all banks receive the UN lists by means of their own internal compliance offices. Operational capability constraints and political considerations sometimes prevented the UAE government from immediately freezing and confiscating terrorist assets absent multilateral assistance.

For further information on money laundering and financial crimes, we refer you to the *2013 International Narcotics Control Strategy Report (INCSR), Volume 2, Money Laundering and Financial Crimes*: http://www.state.gov/j/inl/rls/nrcrpt/index.htm.

Regional and International Cooperation: The UAE is a founding member of the Global Counterterrorism Forum (GCTF). At the GCTF launch in September 2011, the UAE announced that it would open the first-ever international center for training, dialogue, research, and strategic communication on countering violent extremism (CVE): the International Center of Excellence for Countering Violent Extremism, known as Hedayah. Hedayah was formally launched on December 13-14, 2012, at the GCTF's Third Coordinating Committee and Ministerial meetings in Abu Dhabi. The UAE and UK co-chair the GCTF CVE Working Group, whose meetings the UAE had earlier hosted on April 3-4, in Abu Dhabi. The UAE will be the permanent host of Hedayah.

In October, the UAE Ministry of Interior hosted the fifth regional field meeting for the "Project al Qabdah: Counterterrorism for the Middle East and North Africa." The project's goal is to increase information exchange among member countries and the Arab Interior Minister Councils. Participating organizations included the UN Office on Drugs and Crime, Naif Arab University for Security Sciences, Europol, and the Secretariat General of the Corporation Council for Arab States in the Gulf.

The UAE government routinely invited participation from GCC countries at counterterrorism-related training sessions conducted by the FBI in the UAE.

Countering Radicalization and Violent Extremism: In order to prevent violent extremist preaching in UAE mosques, the General Authority of Islamic Affairs and Endowments (Awqaf) provided guidelines for all Friday sermons and monitored compliance. Abroad, Awqaf has trained cohorts of Afghani imams on preaching messages of moderation and tolerance, a program they have conducted since 2010. During key periods of Muslim religious observance, especially the fasting month of Ramadan, the UAE government aired commercials on television warning its Muslim citizens and residents to refrain from donating money at mosques, as the funds could unknowingly go to support terrorist causes. The UAE worked to keep its education system free of radical influences, and it emphasized social tolerance and moderation. Also, the UAE has a cyber crime law criminalizing the use of the internet by terrorist groups to "promote their ideologies and finance their activities." The UAE government repeatedly condemned terrorist acts in Libya, Syria, and elsewhere.

YEMEN

Overview: The Government of Yemen successfully implemented a peaceful change of government and a military campaign against al-Qa'ida in the Arabian Peninsula (AQAP) strongholds in its southern governorates in 2012, while facing multiple challenges including military and police units of varying loyalties, tribal adversaries, anti-government Houthi groups, a southern secessionist movement, and lawlessness in many areas. After their setback in Abyan, AQAP terrorists took advantage of Yemen's climate of instability, employing asymmetric tactics in a campaign of bombings and targeted assassinations against government targets, pro-government tribal militias known as Popular Committees (PCs), as well as civilian and international targets.

The Yemeni government, under President Abdo Rabbo Mansour Hadi, remained a strong U.S. counterterrorism partner. Hadi demonstrated Yemen's commitment as a counterterrorism partner soon after taking office by ordering the military to dislodge AQAP militants from areas they occupied in Abyan and Aden governorates including the towns of Zinjibar, Jaar, and Shuqra. By June, these AQAP forces had been dislodged or withdrawn. AQAP elements continued to remain active in Abyan and Aden governorates, however, as well as in Sanaa and other governorates.

The U.S. conducted counterterrorism operations in Yemen and trained Yemeni forces. Two U.S.-trained counterterrorism units, the Yemen Special Operations Forces (YSOF) and the Counter Terrorism Unit (CTU), remained in the vicinity of Sanaa and did not participate in the early summer campaign against AQAP in the southern governorates. Fractures within the chain of command and reluctance on the part of these units' pro-Saleh leadership to commit forces contributed to this performance. YSOF was under the command of the son of former President Ali Abdullah Saleh, Ahmed Ali Saleh, and the CTU fell under the nephew, Yahya Saleh, Chief of Staff of the Central Security Forces. The CTU deployed to the southern governorates and participated in the counterterrorism fight later in 2012. In December 2012, President Hadi issued a decree that unified some of Yemen's various counterterrorism units and special operations forces under one command as part of a broader military reorganization.

In the spring of 2012, a Yemeni military offensive, with the help of armed residents, regained government control over territory in the south, which AQAP has seized and occupied in 2011. AQAP increasingly turned to asymmetric tactics to target Yemeni government officials, pro-government PCs and their leaders, soldiers, civilians, and U.S. embassy personnel.

Yemeni government officials accused some pro-secessionist members of the Southern Movement (Hirak), of carrying out violent acts in the south. Senior security and military officials accused Hirak in the south and Houthi groups in the north of receiving weapons and funding from Iran in an effort to destabilize Yemen. They also accused Iranian elements of raising political and sectarian tensions through disinformation that promoted and encouraged violent extremism.

2012 Terrorist Incidents: AQAP and AQAP-affiliated groups carried out attacks throughout Yemen using improvised explosive devices (IEDs), ambushes, car bombs, VBIEDs, suicide bombers, and targeted assassinations by gunmen riding motorcycles. The list below is not comprehensive and does not include all of the engagements that occurred almost daily between AQAP and other militants and government forces or pro-government PCs.

- On January 11, in Aden, suspected AQAP gunmen opened fire on a vehicle carrying Yemeni intelligence officers, killing at least one and wounding five.
- On February 25, a suicide car bombing killed 26 Republican Guard troops outside of the presidential palace in Mukalla, the capital of Hadramawt governorate. It occurred while President Abdo Rabbo Mansour Hadi was taking the oath as president in Sanaa. AQAP later claimed responsibility for the attack.
- On March 4, AQAP militants stormed an army base in Kod, south of Abyan's capital, Zinjibar, and then fighting spread to other military posts in the area. The attack reportedly began with coordinated VBIEDs at military posts at Zinjibar's southern and western entrances, which killed at least seven Yemeni soldiers and wounded 12 others. Overall, over 185 Yemeni soldiers were killed in the assault, and over 70 were taken captive by AQAP.
- On March 14, AQAP militants kidnapped a Swiss woman in the port city of al Hodeidah. Two weeks later, they reportedly demanded certain conditions for her release, calling for the release of Usama bin Laden's widows, who were being held in Pakistan, the release of several women being held in Iraq and Saudi Arabia, the release of 100 AQ-affiliated militants from Yemeni jails, and 50 million Euros (approximately US $66 million). Mediation efforts failed, according to a tribal negotiator, because of the prohibitive demands. (The Swiss woman was released in February 2013.)
- On March 18, AQAP gunmen killed American citizen Joel Shrum on his way to work in Taiz. Shrum worked as an administrator and English teacher at a vocational institute. On March 22, AQAP claimed responsibility in a communiqué posted on violent extremist forums.
- On March 28, Abdullah al-Khaldi, the deputy counsel at the Saudi consulate in Aden, was kidnapped on his way to work.
- On April 21, armed tribesmen kidnapped a French employee of the International Committee Red Cross 20 miles outside of Hodeidah. Tribal sources indicated later that he was subsequently handed over to AQAP and was being held in Abyan governorate. He was released on July 14.
- On May 21, a suicide bomber disguised as a soldier struck at a rehearsal for a military parade in Sabeen Square in Sanaa, leaving over 90 soldiers dead. AQAP claimed responsibility for the attack.
- On May 25, a suspected AQAP bomber attacked and killed at least 12 Shia in a bombing of a Houthi mosque in al-Jawf governorate in northern Yemen.
- On June 18, Southern Military Region Commander Major General Salem Qatan was assassinated by a suicide bomber as he was leaving his residence in Aden. AQAP claimed responsibility for the attack.
- On July 11, a suicide bomber targeted cadets at the Sanaa Police Academy as they were leaving class. At least nine were killed in the blast.
- On July 16, suspected AQAP gunmen ambushed the Deputy Director of Taiz Central Prison, killing him and three other persons.
- On August 5, a suicide bomber struck at a funeral in Yemen's southern city of Jaar, killing at least 45 people and wounding dozens more. The attack targeted a local Popular Committee that had sided with the government against AQAP militants.

- On August 18, militants with suspected ties to AQAP attacked a Political Security Organization compound in Aden. The militants first detonated a VBIED and then raided the building. At least 14 members of the security forces were killed and seven others were injured in the attack.
- On August 19, a gunman opened fire on worshippers in a mosque in al-Dhale, killing at least seven people and injuring 11 others. Security sources indicated that the gunman may not have had ties to AQAP.
- On August 19, a suicide bomber with suspected ties to AQAP attacked a group of tribesmen in Mudia in Abyan governorate. The attack killed Nasser Ali Daiheh, leader of the local Popular Committee, along with two of his bodyguards.
- On September 11, Yemen's defense minister Major General Muhammad Nasir Ahmad escaped assassination in a VBIED attack on his motorcade in Sanaa. The attack, which was carried out by suspected AQAP militants, killed 12 people including seven security guards and five civilians.
- On September 13, hundreds of violent protesters broke into the U.S. Embassy compound and looted and vandalized the property. The attack caused an estimated $20 million in damages to U.S. buildings, vehicles, and facilities.
- On October 30, saboteurs bombed the Yemen gas pipeline 300 kilometers north of Balhaf terminal.
- On November 2, a senior officer in the Central Security Forces was shot and killed by masked gunmen in a drive-by shooting near his house in Sayun in Hadramawt governorate.
- On November 24, three worshippers were killed in Sanaa by unknown assailants in an attack on a Houthi gathering commemorating the Shia holy day of Ashura.
- On November 28, a Saudi diplomat and his bodyguard were shot and killed in an ambush in the Hadda district of Sanaa. The attackers, who remained unidentified, reportedly wore Central Security Force uniforms.
- On December 8, eight Yemeni soldiers including one senior officer, were killed in Marib governorate in an ambush by suspected AQAP gunmen.
- On December 10, 17 Yemeni soldiers and officers were killed in an ambush by suspected AQAP militants. The ambush took place in the Wadi Obeida area of Marib province as the soldiers were patrolling the Marib Oil Pipeline.
- On December 11, suspected AQAP militants on a motorcycle shot and killed Deputy Director of the Political Security Organization in Hadramawt governorate, Ahmed Barmadah, as he was leaving his house in Mukalla.
- On December 28, AQAP's media arm al-Mahalem Media Organization posted a *YouTube* video announcing rewards of 3,000 grams of gold for killing the U.S. ambassador to Yemen and five million Yemeni riyals (approximately US $23,000) for killing an American soldier in Yemen. The communiqué was posted on violent extremist websites and reported in public media.

Legislation, Law Enforcement, and Border Security: Parliament has yet to vote on a package of counterterrorism laws first introduced in 2008, despite efforts of the Ministry of Legal Affairs to advocate for the legislation's passage. As a result, the Yemeni government continued to lack a clear legal framework for prosecuting terrorism-related crimes. The government often resorted to charging terrorism suspects with "membership in an armed gang."

There were a number of arrests of terrorist suspects in 2012. However the continued weakness of the Yemeni justice system left many traditional law enforcement counterterrorism responsibilities to the Yemeni military.

A series of decrees by President Hadi in late December marked an important step in implementing some key military and security reforms by establishing a more unified command structure suited to Yemen's security challenges.

Yemen continued to participate in the Department of State's Antiterrorism Assistance program.

Countering Terrorist Finance: Yemen is a member of the Middle East and North Africa Financial Action Task Force (MENAFATF), a Financial Action Task Force (FATF)-style regional body, and enacted its first comprehensive anti-money laundering/combating the financing of terrorism (AML/CFT) law in 2010.

In 2012, the FIU participated in training to enhance its operational capacity. Yemen has a cross-border cash declaration or disclosure requirement for cash amounts over $15,000. Compliance is lax and customs inspectors do not routinely file currency declaration forms if funds are discovered. There are approximately 532 registered money exchange businesses in Yemen. Money transfer businesses are required to register with the Central Bank of Yemen and can open offices at multiple locations. Yemen has a large underground economy. The Yemeni government lacks specific legislation with respect to forfeiture of the assets of those suspected of terrorism.

Since February 2010, Yemen has been publicly identified by the FATF as a jurisdiction with strategic AML/CTF deficiencies, for which it has developed an action plan with the FATF to address these weaknesses. The Yemeni government has since committed to an action plan with the FATF to address these weaknesses. Yemen's Financial Investigations Unit at the Central Bank of Yemen drafted updated legislation to address the recommendations of the MENAFATF.

For further information on money laundering and financial crimes, please refer to the *2013 International Narcotics Control Strategy Report (INCSR), Volume 2, Money Laundering and Financial Crimes*: http://www.state.gov/documents/organization/185866.pdf

Regional and International Cooperation: In February, Yemen participated in the Global Counterterrorism Forum's Horn of Africa region capacity building working group in Dar es Salaam. The Government of Yemen cooperated with U.S., European, Jordanian, and regional partners on counterterrorism issues.

Jordanian and U.S. teams advised the Ministry of Defense as it made plans to restructure Yemen's military and defense forces, and European teams advised the Ministry of Interior on restructuring Yemen's police and interior security forces.

Countering Radicalization and Violent Extremism: Official media published messages from President Hadi and other senior officials highlighting the importance of countering terrorism by addressing the conditions that terrorists exploit. State broadcasters also featured limited messaging designed to raise awareness among the Yemeni people about the dangers of terrorism and violent extremism. They frequently highlighted the threat of terrorism and violent acts on

Yemen's economy and development. Many political leaders and groups (including the former opposition Joint Meeting Party alliance) publicly condemned terrorism and violent attacks, while stressing that a unified army and security service would help to eradicate terrorism. Many Yemeni officials and media professionals have expressed support for expanding messaging efforts aimed at countering violent extremism, but point to a lack of resources and expertise that impede their efforts.

SOUTH AND CENTRAL ASIA

South Asia remained a front line in the battle against terrorism. Although we have seriously degraded the al-Qa'ida (AQ) core in Afghanistan and Pakistan, AQ still has the ability to plan and conduct attacks from its safe havens. AQ looked to consolidate power by forging closer ties with other terrorist organizations in the region such as Tehrik-e Taliban Pakistan (TTP) and the Haqqani Network (HQN). These alliances continued to provide the group with additional resources and capabilities. In 2012, terrorists in South Asia carried out operations in heavily populated areas and attempted to expand networks across the region and beyond.

Afghanistan in particular continued to experience aggressive and coordinated attacks by the Afghan Taliban, HQN, and other AQ-affiliated groups. A number of these attacks were planned and launched from these groups' safe haven in Pakistan. Afghan Security Forces are now providing security throughout most of Afghanistan as the transition to full Afghan leadership on security continues in anticipation of the 2014 withdrawal of U.S. and Coalition Forces (CF). Afghan and CF, in partnership, took aggressive action against terrorist elements in Afghanistan, especially in Kabul, and many of the eastern and northern provinces.

Pakistan continued to experience significant terrorist violence, including sectarian attacks. The Pakistani military undertook operations against groups that conducted attacks within Pakistan such as TTP, but other groups such as Lashkar-e-Tayyiba were able to continue to operate in Pakistan. Pakistan did not directly target the Afghan Taliban or HQN, although it supported efforts to bring both groups into an Afghan peace process.

Although terrorist violence was lower than in previous years, India remained severely impacted by and vulnerable to terrorism, including from groups based in Pakistan. The Government of India, in response, increased its own counterterrorism capabilities and expanded its cooperation and coordination with the international community and regional partners.

Bangladesh, an influential counterterrorism partner in the region, continued to make strides against domestic and international terrorism. The government's ongoing counterterrorism efforts have made it more difficult for transnational terrorists to operate in or use Bangladeshi territory. In addition, Bangladesh and India improved and expanded counterterrorism cooperation.

Despite the absence of major terrorist incidents on their territory, governments in the five Central Asian states were concerned about the possibility of a growing threat connected to changes in the international force presence in Afghanistan in 2014. While some sought to reduce their countries' vulnerability to the perceived terrorist threat, the effectiveness of their efforts was in some cases undercut by failure to distinguish clearly between terrorism on one hand and political opposition, or non-traditional religious practices, on the other.

AFGHANISTAN

Overview: Though the primary responsibility for security in Afghanistan is transitioning from U.S. and international forces to Afghan National Security Forces (ANSF), the United States is committed to continued political, diplomatic, and economic engagement in Afghanistan as a strategic partner. The United States fully supports Afghan efforts to professionalize and modernize the security forces to take ownership of the security and counterterrorism efforts. The United States continued its role as a facilitator in improving Afghanistan's relations with its regional partners, fostering democracy, reintegration, and economic development.

In 2012, the United States and others in the international community provided training and resource assistance to Afghanistan, including democratic institution building, humanitarian relief and assistance, capacity building, security needs, counter-narcotic programs, and infrastructure projects.

The Government of Afghanistan's response to the spate of insider attacks has led directly to an increased focus on the vetting and training of security force personnel. This has led to a more professional force.

2012 Terrorist Attacks: In 2012, insurgents conducted some of the largest vehicle-borne improvised explosive device (VBIED) attacks since 2001, targeting Provincial Reconstruction Teams, large Coalition Forces (CF) bases, and Afghan government buildings, mostly in eastern Afghanistan. The number of insider attacks increased significantly compared to 2011, though actions taken by ISAF and ANSF in response resulted in a significant decrease in these attacks in the latter half of the year. Insurgents across Afghanistan used a variety of tactics to target Afghan security personnel and CF in major cities and rural areas, seeking to expand their territorial influence and control. In major cities, these attacks were well-coordinated, complex attacks to garner media attention while they targeted the ANSF in rural areas. Insurgents carried out several targeted assassinations of Afghan leadership. As in previous years, a greater number of attacks occurred during the summer months. This year, however there were three high-profile attacks in December compared with one in 2011. Helmand, Kandahar, Ghazni, and Kunar represented the most dangerous provinces for Afghan security personnel and CF.

High-profile attacks included:

- On February 25, an Afghan Ministry of Interior officer conducted an insider attack that killed two American military personnel embedded inside the Ministry of Interior compound in Kabul City in Kabul Province.
- On April 15, 14 insurgents embarked on an attack in three separate areas of Kabul City. Insurgents occupied three high-rise buildings in Kabul City in Kabul Province, and attacked the U.S. Embassy, several foreign embassies, Camp Warehouse, and Parliament. Insurgents simultaneously conducted attacks in Jalalabad City in Nangarhar Province against the Provincial Reconstruction Team, in Pul-e Alam District in Logar Province against Afghan government buildings, and in Gardez in Paktiya Province against Afghan government and security locations. The attacks resulted in massive casualties, with at least 50 killed and hundreds wounded in the four provinces.

- On May 2, insurgents conducted an attack consisting of a VBIED and three suicide bombers on foot, against the Green Village camp in Kabul City in Kabul Province, killing nine people and wounding 21.

- On June 20, seven insurgents attacked the Spozhmai Hotel in Kabul, holding over 50 people hostage for almost 12 hours. The attack resulted in the death of at least 18 Afghans, including 14 civilians.

- Also on June 20, insurgents conducted an attack against Forward Operating Base Salerno in Khost Province consisting of a large suicide VBIED and nine suicide bombers wearing U.S. military and Afghan National Army uniforms, killing eight people and wounding 58.

- On July 9, at least 18 insurgents embarked on an attack in several areas of Kandahar City in Kandahar Province, attacking the Afghan National Police headquarters and several Afghan National Police Sub-Stations, killing at least nine people and wounding 39.

- On August 7, insurgents detonated a large VBIED at the Provincial Reconstruction Team at Forward Operating Base Shank in Logar Province, killing four individuals and wounding 28.

- On August 8, two suicide bombers targeted a dismounted movement in Asadabad City in Kunar Province, killing five people, including four Americans, and wounding 15 people, including 10 Americans.

- On September 8, a young Afghan child carrying a backpack full of explosives detonated near the U.S. Embassy inside the Green Zone in Kabul City in Kabul Province, killing six Afghans and wounding five.

- On September 14, 15 insurgents wearing U.S. military and Afghan National Security Force uniforms breached the perimeter of Camp Leatherneck/Camp Bastion in Helmand Province and targeted aircraft and military equipment. The attack resulted in two dead CF soldiers, 15 wounded, and millions of dollars worth of damage.

- On September 18, a suicide VBIED targeted an Aircraft Charter Services convoy traveling toward Kabul International Airport in Kabul City in Kabul Province, killing 10 and wounding three.

- On October 26, a lone suicide bomber entered a mosque in Meymaneh City in Faryab Province and detonated his explosives during a service, killing 41 and wounding at least 50.

- On November 21, two suicide bombers wearing suicide vests detonated at a private security company checkpoint in the Wazir Akbar Khan neighborhood near Camp Eggers and the U.S. Embassy in the Green Zone in Kabul City in Kabul Province, killing four people and wounding seven.

- On December 2, insurgents conducted an attack against Jalalabad Airfield in Nangarhar Province consisting of one VBIED, four suicide bombers on foot, and an unspecified number of insurgents attacking from a considerable stand-off distance. The attack resulted in the deaths of six people and injured 24.

- On December 6, a suicide bomber wearing explosives laced in his underwear and posing as a Taliban peace envoy attempted to assassinate Afghan National Directorate of Security chief Assadullah Khalid in Kabul City in Kabul Province, seriously wounding the Afghan security chief.

- On December 17, insurgents conducted a suicide VBIED attack using a Hino truck against private American company Contrack International in Kabul City in Kabul Province, killing three people and wounding nearly 50.

Legislation, Law Enforcement, and Border Security: The current Afghan Penal Code, enacted in 1976, has gaps, a lack of definitions, disproportionate mandatory fines and sentences, and strict minimum imprisonments that result in overcrowded prisons. A recent workshop established objectives for penal code reform and provided guidance to the Criminal Law Reform Working Group for the future path to revise the Penal Code. The workshop also highlighted some areas for potential concern in the process, such as the influence of radical views regarding Sharia, how gender-related crimes will be addressed in the new penal code, and compliance with international obligations regarding human rights and international treaties and conventions to which Afghanistan is Party. The draft Criminal Procedure Code (CPC) was pending in Parliament at year's end.

The draft Law on the Structure and Jurisdiction of the Attorney General's Office will codify the structure and funding of the existing Anti-Terrorism Protection Directorate in the Attorney General's Office and permit the investigation and prosecution of terrorist and national security cases using internationally accepted methods and evidentiary rules.

Afghanistan continued to process travelers on entry and departure at major points of entry with the Personal Identification Secure Comparison and Evaluation System (PISCES). With support from the United States, Afghan authorities continued to expand PISCES installations at additional locations. Afghanistan remained an important partner nation in the Department of State's Antiterrorism Assistance program, which continued to shift its focus from the Presidential Protective Service to the National Directorate of Security's Detachment 10 security unit, to help the Afghans build broader, self-sustaining capabilities to protect national leadership, government facilities, and diplomatic facilities.

The Governments of Afghanistan and the United States investigated a variety of criminal acts, including kidnappings and conspiracy to commit terrorist acts. On several occasions, U.S. law enforcement bodies assisted the Ministry of Interior, the National Directorate of Security, and other Afghan authorities, which enabled them to take actions to disrupt and dismantle terrorist operations and prosecute terrorist suspects.

In 2012, the Afghan Attorney General's Office continued to investigate and prosecute violations of the laws on crimes against the internal and external security of the state (1976 and 1987), violations of the Law on Combat Against Terrorist Offences (2008), and the Law of Firearms, Ammunition and Explosives (2005), including laws that prohibit membership in terrorist or insurgent groups as well as laws that forbid violent acts committed against the state, hostage taking, murder, and the use of explosives against military forces and state infrastructure. The number of these cases that were investigated and prosecuted increased. A high percentage of these cases, primarily as a consequence of the March 9 Memorandum of Understanding on the Transfer of U.S. Detention Facilities, were tried at the Justice Center in Parwan. Cases were investigated and prosecuted in large numbers in the provinces as well, including a significant number in Kabul.

A number of incidents involving terrorist acts directed at U.S. citizens and interests were investigated and action taken by Afghan authorities. Two highlights included the December kidnapping and hostage recovery of a U.S. person and the November detention and subsequent Foreign Transfer of Custody of an American Unlawful Enemy Combatant.

Countering Terrorist Finance: Afghanistan, a member of the Asia/Pacific Group on Money Laundering (APG), a Financial Action Task Force (FATF)-style regional body, took initial steps to address deficiencies in its anti-money laundering/combating the financing of terrorism (AML/CFT) regime. In June, Afghanistan was publicly identified by FATF as a jurisdiction with strategic AML/CFT deficiencies. At that time, the Central Bank of Afghanistan confirmed by letter to FATF the government's high-level commitment to implement an action plan agreed upon with the FATF to address these deficiencies. The FATF action plan outlined a number of areas that the government needs to address to bring Afghanistan into compliance with international standards, including the enactment of amended AML/CFT legislation. To date, terrorist finance investigations in Afghanistan have been hampered by a weak or non-existent legal and regulatory regime, coupled with lack of capacity and political commitment. For further information on money laundering and financial crimes, we refer you to the *2013 International Narcotics Control Strategy Report (INCSR), Volume 2, Money Laundering and Financial Crimes*: http://www.state.gov/j/inl/rls/nrcrpt/index.htm.

Regional and International Cooperation: Afghanistan consistently emphasized the need to strengthen joint cooperation to fight terrorism and violent extremism in a variety of bilateral and multilateral fora. Notable among such meetings were regular meetings of the U.S.-Afghanistan-Pakistan Core Group; the frequent Istanbul Process meetings; and meetings of the Organization of Islamic Cooperation, the UN Regional Centre for Preventive Diplomacy for Central Asia, the UN Office of Drugs and Crime, the Shanghai Cooperation Organization, and other organizations. Afghanistan supported the UNGA Resolution establishing the UN Centre for Counter-Terrorism as part of the Counter-Terrorism Implementation Task Force.

Afghanistan has driven the Counterterrorism Confidence Building Measure (CBM) of the Istanbul Process, working closely with Turkey and the United Arab Emirates. Throughout 2012, the CBM working group identified activities that will be undertaken to counter terrorism and increase cooperation and mutual confidence.

The Project Global Shield (PGS) partnership focused on monitoring and curtailing the illicit diversion of 14 precursor chemicals used in the production of improvised explosive devices (IEDs), and reported an expansion from 82 to 97 participant countries and international organizations included in the World Customs Organization. The PGS-targeted precursors were used in insurgent IED attacks targeting civilian, Afghan, and ISAF elements in Afghanistan. Afghanistan also continued to work with its NATO-ISAF partners and with its regional neighbors to improve training, capacity, and counterterrorism collaboration. With Turkey and Pakistan, it held a trilateral Summit in December and discussed cooperation and held joint exercises in counterterrorism operations. Besides the Strategic Partnership Agreement signed with the United States in May, Afghanistan signed similar agreements with Italy and France in January 2012, and continued to work on agreements with Turkey and other NATO countries.

Countering Radicalization and Violent Extremism: Afghanistan's programs to counter violent extremism continued through increased engagement with religious communities. According to most estimates, over 90 percent of Afghan mosques and madrassas operated independently of government oversight. Some promoted violent extremist ideology. The Ministry of Hajj and Religious Affairs, as well as the Department of Islamic Education at the Ministry of Education, continued efforts to register more mosques and madrassas with limited success. The National Ulema Council, a quasi-governmental body of religious scholars

156

established by President Karzai in 2002, became more vocal in condemning suicide attacks as un-Islamic.

The Afghanistan Peace and Reintegration Program (APRP) was established by the Government of Afghanistan in 2010, and serves to reintegrate low- and mid-level insurgents back into their communities. The APRP is a National Priority Program of the Afghan government, is managed by the High Peace Council (HPC), and executed at the national level by the Joint Secretariat (JS). The HPC and JS work with the Provincial Peace committees and Provincial Joint Secretariat teams to effectively execute the program at the provincial level. By joining the program, the former fighter makes the commitment to renounce violence and sever all ties with the insurgency, and to abide by the Constitution of Afghanistan. This includes accepting the Government of Afghanistan's laws on women's rights. Since its inception, the APRP has successfully reintegrated over six thousand former combatants across Afghanistan. Community development is a core element of the APRP, serving both to facilitate the reintegrees' return and to encourage good governance and economic development at the local level, thereby increasing community resistance to insurgent influence. By year's end, over 1500 community recovery projects and programs were in various stages of planning and implementation across the country; the Afghan government estimated over 178,000 individuals have benefited from these projects.

BANGLADESH

Overview: The Government of Bangladesh has demonstrated its commitment to combating domestic and transnational terrorist groups, and its counterterrorism efforts made it harder for transnational terrorists to operate in or establish safe havens in Bangladesh. U.S. assistance supports programs for Bangladeshi civilian, law enforcement, and military counterparts to build their capacity to monitor, detect, and prevent terrorism.

Legislation, Law Enforcement, and Border Security: Bangladesh's criminal justice system is in the process of fully implementing the Antiterrorism Act of 2009; however, the judiciary moved slowly in processing terrorism and other criminal cases in general. Bangladesh cooperated with the United States to further strengthen control of its borders and land, sea, and air ports of entry. Bangladesh continued to participate in the Department of State's Antiterrorism Assistance program and cooperated with the Department of Justice's efforts to provide prosecutorial skills training to its assistant public prosecutors, encourage greater cooperation between police and prosecutors, and institute community policing in targeted areas of the country. With financial support from the United States and other partners, Bangladesh established a National Academy for Security Training in 2012 and began to provide counterterrorism training courses.

Countering Terrorist Finance: Bangladesh is a member of the Asia/Pacific Group on Money Laundering, a Financial Action Task Force (FATF)-style regional body. The Bangladesh Bank (the central bank) and its Financial Intelligence Unit/Anti-Money Laundering Section lead the government's effort to comply with the international sanctions regime. FATF has identified Bangladesh's implementation of UNSCRs 1267 and 1373 as a deficiency in its laws. Bangladesh formed an interagency committee to address this issue, and has drafted regulations to implement both of these provisions. While Bangladesh's Anti-Terrorism Act criminalized terrorist financing, FATF has recommended that Bangladesh amend its laws to meet international standards and to clarify remaining ambiguities. The interagency committee mentioned above has begun revising the legislation to satisfy FATF's concerns in this regard. For further information on money laundering and financial crimes, we refer you to the *2013 International Narcotics Control Strategy Report (INCSR), Volume 2, Money Laundering and Financial Crimes*: http://www.state.gov/j/inl/rls/nrcrpt/index.htm.

Regional and International Cooperation: Bangladesh is party to various counterterrorism protocols under the South Asian Association for Regional Cooperation and is bringing the country's counterterrorism efforts in line with the four pillars of the UN Global Counter-Terrorism Strategy. Bangladesh's foreign and domestic policies are heavily influenced by the region's major powers, particularly India. In past years the Indo-Bangladesh relationship provided openings for transnational threats, but the current government has demonstrated its interest in regional cooperation on counterterrorism. Bangladesh was active in the full range of international fora.

In 2012, Bangladesh enacted a mutual legal assistance law that will allow for greater international cooperation. It has also signed memoranda of understanding with a number of countries to share evidence regarding criminal investigations, including investigations related to financial crimes and terrorist financing.

Countering Radicalization and Violent Extremism: Bangladesh uses strategic communication to counter violent extremism, especially among youth. The Ministry of Education provides oversight for madrassas and is developing a standard national curriculum that includes language, math, and science curricula; and minimum standards of secular subjects to be taught in all primary schools, up to the eighth grade. The Ministry of Religious Affairs and the National Committee on Militancy Resistance and Prevention work with imams and religious scholars to build public awareness against terrorism. The Government of Bangladesh is also actively expanding economic opportunities for women as it views economic empowerment for women as a buffer against violent extremist messages of male religious leaders.

INDIA

Overview: According to the South Asia Terrorism Portal, 805 people were killed as a result of terrorist attacks in India in 2012. While this figure represents a 25 percent decrease from the previous year, India remained subject to violent terrorist attacks and continued to be one of the most persistently targeted countries by transnational terrorist groups such as Lashkar-e-Tayyiba (LeT). Included in the total number of fatalities were the 364 deaths ascribed to left-wing violent extremism, almost 80 percent of which were Communist Party of India Maoist or Maoist/ Naxalite violence, which the Indian government considers its most serious internal security threat. To date, those groups have not specifically targeted U.S. or other international interests.

In 2012, Indian sources continued to attribute violence and deaths in Jammu and Kashmir to transnational terrorist groups it alleges are backed by Pakistan. India and Pakistan attempted to decrease tensions in their bilateral relationship by increasing official dialogue between their two governments, lessening trade restrictions, and relaxing some visa requirements in 2012. Continued allegations of violations of the Line of Control between India and Pakistan (the border along Jammu and Kashmir), however, and Indian concerns about Pakistani-based terrorist groups remained impediments to normalizing relations.

In December, the Indian government reached an agreement with the Pakistani government for a second visit of a Pakistan Judicial Commission to visit India to cross-examine witnesses for the Mumbai attack prosecutions in Pakistan, but the visit must be approved by the courts in both countries; this had not occurred by year's end. Terrorist opponents of better India-Pakistan relations, including LeT and its leader Hafiz Saeed, continued to call for violent attacks against India.

The United States and India increased counterterrorism capacity building efforts and cooperation, with the Indians participating in several courses provided by the Department of State's Antiterrorism Assistance program, along with other regional capacity building programs. The annual U.S.-India Counterterrorism Joint Working Group meeting allowed both countries to share counterterrorism perspectives and policies, as well as propose initiatives for future cooperation. In addition, the U.S. Federal Bureau of Investigation, through the Office of the Legal Attaché, conducted additional exchanges with Indian law enforcement personnel, and DHS, through the Homeland Security Dialogue with the Ministry of Home Affairs, expanded its interaction with Indian officials on cyber security, counterfeit Indian currency that could be used to finance terrorism, port security, and megacity policing initiatives.

2012 Terrorist Incidents: Apart from Maoist violence, there were two significant terrorist incidents:

- On February 13, the wife of an Israeli diplomat was severely injured when a bomb was placed on the back of her car as she drove in New Delhi in an area near both the Prime Minister's residence and the diplomatic enclave. Similar attempts to bomb Israeli targets in other countries around the same time led many to believe that Iran might be responsible for the attack.
- On August 1, 30 roadside bombs were discovered in Pune, Maharashtra. One of the bombs exploded causing injuries, and Antiterrorism Assistance program-trained law enforcement officials helped disarm the remaining bombs. By December, Indian police had arrested eight suspected members of the Indian Mujahedeen on suspicion of having planted the bombs.

Legislation, Law Enforcement, and Border Security: In late June, Indian authorities in New Delhi arrested LeT member Sayeed Zabiuddin Ansari, alias Abu Jindal, one of the instigators of the November 2008 Mumbai attack. Jindal's voice was recorded by the Indian authorities monitoring the phone calls, which has directly implicated him in the massacre. In November, just before the fourth anniversary of the Mumbai attack, Mohammad Ajmal Amir Kasab, the lone surviving Pakistani gunman in those attacks, was executed.

As part of its strategy to increase border security, the Ministry of Home Affairs Department of Border Management is building fences and roads and installing floodlights along both the Indo-Pakistan border and the Indo-Bangladesh border. In 2012, land was identified for the establishment of 116 of 131 new coastal police stations and the land acquisition process began for 74 of those stations as part of the government's Coastal Security Plan.

The Government of India's efforts to establish a National Counterterrorism Center were stalled when Chief Ministers from several states objected to its establishment on the grounds that it infringed upon the states' constitutional rights and responsibilities to maintain law and order.

Earlier 2009 initiatives to establish a National Intelligence Grid, a platform for information-sharing between law enforcement, intelligence services, and other government agencies, and a national crime record database had not been implemented by year's end, but some progress was reported. The Crime and Criminal Tracking Network and Systems will create a nation-wide environment for the real-time sharing of crime and criminal information.

Countering Terrorist Finance: India is a member of the Financial Action Task Force (FATF) and two FATF-style regional bodies; the Eurasian Group on Combating Money Laundering and Terrorist Financing and the Asia/Pacific Group on Money Laundering. The international community has targeted LeT individuals and entities under terrorism sanctions, and through FATF, the United States has worked with India to help improve its anti-money laundering/combating the financing of terrorism regime. The number of cases under investigation has continued to increase, but the number of persons convicted has remained low in comparison with the terrorism finance risk faced by India. For further information on money laundering and financial crimes, we refer you to the *2013 International Narcotics Control Strategy Report (INSCR) Volume 2, Money Laundering and Financial Crimes:* http://www.state.gov/j/inl/rls/nrcrpt/index.htm.

Regional and International Cooperation: India is a founding member of the Global Counterterrorism Forum (GCTF) and was an active participant in the GCTF and other UN forums on counterterrorism throughout the year. The Indian and Bangladeshi governments agreed in December to enhance cooperation under their bilateral Coordinated Border Management Plan to control illegal cross-border activities and reviewed the functioning of their system for sharing information on security-related matters.

Countering Radicalization and Violent Extremism: India's counter radicalization and violent extremism efforts are mostly directed by state and local authorities; under the Indian Constitution police and public order issues are state functions. The Indian government has programs that attempt to rehabilitate and integrate various groups, mostly insurgents, back into the mainstream of society, such as the "Scheme for Surrender cum-Rehabilitation of militants in North East." While not a counter radicalization scheme per se, it is directed at disaffected members of Indian society who support separatist and at times violent movements. Indian government officials have raised concerns about how social media and the internet can be used to stir communal unrest and radicalization. However, there was no national program or policy on countering radicalization or violent extremism.

KAZAKHSTAN

Overview: Kazakhstani officials continued to exhibit concern about violent extremism. Several small explosions and gun battles between security forces and suspected violent extremists kept the government on high alert, but terrorist groups have yet to mount a successful, large-scale attack in Kazakhstan. Critics claimed that official measures to counter radicalization and violent extremism were often too heavy-handed, and could result in increasing radicalization. In 2012, the government increasingly used the threat of violent extremism to justify limitations on political opposition and media outlets.

2012 Terrorist Incidents: Security incidents attributed to terrorists or violent extremists generally involved small explosive devices or small arms ambushes, primarily targeting government infrastructure or armed policemen. In several cases, explosions with no reported civilian casualties were attributed to accidental detonations of explosive devices by terrorist groups. Security forces periodically released reports of shootouts with people they described as terrorists. It was unclear, however, how security forces distinguished between terrorist or violent extremist groups and criminal groups. Analysts believe that violent extremist networks in Kazakhstan likely did not physically interact with their counterparts in other regions, but received online training and instructions. Significant incidents included:

- On July 11, a blast in a village outside Almaty killed eight people. Security forces stated that the explosion occurred in a safe-house where a violent extremist group was attempting to build a bomb. In an August 17 follow-up operation, Kazakhstani security forces killed nine suspected violent extremists who reportedly refused to surrender.
- On September 12, a week after suspected violent extremists set off an accidental explosion that killed one of their own, Kazakhstani security forces killed at least two more during a raid on an apartment building in Kulsary in western Kazakhstan.

Legislation, Law Enforcement, and Border Security: In December, Kazakhstan's parliament approved new legislation intended to clearly delineate and regulate the authorities and responsibilities of government agencies in matters of counterterrorism, and to establish regional counterterrorism commissions.

In April, representatives of border control agencies from Kazakhstan, Kyrgyzstan, Russia, Tajikistan, and Uzbekistan announced plans to establish an automated system of information exchange in order to more effectively implement counterterrorism measures across their borders.

Throughout the year, Kazakhstani security forces, prosecutors, and courts actively arrested, tried, and convicted dozens of people on charges of terrorism or extremism, including convictions for providing material support to terrorist groups and for dissemination of so-called "extremist materials."

In April, five people were convicted of organizing a November 2011 terrorist attack in Taraz, although the incident involved only a lone gunman. Their sentences ranged from five years to life in prison. In two separate trials in April, 47 defendants were found guilty of organizing bombing attacks on government buildings in Atyrau on October 31, 2011, and sentenced to prison terms ranging from five to 15 years. The violent extremist group Jund al-Khilafah (Soldiers of the Caliphate) claimed responsibility for that attack.

Government and law enforcement officials in Kazakhstan were motivated to act against perceived terrorist and violent extremist threats in the country. There were concerns, however, regarding Kazakhstan's sometimes heavy-handed response to perceived threats, which critics claimed could exacerbate the spread of extremism. For example, several opposition media outlets were convicted of extremism and ordered to stop operations in 2012 without compelling evidence of involvement in terrorism.

In September, Kazakhstani parliamentarians criticized law enforcement bodies for their tendency to kill all suspected terrorists in shootouts, rather than capture them alive for questioning.

Countering Terrorist Finance: Kazakhstan is a member of the Eurasian Group on Combating Money Laundering and Financing of Terrorism, a Financial Action Task Force-style regional body. In June, Kazakhstan adopted several changes and amendments to its existing terrorist finance laws to eliminate gaps and contradictions in previous legislation. The Prosecutor General's Office has indicated that it has plans to make lists of organizations that finance terrorism based on information submitted by special services and law enforcement agencies with counterterrorism responsibilities. Based on this information, the Prosecutor General's Office would be able to request that the Financial Monitoring Committee monitor the financial operations of the organization in question.

In October, the Senate ratified a Customs Union treaty on money laundering and terrorist finance. The Customs Union consists of Kazakhstan, Russia, and Belarus.

In October, three defendants in Uralsk were convicted under terrorist finance laws of providing financial support to the Islamic Jihad Union.

For further information on money laundering and financial crimes, we refer you to the *2013 International Narcotics Control Strategy Report (INCSR), Volume 2, Money Laundering and Financial Crimes*: http://www.state.gov/j/inl/rls/nrcrpt/index.htm.

Regional and International Cooperation: Kazakhstan is an active participant in regional counterterrorism efforts, and aspires to be a key regional leader in counterterrorism cooperation. In June, regional representatives met in Almaty to discuss a joint plan of action for the implementation of the UN Global Counter-Terrorism Strategy in Central Asia. In August, expert consultants from the Shanghai Cooperation Organization met in Almaty to discuss upcoming joint activities. In August, Kazakhstani security forces conducted joint counterterrorism drills with counterparts from Russia and Ukraine.

Countering Radicalization and Violent Extremism: The Government of Kazakhstan has undertaken a number of efforts to address radicalization, including some that have negative implications for the country's efforts to meet international human rights norms. For example, a new law on religion mandated the registration of religious groups throughout the country. According to a representative of the Committee for National Security, the registration process did not reveal any terrorist organizations in Kazakhstan, but several religious communities with no links to violent registration complained that authorities denied them registration under the new law. We refer you to the Department of State's *Annual Report to Congress on International Religious Freedom* (http://www.state.gov/j/drl/rls/irf/) for further information.

According to a spokesperson, the Agency for Religious Affairs scrutinized 1,800 websites for violent extremist content in the first nine months of the year. A representative of Kazakhstan's National Security Council claimed that 950 websites that promoted violent extremism have been shut down since 2010. As part of the government's plan to conduct a large-scale campaign to counter radicalization in society, new legislation requires all media outlets in Kazakhstan to assist state bodies in counterterrorism efforts; one consequence of this legislation is that several legitimate opposition media outlets were declared "extremist" by Kazakhstani courts and ordered to stop operations. We refer you to the Department of State's *Annual Country Reports on Human Rights Practices* (http://www.state.gov/j/drl/rls/hrrpt/) for further information.

KYRGYZSTAN

Overview: 2012 was a year of relative stability in Kyrgyzstan following the inauguration of President Almazbek Atambayev in December 2011, which marked the first democratic transfer of presidential power in the nation's history. There were no reported terrorist attacks in Kyrgyzstan in 2012 and no large-scale inter-ethnic clashes. Kyrgyz security forces, however, conducted continuing special operations against individuals allegedly affiliated with terrorist organizations. The Kyrgyz government remained attuned to the potential for terrorism and was involved in numerous international cooperative counterterrorism efforts.

Legislation, Law Enforcement, and Border Security: With funding from Embassy Bishkek's Export Control and Related Border Security Assistance (EXBS) office, the Kyrgyz government constructed several border guard towers along the country's southern border with Tajikistan. EXBS worked with Kyrgyzstan's Border Guards to utilize more modern border surveillance techniques and equipment, including ground sensors, and also funded training programs for Kyrgyzstan's Customs Services to improve pedestrian, passenger, and vehicle inspection. The Kyrgyz government does not gather biometric data at its border posts.

In 2012, the State Committee for National Security (GKNB), the main government organization tasked with counterterrorism, arrested several individuals based on their alleged connections to terrorist organizations. Throughout the year, the GKNB periodically arrested alleged members of Hizb-ut-Tahrir, which the Kyrgyz government designated as a terrorist organization in 2003. The GKNB claimed to discover extremist materials during the arrests.

There was positive U.S. cooperation with Kyrgyzstan's main counterterrorism bodies – the GKNB and the Ministry of Internal Affairs (MVD). The GKNB and MVD proactively notified the United States about possible security threats to the U.S. military-operated Transit Center at Manas International Airport and to the U.S. Embassy, usually in the form of protests. They deployed a relatively large number of troops along Bishkek's main thoroughfare (on which the Embassy is located) to deter large crowds from gathering at the Embassy.

Deterrents to more effective host government law enforcement measures against terrorism included rivalry and a lack of coordination between the GKNB and the MVD, as well as budgetary constraints which resulted in a lack of modern military and law enforcement equipment. Inefficient bureaucratic structures left over from the Soviet era, as well as low salaries and frequent personnel turnover hampered law enforcement efforts. Kyrgyz counterterrorist units remained largely untested in combat situations.

In September, the President signed an order making the Border Service independent from the GKNB. While this move may have some institutional benefits for the Border Service, it created another independent security service competing for resources. Bureaucratic friction is likely to weaken cooperation between the GKNB and the Border Service.

Kyrgyzstan continued to participate in the Department of State's Antiterrorism Assistance program, which provided training to help Kyrgyz law enforcement deter, detect, and respond to terrorist activities.

Countering Terrorist Finance: Kyrgyzstan is a member of the Eurasian Group on Combating Money Laundering and Financing of Terrorism, a Financial Action Task Force-style regional body. Its Financial Intelligence Unit (FIU) belongs to the Egmont Group of FIUs. On May 28, the Kyrgyz government established a Commission on Combating Financing of Terrorism. The Commission will function as a consultative body under the government to coordinate activities between relevant state bodies on combating terrorist financing and the laundering of criminal earnings. The Government of Kyrgyzstan did not report any efforts to seize terrorist assets in 2012. For further information on money laundering and financial crimes, we refer you to the *2013 International Narcotics Control Strategy Report (INCSR), Volume 2, Money Laundering and Financial Crimes*: http://www.state.gov/j/inl/rls/nrcrpt/index.htm.

Regional and International Cooperation: In 2012, Kyrgyzstan participated in counterterrorism activities organized by the OSCE, the Commonwealth of Independent States Anti-Terrorism Center, and the Collective Security Treaty Organization.

MALDIVES

Overview: Maldives is a strategically located series of atolls in the heart of the Indian Ocean. Since 2010, there has been growing concern about the activities of a small number of local extremists who support violence and their involvement with transnational terrorist groups. There has been particular concern that young Maldivians may be at risk of becoming radicalized and that some are joining violent extremist groups, including those with ties to Laskhar-e-Tayyiba (LeT) and al-Qa'ida (AQ).

Recent arrests in Pakistan of Maldivian citizens connected to terrorist groups have heightened the concern over radicalization. The Government of Maldives has been an enthusiastic partner with the United States to strengthen its law enforcement capacity and to conduct community outreach to counter violent extremism.

While Pakistan has been a traditional destination for education, young Maldivians have increasingly sought Islamic education in Saudi Arabia, Yemen, and Sudan due to perceived physical security risks associated with traveling in Pakistan. Some have expressed concern that students studying in the Gulf countries are bringing home radical ideology.

Legislation, Law Enforcement, and Border Security: There were no successful prosecutions of individuals promoting violent extremism and terrorism in 2012, as existing laws severely limited the ability of law enforcement agencies to prosecute such cases.

Maldives became a new partner nation in the Department of State's Antiterrorism Assistance (ATA) program in 2011, and 2012 programming efforts focused on building capacity in counterterrorism leadership and management, critical target protection, and regional cooperation. The police participated in five ATA courses in 2012.

On December 17, the Maldivian Parliament approved Maldives' accession to the UN Convention Against Transnational Organized Crime. At year's end, the Attorney General was reviewing the convention, after which the President will ratify it.

Countering Terrorist Finance: Maldives is a member of the Asia/Pacific Group on Money Laundering, a Financial Action Task Force-style regional body, and has submitted annual status reports. The UN 1267/1989 and 1988 consolidated lists for individuals and entities associated with the Taliban and AQ were sent to the Ministry of Foreign Affairs for forwarding to the Maldives Monetary Authority (MMA), which then instructed banks and creditors to take action and report back within a specified time period.

According to the Government of Maldives, capacity building of relevant supervisory and regulatory authorities (MMA and the Capital Market Development Authority), as well as other law enforcement authorities (Anti-Corruption Commission, Department of Immigration and Emigration, Maldives Customs Service, and Maldives Police Service), and the judiciary is needed in order to properly counter money laundering and terrorist financing. For further information on money laundering and financial crimes, we refer you to the *2013 International Narcotics Control Strategy Report (INCSR), Volume 2, Money Laundering and Financial Crimes*: http://www.state.gov/j/inl/rls/nrcrpt/index.htm.

Regional and International Cooperation: The Maldivian government cooperated closely with Indian security forces, and the Indian military offered regular support in the form of assets and training to Maldivian security forces. The Maldivian government also cooperated closely with the Sri Lankan government.

Countering Radicalization and Violent Extremism: The Government of Maldives recognizes that counter-radicalization efforts form a critical component to long-term success against violent extremism and has pursued initiatives in this area. The Ministry of Islamic Affairs implemented a program designed to mobilize religious and social leaders to work against all forms of violence in society, including the religious extremism that can lead to violence. The Ministry conducted over 15 seminars and workshops for religious leaders, educators, and local government officials. Several of these workshops included participants from across the country.

NEPAL

Overview: Nepal experienced no significant acts of international terrorism in 2012, although Nepal's open border with India and weak controls at Kathmandu's Tribhuvan International Airport raised concerns. On September 6, the Department of State revoked the designations of the Communist Party of Nepal (Maoist) (CPN(M)) under E.O. 13224 and as a "terrorist organization" from the Terrorist Exclusion List under the Immigration and Nationality Act, after the Department determined that the CPN(M) was no longer engaged in terrorist activity that threatened the security of U.S. nationals or U.S. foreign policy. (Note: the CPN(M) split into two successor parties in June 2012.)

2012 Terrorist Incidents: More than 47 improvised explosive devices (IEDs) detonated in 2012, but the majority of these incidents had no or few casualties. There were, however, two exceptions:

- On February 27, three people were killed and seven people were injured in Kathmandu when an IED was detonated outside the gate of the Nepal Oil Corporation. In March, police arrested six individuals suspected to have close links to the United Ethnic Liberation Front Nepal (UELFN), which claimed responsibility for the bombing.

- On April 30, an IED attack in Janakpur targeted participants at a sit-in protest demanding representation in negotiations over a new federal constitution. The blast killed four and injured two dozen others. The Janatantrik Tarai Mukti Morcha claimed responsibility for the bombing.

Legislation, Law Enforcement, and Border Security: Other than the ULEFN suspects, described above, there were no arrests or prosecutions of known terrorists in 2012. An open border with India, relatively weak airport security, and rampant corruption remained deterrents to more effective counterterrorism policing. The United States sponsored or hosted capacity-building programs for Nepali security forces, including 14 training courses to Nepali law enforcement, through the Department of State's Antiterrorism Assistance program.

Countering Terrorist Finance: Nepal is a member of the Asia/Pacific Group (APG) on Money Laundering, a Financial Action Task Force (FATF)-style regional body. Nepal has taken a number of steps toward compliance with the requirements of APG. In June, the government passed ordinances on Mutual Legal Assistance and Extradition, as required by the FATF, but did not pass legislation covering organized crime. The FATF has also recommended that Nepal amend its Anti-Money Laundering Act, and a draft was reportedly being finalized at year's end. A group of government finance experts has been working to finish draft legislation that would replace the 2008 Assets Laundering Protection Act. Nepal did not prosecute any terrorist financing cases in 2012.

The Government of Nepal implemented UNSCRs 1267/1989, 1988, and 1373 through Nepal Rastra Bank (NRB)-issued directives to the banking and financial sector. The NRB licenses and monitors money and business services that receive remittances. The Financial Regulation Control Act allows only banks and financial institutions (BFI) registered with the NRB to engage in receiving foreign currency transfers (and only banks are allowed to open letters of credit to remit currency overseas). Any transactions by unauthorized BFIs to transfer or receive money (such as *hundi* or *hawala*) are considered a criminal money laundering offense, but it is difficult for the government to investigate these informal money transfer systems.

Non-profit organizations are not covered by NRB Financial Information Unit directives, unless they are involved in money laundering or terrorist financing. The Government of Nepal approved a National Strategy and Action Plan for anti-money laundering/combating the financing of terrorism and was working on new laws and supervisory systems to cover non-profit organizations and other non-financial actors gradually. It may take two to three years before nonprofit organizations will be fully covered and monitored.

For further information on money laundering and financial crimes, we refer you to the *2013 International Narcotics Control Strategy Report (INCSR), Volume 2, Money Laundering and Financial Crimes*: http://www.state.gov/j/inl/rls/nrcrpt/index.htm.

PAKISTAN

Overview: In 2012, Pakistan remained an important partner in counterterrorism efforts against al-Qa'ida (AQ). Pakistan also undertook operations against terrorist groups that carried out attacks within Pakistan, such as the Tehrik-e Taliban Pakistan (TTP or Pakistani Taliban). Pakistan did not take significant action against some other violent extremist groups, including

Lashkar-e-Tayyiba (LeT), which continued to operate and raise funds openly in Pakistan through its political and charitable wing, Jamaat ud Dawa (JuD). The Afghan Taliban and Haqqani Network (HQN) continued to conduct operations against U.S. and Coalition Forces in Afghanistan from Pakistan. Pakistan took steps to support an Afghan peace process and publicly called on the Taliban to enter into talks with the Afghan government. Hundreds of terrorist attacks occurred nationwide against all sectors of society, including Pakistani military and security personnel.

Pakistani officials continued to make public statements against terrorism and violent extremism. The widely publicized shooting of a 14-year-old girl, Malala Yousufzai, by the TTP led to public calls for the government to do more against terrorist groups. In March, Pakistan's parliament affirmed its commitment to eliminating terrorism and countering violent extremism. The Government of Pakistan also moved forward several pieces of counterterrorism legislation.

Some banned organizations openly participated in political rallies and forged alliances with religious political parties. In September and October, militant groups and religious parties joined forces to protest and conduct public demonstrations nationwide over the video *The Innocence of Muslims*. Violence occurred during the early days of the protests. The government and security agencies undertook enhanced security measures during the protests and sought to convince the militant groups to participate peacefully.

Pakistan's Shia minority continued to be targeted in large-scale sectarian attacks, including in Karachi, Balochistan, and northwest Pakistan. Targeted killings of both Shia and Sunni activists occurred in Karachi. The TTP claimed credit for some sectarian attacks during the Shia holiday of Moharram, although increased levels of security prevented many TTP-planned suicide attacks on Shia processions and mosques, according to law enforcement reports. Despite the government's stringent security measures, including a ban on both cell phone usage and motorbikes, a series of four major bombings in Karachi, Dera Ismail Khan, and Rawalpindi marred the Moharram religious week.

2012 Terrorist Incidents: Over 2,000 Pakistani civilians and 680 security forces personnel were killed in terrorist-related incidents in 2012. Terrorist incidents occurred in every province. Terrorists attacked Pakistani military units, police stations, and border checkpoints, and conducted coordinated attacks against two major military installations. Terrorists displayed videos on the internet of the murders and beheadings of security forces. Terrorist groups also targeted police and security officials with suicide bombings and improvised explosive devices (IEDs). Terrorist groups targeted and assassinated tribal elders, members of peace committees, and anti-Taliban government officials. The TTP often claimed responsibility for attacks targeting civilians and security personnel in Pakistan.

Representative incidents included:

- On February 17, a suicide bomber killed 41 people in a bazaar near a Shia mosque in Parachinar, Kurram Agency. A splinter group of the TTP claimed responsibility for the blast.
- On February 23, a remote-controlled bomb inside a parked car exploded outside a bus station in Peshawar. The blast killed 13 people and injured 38.

- On April 24, a five-kilogram bomb in a bag exploded at the Lahore Railway Station. The blast killed three people and injured 58.
- On July 12, the TTP stormed a police training facility in Lahore and executed nine police cadets.
- On August 16, the TTP launched a coordinated assault with armed commandos and suicide bombers on the Kamra Air Force Base in Attock, Punjab. One security official was killed in the attack.
- On August 29, terrorists attacked a Pakistani military post near the Afghan border in South Waziristan and killed 12 soldiers. TTP uploaded video to the internet of some of the soldiers being beheaded.
- On September 3, a suicide bomber detonated an explosive-laden vehicle next to a Consulate General Peshawar motorcade near the entrance to the Consulate's University town housing area. The blast killed one bystander and injured at least 20 others. Two U.S. diplomatic personnel were injured along with three local staff members and two Pakistani Police officers.
- On November 21, a suicide bomber detonated his jacket near a Moharram religious procession in Rawalpindi. The blast killed 23 people and injured 62.
- On December 15, terrorists attacked Peshawar Airport, killing nine people and injuring 42.
- On December 22, at least nine people, including a provincial Minister, were killed and over 18 others were injured when a suicide bomber attacked a political gathering in Peshawar.
- On December 29, 22 Pakistani soldiers were killed by TTP elements outside Peshawar.

Legislation, Law Enforcement, and Border Security: In November, the Cabinet approved the National Counter Terrorism Authority Act of 2012, which was designed to strengthen counterterrorism coordination and information-sharing between security agencies and provincial police and provide a vehicle for national counterterrorism policy and strategy formulation. In December, Pakistan's National Assembly approved the Fair Trial Act, which was designed to provide the necessary legal tools to intelligence agencies, law enforcement agencies, and prosecutors to detect, disrupt, and dismantle terrorist activities and organizations. The law authorizes trial courts to use evidence obtained by electronic interception and surveillance.

Pakistani security forces conducted counterterrorism operations in Khyber Pakhtunkhwa province and throughout the Federally Administered Tribal Areas that resulted in the detention or arrest of thousands of militants. Security forces intercepted large stockpiles of weapons and explosives, and discovered bomb-making facilities.

Pakistan's Anti-Terrorism Courts have a high acquittal rate. Witnesses routinely recant their statements or fail to appear because of threats against them and their families. In June, an Anti-Terrorism Court acquitted four men accused of assisting Faisal Shahzad, the TTP-trained militant who attempted to explode a car bomb in New York City's Times Square in 2010, claiming a lack of evidence. The court would not accept evidence collected by electronic surveillance. The Fair Trial Act, approved by parliament in December, will allow evidence obtained by electronic interception and surveillance to be admitted as evidence in the courts system.

Pakistan did not conclude the trials of seven alleged perpetrators of the 2008 Mumbai attacks, although it continued to maintain a dialogue with India on steps both sides need to take to enable the prosecutions to move forward.

Information sharing and counterterrorism activities with Pakistan's security establishment continued. Pakistani law enforcement reinforced security at U.S. facilities in Pakistan during the protests over the *Innocence of Muslims* video in September 2012, and took steps to ensure the security of U.S. personnel. Long delays in visa processing for U.S. personnel impeded counterterrorism-related assistance and training for security forces and prosecutors.

Pakistan remained a partner nation in the Department of State's Antiterrorism Assistance program, which provided tactical and investigative training at the federal and provincial levels.

Countering Terrorist Finance: Pakistan is a member of the Asia/Pacific Group on Money Laundering, a Financial Action Task Force (FATF)-style regional body. The FATF named Pakistan on its public statement in February due to Pakistan's failure to address strategic deficiencies in its anti-money laundering/combating the financing of terrorism (AML/CFT) regime. The FATF recommended Pakistan enact legislation to strengthen authorities to prosecute terrorist financing as well as to identify, freeze, and confiscate terrorist assets. The Anti-Terrorism (Amendment) Act of 2012 introduced in Parliament in December includes several of the recommended changes but still failed to bring Pakistan into compliance with international AML/CFT standards.

In April, the Federal Board of Revenue (FBR), Pakistan's customs and tax authority, established Currency Detection Units in Pakistan's 12 international airports to counter bulk cash smuggling. The FBR also instituted improved information-sharing protocols on counterterrorism-related arrests and seizures.

UN-designated terrorist organizations continued to avoid sanctions by reconstituting themselves under different names, often with little effort to hide their connections to previously banned groups. Although Pakistan added some named groups to its proscribed organizations list, Pakistan needs to take additional steps to implement and enforce UNSCRs 1267/1989, 1988, and 1373. For further information on money laundering and financial crimes, we refer you to the *2013 International Narcotics Control Strategy Report (INCSR), Volume 2, Money Laundering and Financial Crimes*: http://www.state.gov/j/inl/rls/nrcrpt/index.htm.

Regional and International Cooperation: Pakistan actively participated in regional and international counterterrorism efforts, including the Global Counterterrorism Forum and the Global Initiative to Combat Nuclear Terrorism. Pakistan commanded Combined Task Force 151, an international naval task force set up to conduct counter-piracy operations in the Gulf of Aden. Pakistan was a partner in the UK's Counterterrorism Prosecution Reform Initiative and the UN Development Program, which worked with provincial governments on rule of law programs in Punjab and Malakand. Pakistan participated in South Asian Association for Regional Cooperation meetings on counterterrorism and participated in multilateral groups where counterterrorism cooperation was discussed, including the Shanghai Cooperation Organization (as an observer) and the D-8, a group of developing nations with large Muslim populations. In October, Pakistan's Interior Minister participated in a Law Enforcement and Counterterrorism working group in Washington, DC.

Countering Radicalization and Violent Extremism: Pakistan's military worked with civil society leaders to operate the Sabaoon Rehabilitation Center, a de-radicalization program in Mingora, Swat where radicalized youth are rehabilitated through education and counseling.

SRI LANKA

Overview: In 2009, the Government of Sri Lanka militarily defeated the Liberation Tigers of Tamil Eelam (LTTE), which was seeking an independent homeland for Sri Lanka's Tamil population. The Sri Lankan government's comprehensive and aggressive counterterrorism stance is a direct result of its experience in this nearly three decades-long conflict. Counterterrorism cooperation and training with the United States in 2012 was limited, however, due to statutory and policy restrictions based on concerns about alleged past human rights abuses committed by Sri Lankan security forces.

The Sri Lankan government claimed that it continued to uncover abandoned weapons and explosives in areas of the country formerly controlled by the LTTE. Although there were no known LTTE activities in Sri Lanka in 2012, the government asserted that peaceful protests at Jaffna University in November were organized by students trained by overseas LTTE supporters and made several arrests.

The Government of Sri Lanka remained concerned that the LTTE's international network of financial support was still functioning; many counterterrorism activities undertaken by the government targeted alleged LTTE finances. Also, the Sri Lankan government maintained a strong military presence in post-conflict areas and voiced concern about the possible re-emergence of pro-LTTE sympathizers.

Legislation, Law Enforcement, and Border Security: Counterterrorism legislation in Sri Lanka has focused on eliminating the remnants of the LTTE and enforcing general security throughout the island. The Sri Lankan government continued to implement the Prevention of Terrorism Act of 1978, which was made a permanent law in 1982 and remains in force.

The Sri Lankan government is a proactive partner with the U.S. Departments of State, Homeland Security, Defense, and Energy on securing its maritime border. In October, the U.S. Coast Guard, under the Department of State's Export Control and Related Border Security program, trained Sri Lankan Coast Guard and Navy personnel on border and export control matters. The Sri Lankan government also cooperated with U.S. Customs and Border Protection through the Container Security Initiative. Further, in 2012, the International Organization for Migration (IOM) trained over 50 immigration officers in techniques to improve border surveillance and combat human trafficking. IOM, in conjunction with the Australian government, provided specialized training to 16 Sri Lankan immigration personnel to reinforce intelligence and data collection efforts to secure the border. A specific Sri Lankan immigration border intelligence unit was established and used improved database processing to target forgeries and the use of counterfeit documents.

Countering Terrorist Finance: Sri Lanka is a member of the Asia/Pacific Group on Money Laundering, a Financial Action Task Force (FATF)-style regional body. Although the LTTE has been militarily defeated, the Government of Sri Lanka asserted that sympathizers and organizational remnants have continued to raise funds in many countries. Sri Lanka was blacklisted by the FATF in June 2011 for significant anti-money laundering/combating the financing of terrorism (AML/CFT) deficiencies. Since then, Sri Lanka has made significant progress in addressing the FATF action plan by passing AML/CFT legislation. Based on largely completing its FATF action plan, Sri Lanka will be considered by the FATF for removal from the blacklist in June 2013, pending successful completion of the on-site visit.

In the past, the LTTE has used a number of non-profit organizations for fundraising purposes, including the Tamil Rehabilitation Organization. The Sri Lankan government continued to actively search for other financial links to the LTTE.

For further information on money laundering and financial crimes, we refer you to the *2013 International Narcotics Control Strategy Report (INCSR), Volume 2, Money Laundering and Financial Crimes*: http://www.state.gov/j/inl/rls/nrcrpt/index.htm.

Regional and International Cooperation: The Sri Lankan government remained committed to the counterterrorism efforts of multilateral institutions, such as the UN. In December, the Sri Lankan government held the 2012 Galle Dialogue, which featured multilateral discussion by international security force representatives on issues of regional security in South Asia, including successful actions against terrorists within the last 10 years.

TAJIKISTAN

Overview: In 2012, Tajikistan continued to correct weaknesses in its counterterrorism strategy and demonstrated its ability to conduct counterterrorism operations. Tajikistan's counterterrorism policies were focused on marginalizing radical Islamic groups in Tajik society, but in some cases targeted non-extremist Islamic groups. These policies also sought to increase the capacity of Tajikistan's military and law enforcement community to conduct tactical operations through bilateral and multilateral assistance programs.

Legislation, Law Enforcement, and Border Security: There have been successful prosecutions of terrorists under the Law on Combating Terrorism. However, a corrupt judicial system and misuse of counterterrorism statutes to suppress legitimate political opposition hampered the effectiveness of the government's counterterrorism efforts.

On June 20, the Parliament of Tajikistan adopted amendments to the "Law on the Fight Against Terrorism" that were then signed by President Emomali Rahmon. The amendments clarify the process by which terrorist lists are compiled and that provide new powers of asset seizure. In 2012, 14 groups were labeled as terrorist organizations by Tajik authorities.

Resource constraints, corruption, lack of training for effective law enforcement and border security officials and general capacity issues continued to plague the Tajik government's ability to interdict possible terrorists. Despite these deficiencies, the Tajik government sought to address terrorism and possible terrorist threats to the extent of its capabilities.

Tajikistan has made progress in improving border security with bilateral and multilateral assistance, though effectively policing the Tajik/Afghan border is a monumental task requiring more resources and capabilities than the Tajik government has. The International Organization on Migration and the OSCE worked to improve travel document security. The OSCE has funding to link Tajikistan's existing passport data scanners at airports and land ports of entry to the Interpol database.

Tajikistan is an active participant in the Department of State's Antiterrorism Assistance program, U.S. military training programs, and other U.S.-sponsored counterterrorism training programs. The State Committee on National Security (GKNB) cooperated with the United States and international organizations to reduce Tajikistan's vulnerability to terrorist threats.

The Ministry of Interior's elite Militia Detachment for Special Purposes, the Dushanbe City Police Department, the GKNB Embassy Protection Service, the Committee of Emergency Situations and Civil Defense, and the U.S. Embassy participated in several drills that simulated a terrorist attack against the U.S. Embassy.

Countering Terrorist Finance: Tajikistan is a member of the Eurasian Group on Combating Money Laundering and Financing of Terrorism (EAG), a Financial Action Task Force (FATF)-style regional body. Through the EAG, Tajikistan received assistance and other resources towards improving legislative and regulatory frameworks and operational capabilities.

Terrorist financing and money laundering were illegal, but existing laws are not comprehensive and do not meet international standards. Despite pressure from the international community, and the Government of Tajikistan's efforts to improve its anti-money laundering/combating the financing of terrorism regime, through the implementation of its FATF "Action Plan" and new legislation – such as the law "On Counteraction Against Legalization (Laundering) of Incomes Received In a Criminal Way and Combating Terrorism Financing" – severe deficiencies remained. Tajikistan's inadequate criminalization of terrorist financing and money laundering and its inability to effectively identify and investigate suspicious transactions was of particular concern. Deficiencies included: inadequate criminalization of money laundering, inadequate procedures for confiscation of criminal proceeds, lack of requirements for comprehensive customer due diligence, lack of adequate record keeping, and the lack of an effective Financial Intelligence Unit. Endemic corruption also prevented significant reform in this area.

For further information on money laundering and financial crimes, we refer you to the *2013 International Narcotics Control Strategy Report (INCSR), Volume 2, Money Laundering and Financial Crimes*: http://www.state.gov/j/inl/rls/nrcrpt/index.htm.

Regional and International Cooperation: Tajikistan is an active member of the OSCE, working with that organization primarily on border security, and is a member of the Collective Security Treaty Organization. The EU provided funding for border security programs in Tajikistan. In September, Tajikistan participated in regional counterterrorism exercises with Shanghai Cooperation Organization partner nations.

Countering Radicalization and Violent Extremism: Stemming violent extremism and radicalization in Tajikistan is a top priority for the Tajik government. Many of the government's measures, however, had an impact on basic religious freedoms, including banning women from attending mosque and wearing the hijab in school, and prohibiting children under 18 from attending mosque or other public religious services. We refer you to the Department of State's

Annual Report to Congress on International Religious Freedom
(http://www.state.gov/j/drl/irf/rpt/index.htm) for further information.

Tajikistan has no programs for the rehabilitation or reintegration into society of terrorists. Leaders of Tajikistan's officially sanctioned religious establishment claimed there was no radicalization threat in its prison system.

TURKMENISTAN

Overview: The Government of Turkmenistan continued its efforts to improve the capacity of law enforcement agencies to counter terrorism, ensure border security, and detect terrorist financing. The Financial Action Task Force (FATF) released Turkmenistan from its global anti-money laundering/combating the financing of terrorism (AML/CFT) compliance monitoring process in recognition of its significant progress in this area.

Legislation, Law Enforcement, and Border Security: There was significant political will in Turkmenistan to counter terrorism and ensure border security. Petty corruption, however, sometimes hampered effective law enforcement. State Border Service officers demonstrated significantly improved professionalism in 2012, and the Government of Turkmenistan opened several new frontier garrisons on its borders with Iran and Afghanistan. Turkmenistan participated in the State Department's Antiterrorism Assistance program.

Countering Terrorist Finance: Turkmenistan is a member of the Eurasian Group on Combating Money Laundering and Financing of Terrorism, a FATF-style regional body. The Ministry of Finance continued to work with advisors from the U.S. Treasury Department's Office of Technical Assistance (OTA), under a bilateral agreement signed in December 2011. As part of this initiative, OTA trained Ministry of Finance officials in financial analytical techniques, customs and financial investigative techniques, detecting and investigating financial crimes, money laundering, and combating terrorist financing. The Ministry's Financial Monitoring Department improved cross-border reporting of currency and monetary instruments and brought cash reporting requirements in-line with FATF recommendations. Turkmenistan continued to express interest in gaining admission to the Egmont Group of Financial Intelligence Units. There were no reported prosecutions of terrorist financing cases during the year. For further information on money laundering and financial crimes, we refer you to the *2013 International Narcotics Control Strategy Report (INCSR), Volume 2, Money Laundering and Financial Crimes*: http://www.state.gov/j/inl/rls/nrcrpt/index.htm.

Regional and International Cooperation: In June, the Government of Turkmenistan participated in consultations with other Central Asian governments to implement the UN Counterterrorism Strategy for Central Asia. The consultations were organized by the UN Regional Center for Preventative Diplomacy in Central Asia.

Turkmenistan signed agreements with the Commonwealth of Independent States, Turkey, and Tajikistan to coordinate counterterrorism activities and counter terrorist financing. Government officials participated in OSCE-sponsored training on border security, anti-money laundering/combating the financing of terrorism, and protecting human rights while countering terrorism.

Countering Radicalization and Violent Extremism: Turkmenistan's law enforcement and security agencies exercised stringent control over the population. The Government of Turkmenistan reportedly views conservative Islam with suspicion. Since the country's independence, mosques and Muslim clergy have been state-sponsored and financed. We refer you to the Department of State's *Annual Report to Congress on International Religious Freedom* (http://www.state.gov/j/drl/irf/rpt/index.htm) for further information.

UZBEKISTAN

Overview: The Government of Uzbekistan continued to rank counterterrorism within its borders as one of its top three security priorities, together with counternarcotics and countering violent extremism. The Government of Uzbekistan shares many U.S. counterterrorism goals and objectives in the region, but has employed methods that are in some cases inconsistent with respect for the fundamental rights of citizens and the rule of law.

Sharing a land border with Afghanistan, the Uzbek government continued to express concern about the potential for a "spillover effect" of terrorism, with the scheduled drawdown of U.S. troops by the end of 2014. The government was confident that it could control its border with Afghanistan but was less sure about its neighbors' ability to do so and was particularly concerned about infiltration of extremists through Uzbekistan's long, rugged border with Tajikistan.

Legislation, Law Enforcement, and Border Security: Law enforcement and judicial bodies used charges of terrorism and alleged ties to extremist organizations not only as grounds to arrest, prosecute, and convict suspected terrorists and extremists, but also to suppress legitimate expression of political or religious beliefs. The government perceives extremism as a threat to security and stability and bans organizations it broadly deems "extremist" and criminalizes membership in them. Nur, founded by Kurdish Mullah Said Nursi and associated with the religious teachings of Turkish scholar Fethullah Gullen, for example, is considered a banned organization, despite its consistent condemnations of violent extremism. The Initiative Group of Independent Human Rights Defenders of Uzbekistan estimated that more than 250 Muslim believers were imprisoned during the year on charges of religious extremism.

The government continued to issue biometric passports to citizens needing them for travel outside of Uzbekistan. The biometric data includes a digital photo, fingerprints, and biographical data.

Countering Terrorist Finance: Uzbekistan is a member of the Eurasian Group on Combating Money Laundering and Financing of Terrorism, a Financial Action Task Force-style regional body. The Government of Uzbekistan did not report any efforts to seize terrorist assets in 2012. However, in one case, the government froze the account of a citizen of Uzbekistan in connection with a joint Russian/Uzbek terrorism-related investigation. For further information on money laundering and financial crimes, we refer you to the *2013 International Narcotics Control Strategy Report (INCSR), Volume 2, Money Laundering and Financial Crimes*: http://www.state.gov/j/inl/rls/nrcrpt/index.htm.

Regional and International Cooperation: Although the Uzbek government preferred bilateral engagement in its security-related cooperation, it is a member of several regional organizations that address terrorism, including the Shanghai Cooperation Organization (SCO), with the Regional Anti-Terrorism Structure (RATS) of the SCO headquartered in Tashkent. Uzbekistan continued to work with several multilateral organizations such as the OSCE, the EU, and the UN Office on Drugs and Crime on general security issues, including border control. However, in 2012 Uzbekistan suspended its membership in the Collective Security Treaty Organization.

In December, at the Commonwealth of Independent States (CIS) Summit held in Ashgabat, Turkmenistan, CIS members, including Uzbekistan, signed an agreement on counterterrorism training cooperation.

Countering Radicalization and Violent Extremism: Official government media continued to produce documentaries, news articles, and full-length books about the dangers of Islamist religious extremism and terrorist organizations. This messaging generally targeted the 15-40 year old male population, which the Government of Uzbekistan considers the most susceptible to recruitment by violent extremist groups, although some campaigns have focused on female audiences. One of Uzbekistan's state-run television channels aired a program that urged citizens to read only state-authorized religious books, noting that there are two government authorized publishers of religious literature in Uzbekistan. The program highlighted inspections by law enforcement agencies of bookshops, publishing houses, and border checkpoints to stop the circulation of unauthorized so-called "extremist" literature. Some non-governmental religious experts continued to suggest that greater freedom to circulate mainstream, non-extremist Islamic and other religious materials could be more effective in countering violent extremism than the current policy of maintaining a government monopoly over religious publications. We refer you to the Department of State's *Annual Report to Congress on International Religious Freedom* (http://www.state.gov/j/drl/irf/rpt/index.htm) for further information.

WESTERN HEMISPHERE

Governments in the Western Hemisphere took modest steps to improve their counterterrorism capabilities and tighten border security. The primary impediments to effective action in some countries included corruption, weak governmental institutions, insufficient interagency cooperation, weak or non-existent legislation, and a lack of resources. Most countries made efforts to investigate possible connections between transnational criminal organizations and terrorist organizations.

Iran continued to try to expand its presence and bilateral relationships within the Western Hemisphere. Iranian President Ahmadinejad visited Cuba, Ecuador, Nicaragua, and Venezuela in 2012. The United States continued to monitor such initiatives.

The United States collaborated with both Canada and Mexico to protect our shared borders through regular exchanges of intelligence and other information.

In 2012, the majority of terrorist attacks within the Western Hemisphere were committed by the Revolutionary Armed Forces of Colombia. The threat of a transnational terrorist attack remained low for most countries in the Western Hemisphere.

There were no known operational cells of either al-Qa'ida or Hizballah in the hemisphere, although ideological sympathizers in South America and the Caribbean continued to provide financial and ideological support to those and other terrorist groups in the Middle East and South Asia. The Tri-Border area of Argentina, Brazil, and Paraguay continued to be an important regional nexus of arms, narcotics, and human smuggling, counterfeiting, pirated goods, and money laundering – all potential funding sources for terrorist organizations.

ARGENTINA

Overview: Argentina continued to focus on the challenges of policing its remote northern and northeastern borders – including the Tri-Border Area (TBA), where Argentina, Brazil, and Paraguay meet – against such threats as illicit drug and human trafficking, contraband smuggling, and other forms of transnational crime. Law enforcement and security cooperation with Argentina was significantly curtailed in February 2011 after Argentine authorities seized sensitive U.S. equipment intended to support an approved bilateral training exercise with the Argentine Federal Police's counterterrorism unit. Bilateral cooperation now continues at the operational level but is more modest than in the past, and is focused primarily on information sharing, training, and other forms of bilateral law enforcement cooperation.

2012 Terrorist Incidents: On May 23, a homemade explosive device was found in the ceiling of the Rex Theater in Buenos Aires. An investigation revealed that the device was set to go off that day during an event that former Colombian president Alvaro Uribe was scheduled to attend. The investigation has produced neither leads nor arrests.

On December 30, a homemade explosive device was detonated in front of the Department of Corrections Headquarters in Buenos Aires. There were no injuries and only minor damage to the headquarters; no one claimed responsibility.

Legislation, Law Enforcement, and Border Security: The Argentine government implemented an identification security system (similar to the Automated Fingerprint Identification System, or AFIS) that uses a fingerprint database created via the implementation of a new national identity card (DNI). The Argentine government is now able to compare the fingerprints of DNI applicants with those existing in the Federal Police, Gendarmeria, Coast Guard, and Airport Security Police databases. The new system will also allow Argentine provinces to compare the DNI fingerprint data base with unidentified prints that were taken at provincial crime scenes, thus facilitating the identification of criminals. This AFIS-type system was deployed at all Argentine international airports, along with a program that requires the taking of photos and fingerprints of all travelers upon arrival and departure. The Ministry of Interior started issuing new e-passports in June that include a new passport book numbering system that facilitates the reporting of lost and stolen passports to Interpol.

The Argentine government continued its efforts to bring to justice those suspected in the July 18, 1994 terrorist bombing of the Argentine-Jewish Mutual Association (AMIA) community center in Buenos Aires that killed 85 and injured more than 150 people. In a marked policy shift, President Cristina Fernandez de Kirchner announced at the September 2011 UN General Assembly that Argentina had accepted Iran's offer to have the two nations' foreign ministers meet to explore ways to move forward on a case for which several senior Iranian officials, including Iran's current Defense Minister, have outstanding Interpol arrest warrants. Foreign Minister Hector Timerman met with his Iranian counterpart and agreed to launch a dialogue designed to clarify Iran's alleged role in the bombing. Two subsequent rounds of negotiations took place in Switzerland. Argentine Jewish community and other opinion leaders publicly opposed the bilateral dialogue, especially in light of Argentina's continuing judicial investigation, and criticized the government for failing to share information about the talks.

On December 10, security forces arrested Peruvian national Rolando Echarri Pareja, a member of the Movement for Amnesty and Fundamental Rights, an organization with strong links to the Shining Path, a designated Foreign Terrorist Organization based in Peru. Echarri was reportedly subject to an Interpol Red Notice for terrorism-related charges in Peru.

Countering Terrorist Finance: Argentina is a member of the Financial Action Task Force (FATF) and the Financial Action Task Force on Money Laundering in South America, a FATF-style regional body. A new law passed in 2011 broadened the definition of terrorism and increased monetary fines and prison sentences for crimes linked to terrorist financing. It closed several loopholes in previous legislation and empowered the Argentine Financial Intelligence Unit to freeze assets, and criminalized the financing of terrorist organizations, individuals, and acts. To date this law has been applied only to human rights cases dating back to Argentina's military dictatorship of thirty-plus years ago.

UNSCRs 1267 and 1373 have not been used to prosecute terrorist finance cases. For further information on money laundering and financial crimes, we refer you to the *2013 International Narcotics Control Strategy Report (INCSR), Volume 2, Money Laundering and Financial Crimes*: http://www.state.gov/j/inl/rls/nrcrpt/index.htm.

Regional and International Cooperation: Argentina participated in meetings of the OAS Inter-American Committee Against Terrorism and the Southern Common Market Special Forum on Terrorism. Argentina, Brazil, and Paraguay coordinated law enforcement efforts in the Tri-Border Area via their "Trilateral Tri-Border Area Command."

BRAZIL

Overview: The Brazilian government continued to support counterterrorism-related activities, including investigating potential terrorist financing and document forgery networks. Operationally, security forces of the Brazilian government worked with U.S. law enforcement and financial agencies regarding terrorist suspects. Brazil's security services have sought to address concerns that terrorists could exploit Brazilian territory to support and facilitate terrorist attacks, whether domestically or abroad, focusing their efforts in the areas of Sao Paulo; the tri-border areas (TBAs) of Brazil, Argentina, and Paraguay; Brazil, Peru, and Colombia; and the Colombian and Venezuelan borders. In preparation for hosting the 2014 World Cup and 2016 Olympic Games, the Government of Brazil created the Special Secretariat for Security for Great Events.

Legislation, Law Enforcement, and Border Security: In 2012, the Chamber of Deputies considered two counterterrorism bills pending in committee; one would deny visas to persons convicted or accused of a terrorist act in another country, and the other would provide the ability to prevent, investigate, and prosecute terrorist organizations. Since 2009, Brazilian authorities have worked with other concerned nations, particularly the United States, in combating document fraud. Since 2009, multiple regional and international joint operations with U.S. authorities successfully disrupted a number of document vendors and facilitators.

The work of the U.S.-Brazil Container Security Initiative (CSI) in Santos continued throughout 2012, as it has since its inception in 2005. The CSI was created to promote secure containerized cargo to the United States by co-locating CBP personnel overseas to work with a foreign customs administration to detect high risk cargo.

The Brazilian government continued to invest in border and law enforcement infrastructure and has worked to undertake new initiatives to control the flow of goods – legal and illegal – through the TBA of Brazil, Argentina, and Paraguay.

In light of Brazil's plans to host the upcoming 2014 World Cup and the 2016 Olympic Games, a key focus for the Department of State's 2012 Antiterrorism Assistance program in Brazil was major event security management. Additional strategic objectives for the program were to help Brazil build law enforcement capacity to secure land, air, and maritime borders, and to conduct terrorism-related investigations.

Countering Terrorist Finance: Brazil is a member of the Financial Action Task Force (FATF) and is also a member of the Grupo de Acción Financiera de Sudamérica (FSRB), a FATF-style regional body. Brazil gives FATF recommendations high priority and has created a working group chaired by the Ministry of Justice to incorporate these recommendations into legislation and regulation. Brazil sought to play an active leadership role in the FSRB and has offered technical assistance to Argentina to implement FATF recommendations.

Brazil monitored domestic financial operations and effectively used its Financial Intelligence Unit, the COAF, to identify possible funding sources for terrorist groups. Terrorist financing is not an autonomous offense in Brazil, but it is a predicate offense to money laundering. COAF does not have the authority to unilaterally freeze assets without a court order. The FATF has recommended that COAF create a standard operating procedure for freezing funds, which COAF has prioritized but not yet completed.

Through COAF, which is a largely independent entity within the Finance Ministry (Fazenda), Brazil has carried out name checks for persons and entities on the UNSC 1267/1989 and 1988 Sanctions Committees' consolidated lists, but it has so far not reported any assets, accounts, or property in the names of persons or entities on the UN lists. The Brazilian government has generally responded to U.S. efforts to identify and block terrorist-related funds. For further information on money laundering and financial crimes, we refer you to the *2013 International Narcotics Control Strategy Report (INCSR), Volume 2, Money Laundering and Financial Crimes*: http://www.state.gov/j/inl/rls/nrcrpt/index.htm.

Regional and International Cooperation: Brazil's intelligence and law enforcement forces work with regional and international partners. Brazil participates in regional counterterrorism fora such as the OAS Inter-American Committee Against Terrorism. Brazil is involved in the Union of South American Nations and Mercosur's working group on terrorism and the sub-working group on financial issues, the latter of which discusses terrorist financing and money laundering among the Mercosur countries.

CANADA

Overview: Canada is an indispensable counterterrorism partner. Canada and the United States cooperated bilaterally through the Cross Border Crime Forum sub-group on counterterrorism and the Bilateral Consultative Group on Counterterrorism. In addition to close bilateral cooperation, as embodied in the Beyond the Border Agreement and numerous cooperative law enforcement and homeland security programs, the U.S. and Canada work together in crucial multilateral settings such as the Global Counterterrorism Forum (GCTF). Canadian diplomats played a key role in international efforts to counter terrorist threats, and the Government of Canada consistently worked to strengthen the rule of law in other countries. Canadian contributions to the Australia Group and the Missile Technology Control Regime help to prevent terrorist organizations from gaining access to weapons of mass destruction.

Legislation, Law Enforcement, and Border Security: In February 2012, Canada's Ministry of Public Safety announced Canada's first official Counterterrorism Strategy. The Strategy includes a terrorism threat analysis and a summary of federal priorities and actions to combat domestic and international terrorism. The Canadian government passed two counterterrorism-related bills in 2012 and introduced three others that were under consideration at year's end. The *Safe Streets and Communities Act*, C-10, received Royal Assent on March 13. The Act rolled together nine draft crime and national security bills from the 40th Parliament into one omnibus crime bill. It included the former S-7, *An Act to Deter Terrorism and Amend the State Immunity,* to allow terrorism victims to sue terrorists and terrorist entities (and in some cases foreign states that have supported terrorist entities) for loss or damage suffered as a result of their acts. These provisions entered into force on receipt of Royal Assent.

On June 29, legislation implementing the Framework Agreement on Integrated Cross-Border Maritime Law Enforcement Operations [Ship Rider] between Canada and the United States received Royal Assent, enabling this bilateral agreement to enter into force in October 2012. The legislation was included in budget legislation, Bill C-38.

Law enforcement actions:

- On April 25, the Federal Court of Appeal ordered a new hearing of the reasonableness of an immigration security certificate against Ottawa resident Mohamed Harkat which the Federal Court had upheld in 2010 on the basis that Harkat constituted a threat to national security. Authorities alleged that Harkat was an al-Qa'ida sleeper agent. The Appeal Court ruled that the withholding of sensitive information against Harkat violated his right to a fair defense, ordered the exclusion of the evidence to which he was not privy, and referred his case back to the Federal Court for reassessment. The appeal stayed a deportation order against Harkat. On November 22, the Supreme Court granted leave to appeal the Federal Court ruling and the constitutionality of the security certificate process. At year's end, the Supreme Court had not set a date for the hearing.
- On December 14, the Supreme Court dismissed an appeal by former Ottawa resident Momin Khawaja of his terrorist conviction under the anti-terrorism law and his challenge to the constitutionality of the legislation. Khawaja was convicted in 2008 and sentenced to 15 years for financing and facilitating a British bomb plot minus credit for time served, for an effective sentence of 10.5 years. The Ontario Court of Appeal increased this sentence to life in prison in 2010 with no eligibility for parole for 10 years. The Supreme Court upheld Khawaja's life sentence as appropriate to the gravity of his offense.

- Also on December 14, the Supreme Court unanimously dismissed an appeal of an extradition order to the United States of Piratheepan Nadarajah and Suresh Sriskandarajah, to stand trial on charges of attempting to purchase surface-to-air missiles and other weaponry in the United States for the Liberation Tigers of Tamil Eelam. The court ordered the men surrendered to U.S. authorities. Delivered in conjunction with the ruling in the Khawaja case, the court rejected the appellants' arguments that the definition of terrorist activity in the 2001 Anti-terrorism Act was overly broad.

- As of December 2012, three men arrested and charged in August 2010 in an alleged conspiracy to bomb targets in Ottawa, and participate in and facilitate terrorist activity continued to await trial. In 2011 authorities released Misbahuddin Ahmed and Khurram Sher on bail. The third member of the group, Hiva Alizadeh, remained in custody.

- During the year, two other Federal Court reviews continued to determine the reasonableness of security certificates against alleged terrorist suspects Mahmoud Jaballah and Mohamed Zeki Mahjoub.

Cooperation sought during the previous five years in the investigation or prosecution of an act of international terrorism against U.S. citizens or interests included:

- In January 2011, Canadian authorities arrested Canadian-Iraqi citizen Faruq Khalil Muhammad in response to U.S. charges that he helped coordinate Tunisian violent extremists believed responsible for separate suicide attacks in Iraq in 2009 that killed five American soldiers outside a U.S. base and seven people at an Iraqi police complex. The Alberta provincial court ruled in October 2012 there was sufficient evidence to extradite Faruq to the United States; Faruq continued to appeal his extradition.

Authorities use biometric systems at Canadian ports of entry. Canada plans to introduce e-passports containing electronic chips with biometric information and radio frequency identification technology used to authenticate the identity of travelers. Canada has required fingerprints from refugee claimants, detainees, and individuals ordered to be deported from Canada since 1993. The Canada Border Services Agency has been collecting fingerprints from detainees and people under removal order from Canada from the same year. On December 13, 2012, the Canada-U.S. Visa and Immigration Information Sharing Agreement was signed. Once it enters into force after Canadian ratification, and implementing arrangements have been concluded, it is expected that both countries will share biographic and biometric information to assist in decision making in cases where third-country nationals are applying for visas, admission, asylum, or other immigration benefits and in immigration enforcement proceedings. Canada continued to exchange a limited number of fingerprint records with the United States in an effort to counter fraud and reduce the abuse of respective immigration programs as part of the High Value Data Sharing Protocol signed in 2009 with the United States, the UK, Australia, and New Zealand. Canada also works with international partner countries through the Five Country Conference forum on biometric information sharing.

Countering Terrorist Finance: Canada is a member of the Financial Action Task Force, the Egmont Group, the Asia/Pacific Group on Money Laundering, and is a supporting nation of the Caribbean Financial Action Task Force. Canada is also an observer in the Council of Europe's Select Committee of Experts on the Evaluation of Anti-Money Laundering Measures and the Financial Action Task Force of South America against Money Laundering.

Canada has a rigorous detection and monitoring process in place to identify money laundering and terrorist financing activities. The Financial Transactions and Reports Analysis Centre of Canada (FINTRAC) is Canada's Financial Intelligence Unit (FIU) and is responsible for detecting, preventing and deterring money laundering and financing of terrorist activities. Established in 2000, FINTRAC is an independent agency reporting to the Minister of Finance. It was established by and operates within the parameters of the *Proceeds of Crime (Money Laundering) and Terrorist Financing Act (PCMLTFA)*. According to its 2011-2012 Annual Report, FINTRAC continued to aggressively investigate instances of potential money laundering and terrorist finance activities.

FINTRAC signed seven new bilateral agreements in 2011-2012 with foreign FIUs and now cooperates with 80 FIU's globally. These bilateral agreements allow for the exchange of information related to money laundering and terrorist financing. During 2012 FINTRAC prepared three Trends and Typologies reports which provided insight into the latest money laundering and terrorist financing patterns. These reports used sophisticated text mining techniques to analyze the content of suspicious transaction reports allowing for more effective detection of the latest trends in suspicious transactions.

For further information on money laundering and financial crimes, we refer you to the *2013 International Narcotics Control Strategy Report (INCSR), Volume 2, Money Laundering and Financial Crimes*: http://www.state.gov/j/inl/rls/nrcrpt/index.htm.

Regional and International Cooperation: Canada prioritizes collaboration with international partners to counter terrorism and international crime and regularly seeks opportunities to lead. Canada is a founding member of the GCTF and was also active in fora dealing with counterterrorism, including the OSCE, UN, G-8, APEC, ASEAN and the ASEAN Regional Forum, Commonwealth, International Civil Aviation Organization, International Maritime Organization, and the OAS. Canada co-sponsored the ASEAN Intersessional Meeting on Counterterrorism and Transnational Crime in 2012 and co-chaired the GCTF's Sahel Regional Capacity Building Group.

Canada's Department of Foreign Affairs and International Trade created the Counterterrorism Capacity Building Program in 2005 as a key part of Canada's international terrorism prevention efforts. The Program provided training, funding, equipment, and technical and legal assistance to states to enable them to prevent and respond to terrorist activity in seven areas: border security; transportation security; legislative, regulatory and legal policy development, legislative drafting, and human rights and counterterrorism training; law enforcement, security, military and intelligence training; chemical/biological/radiological/nuclear and explosives terrorism prevention, mitigation, preparedness, response and recovery; combating the financing of terrorism; and cyber security and protecting critical infrastructure.

Countering Radicalization and Violent Extremism: The Royal Canadian Mounted Police's National Security Community Outreach program promoted interaction and relationship-building with at-risk communities. The Department of Public Safety's Cross-Cultural Roundtable on Security fostered dialogue on national security issues between the government and community leaders. Both of these initiatives are encapsulated in Canada's aforementioned 2012 Counterterrorism Strategy, which seeks specifically to reduce the risk of individuals succumbing to violent extremism and radicalization, challenge violent extremist ideology by producing effective counter-narratives, and increase the resilience of communities to violent extremism. The government continued to work with non-governmental partners and concerned communities to deter violent extremism through preventative programming and community outreach.

COLOMBIA

Overview: Despite significant successes in its campaign against the Revolutionary Armed Forces of Colombia (FARC) and the beginning of peace talks, Colombia experienced a year of increased terrorist activity in 2012. As was the case in 2011, the number of total terrorist incidents, casualties caused by acts of terrorism, and economic losses due to terrorism increased in 2012, albeit with a significant drop in attacks during the second half of the year. Unlike 2011, however, the number of members of the FARC and National Liberation Army (ELN) killed or captured in combat went up by 11 percent and 53 percent, respectively. The implementation of a new counterinsurgency plan in June and the announcement in September of peace talks between the government and the FARC, along with a FARC temporary unilateral ceasefire, may have contributed to this increase.

2012 Terrorist Incidents: Until the declaration of a unilateral cease-fire by the FARC in November, terrorist attacks were an almost daily occurrence in Colombia. The FARC's declaration of a unilateral ceasefire for the period November 20 to January 20 did not completely stop FARC attacks, and had no impact on the activities of the ELN. The most common forms of terrorist activity were the launching of mortars at police stations or the military, explosive devices placed near roads or paths, sniper attacks, and ambushes. There was an increase in infrastructure attacks, particularly on oil and gas pipelines and equipment, by both the FARC and the ELN. Security forces and government buildings were the most common targets, though civilian casualties occurred throughout the year. Attacks were most common along the Venezuelan border in the departments of Arauca and Norte de Santander, in the southwest region of the country in the departments of Narino and Cauca, and in the northwestern department of Antioquia.

As of October 31, Colombian government statistics showed a 52 percent increase in attacks over 2011, with 716 terrorist attacks around the country compared to 472 attacks over the same period in the previous year. There was a 173 percent increase in the number of attacks on oil pipelines. Among the over 700 terrorist attacks recorded in the first 10 months of the year, several were notable for their severity or significant press coverage:

- A January 20 attack by an estimated 100 FARC guerrillas against a radar station outside the village of El Tambo, Cauca Department, took the lives of two members of the Colombian National Police (CNP) and disrupted air traffic control service for flights into the nearby city of Cali.
- On February 1, a motorcycle bomb targeting the local police station exploded in the port town of Tumaco, Narino Department. The explosion killed seven and wounded more than 20. The explosion was the culmination of a period of violence in the region, and sparked a number of protests against the FARC and criticism of the government for its failure to provide security.
- On March 17, FARC forces ambushed a Colombian army patrol in the department of Arauca, killing 11 soldiers and wounding two others.

- On April 27, in a complex attack in the area of Puerto Rico, Caqueta Department, four soldiers and one police sergeant were killed in an ambush. In a separate attack on the police station in Puerto Rico, two civilian adults and their baby were killed when one of five improvised mortars fell short and landed in their house.

Legislation, Law Enforcement, and Border Security: Law enforcement cooperation between Colombia and the United States remained outstanding. Colombia extradited 183 individuals to the United States. Evidence sharing and joint law enforcement operations occurred in a fluid and efficient manner, with information gathered in Colombia contributing to hundreds of prosecutions of U.S.-based criminals and organizations.

In June, the Colombian Congress passed and President Santos signed the Legal Framework for Peace, a groundbreaking piece of legislation meant to lay the groundwork for future legislation on transitional justice. The legislation, which was facing a challenge in the country's constitutional court, will allow the Colombian justice system to prioritize the prosecution of key terrorist leaders.

Colombian border security remained an area of vulnerability. The CNP does not have uniform policies for vehicle or passenger inspection at land border crossings. Biometric and biographic screening is conducted only at international airports. Improved relations with neighboring Ecuador and Venezuela have led to increased cooperation from those countries on law enforcement issues. Colombia also continued cooperation and information sharing with the Panamanian National Border Service. The CNP does not currently utilize advance passenger name records, but was in the process of designing and procuring a system that will allow it to do so.

Colombian authorities arrested several important FARC members in 2012. Ruben Pena Santacoloma, alias "Ancizar," was arrested for his role in FARC takeovers of several small towns and his cruel treatment of kidnapping victims in his custody. In September, FARC member Angelo "Piloso" Caceres was sentenced to 40 years in prison for his role in the murder of three American citizen indigenous rights advocates in 1999.

Kidnappings as a whole have declined in recent years. In 2010, Colombia saw a 93 percent reduction in kidnappings from 2000. The CNP Anti-Kidnapping and Anti-Extortion Directorate (DIASE, also referred to as GAULA) has formed a four-man international kidnapping unit to address any kidnappings involving foreign nationals. This team primarily exists to investigate kidnapping and extortion matters involving U.S. citizens and entities. Additionally, the FBI and GAULA are working together to form a formal vetted team, consisting of 10 to 12 members, that will focus on kidnapping, extortion, and other terrorism-related matters of interest to the U.S. and Colombia.

Colombia continued to participate in the Department of State's Antiterrorism Assistance (ATA) program. ATA provided Colombia with instructor development and crisis response team training to enable it to expand its role both as a regional provider of counterterrorism training to other countries in the Western Hemisphere, and as a senior participant in joint trainings with other ATA partner nations.

Countering Terrorist Finance: Colombia is a member of the Financial Action Task Force of South America against Money Laundering, a Financial Action Task Force (FATF)-style regional body. Colombia stands out as a regional leader in the fight against terrorist financing and has become a key part of a regional Financial Intelligence Unit initiative aimed at strengthening information sharing among Latin American countries.

In September, the Ministries of Foreign Affairs, Justice, and Finance signed an interagency memorandum of understanding (MOU), which gives legal authority to the Prosecutor General's Office to implement the necessary seizure orders under existing Colombian asset forfeiture law against the assets of individuals and entities on the UNSC 1267/1989 and 1988 Sanctions Committees' consolidated list, as well as to adhere to FATF recommendations to freeze the funds of designated terrorists, terrorist financiers, and terrorist groups. The Government of Colombia worked extensively with U.S. law enforcement agencies to identify, target, and prosecute groups and individuals engaged in financial crimes.

In November, the Prosecutor General's Office took steps to seize the property of retired General Mauricio Santoyo, head of security for former President Alvaro Uribe (2002-2010), due to his ties to the Self-Defense Forces of Colombia (AUC). The Prosecutor General's Office seized property including nine farms, five vehicles, a commercial establishment, and a factory. The Prosecutor General's Office Justice and Peace Division developed a special asset forfeiture unit in May 2011 to identify and seize assets belonging to armed illegal groups, such as the AUC and the FARC (both U.S.-designated terrorist organizations). In 2012, this specialized unit of prosecutors seized 130 assets valued at approximately US $50 million; the money will be used for victim reparations in Colombia.

For further information on money laundering and financial crimes, we refer you to the *2013 International Narcotics Control Strategy Report (INCSR), Volume 2, Money Laundering and Financial Crimes*: http://www.state.gov/j/inl/rls/nrcrpt/index.htm.

Regional and International Cooperation: Colombia is actively involved in the UN, the OAS, the Pacific Alliance, the Union of South American Nations, and is a founding member of the Global Counterterrorism Forum. The Colombian government frequently integrates the recommendations of the UN and OAS into its security and human rights decisions. Colombia's term as a non-permanent member of the UNSC ended on December 31. The CNP operates an Interpol office of approximately 70 analysts, agents, and support staff. Colombia also led the creation of Ameripol, the American Police Community, and CNP Director General Jose Roberto Leon served as Ameripol's secretary-general in 2012. Colombia also maintained strong bilateral relations with the UK, Canada, and Spain, and coordinated arrests and deportations with those countries on a regular basis.

Colombia is becoming a key leader in providing security training and assistance to countries from around the world. It provided judicial training to judges and prosecutors in handling drug trafficking and terrorism cases, basic and advanced helicopter training to pilots from countries throughout Latin America, and frequently opened up its elite "Lancero" and "Jungla" special forces courses to students from other countries. In 2012, Colombia expanded its assistance to the instruction of better methods of strategic communications and civil-military relations. Officers from Brazil, Mexico, and Ecuador were invited to attend a training course in radio station and loudspeaker operations and community interaction. Colombia also dispatched a subject matter expert to Peru to provide instruction on the capabilities of the "radio-in-a-box," used to disseminate positive radio messages encouraging defections over guerrilla frequencies. Mexico remained the biggest recipient of Colombian counternarcotics and counterterrorism training.

Countering Radicalization and Violent Extremism: Colombia employed a robust and modern multi-agency approach to countering radicalization and violent extremism, with a focus on encouraging members and entire units of the FARC and ELN to demobilize and reintegrate with society. In October, with U.S. assistance, Colombia hosted a conference on ways to better counter FARC and ELN ideology and better focus demobilization efforts. The demobilization program provides medical care, psychological counseling, education benefits, job placement assistance, and periodic checks on demobilized former members of the FARC and ELN. Recidivism rates were low to moderate.

The Colombian armed forces and police employed a number of fixed and mobile radio transmitters to broadcast strategic messaging to potential deserters. Such messaging was also seen in print, television, and alternative media. The Colombian military employed the same media to counter FARC recruitment efforts.

MEXICO

Overview: The Mexican government remained vigilant against domestic and international terrorist threats. International terrorist organizations do not have a known operational presence in Mexico, and no terrorist group targeted U.S. citizens in or from Mexican territory. The Government of Mexico continued to strengthen its law enforcement institutions and to disrupt and dismantle criminal organizations responsible for drug trafficking-related violence. There was no evidence that these criminal organizations had political or ideological motivations, aside from seeking to maintain the impunity with which they conduct their criminal activities.

Legislation, Law Enforcement, and Border Security: The Mexican government continued to improve the abilities of its security forces to counter terrorism. The United States supported these efforts by providing training and equipment to Mexican law enforcement and security agencies, sharing information, and promoting interagency law enforcement cooperation. The United States also supported Mexican efforts to address border security challenges along its southern and northern borders and its ports. The Mexican and U.S. governments shared information and jointly analyzed transnational threats; promoted information and intelligence sharing; deployed enhanced cargo screening technologies; and strengthened passenger information sharing. Mexican and U.S. officials also continued coordinated efforts to prevent the transit of third country nationals who may raise terrorism concerns. On the Mexico-U.S. border, officials increased coordination of patrols and inspections and improved communications across the border. On the Mexico-Guatemala-Belize border, Mexico deployed additional security forces and implemented biometric controls. Mexico remained an important partner nation in the Department of State's Antiterrorism Assistance program, which continued its overall shift in focus from protection of national leadership training to border security, preventing terrorist safe havens, and protecting critical infrastructure.

In support of U.S. efforts to identify and interdict illegitimate travel and travelers, consular Fraud Prevention Units and Regional Security Office investigators throughout Mexico provided training on recognition of fraudulent U.S. and Mexican identity and travel documents to local, state, and federal officials; and bank investigators.

Countering Terrorist Finance: Mexico is a member of the Financial Action Task Force (FATF) and the Financial Action Task Force of South America against Money Laundering, a FATF-style regional body. Mexico's Congress approved long-awaited anti-money laundering legislation in late 2012, and at year's end the law was on track for full implementation in 2013. Through this legislation, records of transactions that would otherwise be undetectable because they are made solely in cash must now be reported to the federal government. This represents a significant advance over previous years that could help track some forms of potential terrorist financing. For further information on money laundering and financial crimes, we refer you to the *2013 International Narcotics Control Strategy Report (INCSR), Volume 2, Money Laundering and Financial Crimes*: http://www.state.gov/j/inl/rls/nrcrpt/index.htm.

Regional and International Cooperation: Mexico entered into an agreement with the OAS' Inter-American Committee Against Terrorism (CICTE) in 2012. CICTE is implementing a two-year work plan in Mexico to address specific weaknesses in legislation, licensing, investigations and prosecution of proliferation violations, and interdiction of weapons of mass destruction (WMD) and their components in an effort to prevent possible WMD terrorism.

PANAMA

Overview: The most direct terrorism threat in Panama was the persistent presence of a small unit of the Revolutionary Armed Forces of Colombia (FARC), which used remote areas of the Darien Region as a safe haven. The Panamanian National Border Service (SENAFRONT) undertook several operations against the FARC in 2012, further degrading the FARC's capabilities in Panama. Panama continued its close cooperation with Colombia and Costa Rica to secure its borders. Additionally, the Panama Canal Authority's vigilance, along with international support, contributed to the canal's security.

Panama's Darien Region is a significant pathway for human smuggling with counterterrorism implications. In an average month, 270 smuggled aliens enter Panama. While the majority of these are Cubans, the Panamanian National Border Service reported a consistent flow of African, Middle Eastern, and South Asian smuggled aliens, including from Syria, Iran, Pakistan, Sri Lanka, Somalia, Eritrea, Bangladesh, and Ethiopia. Further, some smuggling in the Darien was facilitated by FARC elements operating on both sides of the border. Representatives of DHS-Homeland Security Investigations and the Federal Bureau of Investigation worked with Panamanian authorities to identify smuggled aliens with potential terrorism ties.

Legislation, Law Enforcement, and Border Security: The Government of Panama continued its efforts to enforce its sovereignty in the Darien through more aggressive patrolling by security forces. In January, SENAFRONT and FARC members exchanged fire near Alto Tuira, in the Darien. In March, a FARC camp that could support more than two dozen personnel was destroyed. In May, SENAFRONT uncovered a FARC camp near the Colombian border. In early November, SENAFRONT seized arms and ammunition aboard a boat near the town of Barriales. Later in November, SENAFRONT killed one FARC member, arrested eight Colombians, and seized rifles, pistols, and 391 kilograms of cocaine near Mogue in the Darien.

Executive Decree 448 of December 28, 2011 created a Coordination Council Against International Terrorism to review compliance with international terrorism conventions, strategize the implementation of UNSCRs on terrorism, compile information about public institution measures against terrorism, report on actions taken, and recommend new measures. The Coordination Council, which includes one representative each from 16 government agencies, is presided over by the Ministry of Foreign Affairs. In March, the Council formally met for the first time, pledging stronger actions to prevent money laundering and announcing a new cyber security initiative. In July, under the Council's auspices, the Ministry of Foreign Affairs hosted a day-long seminar on international terrorism which focused on UNSCRs and the experiences of other countries, such as Israel and Colombia, in fighting international terrorism.

The United States and Panama continued to plan for incidents that could potentially shut down transit through the Panama Canal. In August, Panama co-hosted the annual PANAMAX exercise, a multinational security training exercise initiated in 2003 that focuses on canal security. The exercise replicated real-world threats and included specific scenarios designed to counter terrorist attacks. Several U.S. government agencies, as well as 17 partner nations, participated.

U.S. Customs and Border Protection (CBP) linked the Panamanian Advance Passenger Information System (APIS) at Tocumen International Airport to its data systems. Through the Joint Security Program, CBP and DHS investigations targeted potentially dangerous and criminal/terrorist-affiliated passengers on all flights in and out of Tocumen. The system became fully operational in 2012 and has already led to the identification of multiple individuals affiliated with terrorism, several fugitive arrests, and the denial of entry into or transit through Panama by many high-risk passengers. Mobile security teams at the airport, with U.S. support have interdicted alien smuggling, narcotics, and illicit bulk cash.

Panama continued its participation in the Container Security Initiative Program at Balboa and Manzanillo, and the Evergreen Colon Container Terminal. Panama Customs officials received Wisconsin Risk Reduction Project instruction and Commodity Identification Training in November.

The U.S. Southern Command (SOUTHCOM) sponsored conferences and training for Panamanian Public Forces, and the relationship between the Government of Panama and the Missouri National Guard under the State Partnership Program continued to expand. The Embassy Office of Defense Cooperation maintained a strong program to help Panama develop and refine its civil affairs and information operations capacity through SOUTHCOM's Civil Affairs and Military Information Support Teams as part of its overall strategy to counter FARC influence in the Darien.

Panama was the recipient of Department of State Antiterrorism Assistance courses in airport security management, crisis negotiations, vital infrastructure security, protection of national leadership, first responder to terrorist incidents, critical incident management and hospital-based management of mass casualty incidents. The program focused on building Panamanian law enforcement capacity to secure borders and vital infrastructure from terrorist threats, and on preventing terrorist safe havens in Panama.

Countering Terrorist Finance: Panama is a member of the Financial Action Task Force of South America against Money Laundering, a Financial Action Task Force-style regional body. The legal and regulatory frameworks that address counterterrorist financing in Panama also address money laundering. Executive Decree 55 of February 1, 2012 expanded the list of regulatory entities and therefore the number of entities covered by terrorist financing laws and regulations. Uneven enforcement of existing anti-money laundering and terrorist finance controls coupled with the weak judicial system remained a problem. Moreover, the Colon Free Zone, the second largest free zone in the world, continued to be vulnerable to exploitation for illicit financial activities, due primarily to weak customs, trade, and financial transactions oversight. For further information on money laundering and financial crimes, we refer you to the *2011 International Narcotics Control Strategy Report (INCSR), Volume 2, Money Laundering and Financial Crimes*: http://www.state.gov/j/inl/rls/nrcrpt/index.htm.

Regional and International Cooperation: Panama participated in UN and regional security initiatives, such as the OAS Inter-American Committee Against Terrorism.

Countering Radicalization and Violent Extremism: The United States and Panama worked together to create opportunities for the residents of the Darien Region to deter local FARC recruitment. Local youth received vocational and technical training to better prepare them to find jobs or start their own businesses, while indigenous entrepreneurs obtained assistance to improve marketing of their crafts. The Embassy worked closely with NGO partners and the Panamanian government to help local Darien farmers better market their produce in Panama City. Four youth centers were constructed to give more options for young people to constructively use their time and energy. In addition, community facilities have been constructed along with sports fields to give residents space for activities.

PARAGUAY

Overview: Since June 22, when President Fernando Lugo was impeached and Federico Franco took office, the Government of Paraguay has more aggressively charged and arrested individuals under counterterrorism laws created in 2010 and 2011; however, successful prosecutions remained elusive. Paraguay continued to be hampered by ineffective immigration, customs, and law enforcement controls along its porous borders, particularly the Tri-Border Area (TBA) with Argentina and Brazil. Limited resources, sporadic interagency cooperation, and corruption within customs, the police, the public ministry, and the judicial sector impeded Paraguay's law enforcement initiatives throughout the country. Paraguay faced continued activity by an internal insurgent group, which resulted in public demands for governmental response and kept terrorism in the policy forefront throughout the year.

The United States provided training to improve law enforcement counterterrorism capabilities through the Department of State's Antiterrorism Assistance program. In addition, through much of 2012, DHS officers were seconded to Paraguay to enhance Paraguay's border controls.

2012 Terrorist Incidents: Since 2008, the leftist Paraguayan People's Army (EPP) has been active in the northern departments of Paraguay abutting the Brazilian border. The EPP proclaims itself as dedicated to a socialist revolution in Paraguay and may have tenuous links to the Revolutionary Armed Forces in Colombia. Membership statistics for the EPP are difficult to establish, but it is believed to be a small, decentralized group operating mainly in Concepción

Department. Estimates of membership range from 20-100 members. It engaged in kidnappings, placement of explosive devices, and multiple shootouts with the police and military. The following activities are believed to have been perpetrated by the EPP in 2012:

- On March 4 and 8, two private estates were attacked and burned in Concepcion Department. A guard was injured in the March 4 attack.
- On May 17, the 19 year-old son of a Brazilian politician from a border town near Capitan Bado was the victim of an attempted kidnapping. The man and his security guard escaped.
- On July 30, in Yby Yau, three armed men attacked a ranch, shot the water tank and the power transformer, and left behind a threatening note that identified them as members of the EPP.
- On August 31, in Paso Tuja and Kuruzu de Hierro, Concepción Department, alleged EPP members burned two soy plantations and left behind a threatening note.
- On September 5, in Azotey, an alleged group of EPP members shot and killed the aunt of an EPP member and then exploded a device inside her mouth. The same day and approximately one kilometer away, another group of men shot at a police post from a moving vehicle, wounding two police officers. One police officer died of his wounds days later.
- On October 4, two people identified as EPP members attacked a private radio station with two explosive devices in Horqueta. Two radio station operators were unharmed; however, the media facilities sustained damage.
- On October 12 in the vicinity of Horqueta, alleged EPP members unsuccessfully attempted to bring down an electrical high-tension power line with improvised explosive devices placed at the bottom of the tower.

Legislation, Law Enforcement, and Border Security: Limited steps were undertaken specifically to address border security issues, particularly with respect to the large and generally unprotected borders with Argentina and Brazil. There were upgrades made at the Silvio Pettirossi Airport in Asuncion to improve immigration controls. The Franco government more aggressively countered EPP threats.

Following the September 5 killing of an alleged police informant, the Public Ministry issued two arrest warrants for the perpetrators and charged them under the 2010 counterterrorism laws, the first time Paraguay used this law.

Countering Terrorist Finance: Paraguay is a member of the Financial Action Task Force of South America against Money Laundering, a Financial Action Task Force-type regional body. In 2012, there were four arrests under the terrorist financing law. In October, the National Police arrested Ruben Dario Lopez Fernandez, who is believed to be an EPP logistician. Lopez also had an outstanding arrest warrant for his arrest on charges of terrorist financing. As of year's end, there were no convictions for terrorist financing cases. For further information on money laundering and financial crimes, we refer you to the *2013 International Narcotics Control Strategy Report (INCSR), Volume 2, Money Laundering and Financial Crimes*: http://www.state.gov/j/inl/rls/nrcrpt/index.htm.

Regional and International Cooperation: Brazil is Paraguay's strongest regional partner in counterterrorism and law enforcement activities, and the two countries cooperated on security initiatives. Paraguay also collaborated with Mercosur and Union of South American Nations partners in border protection initiatives, regional exchanges, and discussions on counterterrorism and law enforcement projects. While bilateral and multilateral relations between Paraguay and its neighbors stalled following Lugo's impeachment, counterterrorism efforts continued.

PERU

Overview: Peru's primary counterterrorism concern remained the Shining Path (Sendero Luminoso or SL). Although Peru nearly eliminated SL in the 1990s, the organization is well-entwined with coca cultivation and narcotics trafficking and remained a threat to Peru's internal security. In February, Peruvian security forces captured Florindo Flores Hala (alias "Comrade Artemio"), the leader of the Upper Huallaga Valley (UHV) faction of SL. Prosecutors charged Flores with aggravated terrorism, drug trafficking, and money laundering. Because of SL's hierarchy, the capture led to a collapse in SL-UHV's structure and capabilities. While SL still operated in the UHV, it has been severely limited in scope.

A much larger and stronger SL faction occupies the government-designated emergency zone (an area in which the government has suspended certain civil rights due to an "exceptional situation") known as the Apurimac, Ene, and Mantaro River Valleys (VRAEM). The emergency zone expanded in 2012 to include additional territory near the Mantaro River due to the concentration of SL leadership in close proximity to this tributary. In June, Peruvian authorities also expanded the VRAEM emergency zone to include portions of the La Convencion Province in the Region of Cusco, which has seen significant expansion of SL activity over the past year. In 2012, SL-VRAEM had several hundred armed members while the number of its supporters in the urban areas was unknown. Although SL-VRAEM's leaders claimed to have split with SL founder Abimael Guzman, the faction continued to use Maoist philosophy to justify its illegal activities. Involvement in drug production, narcotics trafficking, and extortion in the form of "revolutionary taxes" provided SL with funding to conduct operations. The organization's involvement with drug trafficking also allowed SL-VRAEM to improve relations with coca-growing communities in remote areas.

Government efforts to improve interagency cooperation and to strengthen prosecutorial capacity were somewhat successful. Police units specializing in counterterrorism and counternarcotics conducted several operations with the Peruvian Armed Forces. Peru continued talks with its neighbors to strengthen counterterrorism cooperation.

In January, the Movement for Amnesty and Fundamental Rights (MOVADEF), a front organization of the Shining Path founded by Abimael Guzman's lawyers, attempted to register as a political party. The National Election Board denied the registration application, citing the group's links to terrorism. MOVADEF claimed to reject armed violence, but the National Election Board found its link to SL to be clear. It was reported that MOVADEF gained further support throughout the year in trade unions and rural communities. MOVADEF also increased its international presence, staging protests in Argentina, Chile, and Mexico. They reportedly have additional chapters in Bolivia, France, Spain, Sweden, and Uruguay.

The Revolutionary Armed Forces of Colombia (FARC) continued to use remote areas along the Colombian-Peruvian border to regroup and make arms purchases. Peruvian government experts believed the FARC continued to fund coca cultivation and cocaine production among the

Peruvian population in border areas. The Government of Peru sought to cooperate with the Government of Colombia on ways to combat the FARC's presence in under-governed areas of the border region.

2012 Terrorist Incidents: SL carried out 87 terrorist acts that killed one civilian, 13 members of the military, and five police officers. The attacks included:

- On April 9, an SL-VRAEM group kidnapped 36 workers from the Camisea natural gas pipeline just outside the VRAEM emergency zone. In several failed rescue attempts, a total of eight security personnel were killed, 10 others were wounded, and a U.S.-owned helicopter operated by the police was destroyed. On April 14, all 36 workers were released unharmed. Some analysts claimed the Government of Peru or the pipeline operator paid a US $5 million ransom, an assertion strongly refuted by both.
- On June 6, SL-VRAEM members briefly seized 18 Camisea pipeline workers from an area six kilometers away from the April kidnapping incident. SL spray-painted revolutionary slogans on the workers' helicopters, delivered a communiqué, and released the hostages unharmed.
- On August 15, SL ambushed a 32-man Peruvian army patrol in a remote part of the VRAEM near the counterterrorism base of Mazangaro. The attackers killed five soldiers and wounded six others in the deadliest single attack since 2009.
- On September 7, SL terrorists used explosives to damage an above-ground valve on the Camisea gas pipeline near Kepashiato. When a Peruvian Army helicopter approached the valve site to verify the level of damage, ground-based snipers shot and killed a soldier aboard the helicopter.
- On October 6, members of SL-VRAEM blew up three commercial helicopters subcontracted by the Camisea natural gas pipeline operator. The helicopters were located in Echarate, a district in the region of Cusco. The SL combatants delivered a communiqué stating the pipeline operators had failed to pay a "war tax."

Legislation, Law Enforcement, and Border Security: Peru's Congress passed a bill in January banning convicted terrorists on parole from traveling abroad. President Humala continued reauthorizing 60-day states of emergency in parts of seven regions where SL operated, giving the armed forces and police additional authority to maintain public order.

Immigration authorities collected no biometric information from visitors. Citizens of neighboring countries were allowed to travel to Peru by land using national identification cards in lieu of passports. There was no visa requirement for citizens of most countries in Western, Central, and Eastern Europe and the visa requirement for Mexican nationals was abolished. Peruvian immigration used a database called "Movimiento Migratorio" at five points of entry to track entries and exits of travelers, but the database was limited to Interpol and a local database that tracks outstanding warrants. Peruvian immigration did not have access to Passenger Name Record data or a terrorist watch list.

Police detained 233 suspected terrorists during the year. Besides the February capture of "Comrade Artemio," significant law enforcement action included:

- On July 5, security forces rescued 11 children from an SL camp in the VRAEM. The children, called "little pioneers," were allegedly being indoctrinated into the Shining Path. Eleven SL terrorists were also captured.
- On September 5, Peruvian security forces killed the second-most-senior military commander of the SL-VRAEM faction, Victor Hugo Castro Ramirez alias "Comrade William." President Humala characterized his death as a "major blow" against SL.

SL founder and leader Abimael Guzman and key accomplices remained in prison serving life sentences stemming from crimes committed in the 1980s and 1990s. About 600 people remained in prison on terrorism charges or convictions.

Peru continued to participate in the Department of State's Antiterrorism Assistance program, which provided several courses designed to build capacity in border security, terrorism-related investigations, and the role of police leadership in counterterrorism efforts.

Countering Terrorist Finance: Peru is a member of the Financial Action Task Force of South America against Money Laundering, a Financial Action Task Force-style regional body. In October, Peru's Congress passed law 25.475, making terrorist financing a separate crime punishable by up to 35 years in prison. The Government of Peru took several additional steps to implement the May 2011 "National Plan to Combat Money Laundering and Terrorist Financing." This included two pieces of legislation revamping asset forfeiture and anti-money laundering laws, both containing terrorist finance components. The passage of these two legislative decrees achieved the majority of the legislative reform benchmarks set in the National Plan.

Legislative Decree 1106, "Legislation to Fight against Money Laundering and other crimes linked with Illegal Mining and Organized Crime," empowers the Financial Intelligence Unit and the Superintendent of Banks, Insurance, and Pension Funds to freeze bank accounts in cases linked to money laundering or terrorist financing within 24 hours after a judge's approval.

The U.S. Financial Crimes Enforcement Network continued to suspend cooperation with the FIU, because of a leak of sensitive information published by the Peruvian press in April 2011.

For further information on money laundering and financial crimes, we refer you to the *2013 International Narcotics Control Strategy Report (INCSR), Volume 2, Money Laundering and Financial Crimes*: http://www.state.gov/j/inl/rls/nrcrpt/index.htm.

Regional and International Cooperation: Peru was an active member of the OAS and participated in the OAS Inter-American Committee Against Terrorism training and other events. Peru held the rotating presidency of the Union of South American Nations beginning June 29.

Countering Radicalization and Violent Extremism: Peru has a stated goal of increasing state presence in emergency zones with the hope that such presence will be a deterrent to radicalization. The official position of the National Penitentiary Institute is that prison is meant to rehabilitate and reintegrate prisoners, especially terrorists. A psychological evaluation is required of incarcerated terrorists before parole can be granted. Many observers have expressed concern that the program is ineffective and that many convicted terrorists are not rehabilitated, but instead choose to rejoin SL upon release.

VENEZUELA

In May, for the seventh consecutive year, the U.S. Department of State determined, pursuant to section 40A of the Arms Export Control Act, that Venezuela was not cooperating fully with U.S. antiterrorism efforts. The Venezuelan government took no action against senior Venezuelan government officials who have been designated as Foreign Narcotics Kingpins by the U.S. Department of the Treasury for directly supporting the narcotics and arms trafficking activities of the Revolutionary Armed Forces of Colombia (FARC).

Venezuela and Colombia continued their dialogue on security and border issues. On several occasions during the year, President Chávez said, in reference to the FARC and the Colombian group the National Liberation Army (ELN), that the Venezuelan government would not permit the presence of illegal armed groups in Venezuelan territory. Venezuela captured two FARC members during the year; one died following his capture and the other is still in Venezuelan custody.

Venezuela maintained its economic, financial, and diplomatic cooperation with Iran. Iranian President Ahmadinejad visited Venezuela in January, and following his meeting with Chávez, the leaders announced the signing of agreements in the areas of housing materials, construction, agriculture, and shipping. In June, Chávez unveiled an unarmed, unmanned-aerial vehicle that he claimed Venezuela had produced domestically with Iranian technology. The Banco Internacional de Desarrollo, a subsidiary of the Banco de Desarrollo y Exportacion de Iran, continued to operate in Venezuela despite its designation in 2008 by the U.S. Treasury Department under E.O. 13382 ("Blocking Property of Weapons of Mass Destruction Proliferators and their Supporters").

There were credible reports that Hizballah engaged in fundraising and support activity in Venezuela.

Legislation, Law Enforcement, and Border Security: Venezuela captured two FARC members during the year; one died following his capture and the other was in Venezuelan custody at year's end.

Countering Terrorist Finance: Venezuela is a member of the Caribbean Financial Action Task Force, a Financial Action Task Force-style regional body; the Inter-American Drug Abuse Control Commission Anti-Money Laundering Group; and the Egmont Group.

Venezuela enacted an organic law against organized crime and the financing of terrorism (Gazette No. 39.912, April 2012), as well as joint resolution 122 (Gazette No. 39.945, June 2012) and joint resolution 158 (Gazette No. 39.986, August 2012) to address deficiencies in its anti-money laundering/combating the financing of terrorism regime. The organic law criminalized terrorism in a manner consistent with international norms and extended due diligence requirements beyond banks to include securities, insurance, and other financial institutions. The organic law also obligated financial institutions to notify Venezuela's financial intelligence unit of any transactions that might be related to terrorist acts, terrorist financing, money laundering, or organized crime, even when the funds in question come from licit sources. Joint resolution 122 and joint resolution 158 created a mechanism for implementing

UNSC resolutions 1267 and 1373, respectively.

Venezuela had six terrorist finance cases pending as of September, brought under the organized crime legislation in place before the April 2012 organic law. The Venezuelan government indicted nine people on terrorism charges in these six cases. By year's end, two of the cases were under investigation, one was in an intermediate stage, two were in trial, and one had resulted in the conviction of two people. For further information on money laundering and financial crimes, we refer you to the *2013 International Narcotics Control Strategy Report (INCSR), Volume 2, Money Laundering and Financial Crimes*: http://www.state.gov/j/inl/rls/nrcrpt/index.htm.

Regional and International Cooperation: In September, Colombian President Juan Manuel Santos announced that Venezuela, along with Norway, would serve as official observers to the Colombian government's peace negotiations with the FARC. Venezuela designated its Ambassador to the OAS, Roy Chaderton, as its emissary to the negotiations, which are being held in Oslo and Havana.

Chapter 3.
State Sponsors of Terrorism

To designate a country as a State Sponsor of Terrorism, the Secretary of State must determine that the government of such country has repeatedly provided support for acts of international terrorism. Once a country is designated, it remains a State Sponsor of Terrorism until the designation is rescinded in accordance with statutory criteria. A wide range of sanctions are imposed as a result of a State Sponsor of Terrorism designation, including:

- A ban on arms-related exports and sales;
- Controls over exports of dual-use items, requiring 30-day Congressional notification for goods or services that could significantly enhance the designated country's military capability or ability to support terrorism;
- Prohibitions on economic assistance; and
- Imposition of miscellaneous financial and other restrictions.

More information on State Sponsor of Terrorism designations may be found online at http://www.state.gov/j/ct/c14151.htm.

CUBA

Cuba was designated as a State Sponsor of Terrorism in 1982. Reports in 2012 suggested that the Cuban government was trying to distance itself from Basque Fatherland and Liberty (ETA) members living on the island by employing tactics such as not providing services including travel documents to some of them. The Government of Cuba continued to provide safe haven to approximately two dozen ETA members.

In past years, some members of the Revolutionary Armed Forces of Colombia (FARC) were allowed safe haven in Cuba and safe passage through Cuba. In November, the Government of Cuba began hosting peace talks between the FARC and Government of Colombia.

There was no indication that the Cuban government provided weapons or paramilitary training to terrorist groups.

The Cuban government continued to harbor fugitives wanted in the United States. The Cuban government also provided support such as housing, food ration books, and medical care for these individuals.

The Financial Action Task Force (FATF) has identified Cuba as having strategic anti-money laundering/combating the financing of terrorism deficiencies. In 2012, Cuba became a member of the Financial Action Task Force of South America against Money Laundering, a FATF-style regional body. With this action, Cuba has committed to adopting and implementing the FATF Recommendations.

IRAN

Designated as a State Sponsor of Terrorism in 1984, Iran increased its terrorist-related activity, including attacks or attempted attacks in India, Thailand, Georgia, and Kenya. Iran provided financial, material, and logistical support for terrorist and militant groups in the Middle East and Central Asia. Iran used the Islamic Revolutionary Guard Corps-Qods Force (IRGC-QF) and militant groups to implement foreign policy goals, provide cover for intelligence operations, and stir up instability in the Middle East. The IRGC-QF is the regime's primary mechanism for cultivating and supporting terrorists abroad.

In 2012, Iran was implicated in planned attacks in India, Thailand, Georgia, and Kenya. On February 13, in New Delhi, India, a magnetic bomb placed under the vehicle of an Israeli diplomat's wife exploded, seriously injuring her and three Indian nationals. On February 14, a similar device was discovered under a vehicle belonging to the Israeli embassy in Tbilisi, Georgia, and safely defused. Also on February 14, Thai police arrested three Iranian nationals in connection with explosions in a Bangkok private residence that revealed bomb-making materials and makeshift grenades intended for use in attacks against Israeli targets. On June 19, Kenyan authorities arrested two Iranian nationals in connection with explosives stockpiled for a suspected terrorist attack. According to press reports, the individuals were members of the IRGC-QF.

On October 17, Iranian-born U.S. dual-national Mansour Arbabsiar was arrested by U.S. authorities and pled guilty in a New York court to participating in a 2011 plot to murder the Saudi ambassador to the United States. Arbabsiar held several meetings with an associate whom Iranian officials believed was a narcotics cartel member. This associate, in fact, was a confidential source for U.S. law enforcement. Arbabsiar admitted to working on behalf of the IRGC-QF to carry out the plot. An IRGC-QF officer who remains at large was also indicted. The thwarted plot demonstrated Iran's interest in using international terrorism – including in the United States – to further its foreign policy goals.

In 2012, the IRGC-QF trained Taliban elements on small unit tactics, small arms, explosives, and indirect fire weapons, such as mortars, artillery, and rockets. Since 2006, Iran has arranged arms shipments to select Taliban members, including small arms and associated ammunition, rocket propelled grenades, mortar rounds, 107mm rockets, and plastic explosives. Iran has shipped a large number of weapons to Kandahar, Afghanistan, aiming to increase its influence in this key province.

Despite its pledge to support Iraq's stabilization, Iran trained, funded, and provided guidance to Iraqi Shia militant groups. The IRGC-QF, in concert with Lebanese Hizballah, provided training outside of Iraq as well as advisors inside Iraq for Shia militants in the construction and use of sophisticated improvised explosive device technology and other advanced weaponry.

Regarding Syria, Iran provided extensive support, including weapons, funds, and training to assist the Asad regime in its brutal crackdown that has resulted in the death of more than 70,000 civilians. Iran provided weapons, training, and funding to Hamas and other Palestinian terrorist groups, including the Palestine Islamic Jihad and the Popular Front for the Liberation of Palestine-General Command. Since the end of the 2006 Israeli-Hizballah conflict, Iran has assisted in rearming Hizballah, in direct violation of UNSCR 1701. Iran has provided hundreds of millions of dollars in support of Hizballah in Lebanon and has trained thousands of Hizballah fighters at camps in Iran.

Iran actively supported members of the Houthi tribe in northern Yemen, including activities intended to build military capabilities, which could pose a greater threat to security and stability in Yemen and the surrounding region. In July 2012, the Yemeni Interior Ministry arrested members of an alleged Iranian spy ring, headed by a former member of the IRGC.

Iran remained unwilling to bring to justice senior al-Qa'ida (AQ) members it continued to detain, and refused to publicly identify those senior members in its custody. Iran allowed AQ facilitators Muhsin al-Fadhli and Adel Radi Saqr al-Wahabi al-Harbi to operate a core facilitation pipeline through Iran, enabling AQ to move funds and fighters to South Asia and to Syria. Al-Fadhli is a veteran AQ operative who has been active for years. Al-Fadhli began working with the Iran-based AQ facilitation network in 2009 and was later arrested by Iranian authorities. He was released in 2011 and assumed leadership of the Iran-based AQ facilitation network.

Since 2009, the Financial Action Task Force (FATF) has called for its members and the international community to institute countermeasures to protect their respective financial sectors and the global financial system from the risks – in particular the terrorist financing threat – posed by Iran. In October 2012, the FATF strengthened its language and again called for countermeasures against Iran. Iran has had some limited engagement regarding anti-money laundering/combating the financing of terrorism and has responded to overtures by multilateral entities such as the UN's Global Programme against Money Laundering, but it has failed to criminalize terrorist financing and require that financial institutions and other obliged entities file suspicious transaction reports. Iran has not engaged with FATF and was not a member of a FATF-style regional body.

Iran remains a state of proliferation concern. Despite multiple UNSCRs requiring Iran to suspend its sensitive nuclear proliferation activities, Iran continues to violate its international obligations regarding its nuclear program. For further information, see the Report to Congress on Iran-related Multilateral Sanctions Regime Efforts (February 2013), and the Report on the Status of Bilateral and Multilateral Efforts Aimed at Curtailing the Pursuit of Iran of Nuclear Weapons Technology (September 2012).

SUDAN

Sudan was designated as a State Sponsor of Terrorism in 1993. Sudanese officials regularly discussed counterterrorism issues with U.S. counterparts in 2012 and were generally responsive to international community concerns about counterterrorism efforts. Sudan remained a cooperative counterterrorism partner on certain issues, including al-Qa'ida (AQ)-linked terrorism, and the outlook for continued cooperation on those issues remained somewhat positive. The Government of Sudan continued to pursue counterterrorism operations directly involving threats to U.S. interests and personnel in Sudan. Sudanese officials have indicated that they view continued cooperation with the United States as important and recognize the potential benefits of U.S. training and information-sharing. While the counterterrorism relationship remained solid in many aspects, hard-line Sudanese officials continued to express resentment and distrust over actions by the United States and questioned the benefits of continued cooperation. Their assessment reflected disappointment that Sudan's cooperation on counterterrorism, as well as the Sudanese government's decision to allow for the successful referendum on Southern independence leading to an independent Republic of South Sudan in July 2011, have not resulted in Sudan's removal from the list of state sponsors of terrorism. Nonetheless, there was little indication that the government would curtail its AQ-related counterterrorism cooperation despite tensions in the overall bilateral relationship.

Elements of designated terrorist groups, including AQ-inspired terrorist groups, remained in Sudan. The Government of Sudan took steps to limit the activities of these organizations, and has worked to disrupt foreign fighters' use of Sudan as a logistics base and transit point to Mali and Afghanistan. Gaps remained in the government's knowledge of, and ability to identify and capture these individuals, however. There was some evidence to suggest that individuals who were active participants in the Iraqi insurgency have returned to Sudan and are in a position to use their expertise to conduct attacks within Sudan or to pass on their knowledge. There was also evidence that Sudanese extremists participated in terrorist activities in Somalia and Mali, activities that the Sudanese government has also attempted to disrupt.

In May, the U.S. government alerted U.S. citizens residing in Sudan that it had received credible reports that extremists were planning to carry out kidnapping operations targeting westerners in greater Khartoum. No such kidnapping had occurred by year's end. The Government of Sudan was responsive to U.S. concerns about the threat. In September, violent extremists attacked the German and U.S. Embassies in Khartoum to protest an American-made film they deemed offensive to the Prophet Mohammed, as well as a Berlin Administrative Court's decision not to ban the use of images of the Prophet by a right-wing group when its members protested outside of a Berlin-area mosque. Demonstrators caused extensive damage to both embassies, and the press reported that local police killed three demonstrators outside of the U.S. Embassy. The British Embassy also suffered minor damage during the events, due to its proximity to the German Embassy. In December, the Sudanese government announced that its security services had disrupted a terrorist training camp in Sudan's Dinder National Park, approximately 186 miles southeast of the capital. Authorities said they killed 13 violent extremists and arrested another 25. Security officials said the terrorists were planning to assassinate Sudanese government officials and were planning to target Western diplomatic missions in the country.

With the exception of Hamas, the government does not appear to support the presence of violent extremist elements. In November, Hamas political chief Khaled Meshal visited Khartoum during a meeting of Sudan's Islamic Movement, and Meshal met with several senior members of the Sudanese government during his visit.

The United States continued to monitor Sudan's relationship with Iran, itself designated as a State Sponsor of Terrorism. In October 2012, two Iranian warships docked in Port Sudan, which Sudanese officials characterized as a solid show of political and diplomatic cooperation between the two nations.

The kidnapping of foreigners for ransom in Darfur continued in 2012, though no U.S. citizens were kidnapped during the year. These kidnappings have hindered humanitarian operations in Darfur. Abductees have been released unharmed amid rumors of ransoms having been paid.

In June 2010, four Sudanese men sentenced to death for the January 1, 2008 killing of a U.S. diplomat assigned to the Embassy, as well as a locally employed U.S. Embassy staff member, escaped from Khartoum's maximum security Kober prison. That same month Sudanese authorities confirmed that they recaptured one of the four convicts, and a second escapee was reported killed in Somalia in May 2011. The whereabouts of the other two convicts remained unknown at year's end.

Two cases that stemmed from the murder of the two U.S. Embassy employees remained active in 2012. In the first, the Sudanese Supreme Court is deliberating on an appeal filed by defense attorneys of the three men remaining alive who were convicted of the two murders, requesting that their death sentences be commuted. In the second, in April, a Sudanese court reduced the sentence of five men involved in facilitating the 2010 prison escape of all four convicted killers, including Abdul Raouf Abu Zaid, the murderer who was recaptured shortly after his escape. In November, an appeals court threw out the conviction of one man accused of being involved in the escape attempt, though it upheld the convictions of the other four, including Abu Zaid. The Government of Sudan has been active in continuing the investigations but the unusual circumstances surrounding the escape raised widespread concerns of involvement by Sudanese authorities.

Sudan is a member of the Middle East and North Africa Financial Action Task Force (MENAFATF), a Financial Action Task Force (FATF)-style regional body. Since February 2010, Sudan has been publicly identified by the FATF as a jurisdiction with strategic anti-money laundering/combating the financing of terrorism (AML/CFT) deficiencies, for which it has developed an action plan with the FATF to address these weaknesses. Since that time, the Government of Sudan continued to cooperate with the FATF and has taken steps to meet international standards in AML/CTF, but still has strategic deficiencies to address. Sudan was subject to a mutual evaluation conducted by the MENAFATF; this report was adopted by the MENAFATF in November 2012. Sudan continued to cooperate with the United States in investigating financial crimes related to terrorism.

SYRIA

Designated in 1979 as a State Sponsor of Terrorism, Syria continued its political support to a variety of terrorist groups affecting the stability of the region and beyond, even amid significant internal unrest. Syria provided political and weapons support to Lebanese Hizballah and continued to allow Iran to re-arm the terrorist organization. The Syrian regime's relationship with Hizballah and Iran appears to have gotten stronger over the course of the conflict in Syria. President Bashar al-Asad continued to be a staunch defender of Iran's policies while Iran exhibited equally energetic support for Syrian regime efforts to put down the growing protest movement within Syria. Statements supporting terrorist groups, particularly Hizballah, were often in Syrian government speeches and press statements.

President Asad continued to express public support for Palestinian terrorist groups as elements of the resistance against Israel. Damascus provided safe haven in Syria for exiled individuals, although the Palestinian groups were subject to the same level of insecurity as the rest of the Syrian population and fighting has fractured their alliances with the Syrian regime. As part of a broader strategy during the year, the regime has attempted to portray Syria itself as a victim of terrorism, characterizing all its armed opponents as "terrorists."

Syria continued to generate significant concern regarding the role it plays in terrorist financing. Industry experts reported that 60 percent of all business transactions were conducted in cash and that nearly 80 percent of all Syrians did not use formal banking services. Despite Syrian legislation that required money-changers to be licensed by the end of 2007, many money-changers continued to operate illegally in Syria's vast black market, estimated to be as large as Syria's formal economy. Regional *hawala* networks remained intertwined with smuggling and trade-based money laundering and were facilitated by notoriously corrupt customs and immigration officials. This raised significant concerns that some members of the Syrian government and the business elite were complicit in terrorist finance schemes conducted through these institutions.

Syria is a member of the Middle East and North Africa Financial Action Task Force (MENAFATF), a Financial Action Task Force (FATF)-style regional body. Since February 2010, Syria has been publicly identified by the FATF as a jurisdiction with strategic anti-money laundering/combating the financing of terrorism (AML/CFT) deficiencies for which it has developed an action plan with the FATF to address these weaknesses. Since then, Syria has made limited progress on its AML/CFT regime. In February 2012, Syria was named in the FATF Public Statement for its lack of progress in implementing its action plan, including its need to address the deficiencies by providing sufficient legal basis for implementing its S/RES/1373 obligations and implementing adequate procedures for identifying and freezing terrorist assets, and ensuring that appropriate laws and procedures are in place to provide mutual legal assistance.

In 2012, we continued to closely monitor Syria's proliferation-sensitive materials and facilities, including Syria's significant stockpile of chemical weapons, which we assess remains under the Asad regime's control. There is significant concern, given the instability in Syria, that these materials could find their way to terrorist organizations. We are coordinating closely with a number of like-minded nations and partners to prevent Syria's stockpiles of chemical and advanced conventional weapons from falling into the hands of violent extremists.

Chapter 4.
The Global Challenge of Chemical, Biological, Radiological, or Nuclear (CBRN) Terrorism

Nonproliferation efforts have been a top U.S. national security priority for decades – reducing the amount of chemical, biological, radiological, or nuclear (CBRN) material produced and stored by states; restricting the diversion of materials and expertise for illicit use; and preventing the trafficking of CBRN weapons and related material. Yet CBRN materials and expertise remain a significant terrorist threat as evidenced by: terrorists' stated intent to acquire and use these materials; the nature of injury and damage these weapons can inflict; the ease with which information on these topics now flows; and the dual-use nature of many relevant technologies and material. While efforts to secure CBRN material across the globe have been largely successful, the illicit trafficking of these materials persists, including instances involving highly enriched uranium in 2010 and 2011. These examples suggest that caches of dangerous material may exist on the black market and that we must complement our efforts to consolidate CBRN materials and secure facilities with broader efforts to detect, investigate, and secure CBRN materials that have fallen outside of regulatory control. We must remain vigilant if we hope to prevent terrorist groups from obtaining the means and methods for obtaining CBRN weapons.

A number of international partnerships have either the explicit or the implicit purpose to combat the CBRN threat from terrorists. Organizations and initiatives concerned with chemical and biological weapons use international conventions and regulations to reduce stockpiles of material, regulate the acquisition of dual-use technology, and regulate trade of specific goods. Nuclear and radiological initiatives and programs focus on promoting peaceful uses of nuclear material and energy, safeguarding against diversion, and countering the smuggling of radioactive and nuclear material. The United States also provides technical and financial assistance to ensure that partner nations have the ability to adequately protect and secure CBRN-applicable expertise, technologies, and material. U. S. participation within, and contribution to these groups, is vital to ensure our continued safety from the CBRN threat.

The Proliferation Security Initiative (PSI): Launched in 2003, the PSI has increased international capability to address the challenges associated with stopping the trafficking of weapons of mass destruction (WMD), their related components, and their means of delivery. The PSI remains an important tool in the global effort to combat CBRN material transfers to both state and non-state actors of proliferation concern. As of December 31, 2012, 102 states have endorsed the PSI Statement of Interdiction Principles, by which states commit to take specific actions in support of efforts to halt the trafficking of WMD and related materials. In 2012, PSI participants engaged in the following activities:

- U.S. Africa Command-sponsored maritime security Exercise Phoenix Express.
- U.S. Africa Command-sponsored maritime security Exercise Saharan Express.
- U.S. Southern Command-sponsored Panama Canal security exercise PANAMAX.
- Bilateral Air Interdiction tabletop exercise with the United States and Panama in Panama City.
- Germany hosted a PSI outreach workshop in Frankfurt.
- Poland hosted a Critical Capabilities and Practices Workshop in Warsaw.

- Japan hosted an air interdiction exercise, Pacific Shield 2012, in Hokkaido.
- The Republic of Korea hosted a Global Operational Experts Group meeting in Seoul.
- The Republic of Korea hosted a maritime interdiction exercise, Eastern Endeavor 2012, in Seoul.
- U.S. European Command co-hosted an Eastern European Interdiction Workshop with Moldova in Chisinau.

The Global Initiative to Combat Nuclear Terrorism (GICNT): The GICNT, which is co-chaired by the United States and Russia, is an international partnership of 85 nations and four official observers dedicated to strengthening individual and collective capacity to prevent, detect, and respond to a nuclear terrorist event. Partners engage in multilateral activities and exercises designed to share best practices and lessons learned on a wide range of nuclear security and terrorism issues. To date, partners have conducted over 50 multilateral activities, and seven senior-level meetings, in support of these nuclear security goals. In 2012, there were seven activities to promote the sharing of best practices on the topics of nuclear forensics, nuclear detection, and emergency preparedness and response.

Nuclear Trafficking Response Group (NTRG): The NTRG is an interagency group focused on coordinating the U.S. government response to incidents of illicit trafficking in nuclear and radioactive materials overseas, including radiation alarms. The NTRG works with foreign governments, and the international facilities where diversions occurred, to secure smuggled nuclear material, prosecute those involved, and develop information on smuggling-related threats including potential links between smugglers and terrorists. The Department of State chairs the NTRG, which includes representatives from the nonproliferation, law enforcement, and intelligence communities.

Preventing Nuclear Smuggling Program (PNSP): Through the Preventing Nuclear Smuggling Program (PNSP), the United States utilizes outreach and programmatic capabilities to partner with key governments to broadly enhance capabilities to prevent, detect, and respond effectively to nuclear smuggling attempts. The PNSP develops joint action plans with partner governments to specify priority steps to be taken to improve capabilities. It has developed donor partnerships to assist with joint action plan implementations, resulting in foreign contributions of more than $64 million to anti-nuclear smuggling projects. To date, 14 countries have developed joint action plans and PNSP has programmatically engaged 10 countries to enhance nuclear smuggling response and nuclear forensics capabilities. PNSP also leads a U.S. effort aimed at developing specialized counter-nuclear smuggling capabilities for foreign partners that integrate law enforcement, intelligence, prosecution, and technical capabilities. All PNSP efforts advance the objectives in the 2010 Nuclear Security Summit Work Plan and 2012 Communiqué.

Export Control and Related Border Security Program (EXBS): Through the EXBS Program, the Department of State leads the interagency effort to strengthen export control systems to improve national capabilities to detect, deter, interdict, investigate, and prosecute illicit transfers of Weapons of Mass Destruction (WMD), WMD-related items, and advanced conventional arms in over 60 countries. EXBS delivered over 400 information sharing and training activities in 2012, promoting the adoption, implementation, and enforcement of comprehensive strategic trade controls. These activities improve the capability of partner states to prevent transfers of dual-use items to end-users for purposes of proliferation or terrorism. EXBS is also actively involved in efforts to combat WMD smuggling through enhanced border security and has provided equipment and training to develop the ability to detect, deter, and interdict illicit smuggling of radioactive and nuclear materials, WMD components, and other weapons-related items at ports of entry and across borders. In 2012, EXBS conducted 98 bilateral and regional training activities, and delivered detection and identification equipment to bolster border security in 27 countries. EXBS works in harmony with, and complements, the Department of Homeland Security Container Security Initiative, the Department of Energy International Nonproliferation Export Control Program, the Second Line of Defense Program, the Megaports Initiative, and other international donor assistance programs. EXBS programs improve the ability of partner nations to combat WMD proliferation threats and fulfill important U.S. and international commitments, including UNSCR 1540, the Proliferation Security Initiative, and the Global Initiative to Combat Nuclear Terrorism.

Second Line of Defense (SLD): Under its SLD Program, the Department of Energy's National Nuclear Security Administration (DOE/NNSA) cooperates with partner countries to provide radiation detection systems and associated training to enhance their capabilities to deter, detect, and interdict illicit trafficking of special nuclear and radiological materials across international borders. The SLD Program provides mobile radiological detection equipment to selected countries for use at land borders and internal checkpoints and includes two components: the Core Program and the Megaports Initiative. The Core Program began with work in Russia, and has since expanded to include former Soviet states in the Caucasus, Eastern Europe, and other key regions, providing equipment for land border crossings, feeder seaports, and international airports.

Global Threat Reduction (GTR): GTR programs work to prevent terrorists from acquiring CBRN expertise, materials, and technology across the globe. By engaging scientists, technicians, and engineers with CBRN expertise, GTR seeks to prevent terrorist access to knowledge, materials, and technologies that could be used in a CBRN attack against the U.S. homeland. In 2012, GTR was actively engaged in countries and regions where there is a high risk of proliferation and terrorism. GTR programs have expanded to meet emerging CBRN proliferation threats worldwide and focus on promoting biological, chemical, and nuclear security in those countries where there is a high risk of CBRN proliferation.

National Strategy for Countering Biological Threats: In November 2009, President Obama approved a new national strategy to provide greater policy cohesion and coordination for U.S. efforts to prevent state or non-state actors from acquiring or using biological weapons. While efforts to mitigate the consequences of the use of biological weapons are dealt with through other policy and strategic frameworks, federal agencies have developed detailed implementation plans and are actively coordinating efforts in support of the Strategy's seven key objectives:

1. Promote global health security
2. Reinforce norms of safe/responsible conduct
3. Obtain timely/accurate insight on current/emerging risks
4. Take reasonable steps to reduce potential for exploitation
5. Expand our capability to prevent, apprehend and attribute
6. Communicate effectively with all stakeholders
7. Transform international dialogue on biological threats

Biological Weapons Convention Inter-Sessional Work Program: A work program was developed at the December 2011 Five-Year Review Conference to restructure work for the next five years to include:

- Standing agenda items on strengthening national implementation measures, which are critical to nonproliferation, promoting public health, and combating bioterrorism;
- Identifying and responding to relevant developments in science and technology and steps to guard against the misuse of science; and
- Promoting greater cooperation and assistance, particularly in countering and responding to outbreaks of infectious disease.

Chapter 5
Terrorist Safe Havens (Update to 7120 Report)

Terrorist safe havens described in this report include ungoverned, under-governed, or ill-governed physical areas where terrorists are able to organize, plan, raise funds, communicate, recruit, train, transit, and operate in relative security because of inadequate governance capacity, political will, or both.

TERRORIST SAFE HAVENS

AFRICA

Somalia. In 2012, many areas of Somalia remained a safe haven for terrorists, although fewer areas than in 2011. The Transitional Federal Government (TFG) and its successor, the Federal Government of Somalia, with the assistance of the AU Mission in Somalia, AU member states, and allied Somali militia forces, secured areas neighboring Mogadishu and drove al-Shabaab out of many of its strongholds in south-central Somalia. Most notably, the forces gained control of the port city of Kismayo on September 28.

Al-Shabaab continued to control large sections of rural areas in the middle and lower Jubba regions, however, as well as the Bay and Bakol regions. Al-Shabaab also augmented its presence in northern Somalia along the Golis Mountains and within Puntland's larger urban areas. Additionally, Somalia's long unguarded coastline, porous borders, and proximity to the Arabian Peninsula allowed foreign fighters and al-Shabaab members to transit around the region without detection. Areas under al-Shabaab control provided a permissive environment for al-Shabaab and al-Qa'ida operatives to conduct training and terrorist planning with other sympathetic violent extremists, including foreign fighters. The capability of the TFG through August, the Government of Somalia from September on, and other Somali local and regional authorities to prevent and preempt al-Shabaab terrorist attacks remained limited.

The TFG and its successor, the Federal Government of Somalia, cooperated with U.S. counterterrorism efforts.

According to independent sources and NGOs engaged in demining activities on the ground, there was little cause for concern for the presence of weapons of mass destruction in Somalia.

The Trans-Sahara. The primary terrorist threat in this region was al-Qa'ida in the Islamic Maghreb (AQIM). Though its leadership remained primarily based in northeastern Algeria, AQIM factions also operated from a safe haven in northern Mali, from which it launched kidnap for ransom operations, collected arms in the wake of the Libyan Revolution from that country, and attempted to expand its safe haven but was pushed back by Algeria, Mauritania, and Niger.

Mali. In 2012, the Tuareg Rebellion, aided by returning mercenary fighters and arms proliferation stemming from the Libyan Revolution, was followed by the arrival of violent extremist and terrorist groups such as al-Qa'ida in the Islamic Maghreb (AQIM) and the Movement for Oneness and Jihad in West Africa (MUJAO), in northern Mali. The rebel groups, aided by violent extremists in some cases, took advantage of the political chaos in Bamako following the March 2012 coup d'état to capture northern towns and cities and effectively gain control over northern Mali. The key cities in the north – Timbuktu, Gao, and Kidal – were overrun and occupied by violent extremists, who consolidated their gains in northern Mali north of the Niger River, and attempted to implement sharia law, recruit fighters, and establish a governing structure. The international community mobilized and called for: restoration of a civilian government through inclusive and credible democratic elections, negotiations with the rebels but not the terrorists, responding to the profound humanitarian crisis, and countering terrorism.

State Department assistance to the government of Mali for activities that strengthen biological security and reduce the risk of biological weapons acquisition by terrorists or proliferant states was terminated, as required by law, after the March 2012 military coup d'état.

SOUTHEAST ASIA

The Sulu/Sulawesi Seas Littoral. The numerous islands in the Sulawesi Sea and the Sulu Archipelago make it a difficult region for authorities to monitor. A range of licit and illicit activities that occur there – including worker migration, tourism, and trade – pose additional challenges to identifying and countering the terrorist threat. Indonesia, Malaysia, and the Philippines have improved efforts to control their shared maritime boundaries, including through the U.S.-funded Coast Watch South radar network, which is intended to enhance domain awareness in the waters south and southwest of Mindanao. Nevertheless, the expanse remained difficult to control. Surveillance improved but remained partial at best, and traditional smuggling and piracy groups have provided an effective cover for terrorist activities, including movement of personnel, equipment, and funds. The United States has sponsored the Trilateral Interagency Maritime Law Enforcement Working Group since 2008 and this has resulted in better coordination among Malaysia, Indonesia, and the Philippines on issues of interdiction and maritime security.

Asia is vulnerable to exploitation by illicit traffickers and proliferators given the high volume of global trade that ships through the region as well as the existence of smuggling and proliferation networks. Weak strategic trade control legal and regulatory frameworks, and inadequate maritime law enforcement and security capabilities make Southeast Asia an area of concern for weapons of mass destruction proliferation.

The Southern Philippines. The geographical composition of the Philippines, spread out over 7,100 islands, made it difficult for the central government to maintain a presence in all areas. Counterterrorism operations over the past 10 years, however, have been successful at isolating and constraining the activities of domestic and transnational terrorists. Philippine cooperation with U.S. counterterrorism efforts remained strong. Abu Sayyaf Group members, numbering a few hundred, were present in remote areas in Mindanao, especially the islands of the Sulu Archipelago. Jemaah Islamiya members, of whom there were only a small number remaining, were in a few isolated pockets of Mindanao. The Communist People's Party/New People's Army maintained a national presence with a focus in rural and mountainous areas. Continued pressure from Philippine security forces made it difficult, however, for terrorists to organize, plan, raise funds, communicate, recruit, train, and operate.

THE MIDDLE EAST

Iraq. In 2012, the Government of Iraq was aware of the extent of terrorist activities occurring in its territory, and Iraqi leaders and security forces expended considerable effort to counter terrorist groups and deny terrorists safe havens. While the level of counterterrorism pressure exerted by security forces varied by region, overall the central government took strong action to eliminate terrorist safe havens, maintained strong counterterrorism cooperation with the United States, and made progress in preventing the proliferation and trafficking of weapons of mass destruction (WMD) both within and across its borders.

Lax border enforcement by the Kurdistan Regional Government, tensions between the central government and Kurdish security forces, and the ongoing crisis in Syria, however, increased the likelihood that al-Qa'ida in Iraq and its Syria-based front group, al-Nusrah Front, could successfully smuggle WMD, conventional weapons, and operatives across the Kurdish areas of the border into Iraq from Syria.

The Iraqi government made progress in preventing the proliferation and trafficking of WMD. In February 2012, the Government of Iraq passed the Nonproliferation Act, which will serve as the basis to further develop its legal infrastructure to control strategic goods through implementing regulations. The Iraqi government also committed to adopting the EU control list. Furthermore, Iraq has established a radioactive source regulatory infrastructure, the Iraq Radioactive Source Regulatory Authority.

The United States continued to work with Iraq to build Iraqi government capacity to secure potentially dangerous biological and chemical materials and infrastructure housed at Iraqi facilities, while also productively engaging Iraqi scientists and engineers that have WMD or WMD-applicable expertise in peaceful, civilian science.

Lebanon. The Lebanese government does not exercise complete control over all regions in the country or its borders with Syria and Israel. Hizballah militias controlled access to parts of the country, limiting access by Lebanon's security services, including the police and army, which allowed terrorists to operate in these areas with relative impunity. Palestinian refugee camps were also used as safe havens by Palestinian armed groups and were used to house weapons and shelter wanted criminals.

The Lebanese security services conducted frequent operations to eliminate Palestinian violent extremist safe havens and to capture terrorists. They did not target or arrest Hizballah members; although in August, the Internal Security Forces' Information Branch arrested a political ally of Hizballah, former government minister Michel Samaha, on suspicion that he was involved in a plot to carry out terrorist attacks in north Lebanon on orders from Syrian officials. The Lebanese Armed Forces and Internal Security Force continued to participate in U.S. counterterrorism training programs and improved their ability to conduct successful operations.

Lebanon is not a source country for weapons of mass destruction components, but the primary concern is that Lebanon's porous borders will make the country vulnerable for use as a transit and transshipment hub for proliferation-sensitive transfers. The conflict in Syria increases the risk of illicit transfers of items of proliferation concern across the Lebanese border. The United States conducted technical exchanges focusing on drafting comprehensive strategic trade control legislation and adopting and implementing a control list for strategic goods. On border security, the United States conducted numerous trainings and donated equipment to Lebanese Customs to enhance its capabilities to detect illicit cross-border trade in strategic goods and other contraband. Hizballah's continued ability to receive sophisticated munitions via Iran and Syria requires aggressive regular monitoring of this issue.

Libya. In 2012, Libyan internal security suffered significant challenges and setbacks as it sought to reassert central authority following the fall of the Qadhafi regime, though attempts were made to strengthen overall counterterrorism and border capabilities to mitigate the various threats. The resulting instability was punctuated by the attack against a U.S. facility in Benghazi on September 11, which claimed the lives of four U.S. personnel, including J. Christopher Stevens, the U.S. Ambassador to Libya. The Libyan government had serious difficulty in asserting control over portions of the country and adequately manning border posts, particularly in the east and south, resulting in significant levels of known terrorist transit through the country. The Libyan government attempted to assert firmer control over specific areas of the country, and in December declared broad portions of southern Libya a military zone, resulting in border closings across a number of crossing points.

Libya has encountered significant capacity gaps to mitigate the illicit flows of goods, people, and weapons across its borders since the revolution that toppled Qadhafi. While secured at year's end, Libya also maintains stockpiles of declared chemical weapons materials that could prove a proliferation risk given weakened border security. The United States has offered to assist the Libyan authorities with the security and eventual destruction of their chemical weapons stockpiles, in accordance with their obligations as members of the Organization for the Prohibition of Chemical Weapons.

The proliferation of loose weapons from Libya across the country's borders was very concerning. The EU contributed significant border security assistance to the Libyan authorities, and throughout 2012, the United States worked with the Government of Libya to develop a complementary border security assistance package of its own. A delegation of Libyan officials from the Ministry of Defense and Customs Authority visited the United States in mid-September 2012, and expressed deep interest in both U.S. border security best practices and border security technology. They specifically requested U.S. assistance on border security, particularly in the South. Nevertheless, implementation of these programs has been slow, and the Libyan authorities lack the basic training and equipment necessary to monitor their vast land and maritime borders, and to control the flow of people and goods through their airports. Violent extremists continued to exploit these weaknesses, and threatened to destabilize the Middle East and North Africa region.

Yemen. The Government of Yemen, under President Abdo Rabbo Mansour Hadi, remained a strong partner of the United States on counterterrorism issues. Hadi demonstrated Yemen's commitment as a counterterrorism partner soon after taking office by ordering the military to dislodge al-Qa'ida in the Arabian Peninsula (AQAP) militants from areas they occupied in Abyan and Aden governorates including the towns of Zinjibar, Jaar, and Shuqra. By June, these AQAP forces had been dislodged or withdrawn. The Yemeni government relied on pro-government tribal militias known as Popular Committees (PCs) to secure the area after the military sweep. After their setback in Abyan, AQAP terrorists took advantage of Yemen's climate of instability, employing asymmetric tactics in a campaign of bombings and targeted assassinations against government targets, PCs, and civilian and international targets.

Yemen's political instability makes the country vulnerable for use as a transit point for weapons of mass destruction (WMD)-related materials. In the past year the United States resumed training focusing on the development of strategic trade controls. Yemen has identified an inter-ministry group to work on nonproliferation-related issues.

The United States continues to build Yemeni government capacity to secure potentially dangerous biological and chemical materials and infrastructure housed at Yemeni facilities, while also productively engaging Yemeni scientists and engineers that have WMD or WMD-applicable expertise.

SOUTH ASIA

Afghanistan. Several terrorist networks active in Afghanistan, such as al-Qa'ida (AQ), the Haqqani Network, and others, operate largely out of Pakistan. AQ has some freedom of movement in Kunar and Nuristan provinces largely due to a lack of Afghan National Security Forces capacity to control certain border territories in north and east Afghanistan. During 2012, the Afghan government continued to counter the Afghan Taliban and Taliban-affiliated insurgent networks with AQ connections. Specifically, the increased capability of the Afghan Local Police units has increased the ability of the Government of Afghanistan to control territory.

The potential for weapons of mass destruction (WMD) trafficking and proliferation was a concern in Afghanistan because of its porous borders and the presence of terrorist groups. The U.S. government worked with the Government of Afghanistan to implement comprehensive strategic trade controls. The U.S. Border Management Task Force also worked closely with Afghan officials to prevent the proliferation of and trafficking of WMD in and through Afghanistan. The Export Control and Related Border Security Assistance (EXBS) program assisted the Government of Afghanistan in drafting a Strategic Goods Law. This draft legislation was in the final approval stages within the Afghan Ministry of Justice at the end of 2012. In addition, EXBS contributed to strengthening Afghanistan's enforcement capacity through participation in a regional cross-border training program, and training through the Department of Homeland Security's Customs and Border Protection agency.

The United States continued to assist the Afghan government to build capacity needed to secure potentially dangerous biological and chemical materials and infrastructure housed at Afghan facilities, while also productively engaging Afghan scientists and engineers that have WMD or WMD-applicable expertise.

Pakistan. Portions of Pakistan's Federally Administered Tribal Areas, Khyber Pakhtunkhwa province, and Balochistan remained a safe haven for terrorist groups seeking to conduct domestic, regional, and global attacks. Al-Qa'ida, the Haqqani Network, the Afghan Taliban, Lashkar e-Tayyiba, and other groups exploited the inability of Pakistan's security agencies to fully control portions of its own territory to find refuge and plan operations. U.S.-Pakistan discussions on counterterrorism, border security, and political transition in Afghanistan occurred regularly and at high levels.

Pakistan alleged that ISAF and Afghan forces failed to control the Afghan side of the border, allowing safe haven for anti-Pakistan terrorist groups such as the Tehrik-e Taliban Pakistan (TTP or Pakistani Taliban). Pakistan reiterated this concern following the October 2012 shooting of 14-year-old education activist Malala Yousafzai, which Pakistan claimed was planned by TTP elements in eastern Afghanistan.

The potential for weapons of mass destruction (WMD) trafficking and proliferation remained a concern in Pakistan. Export Control and Related Border Security Assistance (EXBS) enabled Pakistani officials to gain expertise in properly classifying items of proliferation concern and learn about export licensing best practices.

The United States continued to reduce the risk posed by potentially dangerous biological and chemical materials in Pakistan by promoting the institutionalization of safe and secure laboratory best practices, productively engaging Pakistani scientists and engineers that have WMD or WMD-applicable expertise, and helping to develop surveillance capabilities to detect and identify possibly catastrophic biological and chemical events.

WESTERN HEMISPHERE

Colombia. Colombia's borders with Venezuela, Ecuador, Peru, Panama, and Brazil include rough terrain and dense forest cover, which coupled with low population densities and historically weak government presence, have often allowed for potential safe havens for insurgent and terrorist groups, particularly the Revolutionary Armed Forces of Colombia (FARC) and the National Liberation Army (ELN). Although Colombia is actively fighting to combat terrorism within its borders, vast swaths of the country are essentially ungoverned and exploited by terrorists and narco-trafficking organizations. Illegal armed groups use the porous borders, remote mountain areas, and jungles to maneuver, train, cultivate and transport narcotics, operate illegal mines, "tax" the local populace, and engage in other illegal activities. The FARC elements in these border regions often engaged the local population in direct and indirect ways, including relying on them for recruits and logistical support. There was seemingly less of this type of cross-border activity in Brazil and Peru where potential safe havens were addressed by stronger government actions. The Government of Peru assigned security forces along the Peru-Colombia border. Both Ecuador and Panama appeared to be strengthening their efforts against Colombian narcotics trafficking and terrorist groups.

Venezuela. The FARC and ELN reportedly continued to use Venezuelan territory to rest and regroup, engage in narcotics trafficking, extort protection money, and kidnap Venezuelans to finance their operations. Throughout the year, the Governments of Venezuela and Colombia continued a dialogue on security and border issues. Venezuela captured at least two FARC members during the year: Luis Freddy Rojas Rincon, who died in custody from injuries sustained during his capture; and William Alberto Chivitia Asprilla, who remains in Venezuelan custody. FARC member Guillermo Enrique Torres Cueter (aka "Julian Conrado"), captured in 2011, remained in Venezuelan custody at year's end despite the Venezuelan government's initial statement that he would be deported to Colombia.

COUNTERING TERRORISM ON THE ECONOMIC FRONT

In 2012, the Department of State designated three new Foreign Terrorist Organizations (FTOs) and amended three existing designations. In addition, the Department listed 18 organizations and individuals as Specially Designated Global Terrorists under E.O. 13224 and amended three existing designations. The Department also revoked the designations of two organizations. The Department of the Treasury also designated organizations and individuals under E.O. 13224.

FTO/E.O. 13224 group designations: See Chapter 6, Foreign Terrorist Organizations, for further information on any of these groups.

- On January 26, the Department of State amended the FTO and E.O. 13224 designations of al-Qa'ida in Iraq (AQI) to include the Islamic State of Iraq as an alias.
- On February 24, the Department of State designated the Jemmah Anshorut Tauhid (JAT) under E.O. 13224 and as a Foreign Terrorist Organization on March 13.
- On May 24, the Department of State designated the Abdallah Azzam Brigades (AAB) under E.O. 13224 and as a Foreign Terrorist Organization on May 30.
- On September 7, the Department of State designated the Haqqani Network (HQN) under E.O. 13224 and as a Foreign Terrorist Organization on September 19.
- On September 28, the Department of State revoked the Mujahedin-e Khalq's (MEK)'s designation as a Foreign Terrorist Organization and as a Specially Designated Global Terrorist under E.O. 13224.
- On October 4, the Department of State amended the designation of al-Qa'ida in the Arabian Peninsula (AQAP) to include Ansar al-Shari'a as an alias under E.O. 13224 and as a Foreign Terrorist Organization on October 5.
- On December 11, the Department of State amended the designation of al-Qa'ida in Iraq (AQI) to include al-Nusrah Front as an alias under E.O. 13224 and as a Foreign Terrorist Organization.

E.O. 13224 designations:
- On January 5, the Department of State designated the al-Qa'ida Kurdish Battalions (AQKB). Established in 2007 from the remnants of other Kurdish terrorist organizations, AQKB believes the leaders of the Kurdistan Regional Government are traitors and has claimed responsibility for a number of attacks against Kurdish targets in Iraq, including a May 2007 attack in Erbil, Iraq, in which 19 people were killed.
- On January 26, the Department of State designated German citizens Yassin and Monir Chouka, who are fighters, recruiters, facilitators, and propagandists for the Islamic Movement of Uzbekistan (IMU), operating along the Afghanistan-Pakistan border. The Chouka brothers are also senior members of Jundallah Media, the IMU's media production arm, and have claimed responsibility for numerous IMU attacks, including one which killed 17 people, including five Americans.
- On January 26, the Department of State designated Mevlut Kar, a facilitator and recruiter for the Islamic Jihad Union (IJU). He is currently wanted by the Government of Lebanon and was sentenced in absentia to 15 years in prison for attempting to establish an al-Qa'ida cell in Lebanon. Kar is also implicated in the 2007 bomb plot targeting U.S. military installations and American citizens in Germany, and provided more than 20 explosives detonators to members of the IJU.
- On June 21, the Department of State designated Boko Haram commander Abubakar Shekau and senior operatives Khalid al-Barnawi and Abubakar Adam Kambar. Shekau is the most visible leader of Boko Haram, while Khalid al-Barnawi and Abubakar Adam Kambar have ties to Boko Haram and close links to al-Qa'ida in the Islamic Maghreb. Under their leadership, Boko Haram has claimed responsibility for dozens of attacks on government

assets and civilians in Nigeria, including the August 26, 2011 attack on the UN building in Abuja that killed at least 23 people.

- On June 21, the Department of State designated Basque Fatherland and Liberty (ETA) military leader and explosives expert Aitzol Iriondo Yarza, a long-term member who has engaged in murder, bombings, recruiting, and training for ETA.

- On July 17, the Department of State designated Ahmed Abdulrahman Sihab Ahmed Sihab, (aka Abdulrahman al-Sharqi). The Bahraini citizen has trained members of al-Qa'ida (AQ) in terrorist tactics, techniques, and procedures. Since January 2007, Sihab has been wanted for extradition by the Government of Bahrain where he has been publicly charged with planning terrorist attacks as a member of AQ.

- On August 7, the Department of State designated trainer and senior AQ member Azzam Abdullah Zureik Al-Maulid Al-Subhi (aka Mansur al-Harbi). Al-Harbi travelled to Afghanistan more than a decade ago to join AQ and is responsible for training militants and coordinating foreign fighters who travel to Afghanistan to fight against coalition forces. Mansur al-Harbi is a Saudi citizen currently wanted for extradition by the Government of Saudi Arabia and is accused of being tied to numerous senior AQ leaders.

- On September 6, the Department of State revoked the designations of the Communist Party of Nepal-Maoist (CPN(M)) under E.O. 13224 and as a "terrorist organization" from the Terrorist Exclusion List under the Immigration and Nationality Act, after the Department determined that the CPN(M) is no longer engaged in terrorist activity that threatens the security of U.S. nationals or U.S. foreign policy. The Maoist party has been elected as the head of Nepal's coalition government, has taken steps to dismantle its apparatus for the conduct of terrorist operations, and has demonstrated a credible commitment to pursuing the peace and reconciliation process in Nepal.

- On November 5, the Department of State designated Qari Zakir, the Haqqani Network's (HQN) chief of suicide operations. Zakir is responsible for HQN's training program, which includes instruction in small arms, heavy weapons, and basic improvised explosive device (IED) construction. He has been involved in many of HQN's high-profile suicide attacks, including the September 2011 attack on the U.S. Embassy in Kabul, and is partially responsible for making some of the final determinations on whether or not to proceed with large-scale attacks planned by local district-level commanders.

- On December 7, the Department of State designated the Movement of Unity and Jihad in West Africa (MUJWA or MUJAO), Hamad el Khairy, and Ahmed el Tilemsi. MUJWA was created in September 2011 after members broke off from AQIM, and has been behind violent terrorist attacks and kidnappings in the region, including a March 2012 suicide attack on a police base in Tamanrasset, Algeria that wounded 23 people; an April 2012 kidnapping of seven Algerian diplomats in Gao, Mali; and a June 2012 attack in Ouargla, Algeria that killed one and injured three. Hamad el Khairy has appeared in MUJWA videos to claim operations and make threats against those who oppose the organization. He was a member of AQIM prior to his leadership role in MUJWA, and was involved in planning terrorist operations against Mauritania in 2007. Ahmed el Tilemsi acts as MUJWA's military head, and has directly participated kidnapping operations for both MUJWA and AQIM.

- On December 17, the Department of State designated former Lebanese Minister of Information and Tourism Michel Samaha. Samaha was arrested by Lebanese authorities in August 2012 and has been charged with plotting to assassinate political and religious figures in Lebanon through targeted bombings. The goal of these attacks appears to have been an attempt to incite sectarian clashes in Lebanon on behalf of the Syrian regime. Samaha was also accused of transporting explosives for the planned attacks into Lebanon.

MULTILATERAL EFFORTS TO COUNTER TERRORISM

In 2012, the United States continued to work with key partners and allies to strengthen our diplomatic engagement through multilateral organizations. By deepening and broadening the international multilateral counterterrorism framework, we are drawing on the resources and strengthening the activities of multilateral institutions at the international, regional, and sub-regional levels to counter the threat of violent extremists and build the capacities of countries around the world. Working with and through these institutions increases the engagement of our partners, reduces the financial burden on the United States, and enhances the legitimacy of our counterterrorism efforts.

The Global Counterterrorism Forum (GCTF). The GCTF is composed of a strategic-level Coordinating Committee and five thematic and regional expert-driven working groups focusing on the criminal justice sector and rule of law; countering violent extremism; and capacity building in the Sahel, the Horn of Africa, and Southeast Asia. The GCTF aims to strengthen the international architecture for addressing 21st century terrorism and promotes a strategic, long-term approach to dealing with the threat. Since its launch in September 2011 by then-Secretary of State Hillary Clinton and Turkish Foreign Minister Ahmet Davutoğlu, the GCTF has mobilized over US $200 million to strengthen counterterrorism-related rule of law institutions, in particular, for countries transitioning away from emergency law.

Other accomplishments since the launch include the adoption of three sets of good practices that are intended to both provide practical guidance for countries as they seek to enhance their counterterrorism capacity and bring greater strategic coherence to global counterterrorism capacity building efforts:

- The Rabat Memorandum on Good Practices for Effective Counterterrorism Practice in the Criminal Justice Sector;
- The Rome Memorandum on Good Practices for Rehabilitation and Reintegration of Violent Extremist Offenders; and
- The Algiers Memorandum on Preventing and Denying the Benefits of Kidnappings for Ransom to Terrorists.

In addition, the GCTF has set in motion the development of two international training centers that will provide platforms for delivering sustainable training in the Forum's two areas of strategic priority: countering violent extremism and strengthening rule of law institutions. At the December GCTF ministerial meeting, the UAE Foreign Minister announced the opening of Hedayah – the International Center of Excellence on Countering Violent Extremism in Abu Dhabi. At the June 2012 ministerial, Tunisian Foreign Minister Rafik Abdessalem announced that Tunisia would host the International Institute for Justice and the Rule of Law. The Institute will provide interested governments with the training necessary to strengthen criminal justice and other rule of law institutions. GCTF members are working closely with the Government of Tunisia on the development of the Institute.

The UN is a close partner of and participant in the GCTF and its activities. The GCTF serves as a mechanism for furthering the implementation of the universally-agreed UN Global Counter-

Terrorism Strategy and, more broadly, to complement and reinforce existing multilateral counterterrorism efforts, starting with those of the UN.

The United Nations (UN). Sustained and strategic engagement at the UN on counterterrorism issues is a priority for the United States. In 2012, the UNSC addressed critical international security matters, including the adoption of three resolutions that concerned the conflict in Mali. These included UNSCR 2056, which expressed the Council's full support for the joint efforts of the Economic Community of West African States, the AU, and the transitional authorities in Mali trying to re-establish constitutionality and territorial integrity; and UNSCR 2071, which expressed the Council's readiness to respond positively to a request from Mali regarding an intervention force to assist the Malian armed forces reclaim the northern half of the country, pending a report from the UN Secretary-General. In addition, the United States engaged with a wide range of UN actors on counterterrorism in 2012. These included:

- **The Counter-Terrorism Committee (CTC).** The Committee monitors global counterterrorism efforts following the guidance of UNSCRs 1373 and 1624. Its group of experts, the UN's Counter-Terrorism Executive Directorate (CTED), assists the Committee in its work and is well-suited to bring together experts and officials to identify practical solutions to common counterterrorism challenges. In 2012, the CTC focused on outreach and terrorist finance; it organized a workshop on terrorist financing that called attention to the revised Recommendations of the Financial Action Task Force. The Committee also highlighted the challenges in implementing counterterrorism measures for effective cross-border control of small arms and light weapons and the role of central authorities in enhancing counterterrorism collaboration. The CTC and CTED maintained an ongoing dialogue with member states, donors, and beneficiaries regarding the implementation of technical assistance for capacity-building at the national and sub-regional levels. Additionally, CTED launched a global initiative aimed at helping member states set up effective mechanisms to freeze terrorist assets in accordance with their obligations under UNSCR 1373 and held a variety of workshops in South Asia, Southeast Asia and the Pacific, the Sahel, East Africa, and Southeast Europe that brought together relevant practitioners to address issues such as border security, countering terrorist financing, the investigation and prosecution of terrorist cases, and countering violent extremism. The United States continued to support an initiative that brought together senior prosecutors from across the globe with experience in handling high-profile terrorism cases. The United States also financed training for judges in South Asia.

- **The UNSC 1267/1989 Committee.** For over 10 years, the sanctions regime established by UNSCR 1267/1989 and its successor resolutions – most recently UNSCR 2083 of December 2012 – has been instrumental in ensuring effective multilateral cooperation in global counterterrorism efforts, particularly the threat posed by al-Qa'ida and its affiliates. Subsequent modifications to the 1267/1989 regime have strengthened and improved its fairness and transparency, including the establishment of the office of an independent Ombudsperson. Important efforts are also under way to strengthen member states' implementation of 1267/1989 sanctions and improve its overall effectiveness. As such, the 1267/1989 Committee added 13 new individuals and two new entities to its Consolidated List in 2012. The Committee also worked to ensure the integrity of the list by endeavoring to remove those individuals and entities that no longer meet the criteria for listing. To date, 150 individuals and entities have been delisted and additional information on remaining listings has been provided to assist in the operational implementation of the sanctions.

- **The UNSC 1540 Committee.** UNSCR 1977, adopted in 2011, extended the mandate of the 1540 Committee for 10 years, reaffirming UNSCR 1540's attention to the non-proliferation of chemical, biological, and nuclear weapons. The resolution also encouraged member states to prepare national implementation plans and urged the Committee to strengthen its role in facilitating technical assistance for implementing UNSCR 1540. In 2012, the 1540 Committee's activities included participating in outreach events to share best practices and facilitate capacity-building. The UNSC also passed Resolution 2055 increasing the number of experts assisting the Committee to nine. The Committee's program of work focuses on five main areas: monitoring and national implementation; assistance; cooperation with international organizations, including the UNSC committees established pursuant to UNSCRs 1267 and 1373; transparency and media outreach; and administration and resources. This includes the compilation and general examination of information on the status of States' implementation of UNSCR 1540, in addition to States' efforts at outreach, dialogue, assistance and cooperation. The United States has contributed US $4.5 million to the UN Trust Fund for Global and Regional Disarmament to support UNSCR 1540 implementation. See Chapter 4, for further information about *The Global Challenge of Chemical, Biological, Radiological, and Nuclear (CBRN) Terrorism*.

- **The Counter-Terrorism Implementation Task Force (CTITF).** Since the adoption of the UN Global Counter-Terrorism Strategy in 2006, the Task Force (UN Member States, 30 UN entities across the UN system, and Interpol), has become the focal point for UN efforts to support implementation of the global framework. In 2012, the United States funded a series of workshops to raise awareness of the strategy in key regions, including a regional workshop in Dhaka, Bangladesh in May. To support the implementation of the UN Global Counter-Terrorism Strategy in Central Asia, CTITF and the UN Regional Centre for Preventive Diplomacy for Central Asia (UNRCCA) organized consultations with regional organizations. The United States also provided voluntary funding to support a number of CTITF programs and projects including its Integrated Assistance for Countering Terrorism initiative in Nigeria, which seeks to enhance information sharing and coordination of technical assistance delivery with partnering governments and the different entities of the UN; training and capacity building of law enforcement officials on human rights, the rule of law, and the prevention of terrorism; and a project on targeted financial measures to counter terrorism, aimed at strengthening implementation of the al-Qa'ida sanctions regime.

- **The UN Interregional Crime and Justice Research Institute (UNICRI).** In partnership with the International Centre for Counter-Terrorism – The Hague (ICCT), UNICRI developed study sessions and technical workshops on identifying innovative means to prevent and counter radicalization and terrorist recruitment. In 2012, UNICRI also started an initiative focusing on prisons, with the purpose of supporting member states in their efforts to build effective rehabilitation and disengagement programs for violent extremists and to take steps to ensure that their prisons are not serving as breeding grounds for radicalization. The United States worked with UNICRI and ICCT to develop this international initiative. More than 35 countries, many multilateral organizations, and leading independent experts have participated in this initiative, which is providing policymakers, practitioners, and experts a chance to compare notes and best practices in this area. The best practices developed, known as the Global Counterterrorism Forum (GCTF) Rome Memorandum on Good Practices for Rehabilitation and Reintegration of Violent Extremist Offenders, is a key tool for shaping the capacity building assistance that UNICRI is providing to requesting member states.

- **The International Civil Aviation Organization (ICAO).** ICAO's Universal Security Audit Program (USAP) continued to contribute directly to U.S. homeland security by ensuring that each of ICAO's 191 member states undergo regular security audits and comply with uniform aviation security standards. USAP conducted assistance missions to help states correct security problems revealed by surveys and audits. ICAO, in partnership with UN's Counter-Terrorism Executive Directorate (CTED), has assisted member states in the implementation of UNSCRs on counterterrorism, including border control. The two entities have conducted assessment visits and organized workshops focused on countering terrorism and the use of fraudulent travel documents, and promoting good practices on border control and aviation security. Together with the UN Office on Drugs and Crime, ICAO and CTED have encouraged member states to ratify and implement international counterterrorism treaties.

- **The UN Office on Drugs and Crime's Terrorism Prevention Branch (UNODC/TPB).** The Terrorism Prevention Branch (TPB), in conjunction with the UNODC's Global Program against Money Laundering, continued to provide assistance to countries in its efforts to ratify and implement the universal legal instruments against terrorism. In 2012, the United States supported the TPB by funding programs that provided counterterrorism training to national prosecutors and judges.

The International Atomic Energy Agency (IAEA). The IAEA continued to implement its Nuclear Security Plan (2010-2013) for countering the threat of terrorism involving nuclear and other radioactive material. The United States was actively involved in IAEA efforts to enhance security for vulnerable nuclear and other radioactive materials and associated facilities, and to reduce the risk that such materials could be used by terrorists.

Group of Eight (G-8). The United States, which held the G-8 presidency in 2012, hosted the annual G-8 Summit in Camp David where leaders stressed the need to counter terrorist financing, including kidnapping for ransom and strengthening implementation of the UN al-Qa'ida sanctions regime; and to eliminate support for terrorist organizations and criminal networks. They also urged states to develop necessary capacities in governance, education, and criminal justice systems; and to address, reduce, and undercut terrorist and criminal threats, including violent extremism, while safeguarding human rights and upholding the rule of law. They underscored the central role of the UN and welcomed the Global Counterterrorism Forum and efforts of the G-8 Roma-Lyon Group (RLG) in countering terrorism. The RLG met once in 2012 and advanced projects on cross-cutting threats of terrorism and transnational organized crime, through its expert groups on improvised explosive devices, transportation security, high tech crime, migration, criminal legal affairs, and law enforcement.

Financial Action Task Force (FATF) and FATF-Style Regional Bodies (FSRBs). The FATF develops and promotes standards, known as recommendations, that protect the global financial system against money laundering and terrorist financing when adopted and effectively implemented. FATF recommendations are the internationally-recognized standard for countering money laundering and terrorist financing. Over 180 jurisdictions have committed to implement the FATF recommendations. In 2012, FATF continued to identify high-risk jurisdictions with strategic deficiencies and worked closely with them to address their shortcomings.

In 2012, the United States supported the plenary activities on a range of policy issues, negotiating, and revising the assessment criteria for mutual evaluations under the new standards; and participated in the working groups on implementation and on strengthening the FATF network through the FATF-style regional bodies (FSRBs). The United States continued its co-chair roles with Italy on the International Cooperation Review Group and with Spain on the Working Group on Terrorist Financing and Money Laundering. The United States continued to emphasize the importance of targeted financial sanctions and Special Recommendation III, a provision regarding the freezing and confiscation of assets. Additional work contributed by the United States included examining and revising the FATF-FSRB relationship, looking at guidance on new payment methods and their vulnerabilities, outreach to the private sector, public-private partnerships, maintaining an emphasis on non-financial businesses and professions, and participation in the Contact Group on the Central African Action Group against Money Laundering and engagement with that organization to transition to an FSRB.

The United States played a similar and equally active role in the FSRBs, advising and supporting the work of the FSRB members as well as the Secretariats, by supporting FSRB-executed training and workshops. The United States provided technical assistance to both members and Secretariats and took part in technical assistance working group meetings. Additionally, the United States took part in Contact Groups to guide outreach for new members, and Expert Review Groups to delve into mutual evaluation issues.

European Union (EU). Established in 2010, the new European External Action Service (EEAS) led the EU's engagement with the United States on a range of counterterrorism issues, including terrorist finance, capacity building in third countries, and transatlantic counterterrorism cooperation. EEAS officials, along with counterterrorism officials from the European Commission and the EU Counterterrorism Coordinator's office, participated with their U.S. counterparts in biannual discussions in June and November. Specific developments included:

- In January, the United States and the EU sponsored an experts meeting on countering violent extremism work in Pakistan and with Pakistani diaspora communities.
- In March, the United States and EU held a joint experts conference on explosives. Participants discussed improving information exchange, mitigating the homemade explosive threat posed by chemical precursors, K-9 explosive detection capabilities, threats to transportation and air cargo, and research and development.
- In April, the European Parliament approved a new Passenger Name Record agreement with the United States, which entered into force on July 1, 2012.
- In September, the EU committed to assisting in establishing the International Center for Justice and the Rule of Law – Tunisia.
- In October, as a co-chair of the Global Counterterrorism Forum Working Group on the Horn of Africa, the EU sponsored a workshop for Financial Intelligence Units from 11 African countries that focused on countering terrorist financing. U.S. officials from the Departments of State and Treasury participated.

- In November, the EU held a conference in Brussels regarding their external countering violent extremism programming plan for 2013. U.S. officials from the Department of State, USAID, and DHS participated.

Organization for Security and Cooperation in Europe (OSCE). The OSCE was chaired by Ireland in 2012 and concluded the process of consolidating the organization's counterterrorism mandate and focused efforts on promoting a rule of law-based counterterrorism approach. In November, an OSCE Rule of Law Conference on counterterrorism featured a wide-ranging discussion about how to both best respect human rights in law enforcement counterterrorism actions and promote the implementation of the Global Counterterrorism Forum Rabat Memorandum of Good Practices for Effective Counterterrorism Practice in the Criminal Justice Sector. U.S.-funded border security training in Central Asia, particularly through the OSCE's Border Management Staff College in Dushanbe, also contributed to the capabilities of border and customs officials to counter threats. Through the OSCE's Transnational Threats Department and its Action against Terrorism Unit, the United States continued to support additional initiatives aimed at critical energy infrastructure protection, travel document security, cyber-security, non-proliferation, and promoting the role that women play in countering violent extremism, particularly in Central Asia and South East Europe.

North Atlantic Treaty Organization (NATO). NATO leads ISAF stability operations in Afghanistan. ISAF conducted operations to degrade the capability and will of the insurgency, support the growth in capacity and capability of the Afghan National Security Forces, and to facilitate improvements in governance and socio-economic development to provide a secure environment for stability. For details regarding ISAF contributions by country, see: http://www.isaf.nato.int/troop-numbers-and-contributions/index.php.

NATO's new Policy Guidelines on Counterterrorism were endorsed in May at the NATO Chicago Summit. The guidelines called for the development of an implementation action plan, which is intended to identify initiatives to enhance the prevention of, and resilience to, acts of terrorism with a focus on improved threat awareness, adequate capabilities, and enhanced engagement with partner countries and other international actors in countering terrorism. Under Operation Active Endeavor, NATO conducts maritime operations in the Mediterranean to demonstrate NATO's resolve to deter, defend, disrupt, and protect against terrorism. NATO also focused on the protection of critical infrastructure, including energy infrastructure, as well as harbor security and route clearance. Many of these challenges are being addressed by NATO's Emerging Security Challenges Division.

- **NATO-Russia Council (NRC).** Founded in 2002, the NRC provides a framework for security cooperation to address shared challenges, including NATO-Russia counterterrorism cooperation. Through the NRC's Science for Peace and Security Committee, NATO Allies and Russia are working on the STANDEX ("Stand-off Detection of Explosive Devices") project, which is designed to detect and counter a terrorist threat to mass transit and other public spaces.

The African Union (AU). In 2012, the AU Commission (AUC) provided guidance to its 54-member states and coordinated limited technical assistance to cover member states' counterterrorism capability gaps. The AUC established a Sub-Committee on Terrorism, in part to coordinate submissions to terrorist-related lists, both from the UN and other partners as well as possible AU-originated designations. The AUC participated in the July High-Level Conference on Victims of Terrorism, organized by the Global Counterterrorism Forum in Madrid, Spain.

The African Center for the Study and Research on Terrorism (ACRST), an AU institution based in Algiers, served as a forum for discussion, cooperation, and collaboration among AU member states. The ACRST also served as the AU's central institution to collect information, studies, and analyses on terrorism and terrorist groups; and to develop counterterrorism training programs. In April, the ACRST hosted 40 government officials, members of religious organizations, and representatives of civil society from eight member states for a seminar on developing and implementing counter-radicalization and de-radicalization programs. The AU's Special Representative on Counterterrorism Cooperation and Director of ACSRT led assessments of counterterrorism capacity in Uganda, Burundi, Djibouti, and Burkina Faso.

The AU Mission in Somalia (AMISOM) conducted counterterrorism operations against al-Qa'ida and its affiliates, and al-Shabaab. AMISOM's forces have pushed al-Shabaab out of Mogadishu, as well as other territory in southern Somalia. AMISOM consists primarily of troops from Uganda, Kenya, Burundi, and Djibouti.

Association of Southeast Asian Nations (ASEAN) and ASEAN Regional Forum (ARF). In 2012, the United States worked closely with ASEAN and called for increased international cooperation in countering terrorism and bolstering the capabilities of member countries to address terrorism and other transnational criminal threats, as noted in the November 2012 Joint Statement of the Fourth U.S-ASEAN Leaders' Meeting. The United States and ASEAN engaged on counterterrorism and other law enforcement capacity-building efforts at the annual Senior Officials Meeting on Transnational Crime, held in September 2012.

The United States actively participated in counterterrorism-related activities of the 27-member ARF, including the annual meeting on counterterrorism and transnational crime (CTTC) and provided substantial support in capacity building through ARF institutions. The United States has encouraged inter-and intra-forum information sharing and supported the CTTC work plan, which focuses on illicit drugs; chemical, biological, radiological and nuclear terrorism; cyber-security and countering terrorist use of the internet; and counter-radicalization. The United States, Australia, and the Philippines conducted a workshop on preparedness and response to a biological incident in September 2012 and the United States also co-hosted with Vietnam an ARF workshop on Proxy Actors in Cyberspace in March 2012.

Asia-Pacific Economic Cooperation (APEC). In 2012, APEC reaffirmed its commitment to the comprehensive Counterterrorism and Secure Trade Strategy, adopted in 2011, which endorsed the principles of security, efficiency, and resilience; and advocated for risk-based approaches to security challenges across its four cross-cutting areas of supply chains, travel, finance, and infrastructure. The United States served as the 2011-2012 Chair of the APEC Counterterrorism Task Force and directly led initiatives to build the capacity of APEC members to counter terrorist financing, improve aviation and bus security, and counter terrorist threats against the food supply. The United States also served as the Chair of the APEC Transportation Working Group Sub-Group for Maritime Security and directly led initiatives to build APEC member maritime and port security capacities through enhanced implementation of the International Ship and Port Facility Security Code. Through actively facilitating engagement across APEC fora, the United States was able to enhance overall effectiveness in such areas as trade recovery by fostering an APEC project proposal and facilitating engagement with the World Customs Organization. The United States also enhanced APEC achievements by bringing additional resources to bear such as by facilitating International Maritime Organization sponsorship and funding for U.S.-sponsored APEC maritime security initiatives.

Organization of American States Inter-American Committee against Terrorism (OAS/CICTE). In 2012, the CICTE Secretariat conducted 155 activities, training courses, and technical assistance missions which benefited more than 9,946 participants in five thematic areas: border control; critical infrastructure protection; counterterrorism legislative assistance and terrorist financing; strengthening strategies on emerging terrorist threats (crisis management); and international cooperation and partnerships. The United States has been a major contributor to CICTE's training programs and has directly provided funding and expert trainers for capacity building programs focused on maritime security, aviation security, travel document security and fraud prevention, cybersecurity, counterterrorism legislation, and efforts to counter terrorist financing.

INTERNATIONAL CONVENTIONS AND PROTOCOLS

A matrix of the ratification status of 16 of the international conventions and protocols related to terrorism can be found here: **https://www.unodc.org/tldb/universal_instruments_NEW.html**

LONG-TERM PROGRAMS AND INITIATIVES DESIGNED TO COUNTER TERRORIST SAFE HAVENS

COUNTERING VIOLENT EXTREMISM (CVE). CVE programming seeks to (1) provide positive alternatives to those most at-risk of radicalization and recruitment into violent extremism; (2) counter violent extremist narratives and messaging; and (3) increase international partner capacity (civil society and government) to address the drivers of radicalization. CVE activities put particular emphasis on building capacity at the local level.

The President and the Secretary of State established the **Center for Strategic Counterterrorism Communications (CSCC)** in 2010 to lead an interagency effort to coordinate, orient, and inform government-wide foreign communications activities targeted against terrorism and violent extremism, particularly al-Qa'ida (AQ) and its affiliates and adherents. CSCC, based at the Department of State, collaborates with U.S. embassies and consulates, interagency partners, and outside experts to counter terrorist narratives and misinformation and directly supports U.S. government communicators at our U.S. embassies overseas. CSCC's programs draw on a full range of intelligence information and analysis for context and feedback. CSCC counters terrorist propaganda in the social media environment on a daily basis, contesting space where AQ and its supporters formerly had free reign. CSCC communications have provoked defensive responses from extremists on many of the most popular extremist websites and forums as well as on social media. In 2012, CSCC produced over 6,000 postings, 64 videos, and 65 graphics, and data suggests its videos have been viewed over 2.1 million times. Informed by its strong relationships with partners in the intelligence community, CSCC also engages in a variety of projects directly supporting U.S. government communicators working with overseas audiences in critical regions in Africa, the Middle East, and South Asia, as well as amplifying the voices of survivors and victims of terrorism through a Resilient Communities Grants program.

In general, CVE programming more closely resembles programs for curtailing recruitment into militias or gangs than traditional public diplomacy or development programming. It requires knowledge of where youth are most susceptible to radicalization and why that is so. We ensure that our areas of focus align with the areas of greatest risk by working with foreign partners and other U.S. government agencies to identify hotspots of radicalization and to design programming. Key areas of programming include:

- **Community Engagement.** Through small grants to U.S. embassies and consulates, the Department of State implemented projects that focused on activities that link at-risk youth with responsible influencers and leaders in their communities. These activities include youth sports leagues, leadership development, and problem-solving and conflict-resolution skills. Grants have also supported the establishment of youth support groups for youth in prisons, and amplifying narratives from victims of terrorism and former terrorists that portray the negative effects of violent extremism. Programming supported community and law enforcement leadership linkages to identify and eliminate problems within the community. Credible influencers – both local leaders and government actors – provided educational, technological, and community development training to help develop communities that are resistant to violent messaging, thus empowering participants to strengthen the social fabric of their countries.

- **Engaging Women.** CVE programming places particular emphasis on engaging women; women are uniquely positioned to counter radicalization both at home and in their communities and are therefore a vital component of our efforts. We continued to support the networking of CVE women activists. Lastly, we sought to amplify the voices of victims of terrorism who can credibly articulate the destructive consequences of terrorism, and can thus help to dissuade those contemplating such acts.

- **Prison Disengagement.** We have worked to identify and address key nodes of potential radicalization. One priority area for us has been prisons. Many incarcerated terrorists will eventually be released, and we have been working to take steps to decrease the likelihood that they will return to violence after they are released. There are also real concerns about potential radicalization inside prisons; effective prison management and good correctional practices can help reduce these risks. To deal with this challenge, we worked with the UN's Interregional Crime and Justice Research Institute (UNICRI) and the International Center for Counterterrorism (ICCT), a Dutch NGO, to develop an international initiative on prison rehabilitation and disengagement. More than 35 countries, multilateral organizations, and leading independent experts have participated in this initiative, which provided policymakers, practitioners, and experts a chance to compare notes and develop good practices in this critically important area. These good practices were codified and approved in the GCTF's July 2012 Rome Memorandum.

In addition, we continued to be engaged in the following broader U.S. government and multilateral CVE initiative:

- **Global Counterterrorism Forum (GCTF) CVE Working Group.** The Global Counterterrorism Forum (GCTF) provides a platform for counterterrorism policymakers and experts to work together to identify urgent needs, devise solutions, and mobilize resources for addressing key counterterrorism challenges. GCTF's CVE Working Group, one of five expert-driven groups, started to examine the following areas: (a) using institutions to counter violent extremism; (b) measuring the impact of CVE programs; and c) countering the violent extremist narrative. On December 14, at the GCTF's Third Coordinating Committee and Ministerial meetings in Abu Dhabi, the GCTF inaugurated Hedayah, the first-ever International Center of Excellence on Countering Violent Extremism, with its headquarters in Abu Dhabi, United Arab Emirates. More information on Hedayah can be found here: http://www.thegctf.org/

CAPACITY BUILDING PROGRAMS. As the terrorist threat has evolved and grown more geographically diverse in recent years, it has become clear that our success depends in large part on the effectiveness and ability of our partners. To succeed over the long term, we must increase the number of countries capable of and willing to take on this challenge. We have had important successes in Indonesia and Colombia, but we must intensify efforts to improve our partners' law enforcement and border security capabilities to tackle these threats. Our counterterrorism capacity building programs – Antiterrorism Assistance Program, Counterterrorist Finance, Counterterrorism Engagement, the Terrorist Interdiction Program/Personal Identification Secure Comparison and Evaluation System, and transnational activities under the Regional Strategic Initiatives – are all critically important and work on a daily basis to build capacity and improve political will. For further information on these programs, we refer you to the Annual Report on Assistance Related to International Terrorism, Fiscal Year 2012: http://www.state.gov/j/ct/rls/other/rpt/206686.htm.

REGIONAL STRATEGIC INITIATIVE. Terrorist groups often utilize porous borders and ungoverned areas between countries. The Department of State's Bureau of Counterterrorism created the Regional Strategic Initiative (RSI) to encourage Ambassadors and their Country Teams to develop regional approaches to counterterrorism. RSI operates in key terrorist theaters of operation to assess the threat, pool resources, and devise collaborative strategies, action plans, and policy recommendations. In 2012, RSI groups were in place for Southeast Asia, East Africa, Eastern Mediterranean, Iraq and its Neighbors, South Asia, Western Hemisphere, Central Asia, and the Trans-Sahara.

Examples of RSI programs approved and funded in 2012 include the Resident Legal Advisor programs in Malaysia, Mauritania, and Mali/Niger; ongoing support for the Terrorism and Transnational Task Force within the Indonesian Attorney General's Office; border security initiatives in the Eastern Mediterranean; the Ugandan Police Force Community Policing Outreach program; an anti-kidnapping for ransom workshop for countries of the Trans-Sahara Counterterrorism Partnership (TSCTP); and the provision of vehicles to the Ministry of Interior of Tunisia.

SUPPORT TO PAKISTAN

The United States continues to build a long-term partnership with Pakistan, as we believe that a stable, secure, prosperous, and democratic Pakistan is in our long-term national security interest. To support this partnership, the United States has provided civilian and security assistance totaling more than US $4 billion since 2009, including about US $1 billion in emergency humanitarian assistance. In addition, since 2002 the Department of Defense has reimbursed approximately US $11 billion in Coalition Support Funds for Pakistani expenditures in support of Operation Enduring Freedom. U.S. security assistance to Pakistan is targeted to support Pakistan's counterterrorism and counterinsurgency needs.

Composition and levels of assistance, including security and other assistance. Since the Enhanced Partnership with Pakistan Act (Kerry-Lugar-Berman, KLB) was passed in October 2009, the United States has disbursed over US $3 billion in civilian assistance to Pakistan, including over US $1 billion of emergency humanitarian assistance following floods and conflict. We continue to focus on five sectors determined in consultation with the Pakistani government in 2011: energy; economic growth, including agriculture; stabilization; education; and health. Emphasis on improving democracy, governance, and gender equity are integrated across the portfolio.

Since the passage of the KLB Act, U.S. assistance has added 400 megawatts to Pakistan's electricity grid; 650 km of roads have been constructed in Pakistan's border regions, enabling trade, security, and mobility; 4,500 police and 800 prosecutors across Pakistan have been trained; approximately 10,000 Pakistanis have received scholarships to attend Pakistani universities; and over 7,200 healthcare providers, including 4,300 female health workers, have been trained to improve the quality of family planning at public sector facilities.

($ in thousands)	FY 2011	FY 2012
TOTAL	1,798.2	1969.9
Economic Support Fund	918.9	864.7
Foreign Military Financing	295.4	295.4
Global Health and Child Survival - USAID	28.4	0.0
International Military Education and Training	4.1	5.0
International Narcotics Control and Law Enforcement	114.3	34.0
Nonproliferation, Antiterrorism, Demining and Related Programs	24.8	20.8
Pakistan Counterinsurgency Fund	297.2	750,000.0
Food for Peace	115.1	

Energy. Chronic energy shortages severely limited Pakistan's economic development. Energy is our top assistance priority, supporting our goal of job creation, security, and political stability in Pakistan. We continued to fund major infrastructure rehabilitation projects and provided technical assistance to Pakistani energy companies to improve their performance and reduce energy costs.

Economic Growth. Through a range of programs and public-private partnerships in agriculture and skills-building for Pakistani micro-entrepreneurs, U.S. assistance helped Pakistan create jobs for its oversaturated labor market. In 2012, the United States also announced the Pakistan Private Investment Initiative (PPII), a US $40 million capital commitment to small- and medium-sized Pakistani enterprises to provide much-needed liquidity to their ventures.

Stabilization. The United States supported Pakistan's efforts to ensure its territory is inhospitable to violent extremists by strengthening governance and civilian law enforcement capacity and promoting socio-economic development, particularly in border areas and targeted locations vulnerable to violent extremism. Our efforts included road construction, small community-based grants, police and governance training, and providing equipment to civilian law enforcement.

Education. U.S. education programs focused on increasing the number of students who enroll in and complete courses in primary, secondary, and tertiary educational institutions; and improving the quality of that education for the Pakistani workforce. This furthers economic growth, which is integrally linked to improvements in basic and higher education systems. We are also committed to building bridges between Pakistani and American students and professionals through exchange programs.

Health. The provision of basic health services in Pakistan is inconsistent, particularly for rural populations. U.S. health programs support the Government of Pakistan in delivering high-quality, cost-effective healthcare, particularly in the area of maternal and child health and including healthy birth spacing. U.S. assistance is also used to assist the Government of Pakistan construct health clinics and hospitals and fund the acquisition of medical materials, including contraception.

Humanitarian Assistance. In 2010 and 2011, the United States was the largest bilateral donor of flood assistance. In 2011, we relied on existing KLB-funded implementation partners to immediately begin assisting those in need. In June 2011, the United States provided US $190 million to the Citizens' Damage Compensation Program (CDCP), a Government of Pakistan vehicle designed with the World Bank to provide direct assistance to more than one million families affected by the 2010 floods. The U.S. contribution leveraged over US $500 million to CDCP. Since October 2009, over US $1 billion of emergency humanitarian assistance was provided to Pakistan in response to floods and conflict, above and beyond bilateral KLB assistance.

International Narcotics Control and Law Enforcement. During 2012, Pakistan took important steps to counter violent extremists operating in the border region. These steps included intensifying support to civilian law enforcement and border security agencies. The United States directly supported Pakistan's efforts to build the capacity of its civilian law enforcement and border security agencies by providing training, equipment, infrastructure, and aviation assistance. U.S. assistance built police capacity to hold areas cleared by Pakistan's military, to protect local populations from militant attacks, and to maintain law and order. Collectively, these efforts enhanced the counterinsurgency, law enforcement, and counternarcotics capacities of Pakistan's civilian law enforcement and border security agencies. Improved security will, in turn, facilitate economic development, which is necessary for long-term Pakistani stability and progress.

Nonproliferation, Antiterrorism, Demining, and Related Programs (NADR)/Export Control and Related Border Security. The United States provided assistance to strengthen Pakistan's export control system to prevent transfer of weapons of mass destruction and related technology. NADR/Export Control and Related Border Security funds were used for nonproliferation export control training addressing legal/regulatory reform, export licensing systems, customs enforcement, general inspection, weapons of mass destruction detection training for border control personnel, and procuring specialized radiation/chemical detection equipment. The United States also provided assistance to build Pakistani law enforcement capacity to detect, deter, and respond to terrorist threats. Specifically, the Department of State's Antiterrorism Assistance (ATA) program provided training and equipment to Pakistani law enforcement to build its capacity to secure land borders and more effectively conduct terrorism-related investigations, including through improved police-prosecutorial cooperation. The State Department provided ATA assistance with the goal of institutionalizing such assistance within Pakistan's law enforcement training structure. NADR/Global Threat Reduction Programs (GTR) provided assistance to Pakistan to prevent terrorist access to biological expertise, materials, and technology. GTR engaged scientists to reduce bio-security threats against the United States by supporting pathogen security, safe and secure laboratory conduct, and disease detection and control.

Foreign Military Financing (FMF). FMF promotes the development of Pakistan's long-term counterinsurgency and counterterrorism capabilities to promote security and stability throughout the country, particularly in the conflict affected areas on the western borders with Afghanistan; improves Pakistan's ability to lead and/or participate in maritime security operations; and supports the transformation and modernization of Pakistan's military into a more professional and capable force to meet Pakistan's legitimate defense needs. Since 2011, the bulk of FMF assistance has been restricted from execution due to provisions contained in the Kerry-Lugar-Berman legislation. During that period, however, we delivered significant assistance, including new and upgraded F-16s to the Pakistan Air Force which are being used to support counterterrorism efforts throughout the border region. In addition, we delivered one Oliver Hazard Perry-class frigate which has been consistently used by the Pakistan Navy to support its participation in Combined Task Force (CTF) 150 (counterterrorism operations) and CTF 151 (counter-piracy operations). Funding from FY 2011 through FY 2013 will be directed towards enhancing Pakistan's counterinsurgency and counterterrorism capabilities in the areas of precision strike, battlefield air mobility/combat search and rescue, battlefield communications, night vision, survivability, countering improvised explosive devices, and border control.

International Military Education and Training (IMET). Pakistan's IMET program supported professional military education for Pakistan's military leaders, emphasizing respect for the rule of law, human rights, and democratic values, including civilian control of the military. IMET also supported effective management of Pakistan's defense establishment through training in logistics, defense acquisition, and resource management. As required as part of the Kerry-Lugar-Berman legislation, a significant portion of this funding supports training related to counterterrorism and counterinsurgency operations in Pakistan.

Pakistan Counterinsurgency Fund/Pakistan Counterinsurgency Capability Fund. The Department of Defense's Pakistan Counterinsurgency Fund and the Department of State's successor program, the Pakistan Counterinsurgency Capability Fund (PCCF), assist the

Government of Pakistan in building and maintaining the capability of its security forces to conduct counterinsurgency and counterterrorism operations throughout the frontier regions that are in our mutual interest. PCCF has enabled us to provide critical equipment and training to improve capabilities for the Pakistan Army, Air Force, and Frontier Corps, including counter-improvised explosive devices, night operations, and precision strike. In addition, better equipped security forces will continue to facilitate Pakistan's efforts to support our shared interest in ensuring a stable, secure, and prosperous region as we approach the transitions of 2014.

Measures to ensure that assistance has the greatest long-term positive impact on the welfare of the Pakistani people and their ability to counter terrorism. Roughly half of U.S. civilian assistance is implemented via Pakistani partners, including the Government of Pakistan and private sector actors when practicable. This is done to strengthen local capacity and increase sustainability, providing the greatest possible long-term impact of U.S. assistance on the welfare of the Pakistani people. Increasingly, the Administration is also implementing public-private partnerships in health and economic growth programs to engage the private sector as a long-term partner in Pakistan's development.

COUNTERTERRORISM COORDINATION WITH SAUDI ARABIA

The United States and Saudi Arabia have a strong bilateral relationship. Multiple high-level visits in 2012 deepened this relationship at the personal and institutional level and enabled senior officials from both countries the chance to discuss means of improving coordination. In 2012, then-Secretary of Defense Leon Panetta, National Security Advisor Thomas E. Donilon, then-Assistant to the President for Homeland Security and Counterterrorism John O. Brennan, director of FBI Robert Mueller III, and Deputy Secretary of Treasury Neal Wolin, each visited Saudi Arabia, meeting with King Abdullah and other Saudi officials.

Like other countries in the region, Saudi Arabia sought to find meaningful economic and civic opportunities for its people, over 65 percent of its population is under 25 years old. The King has clearly enunciated an economic development agenda, and Saudi Arabia made progress in addressing economic sources of social discontent, such as housing scarcity, a low public sector minimum wage, and the lack of a private sector unemployment benefit. The King Abdulaziz Center for National Dialogue continued to promote tolerance and respect for diversity through its dialogue and awareness-raising programs. In October, as an extension of Saudi Arabia's efforts to promote tolerance and dialogue, the Saudi government, in cooperation with the Governments of Spain and Austria, launched the King Abdullah International Centre for Interreligious and Intercultural Dialogue in Vienna to offer a permanent platform for dialogue between the world's major religions.

The United States continued to support the Saudis in the reforms they are undertaking by facilitating Saudis studying in the United States and other educational exchanges; by encouraging increased bilateral trade and investment, and urging Saudi Arabia to take actions necessary to attract job-creating partnerships with U.S. companies; and by targeted programming in such areas as judicial reform, local governance, and women's entrepreneurship. The United States encouraged the Saudi government to take concrete steps to increase opportunities for civic participation; in September, the Saudi government held municipal council elections (delayed since 2009); also in September, King Abdullah announced that women would be allowed to participate in future elections (expected in 2015) and that women would be appointed to future sessions of the Consultative Council.

U.S.-Saudi collaboration was not confined to bilateral issues: with political upheaval across the region throughout the year, we consulted closely with the Saudi government on regional stability, including in Yemen, Syria, and Egypt. Working both bilaterally and multilaterally through the Gulf Cooperation Council and the Arab League, the Saudi government provided leadership in promoting peaceful transitions. As part of its strategy to support these transitions and to promote stability throughout the region, the Saudi government significantly increased the scope of its economic and development assistance.

BROADCASTING BOARD OF GOVERNORS INITIATIVES: OUTREACH TO FOREIGN MUSLIM AUDIENCES

This section is provided by the Broadcasting Board of Governors (BBG)

Four of the five broadcast entities under the supervision of the Broadcasting Board of Governors (BBC) – the Voice of America (VOA), the Middle East Broadcasting Networks (Alhurra TV, Radio Sawa, and Afia Darfur), Radio Free Europe/Radio Liberty (RFE/RL), and Radio Free Asia – provided programming for Muslim audiences in 2012.

- Eighteen of RFE/RL's broadcast languages – almost two-thirds of the total – were directed to regions with majority-Muslim populations, including Iran, Iraq, Afghanistan, Azerbaijan, Kosovo, Albania, Kazakhstan, Kyrgyzstan, Pakistan, Tajikistan, Turkmenistan, and Uzbekistan. Additional broadcasting regions in the Russian Federation included the majority Muslim populations of Tatarstan, Bashkortostan, and the North Caucasus.
- VOA has been particularly successful in reaching non-Arabic-speaking Muslim audiences, with strong performances in Nigeria, Indonesia, Afghanistan, and Tanzania.
- The Middle East Broadcasting Networks (MBN) broadcast throughout the region to a Muslim population estimated at 315 million.
- VOA and RFE/RL provided news and information to Afghanistan and the Afghanistan-Pakistan border region in Dari and Pashto. Together, RFE/RL and VOA reached nearly 75 percent of Afghan adults each week.
- Radio Free Asia broadcast to the more than 16 million mainly ethnic Uighur Muslims in the Xinjiang Uighur Autonomous Region of northwestern China and Central Eurasia.

The BBG used the latest communications technologies to avoid jamming and to reach new audiences through digital and other communications tools, such as webchats and blogs.

THE MIDDLE EAST

Arabic. Broadcasting through a network of five bureaus/production centers in the region, a network of regional correspondents, and its main studios in Virginia, the Middle East Broadcasting Networks (MBN) broadcast throughout the region to a Muslim population estimated at 315 million. This represented 92 percent of the region's population and 20 percent of the world's Muslim population. The networks provided a unique, local perspective of breaking news, current events, and topics that are not readily found in domestic media, such as freedom of speech, religion, and the role of women in society and politics. In 2012, MBN focused its coverage on the building of democratic principles throughout the region.

Leading up to presidential elections in Egypt, Alhurra joined with Cairo's top rated Al Hayat TV-2 to co-produce and simultaneous broadcast a series of high-profile interviews of Egyptian presidential candidates. The network's coverage continued through the transfer of power from the military to the newly elected president and through the demonstrations and debates over the national referendum regarding the adoption of a new constitution. Alhurra's local news coverage was supplemented by in-depth analysis and panel discussions regarding controversial sections of the proposed constitution including the powers of the president, the role of the judiciary, and the army. Alhurra's flagship talk show *Free Hour* aired live from Cairo in the week leading up to the vote, and the weekly talk show *Hiwar Cairo* expanded to two hours.

In Libya, Alhurra and Radio Sawa continued to cover the transition to democracy though its newscasts, special event programming, and as a special topic on current affairs programs. Topics included the security situation in Libya and the debate over federalism and the formation of the national army. Radio Sawa's coverage was bolstered by the installation of FM transmitters in Tripoli, Benghazi, and Misratah, the country's three largest cities.

Also in 2012, MBN re-launched its Alhurra and Radio Sawa websites, featuring a cleaner and more user-friendly experience. The sites promoted greater audience interaction by allowing readers to easily post comments on stories and share reports. Through its reinvigorated digital presence and integration with on-air promotion, Alhurra's *Facebook* followers have grown to more than 830,000 and Radio Sawa to more than 775,000.

Radio Sawa's network of stations, broadcasting 24/7, is designed to reach the Arabic-speaking population under the age of 35. It broadcast 325 newscasts per week about the Middle East, the United States, and the world. According to international research firms such as ACNielsen, Radio Sawa had a weekly reach of 13.4 million people in countries where its audience has been measured.

Radio Sawa broadcast on FM in:
- Morocco (Rabat, Casablanca, Tangier, Meknes, Marrakesh, Agadir, and Fes)
- Jordan (Amman and Ajlun – also extending SAWA's reach into southern Syria)
- West Bank and Gaza (Jenin and Ramallah)
- Kuwait (Kuwait City)
- Bahrain (Manama)
- Libya (Tripoli, Benghazi, and Misratah)
- Qatar (Doha)
- United Arab Emirates (Abu Dhabi and Dubai)
- Iraq (Baghdad, Nasiriya, Basra, Mosul, Kirkuk, Sulimaniya, Fallujah, Ramadi, Al-Hilla, Tikrit, Amara, Najaf, Samawa, and Erbil)
- Lebanon (Beirut, North Lebanon, South Lebanon, and Bekaa Valley)
- Djibouti

Radio Sawa also broadcast on medium wave to Egypt, Yemen, Saudi Arabia, and Sudan; and was available on the Arabsat, Nilesat, and Eutelsat satellite systems.

Iraq. Every week, 67 percent of Iraqi adults – some 12.4 million people – listened to or watched one of the four BBG broadcasters serving the country: Alhurra TV, Radio Sawa, RFE/RL's Radio Free Iraq, and VOA Kurdish. Alhurra reached 49 percent of the Iraqi population weekly and Radio Sawa remained the number one radio station among adults. Radio Free Iraq, with 16 percent weekly reach on radio and the internet, was among the top five radio stations for news. VOA Kurdish reached 7.1 percent of Kurdish-speaking Iraqis weekly.

Radio Free Iraq connected with its audience through in-depth reporting on political developments, religious tolerance, Iraqi music and literary traditions, women, youth, and sports. While radio was Radio Free Iraq's primary platform, iraqhurr.org gained online users. The Service also had a mobile version of its website and was active on *Facebook, Twitter*, and *YouTube*. Radio Free Iraq's SMS service increased public interactivity. Listeners' feedback sent in via SMS, as well as via voice mail service, was used to enrich radio programming.

Kurdish. VOA's Kurdish Service has been the only international broadcaster to Iraq's Kurds in their main dialects, Sorani and Kurmanji. Although the primary target audience was the Iraqi Kurd population, the Service expanded its coverage to reach Kurds in Turkey, Syria, and Iran. The Service broadcast three hours of radio programming seven days a week via short wave and FM transmitters in the cities of Sulaimania, Kirkuk, Mosul, Erbil, and Baghdad. Postings on *YouTube, Facebook*, and *Twitter* increased the number of visitors to the service's Sorani and Kurmanji sites. VOA Kurdish expanded its audience by introducing one of its daily radio shows via satellite TV. A 2012 survey indicated an audience increase in the weekly listening rate to over eight percent of Kurdish adults in Iraq.

Iran. Although the Government of Iran worked to jam satellite television signals, audience numbers in Iran increased in 2012. New Gallup data showed that VOA Persian's TV weekly audience grew to 21.4 percent, up from 6.5 percent in 2011. The return of the VOA signal to the popular Hotbird satellite is believed a key factor. With the addition of radio and the internet, VOA's total audience reach in Iran is estimated at 22.1 percent. Under the leadership of a new management team, the Persian Service expanded its prime time programming to six hours daily, and revised its lineup to include several new shows that highlight life in the United States and allow greater audience participation. The Persian Service also produced a two-hour star-studded concert, recorded live, in celebration of Nowruz (the Persian New Year). VOA Persian provided audiences with unrivalled coverage of major U.S. events, including the State of the Union address and the 2012 elections.

RFE/RL's Radio Farda broadcast newscasts at the top of each hour, followed by reports, features, interviews, and regular segments on youth, women, culture, economics, and politics.

Radio Farda regularly debunked false claims by Iranian state media. In early 2012, when state television falsely claimed that the EU had ignored a request by Tehran for preparatory talks ahead of a key nuclear negotiation, Radio Farda landed an exclusive interview with an EU spokesperson, who told listeners that the EU had already responded to Iran's request. Radio Farda's report quickly gained traction on social media and the internet, forcing state-run media to correct its earlier story.

New Radio Farda programs directed attention to the plight of political prisoners. A prisoner released by Iranian authorities told Radio Farda that fellow inmates in Tehran's notorious Evin and Gohardasht prisons followed the daily series "Visit" closely. A second series, "Solitary Confinement" generated interest, particularly within the Iranian journalism community, since many Iranian journalists have been subjected to solitary confinement in prison.

Radio Farda received over 100,000 messages via SMS, email, and voicemail annually, and has one of the most popular Iranian news pages on *Facebook* with almost 215,000 fans. Radio Farda's popular satire show, *Pas Farda*, has its own *Facebook* page with over 80,000 fans. Radio Farda's strategies to fight internet blockage by the Iranian regime are proving successful. From June 2011 to May 2012, Farda's website logged nearly 160 million page views.

SOUTH ASIA

Radio Free Afghanistan. Afghanistan was the only country in RFE/RL's broadcast region where U.S. government-funded broadcasters were the dominant media outlets.
- In June, a Radio Azadi report on complaints by local villagers about an official from Badakhshan province resulted in President Hamid Karzai firing the official and criminal proceedings being opened against him.
- The Service's call-in shows provided an important platform for discussion and debate as well as a means of communicating needs and concerns to Afghan officials.
- Every day the service received between 500-600 voice mails and messages from listeners.
- More than 400,000 Afghans received news twice a day from Radio Azadi on their mobile phones and send citizen journalism reports to the station, via a subscription-based SMS news service RFE/RL launched in 2010 in partnership with local mobile phone service provider Etisalat Afghanistan.

VOA's Afghanistan Service provided radio and television programming to Afghan audiences, reaching a combined radio and television audience of 13 million people (five million via TV and eight million via radio), or 60 percent of the adult population. *Ashna* broadcast nine hours daily to Afghanistan (four hours Dari and four hours Pashto for radio, and one half-hour each of Dari and Pashto on TV). VOA's television service, TV *Ashna*, has become especially popular in urban centers. In Afghanistan's top five cities, TV *Ashna* reached 62 percent of adults weekly, while its total "all-media" audience was over 71 percent; almost half of all adults watch the newscast at least once a week. Special radio programming and segments covered Eid, Ramadan, and the Haj, with correspondent reports on prayers in mosques in both Afghanistan and Washington. In addition to news of Afghanistan, *Ashna* provided news and views from the United States.

Urdu. VOA Urdu's flagship show, "Sana Ek Pakistani" provided a peek into America, its people, culture, politics, sports, food, and government. Urdu has a weekly TV Show, Zindagi (Life) 360, directed towards the youth of Pakistan. A weekly program, Café DC, looked at important personalities in the DC area, including members of congress and executive branch officials. In addition, Urdu does a daily "News Minute" on three different channels. Another weekly 30-minute program, "Access Point", was available on the internet. The Service provided an interactive capability through *Facebook* and *Twitter*, and audiences were invited to send their observations, suggestions, and questions to VOA. Every TV and radio reporter has a *Facebook* page and responded to viewers comments. The Service also provided interactive programming with Pakistani-Americans and Pakistani college students.

The Pakistan/Afghanistan Border Region. VOA's Deewa Radio's daily nine-hour broadcast to approximately 40 million Muslims in Pakistan, and the border regions of Pakistan and Afghanistan, provided accurate and timely news in an area dominated by state-controlled media and Taliban-run Mullah Radio. The Service launched a one hour "Radio on TV" broadcast, providing news, analysis, health, and other issues relevant to internally displaced persons (IDPs). Daily talk shows enriched the audience's understanding of U.S. perspective towards Pakistan, Afghanistan, and the Muslim world by engaging top experts with U.S. think tanks and universities. For example, Deewa's daily program 'Sweet Woman' is engaging educated girls and household women on issues ranging from women rights to the arts.

Deewa's network of 27 stringers report provide extensive daily coverage of the Federally Administered Tribal Area, including live reports from camps that house internally IDPs.

With its extensive network of local reporters, RFE/RL's Radio Mashaal (*Torch*) provided breaking news and in-depth coverage on medical, educational, and cultural issues affecting the region's youth, including the impact of the destruction of schools by terrorists and the need to ensure that children are vaccinated for polio. The Service emphasized interaction with its audience through regular call-in shows.

Bangladesh. VOA's Bangla Service reported on events in both Bangladesh and the United States, and provided coverage of Ramadan/Eid celebrations in Bangladesh, Pakistan, India, and in the Bangladeshi-American community in the United States. Bangla Service coverage of U.S. events included remarks by President Obama, members of Congress, administration officials, and Muslim leaders. The Service produced a special web feature on the *haj* that included remarks from those participating in the pilgrimage. VOA Bangla also covered the Ahmadiya Community's Annual Conference in Pennsylvania; the Islamic Society of North America's annual conference in Washington, DC; and the Bishwa Iztema congregation in Dhaka, Bangladesh.

CENTRAL ASIA

Kazakhstan. RFE/RL's Kazakh Service was delivered primarily through its internet platform but also provided two daily hours of radio programming. The web strategy attracted a younger audience to this bilingual (Kazakh and Russian) site, providing opportunities for interactivity and exploration of new genres such as video reporting. In early 2012, the Kazakh Service distinguished itself with its coverage of the deadly unrest in the town of Zhanaozen, where in December 2011, police killed at least a dozen protesting oil workers. The Service got a correspondent into Zhanaozen before the Kazakh government imposed a media blackout. The coverage of the tragedy became a primary source for media outlets including *The New York Times*, BBC, and Reuters.

Kyrgyzstan. RFE/RL's Kyrgyz Service (Radio Azattyk) was one of the most trusted sources of news and information in Kyrgyzstan, especially during periods of political turmoil. The Service's two TV shows were broadcast during prime time hours on National TV with a combined weekly reach of 25 percent of the population.

Tajikistan. RFE/RL's Tajik Service was the largest independent media outlet in Tajikistan and the top international broadcaster in the country. The Tajik Service was repeatedly criticized by the Tajik government for its coverage, and access to the Service's website was temporarily blocked by the government in late December.

Uzbekistan. In June, the Uzbek Service launched "Liberty Online," an internet-based audio talk show that used *Skype* and *Facebook* to involve interview subjects and listeners in a live discussion. Between May 2011 and May 2012, the number of users of the Service's *YouTube* page rose from 35,000 to 537,000, while the Service's mobile site saw a tenfold increase during the same one-year period. VOA's Uzbek TV program and daily 30-minute radio broadcast featured interviews with U.S. and international sources on topics including terrorism, religious extremism, and U.S.-Uzbek relations. The Service launched *uzmobil.com*, distributing VOA news to mobile phone subscribers. Reports were also accessible on *Twitter*, *YouTube,* and *Facebook.*

Turkmenistan. RFE/RL's Turkmen Service is not allowed to have a bureau or accredited journalists within the country, but despite these restrictions, the Turkmen Service increased its online traffic through new-media techniques including blogging and social networking on *Facebook* and *Twitter*. In June, after reporting that Turkmenistan's universities only had space for 6,000 incoming students, the Service created a webpage that compiled information from NGOs, embassies, and university officials in several countries with information for Turkmen students on studying abroad.

EAST ASIA AND PACIFIC

China. VOA Chinese included daily Mandarin and Cantonese broadcasts via satellite television, radio, online, and mobile channels. These broadcasts delivered news about the world and the United States, including religious and legal issues affecting China's estimated 22 million Muslims.

Radio Free Asia's (RFA) Uighur language service broadcast two hours daily, seven days a week, and was the only international radio service providing news and information in the Uighur language to the potential audience of more than 16 million Uighur Muslims in Western China and Central Eurasia. Consistent with RFA's mandate, the Uighur service acted as a substitute for indigenous media reporting on local events in the region. Its programs included breaking news, analysis, interviews, commentary, a weekly news review, and feature stories.

Despite the Xinjiang Uighur Autonomous Region's (XUAR) continued media blackout enforced by Chinese authorities, RFA broke news with local eyewitness and citizen journalist input. RFA's Uighur service website updated news in all three writing systems used to convey the Uighur language: Arabic, Latin, and Cyrillic. The site streamed the daily RFA broadcast in Uighur and offered ongoing coverage of events in the XUAR in text, image, and video. In a radio and online multimedia series, RFA reported on Uighur men who have been missing since the 2009 unrest. The service won a top award at this year's New York Festival for its breaking coverage of the jailing of four Uighur youths in the aftermath of a deadly incident. RSS feeds were available, making it possible for people to automatically update their newsreaders or web pages with RFA news content. RFA also offered a mobile version of its website as well as Uighur *Twitter* and *Facebook* pages. Despite Chinese censorship, research indicated that Uighur listeners and web users considered RFA an important resource in a controlled media environment.

Indonesia. VOA's 2012 weekly audience in Indonesia was more than 21 million people. VOA Indonesian TV news products were regularly seen on eight of Indonesia's 11 national stations, in addition to more than 30 local and regional stations. The Service produced a weekly TV segment on Islam in the United States for ANTV's Wisata Hati, a popular early morning Muslim-oriented program. During the month of Ramadan, VOA produced a special TV series on Islam in the United States, carried by several national stations. The Service produced more than eight hours daily of original radio programming for a network of more than 300 affiliate FM stations. Radio programming included five-minute *Headline News* reports that aired 32 times a day, seven days a week. The Service's *Facebook* page surpassed one million fans by the end of 2012. In November, the Service held two conferences attended by more than 200 radio, TV, and web affiliates; and it participated in two major off-air events; UrbanFest with 50,000 attendees, and the Media Festival sponsored by the Alliance of Independent Journalists.

EUROPE AND EURASIA

The Russian Federation. VOA's Russian Service has systematically addressed issues related to Islam in key areas. A special section on the Service's website, dedicated to coverage of developments in the North Caucasus region, was regularly updated with reports, interviews, and video features.

Tatarstan/Bashkortostan. The Tatar and Bashkir communities are the two largest Muslim communities in Russia. Radio Free Europe/Radio Liberty's Tatar/Bashkir Service was the only major international broadcaster in the Tatar and Bashkir languages and provided listeners with objective news and analysis. The service's web page was a virtual meeting place for people to discuss these issues. VOA Russian also targeted these communities, who largely rely on Russian language for their news and information. Since May 2010, there were over 100,000 visits to VOA's Russian website for Tatarstan and Bashkortostan.

North Caucasus. Broadcasting in the Avar, Chechen, and Circassian languages, RFE/RL's North Caucasus Service reported the news in a region where media freedom and journalists remained under threat.

Turkey. VOA's Turkish Service, updated with top news seven days a week, offered English teaching programs, a daily web radio program, video and audio clips, and the ability for users to post comments. It was accessible by web-enhanced mobile phones and similar devices, and content was distributed on *YouTube, Twitter*, and *Facebook*. The Service provided 15-minute live TV news and analysis broadcasts four times per week to its TV affiliate, TGRT News Network in Turkey (one of the top five all-news networks in Turkey). VOA Turkish also produced a weekly 30-minute magazine show that was aired on TGRT.

The Balkans. VOA's Balkan services explored the life of Muslims in the United States, multi-ethnic and religious tolerance in the Balkans, and terrorism, including manifestations of that threat in the Balkans. More than 4.7 million adults watched or listened weekly to VOA programs in Albania, Kosovo, Bosnia, Serbia, and Macedonia.

VOA Bosnian featured reports on the sentencing of Bosnian-born U.S. citizen Adis Medunjanin in the 2009 al-Qa'ida plot to bomb the New York subway system, and the trial of Mevlid Jasarevic, jailed for the 2011 terrorist attack on the U.S. Embassy in Sarajevo; interviewed Mustafa Ceric, the Grand Mufti of Bosnia; and presented commentary and analysis from U.S. terrorism experts.

VOA Albanian covered the sentencing of Albanian citizen and Brooklyn resident Agron Hasbajrami for attempting to provide material support to terrorists.

Azerbaijan. VOA Azerbaijani daily TV and Web programming focused on the country's political dynamics as the authorities increased their pressure on political activists and civil-society groups. It regularly programmed reports and interviews targeting the large Azeri population in northern Iran. When it was banned from FM airwaves, RFE/RL's Azerbaijan Service (Radio Azadliq) lost more than half of its reach in Baku. It has turned to the internet and to satellite television to reconnect with listeners.

- In the first half of 2012, Azadliq's website garnered more than 2.5 million visits, 80 percent of which came from within Azerbaijan.
- In May, the Service launched a new weekly 15-minute program that appeared within a partner's program on TurkSat as well as on HotBird.
- The Service began providing live video coverage using the Livestream platform Bambuser, which allowed journalists to cover events even when an internet connection was unavailable. The Service also published a weekly newspaper distributed at Baku subway stations.
- The Service launched a six-month project in January 2012 to enhance its Corruption Meter initiative with a series of weekly debates broadcast live on social media, radio, and the internet.

AFRICA

Nigeria. VOA's Hausa Service has provided extensive coverage of Boko Haram's terrorist activities in Northern Nigeria, including reporting and discussion on attacks and bombings of military check points, schools, police stations, banks, and markets. VOA itself was threatened by Boko Haram as a result of its coverage.

Somalia. VOA's Somali Service produced a weekly Islamic affairs program that covered political, economic, and social changes in Muslim majority countries. Issues covered included the joint military offensive by the Somali government and AU against al-Shabaab; Syria; elections in Egypt, and the September 11 attack on Benghazi.

Swahili. VOA's Swahili Service broadcast to large Muslim populations in Tanzania and Kenya, and to Muslim communities in Uganda, Burundi, and the Democratic Republic of the Congo.

French to Africa. VOA's French to Africa Service provided extensive coverage of the fundamentalist-driven conflict in Mali and its effect on the sub-region. Additionally, weekly

Religion Magazine programs have been dedicated to discussions with Muslim scholars and experts on Islam, the role of women, sectarian differences within Islam, and interfaith dialogues with religious figures.

BASIC EDUCATION IN MUSLIM MAJORITY COUNTRIES

In 2012, USAID's contributed US $654,500,000 to basic education in Muslim majority countries. Approximate amounts for each region were:

- USAID/Asia Bureau: US $363 million; approximately US $320 million of this sum was allocated to predominantly Muslim countries or Muslim majority populations within a country. Countries included Bangladesh, India, Indonesia, Kyrgyzstan, Philippines (Mindanao), and Tajikistan.
- USAID/Middle East Bureau: US $153 million for Egypt, Iraq, Jordan, Lebanon, Morocco, Yemen, and the West Bank and Gaza.
- USAID/Office of Afghanistan and Pakistan Affairs: US $105 million.
- USAID/Europe and Eurasia Bureau: Education assistance for Kosovo totaled US $1,510,000.
- USAID/Africa Bureau: US $272 million; US $75 million was used for Muslim populations in Djibouti, Ethiopia, Kenya, Mali, Nigeria, Senegal, Somalia, and Tanzania, and on regional programs in several other countries.

ASIA

Bangladesh. USAID focused on early childhood development to improve enrollment, retention, and performance in primary schools. The Promoting Talent through Early Education Program developed a pre-school curriculum and increased learning skills and access to educational opportunities for 39,710 preschoolers. Over 2,800 primary school teachers were trained in interactive teaching methodologies that included health, nutrition, and sanitation components. In addition to teacher training, the program trained school administrators to ensure that curriculum and teaching improvements were institutionalized. The US $8.3 million Bangladeshi version of *Sesame Street* was the most widely viewed children's television show in the country, reaching over 10 million Bangladeshi children weekly.

India. While not a Muslim majority country, India has a large Muslim population. USAID's basic education activities helped provide quality education to disadvantaged children including Muslim minorities and promoted the use of technology to improve teaching and learning in the classroom and interventions that link education to employment. The Madrassa Education Program came to a close in 2012 and helped enroll over 51,000 disadvantaged students. More than 200 teachers and 110 administrators were trained in modern pedagogic concepts and effective teaching methods resulting in madrassa leaders assuming new roles in education for youth, particularly girls. A noteworthy achievement has been the mobilization of community support groups and volunteers through training, resulting in formal communication channels being institutionalized between parents and madrassas. In addition, USAID/India's Youth Skill Development Initiative provided education in basic life and employability skills to deprived out-of-school youth, such as computer usage, spoken English, and customer relations. Over 38,000 youth were trained in the states of Delhi, Jharkhand, and Maharashtra. Seventy-five percent of the trainees received employment and many opted for further studies.

Designed as a public-private initiative, the program has leveraged resources from non-USAID sources such as the Centre for Civil Society, the India Islamic Cultural Centre, and Jan Shikshan Sansthan, Kishanganj. Finally, USAID/India implemented a program in over 500 madrassas in Hyderabad, West Bengal, and Andra Pradesh that introduced formal curricula, enrolled and retained out-of-school children, improved the quality of education, and prepared madrassas to meet government standards. Over 50,000 Muslim children were provided with formal education in the two states.

Indonesia. The Decentralized Basic Education initiative expanded the dissemination, replication, and sustainability of best practices. Funds provided by local governments and schools resulted in 75 district governments officially budgeting for Basic Education programs in more than 2,000 schools across 24 districts. The program benefited nearly 30,000 educators, 2,000 administrators, and 200,000 students. USAID also supported *Jalan Sesama*, a Sesame Street Workshop that reached 7.5 million children. The Opportunities for Vulnerable Children Program assisted children with special needs to attend inclusive education programs.

Kyrgyzstan. USAID's education programs benefited more than 80,000 students and 4,000 teachers across the country. The model for school financing and increased accountability continued to spread to schools and administrative units beyond the USAID project areas. Assistance also supported the American University of Central Asia and a Development Credit Authority student loan program that increased access to higher education and vocational training for students, particularly those from rural areas, by creating a replicable, private sector tuition financing model.

Philippines. USAID education program assistance reached more than 387,000 learners and 10,300 teachers and administrators in Mindanao. To improve access to education, 385 classrooms were constructed and repaired. Programs also supported 729 Parent-Teacher-Community Associations and distributed more than 700,000 learning materials. The National Achievement test scores of students in U.S.-supported schools increased by 14 percent, and marked improvements were observed in all skill sets, including reading fluency.

Tajikistan. The USAID Safe School Program assisted the government with anti-gender based violence training modules that were adapted and integrated through the national teacher training institutes. In collaboration with the Tajik government, the School Dropout and Prevention Program began to address school drop-out in three regions; and in collaboration with the Tajik government and the World Bank, USAID-supported school financing and management systems were rolled out nationwide in 68 districts. A new activity promoting positive youth engagement in three high-need regions of the country was launched; through civic education courses, youth development activities, and community development grants, this initiative will reach 900 disadvantaged youth.

THE MIDDLE EAST

Egypt. Over the past year, 44 public primary schools in two districts have worked with the Technology for Improved Learning Outcomes (TILO) team to integrate an intensive technology and training model to improve student learning outcomes through the effective use of technology. Ministry of Education (MOE) officials decided to take an initiative to spread TILO to other districts, and conducted an internal assessment to identify gaps within the system that would need to be addressed before they start implementing the expansion strategy. By September 2012, 525 teachers were trained in 105 schools. Based on the demonstrated impact of the USAID early grade reading package, which improved students' reading fluency by 91 percent, the MOE decided to scale up to all primary schools in Egypt. It now benefits 15,000 primary schools nationwide, benefitting 1.4 million grade one students.

USAID/Egypt continued to provide technical support for the 6-of-October Science, Technology, and Math (STM) School for Boys, to reinforce STM pedagogy and increase awareness of relevant teaching and learning approaches. The MOE and science and mathematics educators will participate in U.S.-based and in-country training, technical assistance and strategies instruction. In March 2012, three U.S.-based active STM teacher trainers representing science, engineering, math, and humanities conducted a six full-day training workshop to provide the Egyptian science and math teachers with a rich understanding and familiarity with inquiry and project-based learning pedagogy. In April/May, 25 STM teachers and MOE Science and Math specialists participated in a two-week U.S.-based training to deepen their understanding of STEM (science, technology, engineering, math) education in the United States and consolidate and build on the knowledge and skills they developed as a result of the training and technical assistance. Additionally, the STM Student Assessment Framework was finalized and endorsed by the MOE, the Ministry of Higher Education, and the Supreme Council of Universities. Accordingly, the Egyptian STM students will be admitted to universities based on a special STM assessment system, which will be informed by the STEM best practices in the United States instead of the traditional secondary school national exam (the Thanaweya Amma).

Finally, due to the Education Support Program (ESP), Egyptian schools have witnessed changes relating to two very important elements of the country's human resources that support education. The first element was a redefinition of the role that school Boards of Trustees play in promoting citizenship, governance, and community participation. The second element was the hiring of thousands of young Egyptians by the Ministry of Education as new assistant teachers. Through ESP, 25,000 Boards of Trustees received an MOE-endorsed training package and 75,000 newly hired teachers will receive the Professional Academy for Teachers certified training package by March 2014.

Iraq. In 2012, USAID partnered with the Iraqi Ministry of Education (MOE) and the Ministry of Higher Education (MOHE) to carry out assessments and analyses on: a) student performance in reading and mathematics, pedagogic practice, and school management in the primary grade level; b) in-service teacher training centers; c) Iraq's education management capacity; and d) Kurdistan's basic education systems, including focus on school management, teacher, parent and community concerns. A key component of the surveys and assessments, in addition to getting data and information to make decisions, was to build the capacity of the MOE to implement the surveys. The United States worked work closely with the ministry in all stages of the survey process and trained MOE staff to adapt the survey instruments; design the sample size; participate in assessor training; and administer the survey, data entry, data cleaning, analysis, and policy dialogue. Results highlighted the need to increase: the number of instructional hours per year; children's access to reading materials, both at school and at home; and parental involvement in primary schooling. The existing education system is too centralized to efficiently address the education needs of all Iraqis. As a result, the MOE will embark on a visioning exercise to discuss how to produce a well-informed and widely owned design for a high-quality, modern education system for Iraq. The survey produced baseline data that will inform the MOE's education policy reforms and development and enable monitoring of the progress of education activities.

Jordan. USAID oversaw an Education Reform Support Program (ERSP) that directly supported the Government of Jordan's Education Reform for a Knowledge Economy (ERfKE) program. This project provided technical assistance for early childhood education through kindergarten renovations, thus developing a quality assurance framework. ERSP provided professional development opportunities for teachers, youth activities, data for informed decision making, and the development of an online curriculum for the exam administered at the end of secondary school. Jordan also has a School Construction and Rehabilitation project that aims to build 28 new schools and renovate 100 schools by September 2013. This is in direct support of ERfKE to reduce over-crowding, double shifted schools, and rented school facilities. The Community Mobilization Project works in the communities where USAID is building and renovating schools to establish community-parent-school coalitions to enhance parent involvement in schools and maintain the positive effects of the school construction and rehabilitation. A Monitoring and Evaluation Partnership Project works with the National Counsel for Human Resource Development (NCHRD), the external body that implements studies to evaluate the effects of ERfKE. USAID is providing capacity building for NCHRD and opportunities to enhance the relationship between NCHRD and the Ministry of Education's (MOE) Monitoring and Evaluation unit. The Learning Environment Technical Support Project is a research-based project to improve the learning environments at 320 at-risk schools addressing violence, vandalism, health matters, and other issues that impede student progress.

Lebanon. USAID supported the Developing Rehabilitation Assistance to Schools and Teacher Improvement (D-RASATI) project, which developed a comprehensive school assessment instrument for gathering information on physical facilities, student-staff ratios, and available equipment available, for example. For the first time, information was gathered for all 1,281 public schools in Lebanon. The project also developed an Information and Communications Technology strategy and created standards for school health and safety in the Effective School Profile for the Ministry of Education and Higher Education. Specialized engineering assessments were completed for 30 schools; the results showed clear risks to student health and safety. As a result, the Council of Ministers allocated US $5 million for repairs in schools with dangerous structural conditions, supplementing D-RASATI efforts.

Nineteen schools were provided with resin tables and eye wash stations for science laboratories. MEHE established a new procurement process following the model based on the science lab equipment procurement process. A proficiency test for 4,065 teachers who use English as the language of instruction was administered, establishing the baseline for necessary training activities. The project developed the progress scale teacher observation tool for unbiased assessments that identify strengths and areas for additional training and mentoring. Finally, training manuals and modules for teacher training in English, math, biology, chemistry and physics were developed, and 68 teacher trainers received training on the methodology of teaching subject matter in English, math, and science.

Morocco. USAID's Improving Training and Quality Advancement in National Education project worked with the Ministry of National Education to improve the quality and relevance of education in middle schools and to reduce school dropout rates. Through support to teacher training institutions, a new cadre of high-quality middle school teachers was trained to provide the youth with skills to succeed in today's changing environments. The project is building the capacity of ministry staff in areas of monitoring and evaluation, use of data for education decision making, and e-learning. The project also works with middle school youth to determine factors that youth themselves identify as the main causes leading them to drop out of school. USAID's civil society program engaged civil society in education improvement at the school level. Given that low quality of education and academic failure in middle school are the main reasons for students dropping out, improving education quality is leading to more students staying in school and enhancing skills and knowledge.

USAID/Morocco has also carried out early grade reading and math assessments. Survey results indicated sub-par reading levels in the lower grades, especially in rural areas. The classroom observation of math and reading instructional practices indicated that teachers rarely focused on some of the crucial foundational skills and exercises necessary to develop good reading and mathematics abilities.

West Bank and Gaza. In close coordination with the Ministry of Education and Higher Education (MOEHE), USAID focused on the professional development of teachers and administrators, increasing access to education by constructing and renovating schools and classrooms, and equipping students with the knowledge and skills necessary to compete in the Palestinian labor market. Programs supported the production of a new series of Sesame Street television shows, radio episodes targeting teachers and parents, and the launch of the *Shara'a Simsim* (Sesame Street) website. USAID partnered with the National Institute for Educational Training to design and accredit the new Principal Leadership Program. Through partnership and dialogue, the MOEHE has embraced a decentralized education system model and delegated decision-making authorities to the district and local levels. One-hundred and 12 classrooms were constructed or rehabilitated at eight schools, while 11 youth centers were renovated in the West Bank, with 3,000 students benefiting from increased access to education facilities.

Yemen. USAID worked to strengthen the capacity of communities, schools, and the Ministry of Education to sustain educational improvements. Education program activities included school renovations, adult literacy support, support to increase community participation in school management, and professional development for teachers in reading, writing, and mathematics. The program established baseline data on target student competencies in math and science.

SOUTH ASIA

Afghanistan. USAID's basic education program, totaling US $97,000,000, continued to extend access to quality education to all Afghans by improving the government's service provision capacity, targeting educational access for girls, training teachers, and helping to establish vocational education opportunities. Critical support to the Ministry of Education's operating fund ensured an adequate number of teachers to support increased enrollment. Approximately 850,000 Afghan children, including 256,000 girls, benefitted from U.S. programs in the education sector. Of these, 7,000 students, nearly all girls, were supported in secondary schools, greatly increasing the number of students able to matriculate into higher education programs. The USAID-supported International School of Kabul, which provides an American-style education, enrolled 375 students, 80 percent of whom are Afghans and 38 percent of whom are female. Projects expanded access to education by establishing new schools applying the nationally-approved curriculum, and focused on the professional development of teachers, particularly female teachers. USAID provided 18,567 teachers with complete in-service training to improve their classroom performance and further their professional development. There were also 11,000 education administrators trained to improve school management and performance. USAID's pre-service teacher education program awarded Master of Education degrees to 21 teachers. In 2012, 13 million textbooks were printed as a component of a new three-year, on-budget agreement with the Ministry of Education. USAID's community-based education program, which is transitioning to a new on-budget program aligned with the Ministry of Education, supported approximately 40 supervisory staff, who supported the more than 60,000 students in rural community schools.

EUROPE AND EURASIA

Kosovo. USAID continued its basic education program, a five-year US $9,791,000 initiative designed to benefit all public primary and lower secondary schools in Kosovo, grades one through nine. The project has three components: to enhance school management capacities in a decentralized environment, strengthen the assessment of learning outcomes, and improve in-service teacher development. In 2012, 118,000 students benefited from the project activities; of these, 61,360 were girls. The project trained 3,735 teachers, 707 members of school boards and student and teacher councils, and 45 Ministry of Education and Science officials. The project also adapted an early grade reading assessment to the Albanian language. The project established partnerships with 15 local and international partners and closely collaborated with local municipalities and communities to refurbish 52 classrooms. Collaboration and cooperation with donors and the private sector includes partnerships with the Teacher Training Project of Deutsche Gessellschaft fur Zuzammenarbeit and the EU, with the Swedish International Development Cooperation Agency-supported Education Technology program. Intel and Microsoft will integrate technology in classrooms.

SUB-SAHARAN AFRICA

Djibouti. Basic education funding in 2012 continued to assist the Ministry of Education (MENFOP) in achieving its education-for-all goal for all school-aged Djiboutian children. USAID's basic education program focused on improving the education system through decentralized teacher training, strategic planning and budgeting, enhanced community participation, improving the Education Management Information System (EMIS), and increasing learning for out-of-school youth. Host country strategic information capacity was improved through the establishment of a software application that accurately captures statistical data. EMIS focused on building the capacity of MENFOP staff at national and regional levels; decentralized planning deepened MENFOP skills both at central and regional levels to collect and analyze education data. Under the community mobilization component, 50 school improvement projects were implemented by Parent-Teacher Associations (PTAs), and 101 PTAs benefitted from training that focused on improving reading in primary education and enhancing gender equality. Assistance also focused on activities that improve children's reading abilities and learning outcomes. It introduced the Early Grade Reading Assessment (EGRA) tool to assess reading skills and determine a baseline for future programming. EGRA experts introduced the tool to more than 433 teachers through school-based trainings emphasizing the need to develop relevant strategies to cope with children's reading difficulties in grades two, three, and five. To address Djibouti's chronically high unemployment rate and enable the Djiboutian people to leverage their own skills for continued economic growth, the program supported MENFOP in its efforts to prepare school drop-outs to transition to the workforce. The project provided vocational and professional education training for 112 female out-of-school youth, focused primarily in the hotel and food service sector. The USAID education project supported the Girls' Scholarship Program (GSP) which had a significant impact on girls' retention in middle and secondary school and in achievement rates for underprivileged male and female youth. In FY 2012, 539 girls received scholarship packages. In addition to school supplies, tuition, and transportation fees, the GSP conducted mentoring sessions on HIV/AIDS and other important topics to support beneficiaries' academic success and social development. The program promoted community service and the beneficiaries were required to help other students in their communities by volunteering at local libraries and tutoring school children to improve their reading and writing skills. USAID also worked in close coordination with the U.S. military on the rehabilitation and refurbishment of primary school infrastructure.

Education activities also supported the enhancement of English language training in middle schools through the development of appropriate pedagogical materials and curricula. USAID provided significant support to MENFOP in the review and development of middle school English textbooks and provided training to middle school teachers to improve the production of materials. In collaboration with school pedagogical advisors, technical assistance helped develop a Grade 10 textbook to support secondary schools on curricula reform.

Ethiopia. USAID implemented a nationwide program aimed at improving the reading skills of all students in Ethiopia; the Muslim student population is estimated at 35 percent of the total 18 million primary school students. USAID-supported activities in the Somali, Afar, Benishangul, Gumuz, and Oromia regions included teacher training to improve the quality of primary education; training for Parent-Teacher Associations and community members to increase parent and community involvement in school management; grants to schools to enhance learning and teaching and to build the capacity of education officers to plan and manage the education system; establishment and expansion of alternative basic education centers to provide non-formal primary education to children, especially girls; and adult literacy classes for illiterate adults. Materials, tutoring, counseling, and training were also provided to support and help young Muslim women succeed in both high school and universities.

Kenya. USAID's Education for Marginalized Children program concentrated on the predominantly Muslim North Eastern and Coast Provinces, reaching nearly 377,000 children in both provinces. Approximately 250 Early Childhood Development Centers were supported and over 13,000 teachers were trained in child-centered teaching and early grade reading methods. USAID/Kenya's Education & Youth Office also oversaw the Garissa Youth Project, which provided livelihood and workforce readiness programs for ethnic-Somali youth at-risk of al-Shabaab recruitment. The Garissa program partnered with USAID's Office of Military Affairs to pilot the District Stability Framework, a tool to gauge the level of instability within Garissa and to help coordinate an interagency response, as well as coordinate action by the youth themselves through a US $800,000 youth fund. This was the first pilot of the framework outside of Iraq, Afghanistan, or Yemen.

Mali. In support of the Trans-Sahara Counterterrorism Partnership (TSCTP), USAID/Mali's basic education program focused on supporting moderate Islamic schools and improving the quality of primary education for Mali's predominantly Muslim population. In 2012, US $2.2 million TSCTP and US $1 million Basic Education funds were allocated to serving out-of-school youth with vocational training, remedial academic skills, and civic engagement.

Nigeria. While education indicators were poor nationwide, they were worse in the predominantly Muslim north, where poor education contributed to the marginalization of Muslim communities. An estimated 10 million children were not enrolled in school, and with no vocational skills have little hope of ever joining the formal workforce. USAID implemented interventions that targeted both access to education services for the vulnerable, increased quality for those in school, and strengthened systems for increased accountability and transparency. In FY 2012, USAID worked in Islamic and Quranic schools benefitting 79,766 pupils (45,003 male and 34,763 female), out of which 15,190 (9,350 male; 5,840 female) were identified as orphans and vulnerable children. The vulnerable children received support materials to allow them to attend school. A total of 200 of these children acquire vocational and life skills annually by participating in the skills program.

Senegal. One of USAID's largest education programs helped 50,000 vulnerable children gain access to a quality education or professional and vocational training. This was achieved by improving the living and learning conditions of children through construction and renovation of Quranic schools, and providing children with an education that will allow them to either continue in the formal schooling system or join the professional workforce. In collaboration with Senegal's Ministry of Education, USAID introduced an educational program aligned to the elementary education curriculum that teaches children basic skills in French, math, science, history, geography, and life skills. The "community daara" model developed and implemented by USAID for the past four year includes: 1) a three year educational program that teaches French and Math skills; 2) renovation of the daara's learning space using a standardized classroom model, blackboards, school desks and/or mats, gender separate toilets and access to water where there is none; 3) a management committee comprised of community members to help govern, manage, and increase resources to the daaras; and 4) support and monitoring from education authorities and community-based organizations. To date, more than 17,000 children, ages six to 12, in 350 daaras have benefitted from the program, and there was evidence that 50 to 60 percent of the children were achieving desired levels of competencies in the subjects taught. Improvements in the living conditions of the daaras were seen in the better nutrition, clothing, and hygiene of the children.

Somalia. A dual approach was taken in Somalia. For those enrolled in schools – 20 percent of school-aged children – USAID provided learning materials, improved the physical and sanitary environments of schools, and the quality of teachers and administrators. Achievements for in-school children included the rehabilitation of 102 classrooms and the construction of 68 new classrooms in 25 schools in Somaliland, Puntland, and South Central Somalia; the training of 505 teachers and 43 head teachers in improved teaching practices; the training of 351 Community Education Committee members on improved school management techniques; the distribution of 11,221 school kits and teaching/learning charts; the rehabilitation of three health centers; the training of 296 health workers and eight community health committees; the construction of numerous latrines, water tanks, shallow wells, and hand-washing facilities and the associated water quality testing and training; and the airing of three health promotion programs. As an integral part of improving school environments, improvements in water and sanitation infrastructure were funded in schools and their communities. Part of the rationale for this was the finding that the lack of sanitary facilities for girls was preventing many of them from attending school. As a result, 9,130 people (5,444 male and 3,686 female) were provided with access to clean water and improved sanitation facilities and better knowledge of good hygiene practices. For the remaining 80 percent of school-aged children not enrolled in school, an interactive radio instruction program using distance learning techniques through radio-based programs was employed for those most at-risk, primarily women and girls, youth, internally displaced persons, and illiterate urban youth. Through this initiative, USAID helped enroll an additional 1,337 new learners, trained 1,513 educators, and distributed 102,861 text books and learning materials.

Tanzania. USAID assistance supported improving student outcomes in reading in the early primary grades in underserved, primarily Muslim communities in Zanzibar and mainland Tanzania, through better classroom instruction in foundational subjects and better planning and management for reading instruction. USAID's public-private partnerships with Cisco, Intel, Microsoft, and two local internet service partners, UhuruOne and Zantel, leveraged US $45 million in matching funds and contributed directly to improving lower primary education in reading in Mtwara and Zanzibar. USAID is leveraging US $100 million in Global Partnership for Education (GPE) funding to scale up this innovative reading program to all grade one to four students in Tanzania. The education program emphasizes reading in the local language (Swahili) for grades one to four, and integrates math, English, and science instruction into its reading program through a "reading across the curriculum" approach. The Mission is strengthening policies, information and management, and Education Management Information System (EMIS) development and application. The Mission has completed its design of the computer-based EMIS that has been installed on computers which are being delivered to every primary school in Mtwara and Zanzibar. Teachers and administrators are being trained on data entry and analysis, including indicators pertinent to education quality, student performance, and reading achievement.

Chapter 6.
Foreign Terrorist Organizations

Foreign Terrorist Organizations (FTOs) are designated by the Secretary of State in accordance with section 219 of the Immigration and Nationality Act (INA). FTO designations play a critical role in the fight against terrorism and are an effective means of curtailing support for terrorist activities.

In 2012, the following FTOs were designated by the Department of State: Jemmah Anshorut Tauhid on March 13, the Abdallah Azzam Brigades on May 30, and the Haqqani Network on September 19. In addition, the following FTO designations were amended: al-Qa'ida in Iraq to include the Islamic State of Iraq as an alias on January 26, al-Qa'ida in the Arabian Peninsula to include Ansar al-Shari'a as an alias on October 5, and al-Qa'ida in Iraq to include al-Nusrah Front as an alias on December 11. Also in 2012, the Department of State revoked the Mujahadin-e Khalq's designation as an FTO on September 28.

Legal Criteria for Designation under Section 219 of the INA as amended:

1. It must be a *foreign organization.*
2. The organization must *engage in terrorist activity*, as defined in section 212 (a)(3)(B) of the INA (8 U.S.C. § 1182(a)(3)(B)), or *terrorism*, as defined in section 140(d)(2) of the Foreign Relations Authorization Act, Fiscal Years 1988 and 1989 (22 U.S.C. § 2656f(d)(2)), *or retain the capability and intent to engage in terrorist activity or terrorism.*
3. The organization's terrorist activity or terrorism must threaten the security of U.S. nationals or the national security (national defense, foreign relations, or the economic interests) of the United States.

U.S. Government Designated Foreign Terrorist Organizations

Abdallah Azzam Brigades (AAB)
Abu Nidal Organization (ANO)
Abu Sayyaf Group (ASG)
Al-Aqsa Martyrs Brigade (AAMB)
Ansar al-Islam (AAI)
Army of Islam (AOI)
Asbat al-Ansar (AAA)
Aum Shinrikyo (AUM)
Basque Fatherland and Liberty (ETA)
Communist Party of Philippines/New People's Army (CPP/NPA)
Continuity Irish Republican Army (CIRA)
Gama'a al-Islamiyya (IG)
Hamas
Haqqani Network (HQN)
Harakat ul-Jihad-i-Islami (HUJI)

Harakat ul-Jihad-i-Islami/Bangladesh (HUJI-B)
Harakat ul-Mujahideen (HUM)
Hizballah
Indian Mujahedeen (IM)
Islamic Jihad Union (IJU)
Islamic Movement of Uzbekistan (IMU)
Jaish-e-Mohammed (JEM)
Jemaah Ansharut Tauhid (JAT)
Jemaah Islamiya (JI)
Jundallah
Kahane Chai
Kata'ib Hizballah (KH)
Kurdistan Workers' Party (PKK)
Lashkar e-Tayyiba (LT)
Lashkar i Jhangvi (LJ)
Liberation Tigers of Tamil Eelam (LTTE)
Libyan Islamic Fighting Group (LIFG)
Moroccan Islamic Combatant Group (GICM)
National Liberation Army (ELN)
Palestine Islamic Jihad – Shaqaqi Faction (PIJ)
Palestine Liberation Front – Abu Abbas Faction (PLF)
Popular Front for the Liberation of Palestine (PFLP)
Popular Front for the Liberation of Palestine-General Command (PFLP-GC)
Al-Qa'ida (AQ)
Al-Qa'ida in the Arabian Peninsula (AQAP)
Al-Qa'ida in Iraq (AQI)
Al-Qa'ida in the Islamic Maghreb (AQIM)
Real IRA (RIRA)
Revolutionary Armed Forces of Colombia (FARC)
Revolutionary Organization 17 November (17N)
Revolutionary People's Liberation Party/Front (DHKP/C)
Revolutionary Struggle (RS)
Al-Shabaab (AS)
Shining Path (SL)
Tehrik-e Taliban Pakistan (TTP)
United Self-Defense Forces of Colombia (AUC)

ABDALLAH AZZAM BRIGADES

aka Abdullah Azzam Brigades; Ziyad al-Jarrah Battalions of the Abdallah Azzam Brigades; Yusuf al-'Uyayri Battalions of the Abdallah Azzam Brigades

Description: The Abdallah Azzam Brigades (AAB) was designated as a Foreign Terrorist Organization on May 30, 2012. AAB formally announced its establishment in a July 2009 video statement claiming responsibility for a February 2009 rocket attack against Israel. The group is divided into two branches: the Arabian Peninsula-based Yusuf al-'Uyayri Battalions of the Abdullah Azzam Brigades, named after the now-deceased founder of al-Qa'ida in the Arabian Peninsula; and the Lebanon-based Ziyad al-Jarrah Battalions of the Abdallah Azzam Brigades, named after Ziad al Jarrah, a Lebanese citizen who was one of the masterminds of the September 11 attacks on the United States. In a June 2012 video statement, the group named its leader as Majid bin Muhammad al Majid, a Saudi citizen who is on the Saudi government's list of 85 Most Wanted Terrorists for his links to al-Qa'ida.

Activities: AAB has relied primarily on rocket attacks against Israeli civilians, and is responsible for numerous rocket attacks fired into Israeli territory from Lebanon. These attacks have targeted population centers in Israel and have included incidents such as the September 11, 2009 double rocket attack on Nahariya and an April 2011 rocket attack on Ashkelon. In addition to rocket attacks, AAB carried out a July 2010 suicide bombing attack against the Japanese-owned oil tanker M/V M. Star in the Strait of Hormuz. According to a statement released online, AAB claimed that the attack was carried out by its Arabian Peninsula Branch. AAB has repeatedly articulated its intent to carry out attacks against Western interests in the Middle East. In 2010, for example, the group expressed an interest in kidnapping U.S. and British tourists in the Arabian Peninsula.

Strength: Unknown

Location/Area of Operation: AAB is based in both Lebanon and the Arabian Peninsula.

Funding and External Aid: Unknown

ABU NIDAL ORGANIZATION

aka ANO; Arab Revolutionary Brigades; Arab Revolutionary Council; Black September; Fatah Revolutionary Council; Revolutionary Organization of Socialist Muslims

Description: Designated as a Foreign Terrorist Organization on October 8, 1997, the Abu Nidal Organization (ANO) was founded by Sabri al-Banna (aka Abu Nidal) after splitting from the Palestine Liberation Organization (PLO) in 1974. In August 2002, Abu Nidal died in Baghdad. Present leadership of the organization remains unclear. ANO advocates the elimination of Israel and has sought to derail diplomatic efforts in support of the Middle East peace process.

Activities: The ANO has carried out terrorist attacks in 20 countries, killing or injuring almost 900 persons. It has not staged a major attack against Western targets since the late 1980s and was expelled from its safe haven in Libya in 1999. Major attacks included those on the Rome and Vienna airports in 1985, the 1986 Neve Shalom Synagogue in Istanbul, the hijacking of Pan Am Flight 73 in Karachi in 1986, and the City of Poros day-excursion ship attack in Greece in 1988. The ANO was suspected of assassinating PLO Deputy Chief Abu Iyad and PLO Security Chief Abu Hul in Tunis in 1991, and a senior Jordanian diplomat in Beirut in 1994. In 2008, a Jordanian official reported the apprehension of an ANO member who planned to carry out attacks in Jordan. There were no known ANO attacks in 2012.

Strength: Current strength is unknown.

Location/Area of Operation: ANO associates are presumed present in Lebanon.

Funding and External Aid: The ANO's current access to resources is unclear, but it is likely that the decline in support previously provided by Libya, Syria, and Iran has had a severe impact on its capabilities.

ABU SAYYAF GROUP

aka al Harakat al Islamiyya (the Islamic Movement)

Description: The Abu Sayyaf Group (ASG) was designated as a Foreign Terrorist Organization on October 8, 1997. ASG is the most violent of the terrorist groups operating in the Philippines and claims to promote an independent Islamic state in western Mindanao and the Sulu Archipelago. The group split from the much larger Moro Islamic Liberation Front (MILF) in the early 1990s under the leadership of Abdurajak Abubakar Janjalani, who was killed in a clash with Philippine police in December 1998.

Activities: The ASG engages in kidnappings for ransom, bombings, beheadings, assassinations, and extortion. In April 2000, an ASG faction kidnapped 21 people, including 10 Western tourists, from a resort in Malaysia. In May 2001, the ASG kidnapped three U.S. citizens and 17 Philippine nationals from a tourist resort in Palawan, Philippines. Several of the hostages, including U.S. citizen Guillermo Sobero, were murdered. A Philippine military hostage rescue operation in June 2002 freed U.S. hostage Gracia Burnham, but her husband, U.S. national Martin Burnham, and Deborah Yap of the Philippines were killed. Philippine and U.S. authorities blamed the ASG for a bombing near a Philippine military base in Zamboanga in October 2002 that killed a U.S. serviceman. In one of the most destructive acts of maritime violence, the ASG bombed SuperFerry 14 in Manila Bay in February 2004, killing at least 116 people.

In 2012, ASG remained active, particularly with kidnappings for ransom, an increase in the use of improvised explosive device (IED) attacks, and armed attacks on civilian and police personnel. In January, the ASG was linked to the bombing of a bridge in a town of Sulu province. In March, police linked the ASG to the bombing of a commercial district on the island of Jolo that caused two deaths and 13 injuries. In April, 22 Philippine soldiers were wounded when suspected ASG members detonated an IED while patrolling in Basilan province. In November, police in the southern Philippines thwarted a bomb attack in a heavy populated urban area when they arrested three ASG members and seized two motorcycles, one of which was rigged with explosives.

Philippine police captured or killed a number of ASG leaders in 2012. In February, Philippine police forces arrested Abdulpattah Ismael, who was involved in the 2007 beheadings of 10 Philippine marines and a 2009 prison break, and arrested ASG sub-commander, Abdulhan Ussih. In March, Philippine troops captured ASG militants, Anni Idris and Serham Akalon, who were implicated in beheadings and kidnappings.

Strength: ASG is estimated to have 400 members.

Location/Area of Operation: The ASG operates primarily in the provinces of the Sulu Archipelago, namely Basilan, Sulu, and Tawi-Tawi. The group also operates on the Zamboanga Peninsula.

Funding and External Aid: The ASG is funded through kidnapping for ransom operations and extortion, and may also receive funding from external sources such as remittances from overseas Philippines workers and Middle East-based violent extremists. In the past, the ASG has also received assistance from regional terrorist groups such as Jemaah Islamiya, whose operatives provided training to ASG members and helped facilitate several ASG terrorist attacks.

AL-AQSA MARTYRS BRIGADE

aka al-Aqsa Martyrs Battalion

Description: Designated as a Foreign Terrorist Organization on March 27, 2002, the al-Aqsa Martyrs Brigade (AAMB) is composed of an unknown number of small cells of Fatah-affiliated activists that emerged at the outset of the al-Aqsa Intifada, in September 2000. AAMB's goal is to drive the Israeli military and West Bank settlers from the West Bank in order to establish a Palestinian state loyal to the Fatah.

Activities: AAMB employed primarily small-arms attacks against Israeli military personnel and settlers as the intifada spread in 2000, but by 2002 turned increasingly to suicide bombings against Israeli civilians inside Israel. In January 2002, the group claimed responsibility for the first female suicide bombing inside Israel. In 2010, AAMB launched numerous rocket attacks on communities in Israel, including the city of Sederot and areas of the Negev desert. Again in December 2011, AAMB launched rockets aimed at communities in the Negev. The attack caused no injuries or damage. In November 2012, two men recruited by AAMB were arrested in connection with a stabbing attack on a student in the Israeli city of Beersheba. Also in November, AAMB claimed that they had fired more than 500 rockets and missiles into Israel during Operation Pillar of Defense, the week-long Israeli Defense Force operation in Gaza.

Strength: A few hundred members.

Location/Area of Operation: Most of AAMB's operational activity is in Gaza but the group also planned and conducted attacks inside Israel and the West Bank. The group also has members in Palestinian refugee camps in Lebanon.

Funding and External Aid: Iran has exploited AAMB's lack of resources and formal leadership by providing funds and guidance, mostly through Hizballah facilitators.

ANSAR AL-ISLAM

aka Ansar al-Sunna; Ansar al-Sunna Army; Devotees of Islam; Followers of Islam in Kurdistan; Helpers of Islam; Jaish Ansar al-Sunna; Jund al-Islam; Kurdish Taliban; Kurdistan Supporters of Islam; Partisans of Islam; Soldiers of God; Soldiers of Islam; Supporters of Islam in Kurdistan

Description: Designated as a Foreign Terrorist Organization on March 22, 2004, Ansar al-Islam's (AI's) goals include expelling western interests from Iraq and establishing an independent Iraqi state based on Sharia law. AI was established in 2001 in Iraqi Kurdistan with the merger of two Kurdish extremist factions that traced their roots to the Islamic Movement of

Kurdistan. On May 4, 2010, Abu Abdullah al-Shafi'i, Ansar al-Islam's leader, was captured by U.S. forces in Baghdad and remains in prison. On December 15, 2011 AI announced a new leader, Abu Hashim Muhammad bin Abdul Rahman al Ibrahim.

Mullah Krekar (aka Najmuddin Faraj Ahmad), an Iraqi citizen and the founder of Ansar al-Islam, continued to reside in Norway on a long-term residence permit. In March 2012, a trial court convicted Krekar of issuing threats and inciting terrorism, and sentenced him to six years in prison. Krekar appealed, and in December an appeals court affirmed his convictions for issuing threats and intimidating witnesses, but reversed his conviction for "inciting terrorism." The appeals court reduced his sentence to two years and 10 months in prison.

Activities: AI has conducted attacks against a wide range of targets including Iraqi government and security forces, and U.S. and Coalition Forces. AI has conducted numerous kidnappings, executions, and assassinations of Iraqi citizens and politicians. The group has either claimed responsibility or is believed to be responsible for attacks in 2011 that killed 24 and wounded 147.

Strength: Though precise numbers are unknown, AI is considered one of the largest Sunni terrorist groups in Iraq.

Location/Area of Operation: Primarily northern Iraq, but also maintains a presence in western and central Iraq.

Funding and External Aid: AI receives assistance from a loose network of associates in Europe and the Middle East.

ARMY OF ISLAM

aka Jaysh al-Islam; Jaish al-Islam

Description: Designated as a Foreign Terrorist Organization on May 19, 2011, the Army of Islam (AOI) is a Gaza-based terrorist organization founded in late 2005 responsible for numerous terrorist acts against the Governments of Israel and Egypt, as well as American, British, and New Zealander citizens. Led by Mumtaz Dughmush, AOI primarily operates in Gaza. It subscribes to an extremist Salafist ideology together with the traditional model of armed Palestinian resistance. AOI has previously worked with Hamas and is attempting to develop closer al-Qa'ida contacts.

Activities: AOI's terrorist acts include a number of rocket attacks on Israel, the 2006 kidnapping of two journalists in Gaza (an American and a New Zealander), and the 2007 kidnapping of a British citizen, journalist Alan Johnston, in Gaza. AOI is also responsible for early 2009 attacks on Egyptian civilians in Cairo and Heliopolis, Egypt. In 2011, AOI was alleged to have planned the January 1 Alexandria attack on a Coptic Christian church that killed 25 and wounded 100. On May 7, 2011, the group released a eulogy for Usama bin Laden via its al-Nur Media Foundation. On July 28, 2012, AOI released a statement that one of its members, Nidal al 'Ashi, was killed fighting in Syria.

Strength: Membership is estimated in the low hundreds.

Location/Area of Operation: Gaza, with attacks in Egypt and Israel.

Funding and External Aid: AOI receives the bulk of its funding from a variety of criminal activities in Gaza.

ASBAT AL-ANSAR

aka Asbat al-Ansar; Band of Helpers; Band of Partisans; League of Partisans; League of the Followers; God's Partisans; Gathering of Supporters; Partisan's League; AAA; Esbat al-Ansar; Isbat al-Ansar; Osbat al-Ansar; Usbat al-Ansar; Usbat ul-Ansar

Description: Designated as a Foreign Terrorist Organization on March 27, 2002, Asbat al-Ansar is a Lebanon-based Sunni extremist group composed primarily of Palestinians with links to al-Qa'ida (AQ) and other Sunni extremist groups. Some of the group's stated goals include thwarting perceived anti-Islamic and pro-Western influences in the country, though the group remains largely confined to Lebanon's refugee camps.

Activities: Asbat al-Ansar first emerged in the early 1990s. In the mid-1990s, the group assassinated Lebanese religious leaders and bombed nightclubs, theaters, and liquor stores. The group has also plotted against foreign diplomatic targets. In October 2004, Mahir al-Sa'di, a member of Asbat al-Ansar, was sentenced in absentia to life imprisonment for his 2000 plot to assassinate then-U.S. Ambassador to Lebanon David Satterfield. Asbat al-Ansar has no formal ties to the AQ network, but the group shares AQ's ideology and has publicly proclaimed its support for al-Qa'ida in Iraq. Members of the group have traveled to Iraq since 2005 to fight Coalition Forces. Asbat al-Ansar has been reluctant to involve itself in operations in Lebanon due in part to concerns over losing its safe haven in the Ain al-Hilwah refugee camp. AAA did not stage any known attacks in 2012.

Strength: The group has fewer than 2,000 members.

Location/Area of Operation: The group's primary base of operations is the Ain al-Hilwah Palestinian refugee camp near Sidon in southern Lebanon.

Funding and External Aid: It is likely that the group receives money through international Sunni extremist networks.

AUM SHINRIKYO

aka A.I.C. Comprehensive Research Institute; A.I.C. Sogo Kenkyusho; Aleph; Aum Supreme Truth

Description: Aum Shinrikyo (AUM) was designated as a Foreign Terrorist Organization on October 8, 1997. Jailed leader Shoko Asahara established AUM in 1987, and the organization received legal status in Japan as a religious entity in 1989. The Japanese government revoked its recognition of AUM as a religious organization following AUM's deadly 1995 sarin gas attack in Tokyo. Despite claims of renunciation of violence and Asahara's teachings, members of the group continue to adhere to the violent and apocalyptic teachings of its founder.

Activities: In March 1995, AUM members simultaneously released the chemical nerve agent sarin on several Tokyo subway trains, killing 12 people and causing up to 6,000 to seek medical treatment. Subsequent investigations by the Japanese government revealed the group was responsible for other mysterious chemical incidents in Japan in 1994, including a sarin gas attack on a residential neighborhood in Matsumoto that killed seven and hospitalized approximately 500. Japanese police arrested Asahara in May 1995; in February 2004, authorities sentenced him to death for his role in the 1995 attacks. In September 2006, Asahara lost his final appeal against the death penalty and the Japanese Supreme Court upheld the decision in October 2007. In 2010 and 2011, several death sentences for other AUM senior members were finalized or affirmed by Japanese courts. In 2012, the final three AUM fugitives were arrested after 17 years on the run.

Since 1997, the group has split into two factions, both of which have recruited new members, engaged in commercial enterprises, and acquired property. In July 2001, Russian authorities arrested a group of Russian AUM followers who had planned to detonate bombs near the Imperial Palace in Tokyo as part of an operation to free Asahara from jail and smuggle him to Russia. In August 2012, a Japan Airlines flight to the United States was turned back after receiving a bomb threat demanding the release of Asahara.

Though AUM has not conducted a terrorist attack since 1995, concerns remain regarding its continued adherence to the violent teachings of Asahara.

Strength: According to a study by the Japanese government issued in December 2009, AUM membership in Japan is approximately 1,500 with another 200 in Russia. In 2012, it is believed that AUM recruited approximately 255 new members. As of December 2012, AUM continues to maintain at least 29 facilities in 15 prefectures in Japan and may continue to possess a few facilities in Russia. At the time of the Tokyo subway attack, the group claimed to have as many as 40,000 members worldwide, including 9,000 in Japan and 30,000 members in Russia.

Location/Area of Operation: AUM's principal membership is located in Japan; a residual branch of about 200 followers live in Russia.

Funding and External Aid: Funding primarily comes from member contributions.

BASQUE FATHERLAND AND LIBERTY

aka ETA; Askatasuna; Batasuna; Ekin; Euskal Herritarrok; Euzkadi Ta Askatasuna; Herri Batasuna; Jarrai-Haika-Segi; K.A.S.; XAKI

Description: Designated as a Foreign Terrorist Organization on October 8, 1997, Basque Fatherland and Liberty (ETA) was founded in 1959 with the aim of establishing an independent homeland based on Marxist principles encompassing the Spanish Basque provinces of Vizcaya, Guipuzcoa, and Alava; the autonomous region of Navarra; and the southwestern French territories of Labourd, Basse-Navarre, and Soule. ETA is listed as a terrorist organization by Spain and the EU. In 2002, the Spanish Parliament banned the political party Batasuna, ETA's political wing, charging its members with providing material support to the terrorist group. The European Court of Human Rights in June 2009 upheld the ban on Batasuna. In September 2008, Spanish courts also banned two other Basque independence parties with reported links to

Batasuna. In 2010, when Batasuna continued to try to participate in regional politics, splits between parts of ETA became publicly apparent.

Activities: ETA primarily has conducted bombings and assassinations. Targets typically have included Spanish government officials, businessmen, politicians, judicial figures, and security and military forces, but the group has also targeted journalists and tourist areas. The group is responsible for killing 829 civilians and members of the armed forces or police, and injuring thousands since it formally began a campaign of violence in 1968.

ETA has committed numerous attacks in the last four decades. Some of the group's high profile attacks include the February 2005 ETA car bombing in Madrid at a convention center where Spanish King Juan Carlos and then Mexican President Vicente Fox were scheduled to appear, wounding more than 20 people. In December 2006, ETA exploded a massive car bomb that destroyed much of the covered parking garage at Madrid's Barajas International Airport. ETA marked its fiftieth anniversary in 2009 with a series of high profile and deadly bombings, including the July attack on a Civil Guard Barracks that injured more than 60 people, including children.

In March 2010, a Spanish judge charged ETA and Revolutionary Armed Forces of Colombia members of terrorist plots, including a plan to assassinate Colombian President Alvaro Uribe. Spanish authorities arrested more than 400 ETA members between 2007 and 2010 and arrested an additional 52 in 2011. In 2012, a number of ETA fugitives were arrested. In June, an ETA operative was apprehended in London and two in France. In August, another ETA fugitive, who had been a target of a European arrest warrant since 2001, was arrested in London.

In October 2011, the militarily weakened and politically isolated ETA announced a "definitive cessation" of armed activity. Given that the group has made and broken several past cease-fires, Madrid rejected this announcement and demanded that ETA disarm and disband.

Strength: Estimates put ETA membership, of those who have not been captured by authorities, at fewer than 100. Spanish and French prisons together hold approximately 750 ETA members.

Location/Area of Operation: ETA operates primarily in the Basque autonomous regions of northern Spain and southwestern France, but has attacked Spanish and French interests elsewhere. The group also maintains a low profile presence in Cuba and Venezuela.

Funding and External Aid: ETA is probably experiencing financial shortages given that the group announced publicly in September 2011 that it had ceased collecting "revolutionary taxes" from Basque businesses. This extortion program was a major source of ETA's income.

COMMUNIST PARTY OF PHILIPPINES/NEW PEOPLE'S ARMY

aka CPP/NPA; Communist Party of the Philippines; the CPP; New People's Army; the NPA

Description: The Communist Party of the Philippines/New People's Army (CPP/NPA) was designated as a Foreign Terrorist Organization on August 9, 2002. The military wing of the Communist Party of the Philippines (CPP), the New People's Army (NPA), is a Maoist group formed in March 1969 with the aim of overthrowing the government through protracted guerrilla warfare. Jose Maria Sison, the Chairman of the CPP's Central Committee and the NPA's founder, reportedly directs CPP and NPA activity from the Netherlands, where he lives in self-imposed exile. Luis Jalandoni, a fellow Central Committee member and director of the CPP's overt political wing, the National Democratic Front (NDF), also lives in the Netherlands and has become a Dutch citizen. Though primarily a rural-based guerrilla group, the NPA had an active urban infrastructure to support its terrorist activities and, at times, used city-based assassination squads.

Activities: The CPP/NPA primarily targeted Philippine security forces, government officials, local infrastructure, and businesses that refused to pay extortion, or "revolutionary taxes." The CPP/NPA charged politicians running for office in CPP/NPA-influenced areas for "campaign permits." Despite its focus on Philippine governmental targets, the CPP/NPA has a history of attacking U.S. interests in the Philippines. In 1987, the CPP/NPA conducted direct actions against U.S. personnel and facilities killing three American soldiers in four separate attacks in Angeles City. In 1989, the CPP/NPA issued a press statement claiming responsibility for the ambush and murder of Colonel James Nicholas Rowe, chief of the Ground Forces Division of the Joint U.S.-Military Advisory Group.

For many years, the CPP/NPA carried out killings, raids, acts of extortion, and other forms of violence. In 2011 and 2012, the CPP/NPA's attacks and kidnappings continued unabated. In 2011, the CPP/NPA was responsible for detonating a landmine improvised explosive device in Illuro Sur, Philippines, that killed five and injured two police officers; killing two civilians when 50 CPP/NPA assailants fired upon a police checkpoint in Trento, Philippines; and kidnapping the Mayor of Lingig and two of his bodyguards before releasing the hostages in a prisoner swap.

In early January 2012, the group attacked a Philippine Army Patrol Base on the island of Mindanao. In May, an attack resulted in the CPP/NPA capturing one Philippine soldier and wounding four civilians, including one child. Further clashes between the CPP/NPA and government caused the displacement of approximately 700 individuals from their homes. Peace talks between the government and CPP/NPA were halted in the summer of 2012.

Strength: The Philippines government estimates there are 4,000 members.

Location/Area of Operation: The CPP/NPA operates in rural Luzon, Visayas, and parts of northern and eastern Mindanao. There are also cells in Manila and other metropolitan centers.

Funding and External Aid: The CPP/NPA raises funds through extortion.

CONTINUITY IRISH REPUBLICAN ARMY

aka Continuity Army Council; Continuity IRA; Republican Sinn Fein

Description: Designated as a Foreign Terrorist Organization on July 13, 2004, the Continuity Irish Republican Army (CIRA) is a terrorist splinter group formed in 1994 as the clandestine armed wing of Republican Sinn Fein; it split from Sinn Fein in 1986. "Continuity" refers to the group's belief that it is carrying on the original Irish Republican Army's (IRA) goal of forcing the British out of Northern Ireland. CIRA cooperates with the larger Real IRA (RIRA).

In 2012, CIRA released a statement claiming it had new leadership, after previous leadership was ousted over allegations that it was acting to the detriment of the organization.

Activities: CIRA has been active in Belfast and the border areas of Northern Ireland, where it has carried out bombings, assassinations, kidnappings, hijackings, extortion, and robberies. On occasion, it provided advance warning to police of its attacks. Targets have included the British military, Northern Ireland security forces, and Loyalist paramilitary groups. CIRA did not join the Provisional IRA in the September 2005 decommissioning and remained capable of effective, if sporadic, terrorist attacks. On April 21, 2011, authorities defused an explosive device planted by CIRA near a statue of the Duke of Wellington in Trim, Meath, Ireland.

In December 2012, a plot by CIRA to murder an Irish national serving in the British army was foiled by Irish police.

Strength: Membership is small, with possibly fewer than 50. Police counterterrorism operations have reduced the group's strength.

Location/Area of Operation: Northern Ireland and the Irish Republic.

Funding and External Aid: CIRA supported its activities through criminal activities, including smuggling.

GAMA'A AL-ISLAMIYYA

aka al-Gama'at; Egyptian al-Gama'at al-Islamiyya; GI; Islamic Gama'at; IG; Islamic Group

Description: Gama'a al-Islamiyya (IG) was designated as a Foreign Terrorist Organization on October 8, 1997. Once Egypt's largest militant group, IG was active in the late 1970s, but is now a loosely organized network. It formed the Building and Development political party that competed in the 2011 parliamentary elections, winning 13 seats. Egypt-based members of IG released from prison prior to the revolution have renounced terrorism, though some members located overseas have worked with or joined al-Qa'ida (AQ). Hundreds of members who may not have renounced violence were released from prison in 2011. The external wing, composed of mainly exiled members in several countries, maintained that its primary goal was to replace the Egyptian government with an Islamic state. IG's "spiritual" leader, the "blind Sheikh," Umar Abd al-Rahman, is serving a life sentence in a U.S. prison for his involvement in the 1993 World Trade Center bombing. Supporters of al-Rahman have called for reprisal attacks in the event of his death in prison.

Activities: In the 1990s, IG conducted armed attacks against Egyptian security, other government officials, and Coptic Christians. IG claimed responsibility for the June 1995 assassination attempt on Egyptian President Hosni Mubarak in Addis Ababa, Ethiopia. The group also launched attacks on tourists in Egypt, most notably the 1997 Luxor attack. In 1999, part of the group publicly renounced violence.

Strength: At its peak, IG likely commanded several thousand core members and a similar number of supporters. Security crackdowns following the 1997 attack in Luxor and the 1999

cease-fire, along with post-September 11 security measures and defections to AQ, have probably resulted in a substantial decrease in what is left of an organized group.

Location/Area of Operation: The IG maintained an external presence in Afghanistan, Yemen, Iran, the UK, Germany, and France. The IG terrorist presence in Egypt was minimal due to the reconciliation efforts of former local members.

Funding and External Aid: Unknown

HAMAS

aka the Islamic Resistance Movement; Harakat al-Muqawama al-Islamiya; Izz al-Din al Qassam Battalions; Izz al-Din al Qassam Brigades; Izz al-Din al Qassam Forces; Students of Ayyash; Student of the Engineer; Yahya Ayyash Units; Izz al-Din al-Qassim Brigades; Izz al-Din al-Qassim Forces; Izz al-Din al-Qassim Battalions

Description: Designated as a Foreign Terrorist Organization on October 8, 1997, Hamas possesses military and political wings and came into being in late 1987 at the onset of the first Palestinian uprising, or Intifada, as an outgrowth of the Palestinian branch of the Muslim Brotherhood. The armed element, called the Izz al-Din al-Qassam Brigades, conducts anti-Israeli attacks, including suicide bombings against civilian targets inside Israel. Hamas also manages a broad, mostly Gaza-based network of "Dawa" or ministry activities that include charities, schools, clinics, youth camps, fund-raising, and political activities. After winning Palestinian Legislative Council elections in January 2006, Hamas gained control of significant Palestinian Authority (PA) ministries in Gaza, including the Ministry of Interior. At year's end there were no Hamas ministers in the PA and no power-sharing government of the PA in which Hamas is a member. In 2007, Hamas cadres took control of Gaza in a violent confrontation with Fatah, forcing Fatah forces to leave Gaza or go underground. Hamas retains control of Gaza.

A Shura Council based in Damascus, Syria, set overall policy for many years, but the group abandoned its Damascus base in late 2011 following a disagreement with the Syrian government over its use of violence against protestors.

Activities: Prior to 2005, Hamas conducted numerous anti-Israeli attacks, including suicide bombings, rocket launches, improvised explosive device (IED) attacks, and shootings. Hamas has not directly targeted U.S. interests, though U.S. citizens have died and been injured in the group's attacks. The group curtailed terrorist attacks in February 2005 after agreeing to a temporary period of calm brokered by the PA, and ceased most violence after winning control of the PA legislature and cabinet in January 2006. After Hamas staged a June 2006 attack on Israel Defense Forces soldiers near Kerem Shalom, which resulted in two deaths and the abduction of Corporal Gilad Shalit, Israel took steps that severely limited the operation of the Rafah crossing. In June 2007, after Hamas took control of Gaza from the PA and Fatah, the Gaza borders were closed and Hamas increased its use of tunnels to smuggle weapons into Gaza, using the Sinai and maritime routes. Hamas has since dedicated the majority of its activity in Gaza to solidifying its control, hardening its defenses, building its weapons caches, tightening security, and conducting limited operations against Israeli military forces.

Hamas fought a 23-day war with Israel from late December 2008 to January 2009. Throughout 2011, Hamas carried out rocket attacks on southern Israel.

From November 14-21, 2012, Hamas fought a war with Israel during which it claims to have launched more than 1,400 rockets into Israel. Prior to the confrontation, approximately 750 rockets had been fired into Israel from Hamas-governed Gaza. Among those, one hit an apartment building in the Israeli city of Kiryat Malachi and killed three civilians. Following the Egypt-mediated cease-fire between Israel and Hamas, operatives from Hamas and Palestine Islamic Jihad coordinated and carried out a November bus bombing in Tel Aviv that wounded 29 people.

Strength: Several thousand Gaza-based operatives with varying degrees of skills are in its armed wing, the Izz al-Din al-Qassam Brigades, along with its reported 9,000-person Hamas-led paramilitary group known as the "Executive Force."

Location/Area of Operation: Hamas has a presence in every major city in the West Bank and Gaza. The group retains a cadre of leaders and facilitators that conduct political, fundraising, and arms-smuggling activities throughout the region. Hamas also increased its presence in the Palestinian refugee camps in Lebanon, probably with the goal of eclipsing Fatah's long-time dominance of the camps.

Funding and External Aid: Hamas receives funding, weapons, and training from Iran. In addition, the group raises funds in the Persian Gulf countries and receives donations from Palestinian expatriates around the world, through its charities, such as the umbrella fundraising organization, the Union of Good. Some fundraising and propaganda activity also takes place in Western Europe.

HAQQANI NETWORK

aka HQN

Description: Designated as a Foreign Terrorist Organization on September 19, 2012, the Haqqani Network (HQN) has its roots in an offensive formed in the late 1970s, around the time of the former Soviet Union's invasion of Afghanistan. Jalaluddin Haqqani, HQN's founder, established a relationship with Usama bin Laden in the mid-1980s, and joined the Taliban in 1995. After the fall of the Taliban in Afghanistan in 2001, Jalaluddin retreated to Pakistan where, under the leadership of Jalaluddin's son, Sirajuddin Haqqani, the group began participating in the insurgency and became known as the Haqqani Network.

Activities: HQN has planned and carried out a number of significant attacks against U.S. and Coalition Forces in Afghanistan, as well as Afghan government targets and civilians. HQN's most notorious attacks include a January 2008 attack on the Serena Hotel in Kabul, during which the attackers killed eight individuals, including one U.S. citizen; a May 2010 attack on Bagram Airbase using suicide bombers, rockets, and grenades, which killed an American contractor and wounded nine U.S. soldiers; an attack on the Intercontinental Hotel in Kabul in June 2011, which killed 11 civilians and two Afghan policemen; a September 2011 truck bombing in Wardak Province, Afghanistan, which wounded 77 U.S. soldiers; and the 19-hour attack on the U.S.

Embassy and ISAF headquarters in Kabul in September 2011, which killed 16 Afghans, including at least six children.

In 2012, HQN's attacks continued. Attacks included a June suicide bomb attack against Forward Operating Base Salerno, which killed two U.S. soldiers and wounded more than 100; and a 12-hour siege of the Spozhmai Hotel in Kabul, which resulted in the death of at least 18 Afghans, including 14 civilians. Despite HQN's violent attacks, the group suffered a major setback in August with the death of senior leader Badruddin Haqqani.

HQN has also been involved in numerous kidnappings in Afghanistan, including that of *New York Times* reporter David Rohde in November 2008, who escaped in June 2009. HQN was also behind the June 2009 kidnapping of Bowe Bergdahl, a soldier in the U.S. Army, who remained in captivity throughout 2012.

Strength: HQN is believed to have several hundred core members, but it is estimated that the organization is also able to draw upon a pool of upwards of 10,000 fighters with varying degrees of affiliation. HQN also draws strength through cooperation with other terrorist organizations operating in Afghanistan, including the Afghan Taliban, al-Qa'ida, Tehrik-e Taliban Pakistan, the Islamic Movement of Uzbekistan, Lashkar-e Jhangvi, and Jaish-e Mohammad.

Location/Area of Operation: HQN is active along the Afghanistan-Pakistan border and across much of southeastern Afghanistan. The group's leadership maintains a power base in Miram Shah, North Waziristan, Pakistan.

Funding and External Aid: In addition to the support it receives through its connections to other terrorist organizations, HQN receives much of its funds from donors in Pakistan and the Gulf, as well as through criminal activities such as kidnapping, extortion, smuggling, and other licit and illicit business ventures.

HARAKAT-UL JIHAD ISLAMI

aka HUJI, Movement of Islamic Holy War; Harkat-ul-Jihad-al Islami; Harkat-al-Jihad-ul Islami; Harkat-ul-Jehad-al-Islami; Harakat ul Jihad-e-Islami; Harakat-ul Jihad Islami

Description: Designated as a Foreign Terrorist Organization on August 6, 2010, Harakat-ul Jihad Islami (HUJI) was founded in 1980 in Afghanistan to fight against the former Soviet Union. Following the Soviet withdrawal from Afghanistan in 1989, the organization re-focused its efforts on India. HUJI seeks the annexation of Indian Kashmir and expulsion of Coalition Forces from Afghanistan. It also has supplied fighters for the Taliban in Afghanistan. In addition, some factions of HUJI espouse a more global agenda and conduct attacks in Pakistan. HUJI is composed of militant Pakistanis and veterans of the Soviet-Afghan war. HUJI has experienced a number of internal splits and a portion of the group has aligned with al-Qa'ida (AQ) in recent years, including training its members in AQ training camps. Mohammad Ilyas Kashmiri, one of HUJI's top leaders who also served as an AQ military commander and strategist, was killed on June 3, 2011.

Activities: HUJI has been involved in a number of terrorist attacks in recent years. On March 2, 2006, a HUJI leader was behind the suicide bombing of the U.S. Consulate in Karachi, Pakistan, which killed four people, including U.S. diplomat David Foy, and injured 48 others. HUJI was also responsible for terrorist attacks in India including the May 2007 Hyderabad mosque attack, which killed 16 and injured 40; and the March 2007 Varanasi attack, which killed 25 and injured 100. HUJI claimed responsibility for the September 7, 2011 bombing of the New Delhi High Court, which left at least 11 dead and an estimated 76 wounded. HUJI sent an email to the press stating that the bomb was intended to force India to repeal a death sentence of a HUJI member. While HUJI continued its recruitment efforts in 2012, the organization also had several members arrested by authorities.

Strength: HUJI has an estimated strength of several hundred members.

Location/Area of Operation: HUJI's area of operation extends throughout South Asia, with its terrorist operations focused primarily in India and Afghanistan. Some factions of HUJI conduct attacks within Pakistan.

Funding and External Aid: Unknown

HARAKAT UL-JIHAD-I-ISLAMI/BANGLADESH

aka HUJI-B, Harakat ul Jihad e Islami Bangladesh; Harkatul Jihad al Islam; Harkatul Jihad; Harakat ul Jihad al Islami; Harkat ul Jihad al Islami; Harkat-ul-Jehad-al-Islami; Harakat ul Jihad Islami Bangladesh; Islami Dawat-e-Kafela; IDEK

Description: Designated as a Foreign Terrorist Organization on March 5, 2008, Harakat ul-Jihad-i-Islami/Bangladesh (HUJI-B) was formed in April 1992 by a group of former Bangladeshi Afghan veterans to establish Islamic rule in Bangladesh. In October 2005, Bangladeshi authorities banned the group. HUJI-B has connections to Pakistani terrorist groups such as Lashkar e-Tayyiba, which advocate similar objectives. The leaders of HUJI-B signed the February 1998 fatwa sponsored by Usama bin Laden that declared American civilians legitimate targets.

Activities: In December 2008, three HUJI-B members were convicted for the May 2004 grenade attack that wounded the British High Commissioner in Sylhet, Bangladesh. In 2011, Bangladeshi authorities formally charged multiple suspects, including HUJI-B leader Mufti Abdul Hannan, with the killing of former Finance Minister Shah AMS Kibria of Awami League in a grenade attack on January 27, 2005. Though HUJI-B committed no known attacks in 2012, there were indications that the group continued to recruit members, particularly women. Authorities arrested several HUJI-B members.

Strength: HUJI-B leaders claim that up to 400 of its members are Afghan war veterans, but its total membership is unknown.

Location/Area of Operation: The group operates primarily in Bangladesh and India. HUJI-B trains and has a network of madrassas in Bangladesh.

Funding and External Aid: HUJI-B funding comes from a variety of sources. Several international Muslim NGOs may have funneled money to HUJI-B and other Bangladeshi militant groups.

HARAKAT UL-MUJAHIDEEN

aka HUM; Harakat ul-Ansar; HUA; Jamiat ul-Ansar; JUA; al-Faran; al-Hadid; al-Hadith; Harakat ul-Mujahidin

Description: Designated as a Foreign Terrorist Organization on October 8, 1997, Harakat ul-Mujahideen (HUM) seeks the annexation of Indian Kashmir and the expulsion of Coalition Forces in Afghanistan. Reportedly under pressure from the Government of Pakistan, HUM's long-time leader Fazlur Rehman Khalil stepped down and was replaced by Dr. Badr Munir as the head of HUM in January 2005. HUM operated terrorist training camps in eastern Afghanistan until Coalition air strikes destroyed them in 2001. Khalil was detained by Pakistani authorities in mid-2004 and subsequently released in late December of the same year. In 2003, HUM began using the name Jamiat ul-Ansar (JUA). Pakistan banned JUA in November 2003.

Activities: HUM has conducted a number of operations against Indian troops and civilian targets in Kashmir. It is linked to the Kashmiri militant group al-Faran, which kidnapped five Western tourists in Kashmir in July 1995; the five reportedly were killed later that year. HUM was responsible for the hijacking of an Indian airliner in December 1999 that resulted in the release of Masood Azhar, an important leader in the former Harakat ul-Ansar, who was imprisoned by India in 1994 and then founded Jaish-e-Mohammed (JEM) after his release. Another former member of Harakat ul-Ansar, Ahmed Omar Sheik was also released by India as a result of the hijackings and was later convicted of the abduction and murder in 2002 of U.S. journalist Daniel Pearl.

HUM targets Indian security and civilian targets in Kashmir. In 2005, such attacks resulted in the deaths of 15 people. In November 2007, two Indian soldiers were killed in Kashmir while engaged in a firefight with a group of HUM militants. Indian police and army forces have engaged with HUM militants in the Kashmir region, killing a number of the organization's leadership in April, October, and December 2008. In February 2009, Lalchand Kishen Advani, leader of the Indian opposition Bharatiya Janata Party, received a death threat that was attributed to HUM. In December 2012, Pakistani police disrupted militants associated with HUM and Lashkar i Jhangvi who were planning an attack on a congregation hall in Karachi, Pakistan.

Strength: HUM has several hundred armed supporters located in Pakistan-administered Kashmir; India's southern Kashmir and Doda regions; and in the Kashmir valley. Supporters are mostly Pakistanis and Kashmiris, but also include Afghans and Arab veterans of the Afghan war. After 2000, a significant portion of HUM's membership defected to JEM.

Location/Area of Operation: Based in Muzaffarabad, Rawalpindi, and several other cities in Pakistan, HUM conducts insurgent and terrorist operations primarily in Kashmir and Afghanistan. HUM trains its militants in Afghanistan and Pakistan.

Funding and External Aid: HUM collects donations from wealthy and grassroots donors in Pakistan. HUM's financial collection methods include soliciting donations in magazine advertisements and pamphlets.

HIZBALLAH

aka the Party of God; Islamic Jihad; Islamic Jihad Organization; Revolutionary Justice Organization; Organization of the Oppressed on Earth; Islamic Jihad for the Liberation of Palestine; Organization of Right Against Wrong; Ansar Allah; Followers of the Prophet Muhammed

Description: Hizballah was designated as a Foreign Terrorist Organization on October 8, 1997. Formed in 1982 in response to the Israeli invasion of Lebanon, the Lebanese-based radical Shia group takes its ideological inspiration from the Iranian revolution and the teachings of the late Ayatollah Khomeini. The group generally follows the religious guidance of Khomeini's successor, Iranian Supreme Leader Ali Khamenei. Hizballah is closely allied with Iran and the two often work together on shared initiatives, though Hizballah also acts independently. Hizballah shares a close relationship with Syria, and like Iran, the group is providing assistance to Syrian regime forces in the Syrian conflict.

Hizballah has strong influence in Lebanon, especially with the Shia community. Hizballah plays an active role in Lebanese politics, and the group holds 13 seats in the 128-member Lebanese Parliament and two seats in the 30-member Council of Ministers. Hizballah's political strength grew in the wake of the 2006 war with Israel and the group's 2008 takeover of West Beirut, though its reputation and popularity have been significantly undermined by the group's active support for the Asad regime.

Hizballah provides support to several Palestinian terrorist organizations, as well as a number of local Christian and Muslim militias in Lebanon. Besides overt political support, support includes the covert provision of weapons, explosives, training, funding, and guidance.

Activities: Hizballah's terrorist attacks have included the suicide truck bombings of the U.S. Embassy and U.S. Marine barracks in Beirut in 1983; the U.S. Embassy annex in Beirut in 1984; and the 1985 hijacking of TWA flight 847, during which a U.S. Navy diver was murdered. Elements of the group were responsible for the kidnapping, detention, and murder of Americans and other Westerners in Lebanon in the 1980s. Hizballah was implicated, along with Iran, in the 1992 attacks on the Israeli Embassy in Argentina and on the 1994 bombing of the Argentine-Israeli Mutual Association in Buenos Aires. In 2000, Hizballah operatives captured three Israeli soldiers in the Shebaa Farms area and, separately, kidnapped an Israeli non-combatant in Dubai. Though the non-combatant survived, on November 1, 2001, Israeli Army Rabbi Israel Weiss pronounced the soldiers dead. The surviving non-combatant and the bodies of the IDF soldiers were returned to Israel in a prisoner exchange with Hizballah in 2004.

Hizballah and a Palestinian group affiliated with al-Qa'ida blamed each other for a May 2011 roadside bomb attack that wounded six Italian soldiers with the UN Interim Force in Lebanon (UNIFIL). Two other attacks against UNIFIL peacekeepers – an attack in late July that wounded six French citizens and a second attack days later that injured three other French soldiers – were believed to have been carried out by Hizballah. Also in 2011, four Hizballah members were indicted by the U.N.-based Special Tribunal for Lebanon (STL), an international tribunal investigating the 2005 assassination of Lebanese Prime Minister Rafik Hariri. The four Hizballah members indicted by the STL were Mustafa Badreddine Salim Ayyash, Assad Sabra, and Hassan Anise. Identified as the primary suspect in Hariri's assassination, Badreddine is believed to have replaced his cousin, Imad Mugniyeh, as Hizballah's top military commander after Mugniyeh's 2008 death. Hizballah denounced the trial and vowed to retaliate, saying the four indicted Hizballah members would not be handed over.

On January 12, Thai police detained a Hizballah operative on immigration charges as he was attempting to depart Thailand from Suvarnabhumi International Airport. He led police to nearly 10,000 pounds of urea-based fertilizer and 10 gallons of liquid ammonium nitrate in a commercial building about 20 miles south of Bangkok. It was unclear if the materials were intended to be used to carry out terrorist attacks in Thailand – possibly against Israeli tourists – or if they were to be transported to another country. The Hizballah operative was awaiting trial at year's end.

In 2012, Hizballah stepped up the pace of its terrorist plotting, and was implicated in several terrorist plots around the world. In Cyprus, a suspected Lebanese Hizballah operative was detained by the Cypriot authorities on July 7 for allegedly helping plan an attack against Israeli tourists in Cyprus. The trial began in September 2012, and on March 21, 2013, a Cyprus court found a Hizballah operative guilty of charges stemming from his surveillance activities of Israeli tourist targets.

In Bulgaria, on July 18, a terrorist attack was carried out on a passenger bus carrying 42 Israeli tourists at the Sarafovo Airport near the Bulgarian city of Burgas. The explosion killed five Israelis and injured 32, and also killed the Bulgarian bus driver. On February 5, 2013, Bulgarian Deputy Prime Minister Tsvetan Tsevtanov, publically linked Hizballah to the Burgas bombing, citing the involvement of two Hizballah operatives in the plot.

Strength: Several thousand supporters and members.

Location/Area of Operation: Hizballah is based in the southern suburbs of Beirut, the Bekaa Valley, and southern Lebanon. However, as evidenced by Hizballah's activities during the course of 2012, the group is capable of operating around the globe.

Funding and External Aid: Iran continues to provide Hizballah with training, weapons, and explosives, as well as political, diplomatic, monetary, and organizational aid; Syria furnished training, weapons, diplomatic, and political support. Hizballah also receives funding from private donations and profits from legal and illegal businesses. Hizballah receives financial support from Lebanese Shia communities in Europe, Africa, South America, North America, and Asia. As illustrated by the Lebanese Canadian bank case, Hizballah supporters are often engaged in a range of criminal activities that benefit the group financially. These have included smuggling contraband goods, passport falsification, trafficking in narcotics, money laundering, and credit card, immigration, and bank fraud.

INDIAN MUJAHEDEEN

aka Indian Mujahidin; Islamic Security Force-Indian Mujahideen (ISF-IM)

Description: The Indian Mujahedeen (IM) was designated as a Foreign Terrorist Organization on September 19, 2011. An India-based terrorist group with significant links to Pakistani-based terrorist organizations, IM has been responsible for dozens of bomb attacks throughout India since 2005, and has caused the deaths of hundreds of civilians. IM maintains close ties to other U.S.-designated terrorist entities including Pakistan-based Lashkar e-Tayyiba (LeT), Jaish-e-Mohammed, and Harakat ul-Jihad-i-Islami (HUJI). IM's stated goal is to carry out terrorist actions against non-Muslims in furtherance of its ultimate objective, an Islamic Caliphate across South Asia.

Activities: IM's primary method of attack is multiple coordinated bombings in crowded areas against economic and civilian targets to maximize terror and casualties. In 2008, an IM attack in Delhi killed 30 people; that same year, IM was responsible for 16 synchronized bomb blasts in crowded urban centers and a local hospital in Ahmedabad that killed 38 and injured more than 100. IM also played a facilitative role in the 2008 Mumbai attack carried out by LeT that killed approximately 170 people, including six Americans. In 2010, IM carried out the bombing of a popular German bakery in Pune, India, frequented by tourists, killing 17 and injuring over 60.

In 2012, IM conducted multiple bombings killing dozens of innocent civilians and injuring hundreds more. In May, IM was suspected of an improvised explosive device (IED) attack in New Delhi. In July, 25 civilians were killed and 137 wounded in an IM-led IED attack in Mumbai. In August, 30 roadside bombs were discovered in Pune, Maharashtra. One of the bombs exploded causing injuries to authorities disarming the remaining bombs, and police arrested eight suspected members of IM on suspicion of having planted the bombs. In September, 15 civilians were killed, and 91 others injured in a bombing in New Delhi. Indian police arrested three militants in October suspected of planning bomb attacks in New Delhi during the Hindu festival season. In December, four IM operatives were arrested in connection with four coordinated August bombings in Pune that seriously injured a civilian.

Strength: Estimated to have several thousand supporters and members.

Location/Area of Operation: India

Funding and External Aid: Suspected to obtain funding and support from other terrorist organizations, such as LeT and HUJI, and from sources in Pakistan and the Middle East.

ISLAMIC JIHAD UNION

aka Islamic Jihad Group; Islomiy Jihod Ittihodi; al-Djihad al-Islami; Dzhamaat Modzhakhedov; Islamic Jihad Group of Uzbekistan; Jamiat al-Jihad al-Islami; Jamiyat; The Jamaat Mojahedin; The Kazakh Jama'at; The Libyan Society

Description: Designated as a Foreign Terrorist Organization on June 17, 2005, the Islamic Jihad Union (IJU) is a Sunni extremist organization that splintered from the Islamic Movement of Uzbekistan in the early 2000s and is currently based in Pakistan's Federally Administered Tribal Areas. Najmiddin Jalolov founded the organization as the Islamic Jihad Group (IJG) in March 2002, but the group was renamed IJU in May 2005. Though IJU remains committed to overthrowing the Government of Uzbekistan, it also has a global agenda, seen in its attacks on Coalition Forces in Afghanistan and the recruitment of German nationals for the purpose of conducting operations in Europe.

Activities: The IJU primarily operates against American and ISAF Forces in Afghanistan and continues to pose a threat to Central Asia. The group claimed responsibility for attacks in March and April 2004, targeting police at several roadway checkpoints and at a popular bazaar, killing approximately 47 people, including 33 IJU members, some of whom were suicide bombers. In July 2004, the group carried out near-simultaneous suicide bombings of the Uzbek Prosecutor General's office and the U.S. and Israeli Embassies in Tashkent. In September 2007, German authorities disrupted an IJU plot to attack U.S. military bases and personnel by detaining and prosecuting three IJU operatives, including two German citizens. Foreign fighters from Germany, Turkey, and elsewhere in Europe continued to travel to the Afghan-Pakistan border area to join the IJU to fight against U.S. and Coalition Forces. In 2012, the Federal Bureau of Investigation arrested a number of Americans attempting to travel to Turkey to join the IJU.

Strength: 100-200 members.

Location/Area of Operation: Based in Pakistan, IJU members are also scattered throughout Central Asia, Europe, Pakistan, and Afghanistan.

Funding and External Aid: Unknown

ISLAMIC MOVEMENT OF UZBEKISTAN

aka IMU

Description: Designated as a Foreign Terrorist Organization on September 25, 2000, the Islamic Movement of Uzbekistan's (IMU) goal is to overthrow the Uzbek government and establish an Islamic state. For most of the past decade, however, the group recruited members from other Central Asian states and Europe and has focused on fighting in Afghanistan and Pakistan. The IMU has a relationship with al-Qa'ida, the Taliban, and Tehrik-e Taliban Pakistan. In April 2012, IMU leader Abu Usman Adil died and Usman Ghazi was named the group's new leader. IMU's leadership cadre remains based in Pakistan's Taliban-controlled North Waziristan and operates primarily along the Afghanistan-Pakistan border and in northern Afghanistan. Top IMU leaders have integrated themselves into the Taliban's shadow government in Afghanistan's northern provinces. Operating in cooperation with each other, the Taliban and IMU have expanded their presence throughout northern Afghanistan and have established training camps in the region.

Activities: Since the beginning of Operation Enduring Freedom, the IMU has been predominantly focused on attacks against U.S. and Coalition Forces in Afghanistan. In late 2009, NATO forces reported an increase in IMU-affiliated foreign fighters in Afghanistan. In 2010, the IMU continued to fight in Afghanistan and the group claimed credit for the September 19 ambush that killed 25 Tajik troops in Tajikistan. On October 15, 2011, IMU claimed responsibility for a suicide assault on a U.S.-led Provincial Reconstruction Team base in the Afghan province of Panjshir that killed two Afghan civilians and wounded two security guards.

In March 2012, five suspected IMU members were convicted of killing a soldier in Tajikistan. In April, a Tajikistan court convicted 34 alleged members of the IMU for attacks in Kairakkum, attacks at a border post in Isfara, the murder of several police officers, and facilitating a suicide attack against security forces in Khujand. An October 2012 IMU video showed an attack and the death of numerous Pakistani security forces in the Federally Administered Tribal Areas. In December in Paris, nine Europeans were convicted for sending tens of thousands of euros to the IMU.

Strength: 200-300 members

Location/Area of Operation: IMU militants are located in South Asia, Central Asia, and Iran.

Funding and External Aid: The IMU receives support from a large Uzbek diaspora, terrorist organizations, and donors from Europe, Central and South Asia, and the Middle East.

JAISH-E-MOHAMMED

aka the Army of Mohammed; Mohammed's Army; Tehrik ul-Furqaan; Khuddam-ul-Islam; Khudamul Islam; Kuddam e Islami; Jaish-i-Mohammed

Description: Designated as a Foreign Terrorist Organization on December 26, 2001, Jaish-e-Mohammed (JEM) is based in Pakistan. JEM was founded in early 2000 by Masood Azhar, a former senior leader of Harakat ul-Ansar, upon his release from prison in India in exchange for 155 hijacked Indian Airlines hostages. The group's aim is to annex Indian Kashmir and expel Coalition Forces from Afghanistan, and it has openly declared war against the United States. Pakistan outlawed JEM in 2002. By 2003, JEM had splintered into Khuddam-ul-Islam (KUI), headed by Azhar, and Jamaat ul-Furqan (JUF), led by Abdul Jabbar, who was released from Pakistani custody in August 2004. Pakistan banned KUI and JUF in November 2003.

Activities: JEM continued to operate openly in parts of Pakistan despite the 2002 ban on its activities. Since Masood Azhar's 1999 release from Indian custody, JEM has conducted many fatal terrorist attacks in the region. JEM claimed responsibility for several suicide car bombings in Kashmir, including an October 2001 suicide attack on the Jammu and Kashmir legislative assembly building in Srinagar that killed more than 30 people. The Indian government has publicly implicated JEM, along with Lashkar e-Tayyiba, for the December 2001 attack on the Indian Parliament that killed nine and injured 18. In 2002, Pakistani authorities arrested and convicted a JEM member for the abduction and murder of U.S. journalist Daniel Pearl. Pakistani authorities suspect that JEM members may have been involved in the 2002 anti-Christian attacks in Islamabad, Murree, and Taxila that killed two Americans. In December 2003, Pakistan implicated JEM members in the two assassination attempts against President Musharraf. In 2006, JEM claimed responsibility for a number of attacks, including the killing of several Indian police officials in the Indian-administered Kashmir capital of Srinagar. Indian police and JEM members continued to engage in firefights throughout 2008 and 2009. In March 2011, Indian security forces killed chief JEM commander Sajad Afghani and his bodyguard in Sirnagar, Kashmir.

Strength: JEM has at least several hundred armed supporters – including a large cadre of former Harakat ul-Mujahideen members – located in Pakistan, India's southern Kashmir and Doda regions, and in the Kashmir Valley. In 2012, JEM continued its fundraising and recruitment activities in Pakistan.

Location/Area of Operation: Kashmir in India, Afghanistan, and Pakistan, particularly southern Punjab.

Funding and External Aid: To avoid asset seizures by the Pakistani government, since 2007 JEM has withdrawn funds from bank accounts and invested in legal businesses, such as commodity trading, real estate, and production of consumer goods. JEM also collects funds through donation requests in magazines and pamphlets, sometimes using charitable causes to solicit donations.

JEMAAH ANSHORUT TAUHID

aka JAT; Jemmah Ansharut Tauhid; Jem'mah Ansharut Tauhid; Jamaah Ansharut Tauhid; Jama'ah Ansharut Tauhid; Laskar 99

Description: The Department of State designated Indonesia-based group Jemaah Anshorut Tauhid (JAT) as a Foreign Terrorist Organization on March 13, 2012. JAT formed in 2008, seeks to establish an Islamic caliphate in Indonesia, and has carried out numerous attacks on Indonesian government personnel, police, military, and civilians. In 2011, Abu Bakar Ba'asyir, the founder and leader of JAT, was convicted and sentenced to 15 years in prison for his role in organizing a militant training camp in Aceh. Ba'asyir is also the co-founder and former leader of Jemaah Islamiya (JI); JAT maintains close ties to JI and other indigenous terrorist groups in Southeast Asia.

Activities: JAT has conducted multiple attacks targeting civilians and Indonesian officials, resulting in the deaths of several Indonesian police. JAT has robbed banks and carried out other illicit activities to fund the purchase of assault weapons, ammunition, explosives, and bomb-making materials. In September 2011, a JAT suicide bomber detonated explosives inside a church in Central Java, killing the bomber and wounding dozens. Indonesian police arrested other JAT members in connection with this bombing and uncovered a plot for additional suicide attacks. In April 2011, a suicide bomber carried out an attack at a mosque in West Java that injured dozens of police officers and killed the bomber.

In 2012, JAT participated in numerous attacks. In October, two policemen investigating an alleged terrorist camp linked to JAT were tortured and found dead in Poso, and authorities implicated JAT in the killings. In December, four police officers were killed and two wounded in an attack by suspected local JAT members in Central Sulawesi after a group of 10 to 15 gunmen ambushed a police patrol in the area. On December 25, a 10-kilogram nail bomb was planted at a police station in front of the central Poso market. Police suspected the perpetrators belonged to the local JAT cell in Poso.

Strength: JAT is estimated to have several thousand supporters and members.

Location/Area of Operation: JAT is based in Indonesia with suspected elements in Malaysia and the Philippines.

Funding and External Aid: JAT raises funds through membership donations, as well as bank robberies, cyber hacking, and other illicit activities; and legitimate business activities such as operating bookstores and other shops.

JEMAAH ISLAMIYA

aka Jemaa Islamiyah; Jema'a Islamiyah; Jemaa Islamiyya; Jema'a Islamiyya; Jemaa Islamiyyah; Jema'a Islamiyyah; Jemaah Islamiah; Jemaah Islamiyah; Jema'ah Islamiyah; Jemaah Islamiyyah; Jema'ah Islamiyyah; JI

Description: Designated as a Foreign Terrorist Organization on October 23, 2002, Jemaah Islamiya (JI) is a Southeast Asia-based terrorist group co-founded by Abu Bakar Ba'asyir and Abdullah Sungkar that seeks the establishment of an Islamic caliphate spanning Indonesia, Malaysia, southern Thailand, Singapore, Brunei, and the southern Philippines. More than 400 JI operatives have been captured since 2002, including operations chief and al-Qa'ida associate Hambali. In 2006, several members connected to JI's 2005 suicide attack in Bali were arrested; in 2007, Muhammad Naim (a.k.a. Zarkasih) and JI military commander Abu Dujana were arrested; and in 2008, two senior JI operatives were arrested in Malaysia and a JI-linked cell was broken up in Sumatra. In September 2009, JI-splinter group leader Noordin Mohammad Top was killed in a police raid. Progress against JI continued in February 2010, when Indonesian National Police discovered and disbanded a violent extremist training base in Aceh in which members of JI and other Indonesian violent extremist groups participated. The police raid resulted in the capture of more than 60 militants, including some JI operatives, and led authorities to former JI leader Dulmatin, one of the planners of the 2002 Bali bombing. In March 2010, Dulmatin was killed outside of Jakarta. In June 2010, wanted JI commander Abdullah Sunata was captured while planning to bomb the Danish Embassy in Jakarta. In January 2011, JI member Umar Patek was captured in Abbottabad, Pakistan, and put on trial in Indonesia, where he was convicted and sentenced to 20 years in prison in June 2012 for his role in the Bali bombing.

Activities: In December 2001, Singaporean authorities uncovered a JI plot to attack U.S., Israeli, British, and Australian diplomatic facilities in Singapore. Other significant JI attacks include the 2002 Bali bombings, which killed more than 200, including seven U.S. citizens; the August 2003 bombing of the J. W. Marriott Hotel in Jakarta; the September 2004 bombing outside the Australian Embassy in Jakarta; and JI's October 2005 suicide bombing in Bali, which killed 26, including the three suicide bombers.

On July 17, 2009, a JI faction led by Top conducted the group's most recent high-profile attacks, when two suicide bombers detonated explosive devices at the J.W. Marriott and Ritz-Carlton hotels in Jakarta, killing seven and injuring more than 50, including seven Americans. The Philippine military announced it had killed two JI members in separate incidents in the south of the country in late 2012, including one of the group's senior-most representatives to the Philippines.

Strength: Estimates of total JI members vary from 500 to several thousand.

Location/Area of Operation: JI is based in Indonesia and is believed to have elements in Malaysia and the Philippines.

Funding and External Aid: Investigations have indicated that JI is fully capable of its own fundraising through membership donations and criminal and business activities. It has received financial, ideological, and logistical support from Middle Eastern contacts and NGOs.

JUNDALLAH

aka People's Resistance Movement of Iran (PMRI); Jonbesh-i Moqavemat-i-Mardom-i Iran; Popular Resistance Movement of Iran; Soldiers of God; Fedayeen-e-Islam; Former Jundallah of Iran; Jundullah; Jondullah; Jundollah; Jondollah; Jondallah; Army of God (God's Army); Baloch Peoples Resistance Movement (BPRM)

Description: Jundallah was designated as a Foreign Terrorist Organization on November 4, 2010. Since its inception in 2003, Jundallah, which operates primarily in the province of Sistan va Balochistan of Iran, has engaged in numerous attacks, killing and maiming scores of Iranian civilians and government officials. Jundallah's stated goals are to secure recognition of Balochi cultural, economic, and political rights from the Government of Iran, and to spread awareness of the plight of the Baloch situation through violent and nonviolent means.

Activities: In March 2006, Jundallah attacked a motorcade in eastern Iran, which included the deputy head of the Iranian Red Crescent Security Department, who was then taken hostage. The Governor of Zahedan, his deputy, and five other officials were wounded; seven others were kidnapped; and more than 20 were killed in the attack. An October 2009 suicide bomb attack in a marketplace in the city of Pishin in the Sistan va Balochistan province, which killed more than 40 people, was reportedly the deadliest terrorist attack in Iran since the 1980s. In a statement on its website, Jundallah claimed responsibility for the December 15, 2010 suicide bomb attack inside the Iman Hussein Mosque in Chabahar, which killed an estimated 35 to 40 civilians and wounded 60 to 100. In July 2010, Jundallah attacked the Grand Mosque in Zahedan, killing approximately 30 and injuring an estimated 300.

Strength: Reports of Jundallah membership vary from 500 to 2,000.

Location/Area of Operation: Throughout Sistan va Balochistan province in southeastern Iran and the greater Balochistan area of Afghanistan and Pakistan.

Funding and External Aid: Unknown

KAHANE CHAI

aka American Friends of the United Yeshiva; American Friends of Yeshivat Rav Meir; Committee for the Safety of the Roads; Dikuy Bogdim; DOV; Forefront of the Idea; Friends of the Jewish Idea Yeshiva; Jewish Legion; Judea Police; Judean Congress; Kach; Kahane; Kahane Lives; Kahane Tzadak; Kahane.org; Kahanetzadak.com; Kfar Tapuah Fund; Koach; Meir's Youth; New Kach Movement; Newkach.org; No'ar Meir; Repression of Traitors; State of Judea; Sword of David; The Committee Against Racism and Discrimination (CARD); The Hatikva Jewish Identity Center; The International Kahane Movement; The Jewish Idea Yeshiva; The Judean Legion; The Judean Voice; The Qomemiyut Movement; The Rabbi Meir David Kahane Memorial Fund; The Voice of Judea; The Way of the Torah; The Yeshiva of the Jewish Idea; Yeshivat Harav Meir

Description: Kach – the precursor to Kahane Chai – was founded by radical Israeli-American Rabbi Meir Kahane, with the goal of restoring Greater Israel, which is generally used to refer to Israel, the West Bank, and Gaza. Its offshoot, Kahane Chai (translation: "Kahane Lives"), was founded by Meir Kahane's son Binyamin, following his father's 1990 assassination in the United States. Both organizations were designated as Foreign Terrorist Organizations on October 8, 1997. The group has attempted to gain seats in the Israeli Knesset over the past several decades but won only one seat in 1984.

Activities: Kahane Chai has harassed and threatened Arabs, Palestinians, and Israeli government officials, and has vowed revenge for the death of Binyamin Kahane and his wife. The group is suspected of involvement in a number of low-level attacks since the start of the First Palestinian Intifada in 2000. Since 2003, Kahane Chai activists have called for the execution of former Israeli Prime Minister Ariel Sharon, and physically intimidated other Israeli and Palestinian government officials who favored the dismantlement of Israeli settlements. Although they have not explicitly claimed responsibility for a series of mosque burnings in the West Bank, individuals affiliated with Kahane Chai are widely suspected of being the perpetrators. There were no known Kahane Chai attacks during 2012.

Strength: Kahane Chai's core membership is believed to be fewer than 100. The group's membership and support networks are overwhelmingly composed of Israeli citizens that live mostly in West Bank settlements.

Location/Area of Operation: Israel and West Bank settlements, particularly Qiryat Arba in Hebron.

Funding and External Aid: Receives support from sympathizers in the United States and Europe.

KATA'IB HIZBALLAH

aka Hizballah Brigades; Hizballah Brigades in Iraq; Hizballah Brigades-Iraq; Kata'ib Hezbollah; Khata'ib Hezbollah; Khata'ib Hizballah; Khattab Hezballah; Hizballah Brigades-Iraq of the Islamic Resistance in Iraq; Islamic Resistance in Iraq; Kata'ib Hizballah Fi al-Iraq; Katibat Abu Fathel al-A'abas; Katibat Zayd Ebin Ali; Katibut Karbalah

Description: Designated as a Foreign Terrorist Organization on July 2, 2009, Kata'ib Hizballah (KH) was formed in 2006 and is a radical Shia Islamist group with an anti-Western outlook and extremist ideology that has conducted attacks against Iraqi, U.S., and Coalition targets in Iraq. KH has threatened the lives of Iraqi politicians and civilians that support the legitimate political process in Iraq. The group is notable for its extensive use of media operations and propaganda by filming and releasing videos of attacks. KH has ideological ties to Lebanese Hizballah and receives support from that group and its sponsor, Iran.

Activities: KH has been responsible for numerous terrorist attacks since 2007, including improvised explosive device bombings, rocket propelled grenade attacks, and sniper operations. In 2007, KH gained notoriety with attacks on U.S. and Coalition Forces in Iraq. KH was particularly active in summer 2008, recording and distributing video footage of its attacks.

In June 2011, five U.S. soldiers were killed in a rocket attack in Baghdad, Iraq, when KH assailants fired between three and five rockets at U.S. military base Camp Victory. The group remained active in 2012, but has not conducted an attack on U.S. interests since July 2011.

Strength: Membership is estimated at 400 individuals.

Location/Area of Operation: KH's operations are predominately Iraq-based. In 2011, KH conducted the majority of its operations in Baghdad but was active in other areas of Iraq, including Kurdish areas such as Mosul. KH militants were reportedly in Syria, protecting Shia shrines and fighting alongside Syrian President Asad's troops against Syrian opposition forces.

Funding and External Aid: KH is almost entirely dependent on support from Iran and Lebanese Hizballah.

KURDISTAN WORKERS' PARTY

aka the Kurdistan Freedom and Democracy Congress; the Freedom and Democracy Congress of Kurdistan; KADEK; Partiya Karkeran Kurdistan; the People's Defense Force; Halu Mesru Savunma Kuvveti; Kurdistan People's Congress; People's Congress of Kurdistan; KONGRA-GEL

Description: Founded by Abdullah Ocalan in 1978 as a Marxist-Leninist separatist organization, the Kurdistan Workers' Party (PKK) was designated as a Foreign Terrorist Organization on October 8, 1997. The group, composed primarily of Turkish Kurds, launched a campaign of violence in 1984. The PKK's original goal was to establish an independent Kurdish state in southeastern Turkey, but in recent years it has spoken more often about autonomy within a Turkish state that guarantees Kurdish cultural and linguistic rights.

Activities: In the early 1990s, the PKK moved beyond rural-based insurgent activities to include urban terrorism. In the 1990s, southeastern Anatolia was the scene of significant violence; some estimates placed casualties at some 30,000 persons. Following his capture in 1999, Ocalan announced a "peace initiative," ordering members to refrain from violence and requesting dialogue with Ankara on Kurdish issues. Ocalan's death sentence was commuted to life imprisonment; he remains the symbolic leader of the group. The group foreswore violence until June 2004, when the group's hard-line militant wing took control and renounced the self-imposed cease-fire of the previous five years. Striking over the border from bases within Iraq, the PKK has engaged in terrorist attacks in eastern and western Turkey. In 2009 the Turkish government and the PKK resumed peace negotiations. However, talks broke down after a PKK initiated attack on July 14, 2011, that left 13 Turkish soldiers dead. Violence in 2011 and 2012 has marked one of the most deadly time periods in the almost 30 year conflict. Widely publicized peace talks between Ocalan and the Turkish government to resolve the conflict began at the end of 2012.

Primary targets have been Turkish government security forces, local Turkish officials, and villagers who oppose the organization in Turkey. The PKK remained active in 2012: on August 20, a car bomb in the southeastern Turkish city of Gaziantep killed nine people, including four children, and wounded in excess of 70. Similar car bombings occurred in both Hakkari province in January, killing one and injuring 28, and Kayseri province in May, injuring 18.

Strength: Approximately 4,000 to 5,000 members; 3,000 to 3,500 are located in northern Iraq.

Location/Area of Operation: The PKK operate primarily in Turkey, Iraq, and Europe.

Funding and External Aid: The PKK receives financial support from the large Kurdish diaspora in Europe and from criminal activity.

LASHKAR E-TAYYIBA

aka al Mansooreen; Al Mansoorian; Army of the Pure; Army of the Pure and Righteous; Army of the Righteous; Lashkar e-Toiba; Lashkar-i-Taiba; Paasban-e-Ahle-Hadis; Paasban-e-Kashmir; Paasban-i-Ahle-Hadith; Pasban-e-Ahle-Hadith; Pasban-e-Kashmir; Jamaat-ud-Dawa, JUD; Jama'at al-Dawa; Jamaat ud-Daawa; Jamaat ul-Dawah; Jamaat-ul-Dawa; Jama'at-i-Dawat; Jamaiat-ud-Dawa; Jama'at-ud-Da'awah; Jama'at-ud-Da'awa; Jamaati-ud-Dawa; Idara Khidmat-e-Khalq; Falah-i-Insaniat Foundation; FiF; Falah-e-Insaniat Foundation; Falah-e-Insaniyat; Falah-i-Insaniyat; Falah Insania; Welfare of Humanity; Humanitarian Welfare Foundation; Human Welfare Foundation

Description: Designated as a Foreign Terrorist Organization (FTO) on December 26, 2001, Lashkar e-Tayyiba (LeT) is one of the largest and most proficient of the traditionally anti-India-focused militant groups. It has the ability to severely disrupt already delicate regional relations. LeT formed in the late 1980s as the militant wing of the Islamic extremist organization, Markaz Dawa ul-Irshad, a Pakistan-based Islamic fundamentalist mission organization and charity founded to oppose the Soviet presence in Afghanistan. Led by Hafiz Muhammad Saeed, LeT is not connected to any political party. Shortly after LeT was designated as an FTO, Saeed changed the name to Jamaat-ud-Dawa (JUD) and began humanitarian projects to avoid restrictions. LeT disseminates its message through JUD's media outlets. Elements of LeT and Jaish-e-Muhammad (JEM) combined with other groups to mount attacks as "The Save Kashmir Movement." The Pakistani government banned LeT in January 2002, and JUD in 2008, following the Mumbai attack. LeT and Saeed continue to spread terrorist ideology, as well as virulent rhetoric condemning the United States, India, Israel, and other perceived enemies.

Activities: LeT has conducted a number of operations against Indian troops and civilian targets in Jammu and Kashmir since 1993; several high profile attacks inside India; and operations against Coalition Forces in Afghanistan. The group uses assault rifles, machine guns, mortars, explosives, and rocket-propelled grenades.

Indian governmental officials hold LeT responsible for the July 2006 train attack in Mumbai and for multiple attacks in 2005 and 2006. LeT conducted the November 2008 attacks in Mumbai against luxury hotels, a Jewish center, a train station, and a popular café that killed approximately 170 people, including six American citizens, and injured more than 300. India has charged 38 people in the case, including the alleged attacker, Mohammad Ajmal Amir Kasab, who was captured at the scene and later executed for his involvement in the massacre. Most of those charged are at large and thought to be in Pakistan.

In March 2010, Pakistani-American businessman David Headley pleaded guilty in a U.S. court to crimes relating to his role in the November 2008 LeT attacks in Mumbai as well as to crimes relating to a separate plot to bomb the Danish newspaper *Jyllands-Posten*. In May 2011, Headley was a witness in the trial of Tahawwur Rana, who was charged with providing material support to LeT. Rana was convicted for providing material support to LeT in June 2011.

In 2011, LeT was responsible for multiple attacks, most of them in Jammu and Kashmir. The deadliest was a May 27 attack on a private residence in the city of Kupwara that killed two civilians. In a notable 2011 counterterrorism success, police in Indian-administered Kashmir shot and killed a senior LeT operative, Azhar Malik, after they surrounded a house where he was hiding in the town of Sopore.

In June 2012, Indian authorities arrested LeT member Sayeed Zabiuddin Ansari, alias Abu Jindal, one of the instigators of the November 2008 Mumbai attack. In October 2012, LeT claimed responsibility for an attack against an Indian army convoy outside a hotel in Kashmir, which killed one bellboy and injured two others.

Strength: The size of LeT is unknown, but it has several thousand members in Azad Kashmir and Punjab in India; Khyber-Pakhtunkhwa and Punjab Provinces in Pakistan; and in the southern Jammu, Kashmir, and Doda regions. Most LeT members are Pakistanis or Afghans and/or veterans of the Afghan wars.

Location/Area of Operation: LeT has global connections and a strong operational network throughout South Asia. LeT maintains a number of facilities, including training camps, schools, and medical clinics in Pakistan.

Funding and External Aid: LeT collects donations in Pakistan and the Gulf as well as from other donors in the Middle East and Europe, particularly the UK.

LASHKAR I JHANGVI

aka Army of Jhangvi; Lashkar e Jhangvi; Lashkar-i-Jhangvi

Description: Designated as a Foreign Terrorist Organization on January 30, 2003, Lashkar I Jhangvi (LJ) is the militant offshoot of the Sunni Deobandi sectarian group Sipah-i-Sahaba Pakistan. LJ focuses primarily on anti-Shia attacks and other attacks in Pakistan and Afghanistan, and was banned by Pakistan in August 2001, as part of an effort to rein in sectarian violence. Many of its members then sought refuge in Afghanistan with the Taliban, with whom they had existing ties. After the collapse of the Taliban as the ruling government in Afghanistan, LJ members became active in aiding other terrorists, providing safe houses, false identities, and protection in Pakistani cities, including Karachi, Peshawar, and Rawalpindi. LJ works closely with Tehrik-e Taliban Pakistan.

Activities: LJ specializes in armed attacks and bombings and has admitted responsibility for numerous killings of Shia religious and community leaders in Pakistan. In January 1999, the group attempted to assassinate former Prime Minister Nawaz Sharif and his brother Shabaz Sharif, Chief Minister of Punjab Province. Media reports linked LJ to attacks on Christian targets in Pakistan, including a March 2002 grenade assault on the Protestant International Church in Islamabad that killed two U.S. citizens.

LJ was active in 2011 and 2012. The most notable 2011 attack occurred in December, when an LJ suicide bomber detonated an improvised explosive device in a crowd of Shia mourners in Kabul, killing 48 civilians – including 12 children – and wounding 193. LJ attacks in 2012 ranged from suicide bombings to targeted shootings of ethnic Hazaras. In April, LJ members committed a series of shootings that killed 27 ethnic Hazaras over a two-week period. In June, a suicide bombing on a bus of pilgrims travelling from Iran to Pakistan left 14 dead, and 30 wounded. In September, LJ claimed responsibility for killing seven Shia in Hazarganji, and LJ members were arrested by Pakistani authorities when two explosions in Karachi killed seven, including two children, and wounded another 22. In October, the chief of the LJ Karachi branch, Mehmood Babar, was arrested by Pakistani authorities. Pakistani authorities claimed the arrest of the cell leader and his co-conspirators disrupted operational planning of VBIED attacks on a school and prison.

Strength: Assessed in the low hundreds.

Location/Area of Operation: LJ is active primarily in Punjab, the Federally Administered Tribal Areas, Karachi, and Baluchistan.

Funding and External Aid: Funding comes from wealthy donors in Pakistan, as well as the Middle East, particularly Saudi Arabia. The group engages in criminal activity to fund its activities, including extortion and protection money.

LIBERATION TIGERS OF TAMIL EELAM

aka Ellalan Force; Tamil Tigers

Description: Founded in 1976 and designated as a Foreign Terrorist Organization on October 8, 1997, the Liberation Tigers of Tamil Eelam (LTTE) became a powerful Tamil secessionist group in Sri Lanka. Despite its military defeat at the hands of the Sri Lankan government in 2009, the LTTE's international network of sympathizers and financial support persists.

Activities: Though the LTTE has been largely inactive since its military defeat in Sri Lanka in 2009, in the past the LTTE was responsible for an integrated battlefield insurgent strategy that targeted key installations and senior Sri Lankan political and military leaders. It conducted a sustained campaign targeting rival Tamil groups, and assassinated Prime Minister Rajiv Gandhi of India in 1991 and President Ranasinghe Premadasa of Sri Lanka in 1993. Though most notorious for its cadre of suicide bombers, the Black Tigers, LTT also had an amphibious force, the Sea Tigers, and a nascent air wing, the Air Tigers. Fighting between the LTTE and the Sri Lanka government escalated in 2006 and continued through 2008.

In early 2009, Sri Lankan forces recaptured the LTTE's key strongholds, including their capital of Kilinochchi. In May 2009, government forces defeated the last LTTE fighting forces, killed LTTE leader Prahbakaran and other members of the LTTE leadership and military command, and declared military victory over LTTE. There have been no known attacks in Sri Lanka that could verifiably be attributed to the LTTE since the end of the war. LTTE's financial network of support continued to operate throughout 2012, and there were multiple reports of increased LTTE involvement in human smuggling out of refugee camps.

Strength: Exact strength is unknown.

Location/Area of Operation: Sri Lanka and India

Funding and External Aid: The LTTE used its international contacts and the large Tamil diaspora in North America, Europe, and Asia to procure weapons, communications, funding, and other needed supplies. The group employed charities as fronts to collect and divert funds for their activities.

LIBYAN ISLAMIC FIGHTING GROUP

aka LIFG

Description: The Libyan Islamic Fighting Group (LIFG) was designated as a Foreign Terrorist Organization on December 17, 2004. In the early 1990s, LIFG emerged from the group of Libyans who had fought Soviet forces in Afghanistan and pledged to overthrow Libyan leader Muammar al-Qadhafi. In the years following, some members maintained an anti-Qadhafi focus and targeted Libyan government interests. Others, such as Abu al-Faraj al-Libi, who was arrested in Pakistan in 2005, aligned with Usama bin Laden and are believed to be part of the al-Qa'ida (AQ) leadership structure. On November 3, 2007, AQ leader Ayman al-Zawahiri announced a formal merger between AQ and LIFG. However, on July 3, 2009, LIFG members in the UK released a statement formally disavowing any association with AQ. In September 2009, six imprisoned LIFG members issued a 417 page document that renounced violence. More than 100 LIFG members pledged to adhere to this revised doctrine and have been pardoned and released from prison in Libya since September 2009.

Activities: LIFG has been largely inactive operationally in Libya since the late 1990s when members fled predominately to Europe and the Middle East because of tightened Libyan security measures. In early 2011, in the wake of the Libyan revolution and the fall of Qadhafi, LIFG members created the LIFG successor group, the Libyan Islamic Movement for Change (LIMC), and became one of many rebel groups united under the umbrella of the opposition leadership known as the Transitional National Council. Former LIFG emir and LIMC leader Abdel Hakim Bil-Hajj was appointed the Libyan Transitional Council's Tripoli military commander during the Libyan uprisings, and has denied any link between his group and AQ. There were no known attacks carried out by LIFG in 2012.

Strength: Unknown

Location/Area of Operation: Since the late 1990s, many members have fled to southwest Asia, and European countries, particularly the UK.

Funding and External Aid: Unknown

MOROCCAN ISLAMIC COMBATANT GROUP

aka Groupe Islamique Combattant Marocain; GICM

Description: Designated as a Foreign Terrorist Organization on October 11, 2005, the Moroccan Islamic Combatant Group (GICM) is a transnational terrorist group centered in the Moroccan diaspora communities of Western Europe. Its goals include establishing an Islamic state in

Morocco. The group emerged in the 1990s and was composed of Moroccan recruits who trained in armed camps in Afghanistan, including some who fought in the Soviet war in Afghanistan. Former GICM members interact with other North African extremists, particularly in Europe.

Activities: GICM members were believed to be among those responsible for the 2004 Madrid train bombings, which killed 191 people. GICM members were also implicated in the recruitment network for Iraq, and at least one GICM member carried out a suicide attack against Coalition Forces in Iraq. According to open source reports, GICM individuals are believed to have participated in the 2003 Casablanca attacks. However, the group has largely been inactive since these attacks, and has not claimed responsibility for or had attacks attributed to them since the Madrid train bombings in 2004.

Strength: Much of GICM's leadership in Morocco and Europe has been killed, imprisoned, or is awaiting trial. In 2003, alleged leader Mohamed al-Guerbouzi was convicted in absentia by the Moroccan government for his role in the Casablanca attacks but remains free in exile in London.

Location/Area of Operation: Morocco, Western Europe, and Afghanistan.

Funding and External Aid: In the past, GICM has been involved in narcotics trafficking in North Africa and Europe to fund its operations.

NATIONAL LIBERATION ARMY

aka ELN; Ejercito de Liberacion Nacional

Description: The National Liberation Army (ELN) was designated as a Foreign Terrorist Organization on October 8, 1997. The ELN is a Colombian Marxist-Leninist group formed in 1964. It is primarily rural-based, though it also has several urban units. The ELN remains focused on attacking economic infrastructure, in particular oil and gas pipelines and electricity pylons, and extorting foreign and local companies.

Activities: The ELN engages in kidnappings, hijackings, bombings, drug trafficking, and extortion activities. The group also uses intimidation of judges, prosecutors and witnesses and has been involved in the murder of teachers and trade unionists. Historically, the ELN has been one of the most prolific users of anti-personnel mines in Colombia. In recent years, the ELN has launched joint attacks with the Revolutionary Armed Forces of Colombia (FARC), Colombia's largest terrorist organization.

In September 2012, an Ecuadorian hostage escaped from the ELN after two years of captivity. He reported that ELN guerrillas assassinated his father on January 31, after he paid the ransom the group had requested for the release of his son. In November, an ELN bomb killed one person and injured three in El Tarra, Catatumbo, near the Venezuelan border. ELN attacks on Colombia's oil and gas industry continued in 2012, resulting in major economic damage, and numerous deaths and kidnappings. After demanding a nearly $300,000 ransom, the ELN released two kidnapped oil workers after 12 days of captivity in Arauca Department in December. The ELN released another two oil workers within 48 hours.

Strength: Approximately 2,000 armed combatants and an unknown number of active supporters.

Location/Area of Operation: Mostly in the rural and mountainous areas of northern, northeastern, and southwestern Colombia, as well as the border regions with Venezuela.

Funding and External Aid: The ELN draws its funding from the narcotics trade and from extortion of oil and gas companies. Additional funds are derived from kidnapping ransoms. There is no known external aid.

PALESTINE ISLAMIC JIHAD - SHAQAQI FACTION

aka PIJ; Palestine Islamic Jihad; PIJ-Shaqaqi Faction; PIJ-Shallah Faction; Islamic Jihad of Palestine; Islamic Jihad in Palestine; Abu Ghunaym Squad of the Hizballah Bayt al-Maqdis; Al-Quds Squads; Al-Quds Brigades; Saraya al-Quds; Al-Awdah Brigades

Description: Palestine Islamic Jihad (PIJ) was designated as a Foreign Terrorist Organization on October 8, 1997. Formed by militant Palestinians in Gaza during the 1970s, PIJ is committed to both the destruction of Israel through attacks against Israeli military and civilian targets and the creation of an Islamic state in all of historic Palestine, including present day Israel.

Activities: PIJ terrorists have conducted numerous attacks, including large-scale suicide bombings against Israeli civilian and military targets. PIJ continued to plan and direct attacks against Israelis both inside Israel and in the West Bank and Gaza. Though U.S. citizens have died in PIJ attacks, the group has not directly targeted U.S. interests. PIJ attacks between 2008 and 2011 were primarily rocket attacks aimed at southern Israeli cities, and have also included attacking Israeli targets with explosive devices. 2012 saw no deviation from PIJ terrorist tactics. The group is thought to be behind a large number of the record setting 2,300 plus rockets launched from Gaza towards Israel. Additionally, on November 21, 2012, PIJ operatives, working with HAMAS, detonated a bomb on a bus in Tel Aviv, leaving 29 civilians wounded.

Strength: PIJ has fewer than 1,000 members.

Location/Area of Operation: Primarily Gaza with minimal operational presence in the West Bank and Israel. The group's senior leadership resides in Syria. Other leadership elements reside in Lebanon and official representatives are scattered throughout the Middle East.

Funding and External Aid: Receives financial assistance and training primarily from Iran.

PALESTINE LIBERATION FRONT - ABU ABBAS FACTION

aka PLF; PLF-Abu Abbas; Palestine Liberation Front

Description: The Palestinian Liberation Front – Abu Abbas Faction (PLF) was designated as a Foreign Terrorist Organization on October 8, 1997. In the late 1970s, the Palestine Liberation Front (PLF) splintered from the Popular Front for the Liberation of Palestine-General Command (PFLP-GC), and then later split into pro-PLO, pro-Syrian, and pro-Libyan factions. The pro-PLO faction was led by Muhammad Zaydan (a.k.a. Abu Abbas) and was based in Baghdad prior to Operation Iraqi Freedom.

Activities: Abbas's group was responsible for the 1985 attack on the Italian cruise ship *Achille Lauro* and the murder of U.S. citizen Leon Klinghoffer. The PLF was suspected of supporting terrorism against Israel by other Palestinian groups into the 1990s. In April 2004, Abu Abbas died of natural causes while in U.S. custody in Iraq. The PLF took part in the 2006 Palestinian parliamentarian elections but did not win a seat. In 2008, as part of a prisoner exchange between Israel and Hizballah, Samir Kantar, a PLF member, and purportedly the longest serving Arab prisoner in Israeli custody, was released from an Israeli prison.

After going approximately 16 years without claiming responsibility for an attack, PLF claimed responsibility for two attacks against Israeli targets on March 14, 2008. One attack was against an Israeli military bus in Huwarah, Israel, and the other involved a PLF "brigade" firing at an Israeli settler south of the Hebron Mountain, seriously wounding him. On March 28, 2008, shortly after the attacks, a PLF Central Committee member reaffirmed PLF's commitment to using "all possible means to restore" its previous glory and to adhering to its role in the Palestinian "struggle" and "resistance," through its military. There were no known PLF attacks in 2012.

Strength: Estimates have placed membership between 50 and 500.

Location/Area of Operation: PLF leadership and membership are based in Lebanon and the West Bank and Gaza.

Funding and External Aid: Unknown

POPULAR FRONT FOR THE LIBERATION OF PALESTINE

aka PFLP; Halhul Gang; Halhul Squad; Palestinian Popular Resistance Forces; PPRF; Red Eagle Gang; Red Eagle Group; Red Eagles; Martyr Abu-Ali Mustafa Battalion

Description: Designated as a Foreign Terrorist Organization on October 8, 1997, the Popular Front for the Liberation of Palestine (PFLP), a Marxist-Leninist group founded by George Habash, broke away from the Arab Nationalist Movement in 1967. The group earned a reputation for spectacular international attacks in the 1960s and 1970s, including airline hijackings that killed at least 20 U.S. citizens. A leading faction within the PLO, the PFLP has long accepted the concept of a two-state solution but has opposed specific provisions of various peace initiatives.

Activities: The PFLP stepped up its operational activity during the Second Intifada. This was highlighted by at least two suicide bombings since 2003, multiple joint operations with other Palestinian terrorist groups, and the assassination of Israeli Tourism Minister Rehavam Ze'evi in 2001, to avenge Israel's killing of the PFLP Secretary General earlier that year. The PFLP was involved in several rocket attacks, launched primarily from Gaza, against Israel in 2008 and 2009, and claimed responsibility for numerous attacks on Israeli Defense Forces (IDF) in Gaza, including a December 2009 ambush of Israeli soldiers in central Gaza. The PLFP claimed numerous mortar and rocket attacks fired from Gaza into Israel in 2010, as well as an attack on a group of Israeli citizens. In 2011, the group continued to use rockets and mortars to target communities in Israel, including rocket attacks in August and October in Eshkolot and Ashqelon, respectively, which caused no injuries or damage. In October 2011, the PFLP claimed responsibility for a rocket attack that killed one civilian in Ashqelon.

In August 2012, the Israeli Shin Bet security agency arrested a cell of PFLP militants on suspicion of engaging in terrorist activities. The group of militants, three of whom were previously imprisoned, was accused of plotting to carry out shooting attacks on IDF checkpoints in the West Bank, and planning to kidnap an Israeli IDF soldier. In December, Israeli authorities arrested 10 more members of the PFLP and charged them with attempted kidnapping. The suspects were allegedly planning to kidnap an Israeli soldier to use as leverage in a prisoner swap for PFLP head Ahmad Sadaat, who is incarcerated by the Israelis for his role in a number of terrorist attacks.

Strength: Unknown

Location/Area of Operation: Syria, Lebanon, Israel, the West Bank, and Gaza.

Funding and External Aid: Leadership received safe haven in Syria.

POPULAR FRONT FOR THE LIBERATION OF PALESTINE-GENERAL COMMAND

aka PFLP-GC

Description: The Popular Front for the Liberation of Palestine-General Command (PFLP-GC) was designated as a Foreign Terrorist Organization on October 8, 1997. The PFLP-GC split from the PFLP in 1968, claiming it wanted to focus more on resistance and less on politics. Originally, the group was violently opposed to the Arafat-led Palestinian Liberation Organization. Ahmad Jibril, a former captain in the Syrian Army, has led the PFLP-GC since its founding. The PFLP-GC is closely tied to both Syria and Iran.

Activities: The PFLP-GC carried out dozens of attacks in Europe and the Middle East during the 1970s and 1980s. The organization was known for cross-border terrorist attacks into Israel using unusual means, such as hot-air balloons and motorized hang gliders. The group's primary recent focus was supporting Hizballah's attacks against Israel, training members of other Palestinian terrorist groups, and smuggling weapons. The PFLP-GC maintained an armed presence in several Palestinian refugee camps and at its own military bases in Lebanon and along the Lebanon-Syria border. In recent years, the PFLP-GC was implicated by Lebanese security officials in several rocket attacks against Israel. In May 2008, the PFLP-GC claimed responsibility for a rocket attack on a shopping center in Ashqelon that wounded at least 10 people. In 2009, the group was responsible for wounding two civilians in an armed attack in Nahariyya, Northern District, Israel. In 2011, the PFLP-GC targeted Israeli communities in a March 20 rocket attack by its Jihad Jibril Brigades in the city of Eshkolot, Southern District, Israel. The attack caused no injuries or damage.

In November 2012, PFLP-GC claimed responsibility for a bus bombing in Tel Aviv that injured 29 people, although four Palestine Islamic Jihad and Hamas operatives were later arrested for being behind the attack.

Strength: Several hundred.

Location/Area of Operation: Political leadership was headquartered in Damascus, with bases in southern Lebanon and a presence in the Palestinian refugee camps in Lebanon and Syria. The group also maintained a small presence in Gaza.

Funding and External Aid: Received safe haven and logistical and military support from Syria and financial support from Iran.

AL-QA'IDA

aka al-Qa'eda; Qa'idat al-Jihad (The Base for Jihad); formerly Qa'idat Ansar Allah (The Base of the Supporters of God); the Islamic Army; Islamic Salvation Foundation; The Base; The Group for the Preservation of the Holy Sites; The Islamic Army for the Liberation of the Holy Places; the World Islamic Front for Jihad Against Jews and Crusaders; the Usama Bin Laden Network; the Usama Bin Laden Organization; al-Jihad; the Jihad Group; Egyptian al-Jihad; Egyptian Islamic Jihad; New Jihad

Description: Designated as a Foreign Terrorist Organization on October 8, 1999, al-Qa'ida (AQ) was established by Usama bin Laden in 1988. The group helped finance, recruit, transport, and train Sunni Islamist extremists for the Afghan resistance. AQ's strategic objectives are to remove Western influence and presence from the Muslim world, topple "apostate" governments of Muslim countries, and establish a pan-Islamic caliphate governed by its own interpretation of Sharia law that ultimately would be at the center of a new international order. These goals remain essentially unchanged since the group's 1996 public declaration of war against the United States. AQ leaders issued a statement in February 1998 under the banner of "The World Islamic Front for Jihad against the Jews and Crusaders," saying it was the duty of all Muslims to kill U.S. citizens, civilian and military, and their allies everywhere. AQ merged with al-Jihad (Egyptian Islamic Jihad) in June 2001. Many AQ leaders have been killed in recent years, including bin Laden and then second-in-command Atiyah Abd al-Rahman, in May and August 2011, respectively. Al-Rahman's replacement, Abu Yahya al-Libi, was killed in June 2012. Leader Ayman al-Zawahiri remained at large.

Activities: AQ and its supporters conducted three bombings that targeted U.S. troops in Aden in December 1992, and claim to have shot down U.S. helicopters and killed U.S. servicemen in Somalia in 1993. AQ also carried out the August 1998 bombings of the U.S. Embassies in Nairobi and Dar es Salaam, killing up to 300 individuals and injuring more than 5,000. In October 2000, AQ conducted a suicide attack on the USS Cole in the port of Aden, Yemen, with an explosive-laden boat, killing 17 U.S. Navy sailors and injuring 39.

On September 11, 2001, 19 AQ members hijacked and crashed four U.S. commercial jets – two into the World Trade Center in New York City, one into the Pentagon near Washington, DC; and the last into a field in Shanksville, Pennsylvania – leaving over 3,000 individuals dead or missing.

In November 2002, AQ carried out a suicide bombing of a hotel in Mombasa, Kenya that killed 15. In 2003 and 2004, Saudi-based AQ operatives and associated violent extremists launched more than a dozen attacks, killing at least 90 people, including 14 Americans in Saudi Arabia.

Al-Zawahiri claimed responsibility on behalf of AQ for the July 7, 2005 attacks against the London public transportation system. AQ likely played a role in the unsuccessful 2006 plot to destroy several commercial aircraft flying from the UK to the United States using liquid explosives. AQ claimed responsibility for a 2008 suicide car bomb attack on the Danish embassy in Pakistan that killed six, as retaliation for a Danish newspaper re-publishing cartoons depicting the Prophet Muhammad and for Denmark's involvement in Afghanistan.

In January 2009, Bryant Neal Vinas – a U.S. citizen who traveled to Pakistan and allegedly trained in explosives at AQ camps, was captured in Pakistan and extradited to the United States – was charged with providing material support to a terrorist organization and conspiracy to commit murder. Vinas later admitted his role in helping AQ plan an attack against the Long Island Rail Road in New York and confessed to having fired missiles at a U.S. base in Afghanistan. In September 2009, Najibullah Zazi, an Afghan immigrant and U.S. lawful permanent resident, was charged with conspiracy to use weapons of mass destruction, to commit murder in a foreign country, and with providing material support to a terrorist organization as part of an AQ plot to attack the New York subway system. Zazi later admitted to contacts with AQ senior leadership, suggesting they had knowledge of his plans. In February 2010, Zazi pled guilty to charges in the U.S. District Court for the Eastern District of New York.

In a December 2011 video, new AQ leader al-Zawahiri claimed AQ was behind the August kidnapping of American aid worker Warren Weinstein in Pakistan. As conditions for his release, al-Zawahiri demanded the end of U.S. air strikes and the release of all terrorist suspects in U.S. custody. Weinstein remained in AQ custody throughout 2012.

Strength: In South Asia, AQ's core has been seriously degraded. The death or arrest of dozens of mid- and senior-level AQ operatives – including bin Laden in May 2011 – have disrupted communication, financial, facilitation nodes, and a number of terrorist plots. AQ serves as a focal point of "inspiration" for a worldwide network of affiliated groups – al-Qa'ida in the Arabian Peninsula (AQAP), al-Qa'ida in Iraq (AQI), al-Qa'ida in the Islamic Maghreb (AQIM), al-Shabaab – and other Sunni Islamic extremist groups, including the Islamic Movement of Uzbekistan, the Islamic Jihad Union, Lashkar i Jhangvi, Harakat ul-Mujahadin, and Jemaah Islamiya. Tehrik-e Taliban Pakistan and the Haqqani Network also have ties to AQ. Additionally, supporters and associates worldwide who are "inspired" by the group's ideology may be operating without direction from AQ central leadership, and it is impossible to estimate their numbers.

Location/Area of Operation: AQ was based in Afghanistan until Coalition Forces removed the Taliban from power in late 2001. Since then, they have resided in Pakistan's Federally Administered Tribal Areas. AQ's regional affiliates – AQI, AQAP, AQIM, and al-Shabaab – work in Iraq and Syria, Yemen, the Trans-Sahara, and Somalia, respectively.

Funding and External Aid: AQ primarily depends on donations from like-minded supporters as well as from individuals who believe that their money is supporting a humanitarian cause. Some funds are diverted from Islamic charitable organizations.

AL-QA'IDA IN THE ARABIAN PENINSULA

aka al-Qa'ida in the South Arabian Peninsula; al-Qa'ida in Yemen; al-Qa'ida of Jihad Organization in the Arabian Peninsula; al-Qa'ida Organization in the Arabian Peninsula; Tanzim Qa'idat al-Jihad fi Jazirat al-Arab; AQAP; AQY; Ansar al-Shari'a

Description: Al-Qa'ida in the Arabian Peninsula (AQAP) was designated as a Foreign Terrorist Organization (FTO) on January 19, 2010. In January 2009, the leader of al-Qa'ida in Yemen (AQY), Nasir al-Wahishi, publicly announced that Yemeni and Saudi al-Qa'ida (AQ) operatives were working together under the banner of AQAP. This announcement signaled the rebirth of an AQ franchise that previously carried out attacks in Saudi Arabia. AQAP's self-stated goals include establishing a caliphate in the Arabian Peninsula and the wider Middle East, as well as implementing Sharia law.

On September 30, 2011, AQAP cleric and head of external operations Anwar al-Aulaqi, as well as Samir Khan, the publisher of AQAP's online magazine, *Inspire,* were killed in Yemen.

Activities: AQAP has claimed responsibility for numerous terrorist acts against both internal and foreign targets since its inception in January 2009. Attempted attacks against foreign targets include a March 2009 suicide bombing against South Korean tourists in Yemen, the August 2009 attempt to assassinate Saudi Prince Muhammad bin Nayif, and the December 25, 2009 attempted attack on Northwest Airlines Flight 253 from Amsterdam to Detroit, Michigan. AQAP was responsible for an unsuccessful attempt to assassinate the British Ambassador in April 2010, and a failed attempt to target a British embassy vehicle with a rocket in October of that year. Also in October 2010, AQAP claimed responsibility for a foiled plot to send explosive-laden packages to the United States via cargo plane. The parcels were intercepted in the UK and in the United Arab Emirates.

In 2012, the Yemeni government carried out a two-month offensive to uproot AQAP from portions of Abyan Governorate, and Yemeni forces eventually regained control over the towns of Zinjibar and Jaar. However, approximately 3,000 land mines, planted by AQAP militants before they fled, killed 72 residents in the aftermath of AQAP's departure. Other AQAP attacks in 2012 targeted the Yemeni military, including a February 2012 suicide car bombing that killed 26 Yemeni soldiers in Hadramawt Governorate.

The FTO designation for AQAP was amended on October 4, 2012, to include the alias Ansar al-Shari'a (AAS). AAS represents a rebranding effort designed to attract potential followers in areas under AQAP's control. AQAP, operating under the alias AAS, carried out a May 2012 suicide bombing in Sanaa that killed 96 people. AQAP/AAS claimed responsibility for the attack, which targeted Yemeni soldiers rehearsing for a parade to celebrate Yemen's National Day, and said the bombing was intended to target the Yemeni military brass. Also in May, press reported that AQAP allegedly plotted to detonate a bomb aboard a U.S.-bound airliner using an improvised explosive device. Though there was no imminent threat to U.S. jetliners, the device, which was acquired from another government, was similar to devices that AQAP had previously used in attempted terrorist attacks.

Strength: Although it is difficult to assess the number of AQAP's members, the group is estimated to have close to one thousand members.

Location/Area of Operation: Yemen

Funding and External Aid: AQAP's funding primarily comes from robberies and kidnap for ransom operations and to a lesser degree from donations from like-minded supporters.

AL-QA'IDA IN IRAQ

aka al-Qa'ida Group of Jihad in Iraq; al-Qa'ida Group of Jihad in the Land of the Two Rivers; al-Qa'ida in Mesopotamia; al-Qa'ida in the Land of the Two Rivers; al-Qa'ida of Jihad in Iraq; al-Qa'ida of Jihad Organization in the Land of The Two Rivers; al-Qa'ida of the Jihad in the Land of the Two Rivers; al-Tawhid; Jam'at al-Tawhid Wa'al-Jihad; Tanzeem Qa'idat al Jihad/Bilad al Raafidaini; Tanzim Qa'idat al-Jihad fi Bilad al-Rafidayn; The Monotheism and Jihad Group; The Organization Base of Jihad/Country of the Two Rivers; The Organization Base of Jihad/Mesopotamia; The Organization of al-Jihad's Base in Iraq; The Organization of al-Jihad's Base in the Land of the Two Rivers; The Organization of al-Jihad's Base of Operations in Iraq; The Organization of al-Jihad's Base of Operations in the Land of the Two Rivers; The Organization of Jihad's Base in the Country of the Two Rivers; al-Zarqawi Network; Islamic State of Iraq; al-Nusrah Front; Jabhat al-Nusrah; Jabhet al-Nusrah; The Victory Front; al-Nusrah Front for the People of the Levant

Description: Al-Qa'ida in Iraq (AQI) was designated as a Foreign Terrorist Organization on December 17, 2004. In the 1990s, Abu Mus'ab al-Zarqawi, a Jordanian-born militant, organized a terrorist group called al-Tawhid wal-Jihad to oppose the presence of U.S. and Western military forces in the Islamic world and the West's support for and the existence of Israel. In late 2004, he joined al-Qa'ida (AQ) and pledged allegiance to Usama bin Laden. After this, al-Tawhid wal-Jihad became known as AQI. Zarqawi traveled to Iraq during Operation Iraqi Freedom and led his group against U.S. and Coalition Forces until his death in June 2006. In October 2006, AQI publicly re-named itself the Islamic State of Iraq and has since used that name in its public statements. In 2012, AQI was led by Ibrahim Awwad Ibrahim Ali al-Badri, aka Abu Du'a, who was designated by the Department of State under Executive Order 13224 on October 4.

Since late 2011, AQI has also participated in the Syrian conflict through its alias, al-Nusrah Front, which has sought to portray itself as part of the legitimate Syrian opposition. A number of al-Nusrah Front's leaders have been members of AQI and its facilitation network that operated in Syria and Iraq from 2004-2011. [In mid-April 2013, al-Nusrah leader Muhammad al-Jawlani publicly pledged al-Nusrah's fealty to AQ and its leader, Ayman al-Zawahiri.] Al-Nusrah works with other U.S. designated terrorist organizations, such as Lebanon based Fatah al-Islam. Al-Nusrah Front's base of operations is probably Damascus, but the group mirrors the organizational structure of AQI in Iraq, with regional military, administrative, and local media efforts. On December 11, the Department of State amended AQI's designation to include al-Nusrah Front as an alias.

Activities: Since its founding, AQI has conducted high profile attacks, including improvised explosive device (IED) attacks against U.S. military personnel and Iraqi infrastructure; videotaped beheadings of Americans Nicholas Berg (May 11, 2004), Jack Armstrong (September 22, 2004), and Jack Hensley (September 21, 2004); suicide bomber attacks against both military and civilian targets; and rocket attacks. AQI perpetrates the majority of suicide and mass casualty bombings in Iraq using foreign and Iraqi operatives.

Since November 2011, al-Nusrah Front has claimed nearly 600 attacks, ranging from more than 40 suicide attacks to small arms and IED operations in major city centers including Damascus, Aleppo, Hamah, Dara, Homs, Idlib, and Dayr al-Zawr. For example, on September 28, 2012, al-Nusrah Front claimed responsibility for two suicide car bombs at a military complex in Damascus that killed four and wounded 14, including civilians. On October 3, 2012, the group claimed responsibility for four bombings in Aleppo, including two suicide attacks that killed more than 50 people. Al-Nusrah Front followed up those attacks with an October 9 suicide bomb attack on a Syrian Air Force Intelligence compound in a Damascus suburb that killed and wounded at least 100, including civilians.

AQI was also active in Iraq in 2012. In a series of coordinated attacks in March, AQI struck Shia pilgrims in the city of Karbala, set cars on fire near a police headquarters in Kirkuk, and targeted security forces and government officials in Baghdad. In all, AQI struck eight cities in just under six hours, killing 46 people and wounding 200. July was the bloodiest month of AQI attacks in two years, with 325 people killed over the span of multiple bombings and attacks. In August, the Islamic State of Iraq, AQI's political front, released a video detailing a sophisticated attack in March on five locations in Haditha and neighboring Barwana that included dozens of fighters dressed as police commandos. During the raid, AQI fighters killed 27 Iraqi policemen, including two police commanders. In November, at least 166 Iraqi civilians, police, and soldiers were killed in violence across the country, according to the Government of Iraq.

Strength: In Iraq, membership is estimated between 1,000 and 2,000, making it the largest Sunni extremist group in Iraq. Membership in Syria is unknown, though it is likely a small force within the larger Syrian armed opposition.

Location/Area of Operation: AQI's operations are predominately Iraq-based, but it has perpetrated attacks in Jordan. In Syria, al-Nusrah Front has claimed attacks in several major city centers. The group maintains a logistical network throughout the Middle East, North Africa, Iran, South Asia, and Europe.

Funding and External Aid: AQI receives most of its funding from a variety of businesses and criminal activities within Iraq.

AL-QA'IDA IN THE ISLAMIC MAGHREB

aka AQIM; Group for Call and Combat; GSPC; Le Groupe Salafiste Pour La Predication Et Le Combat; Salafist Group for Preaching and Combat

Description: The Salafist Group for Call and Combat (GSPC) was designated as a Foreign Terrorist Organization on March 27, 2002. After the GSPC officially joined with al-Qa'ida (AQ) in September 2006 and became known as al-Qa'ida in the Islamic Maghreb (AQIM), the Department of State amended the GSPC designation on February 20, 2008, to reflect the change. AQIM remains largely a regionally-focused terrorist group. It has adopted a more anti-Western rhetoric and ideology and has aspirations of overthrowing "apostate" African regimes and creating an Islamic Caliphate. Abdelmalek Droukdel, aka Abu Mus'ab Abd al-Wadoud, is the group's leader.

Activities: Since 2007, when AQIM bombed the UN headquarters building in Algiers and an Algerian government building outside of Algiers killing 60 people, AQIM had been relatively quiet and focused on its kidnapping for ransom efforts. In 2011 and 2012, however, AQIM took advantage of the deteriorating security situation in northern Africa to plan and conduct operations. In 2011, AQIM targeted Mauritanian President Muhammad Abdel Aziz and detonated a vehicle-borne improvised explosive device (VBIED) in Nouakchott, injuring nine soldiers, and also claimed responsibility for multiple suicide bomb attacks against Algerian military and police targets, which killed at least 20 people and wounded almost 50 others. In January 2012, Algerian authorities disrupted an AQIM plot targeting U.S. or European ships in the Mediterranean Sea. Some militants with ties to AQIM were involved in the September 11 attack on U.S. facilities in Benghazi that killed J. Christopher Stevens, the U.S. Ambassador to Libya, and three staff members.

In addition to conducting attacks, AQIM also conducted kidnap for ransom operations. The targets are usually Western citizens from governments or third parties that have established a pattern of making concessions in the form of ransom payments for the release of individuals in custody. In September 2010, AQIM claimed responsibility for the kidnapping of seven people working at a uranium mine in Niger. AQIM released three of the hostages in February 2011, but at the end of 2012, four French citizens remained in captivity.

AQIM continued its kidnapping operations in 2012. In May, AQIM killed a German hostage in Nigeria during a military raid. AQIM was also believed to be behind the December kidnapping of a French engineer in northern Nigeria, an operation that resulted in the death of two Nigerians.

Strength: AQIM has under a thousand fighters operating in Algeria with a smaller number in the Sahel. It is attempting to take advantage of the volatile political situation in the Sahel, especially in Mali, to expand its membership, resources, and operations.

Location/Area of Operation: Northeastern Algeria (including but not limited to the Kabylie region) and northern Mali, Niger, and Mauritania.

Funding and External Aid: AQIM members engaged in kidnapping for ransom and criminal activities to finance their operations. Algerian expatriates and AQIM supporters abroad – many residing in Western Europe – may also provide limited financial and logistical support.

REAL IRA

aka RIRA; Real Irish Republican Army; 32 County Sovereignty Committee; 32 County Sovereignty Movement; Irish Republican Prisoners Welfare Association; Real Oglaigh Na hEireann

Description: Designated as a Foreign Terrorist Organization on May 16, 2001, the Real IRA (RIRA) was formed in 1997 as the clandestine armed wing of the 32 County Sovereignty Movement, a "political pressure group" dedicated to removing British forces from Northern Ireland and unifying Ireland. The RIRA has historically sought to disrupt the Northern Ireland peace process and did not participate in the September 2005 weapons decommissioning. In September 1997, the 32 County Sovereignty Movement opposed Sinn Fein's adoption of the Mitchell principles of democracy and non-violence. Despite internal rifts and calls by some jailed members, including the group's founder Michael "Mickey" McKevitt, for a cease-fire and disbandment, the RIRA has pledged additional violence and continued to conduct attacks.

Activities: Many RIRA members are former Provisional Irish Republican Army members who left the organization after that group renewed its cease-fire in 1997. These members brought a wealth of experience in terrorist tactics and bomb making to the RIRA. Targets have included civilians (most notoriously in the Omagh bombing in August 1998), British security forces, and police in Northern Ireland. The Independent Monitoring Commission, which was established to oversee the peace process, assessed that RIRA members were likely responsible for the majority of the shootings and assaults that occurred in Northern Ireland.

The group remained active in 2012. In April, RIRA was accused of planting a bomb near the Newry Canal in south Armagh, Northern Ireland, with the intent of killing a passing police patrol. The bomb weighed approximately 600 lbs.

Strength: According to the Irish government, the RIRA has approximately 100 active members. The organization may receive limited support from IRA hardliners and Republican sympathizers who are dissatisfied with the IRA's continuing cease-fire and with Sinn Fein's involvement in the peace process.

Location/Area of Operation: Northern Ireland, Great Britain, and the Irish Republic.

Funding and External Aid: The RIRA is suspected of receiving funds from sympathizers in the United States and of attempting to buy weapons from U.S. gun dealers. The RIRA was also reported to have purchased sophisticated weapons from the Balkans and to have occasionally collaborated with the Continuity Irish Republican Army.

REVOLUTIONARY ARMED FORCES OF COLOMBIA

aka FARC; Fuerzas Armadas Revolucionarias de Colombia

Description: Designated as a Foreign Terrorist Organization on October 8, 1997, the Revolutionary Armed Forces of Colombia (FARC) is Latin America's oldest, largest, most violent, and best-equipped terrorist organization. The FARC began in the early 1960s as an outgrowth of the Liberal Party-based peasant self-defense leagues, but took on Marxist ideology. Today, it only nominally fights in support of Marxist goals, and is heavily involved in narcotics production and trafficking. The FARC has been responsible for large numbers of kidnappings for ransom in Colombia, and in past years has allegedly held as many as 700 hostages. The FARC's capacity has been degraded by a continuing Colombian military offensive targeting key FARC units and leaders that has, by most estimates, halved the FARC's numbers – estimated at approximately 8,000 – and succeeded in capturing or killing a number of FARC senior and mid-level commanders.

Activities: The FARC has carried out bombings, murders, mortar attacks, sniper attacks, kidnapping, extortion, and hijacking, as well as guerrilla and conventional military acts against Colombian political, military, civilian, and economic targets. The FARC has used landmines extensively. The FARC has well-documented ties to the full range of narcotics trafficking activities, including extortion, cultivation, and distribution.

Over the years, the FARC has perpetrated a large number of high profile terrorist acts, including the 1999 murder of three U.S. missionaries working in Colombia, and multiple kidnappings and assassinations of Colombian government officials and civilians. In July 2008, the Colombian military made a dramatic rescue of 15 high-value FARC hostages including U.S. Department of Defense contractors Marc Gonsalves, Keith Stansell, and Thomas Howe, who were held in captivity for more than five years, along with former Colombian presidential candidate Ingrid Betancourt.

FARC attacks in 2012 increased by more than 50 percent over 2011. The implementation of a new counterinsurgency plan in June and the September peace talks between the Colombian government and the FARC, however, contributed to a drop in attacks in the last six months of the year. In January, around 100 FARC guerrillas destroyed a radar installation used to monitor drug trafficking. The attack killed two police officers and disrupted civil aviation in Colombia's south and west regions. In February, the FARC killed nine and injured 72 in an attack on a police station in Tumaco, Narino. In another incident, the FARC killed six and injured 20 in an attack against the police station in Villa Rica, Cauca. In March, the FARC killed 11 army soldiers in an ambush in the department of Arauca. In April, the FARC killed five Colombian security force members in an ambush in Puerto Rico, Caqueta. In a separate attack on the police station in Puerto Rico, two civilian adults and a baby were killed by a mortar. In April, the FARC kidnapped a French freelance journalist, while he was accompanying Colombian security forces on an antidrug mission. Four security force members were killed in the attack. After more than four weeks of captivity, the journalist was released on May 30.

Strength: Approximately 8,000 to 9,000 combatants, with several thousand more supporters.

Location/Area of Operation: Primarily in Colombia. Activities including extortion, kidnapping, weapons sourcing, and logistical planning took place in neighboring countries.

Funding and External Aid: Cuba provided some medical care, safe haven, and political consultation. The FARC often use Colombia's border areas with Venezuela, Panama, and Ecuador for incursions into Colombia; and used Venezuelan and Ecuadorian territory for safe haven.

REVOLUTIONARY ORGANIZATION 17 NOVEMBER

aka Epanastatiki Organosi 17 Noemvri; 17 November

Description: Designated as a Foreign Terrorist Organization on October 8, 1997, the Revolutionary Organization 17 November (17N) is a radical leftist group established in 1975. Named for the student uprising in Greece in November 1973 that protested the ruling military junta, 17N is opposed to the Greek government, the United States, Turkey, and NATO. It seeks the end of the U.S. military presence in Greece, the removal of Turkish military forces from Cyprus, and the severing of Greece's ties to NATO and the EU.

Activities: Initial attacks consisted of assassinations of senior U.S. officials and Greek public figures. Between 1975 and 1991, four American citizens were killed by 17N. The group began using bombings in the 1980s. 17N's most recent attack was a bombing attempt in June 2002 at the port of Piraeus in Athens. After the attempted attack, Greek authorities arrested 19 17N members, including a key leader of the organization. The convictions of 13 of these members have been upheld by Greek courts. There were no known 17N attacks in 2012.

Strength: Unknown

Location/Area of Operation: Athens, Greece

Funding and External Aid: Unknown

REVOLUTIONARY PEOPLE'S LIBERATION PARTY/FRONT

aka DHKP/C; Dev Sol; Dev Sol Armed Revolutionary Units; Dev Sol Silahli Devrimci Birlikleri; Dev Sol SDB; Devrimci Halk Kurtulus Partisi-Cephesi; Devrimci Sol; Revolutionary Left

Description: Designated as a Foreign Terrorist Organization on October 8, 1997, the Revolutionary People's Liberation Party/Front (DHKP/C) was originally formed in 1978 as Devrimci Sol, or Dev Sol, a splinter faction of Dev Genc (Revolutionary Youth). It was renamed in 1994 after factional infighting. "Party" refers to the group's political activities, while "Front" is a reference to the group's militant operations. The group advocates a Marxist-Leninist ideology and opposes the United States, NATO, and Turkish establishments. Its goals are the establishment of a socialist state and the abolition of harsh high-security Turkish prisons.

Activities: Since the late 1980s, the group has primarily targeted current and retired Turkish security and military officials, though it has conducted attacks against foreign interests, including U.S. military and diplomatic personnel and facilities, since 1990. The DHKP/C has assassinated two U.S. military contractors, wounded a U.S. Air Force officer, and bombed more than 20 U.S. and NATO military, diplomatic, commercial, and cultural facilities. DHKP/C added suicide bombings to its repertoire in 2001, with attacks against Turkish police in January and September that year. Since the end of 2001, DHKP/C has typically used improvised explosive devices against official Turkish targets and U.S. targets of opportunity.

Operations and arrests against the group have weakened its capabilities, though attacks continued. In late June 2004, the group was suspected of a bus bombing at Istanbul University, which killed four civilians and wounded 21. In July 2005, in Ankara, police intercepted and killed a DHKP/C suicide bomber who attempted to attack the Ministry of Justice. In June 2006, the group killed a police officer in Istanbul; four members of the group were arrested the next month for the attack.

The DHKP/C was dealt a major ideological blow when Dursun Karatas, leader of the group, died in August 2008. After the loss of their leader, the DHKP/C reorganized in 2009 and was reportedly competing with the Kurdistan Workers' Party for influence in both Turkey and with the Turkish diaspora in Europe.

The DHKP/C remained active in 2012, despite Turkish police operations against the organization. In late March, Turkish police arrested nine suspected DHKP/C members for plotting to assassinate Turkey's Justice Minister. In June, the DHKP/C claimed responsibility for a small arms attack on a Turkish police station, and in September the group conducted a suicide bombing of a police station in Istanbul, killing one police officer and wounding seven others.

Strength: Probably several dozen members inside Turkey, with a limited support network throughout Europe.

Location/Area of Operation: Turkey, primarily in Istanbul, Ankara, Izmir, and Adana. Many members also live and plan operations in European countries.

Funding and External Aid: The DHKP/C finances its activities chiefly through donations and extortion, and raises funds primarily in Europe.

REVOLUTIONARY STRUGGLE

aka RS; Epanastatikos Aghonas; EA

Description: Designated as a Foreign Terrorist Organization on May 18, 2009, Revolutionary Struggle (RS) is a radical leftist group with Marxist ideology that has conducted attacks against both Greek and U.S. targets in Greece. RS emerged in 2003 following the arrests of members of the Greek leftist groups 17 November and Revolutionary People's Struggle.

Activities: RS first gained notoriety when it claimed responsibility for the September 5, 2003 bombings at the Athens Courthouse during the trials of 17 November members. From 2004 to 2006, RS claimed responsibility for a number of improvised explosive device (IED) attacks, including a March 2004 attack outside of a Citibank office in Athens. RS claimed responsibility for the January 12, 2007 rocket propelled grenade (RPG) attack on the U.S. Embassy in Athens, which resulted in damage to the building. In 2009, RS increased the number and sophistication of its attacks on police, financial institutions, and other targets. RS successfully bombed a Citibank branch in Athens in March 2009, but failed in its vehicle-borne IED attack in February 2009 against the Citibank headquarters building in Athens. In September 2009, RS claimed responsibility for a car bomb attack on the Athens Stock Exchange, which caused widespread damage and injured a passerby.

In 2010, the Greek government made significant strides in curtailing RS's terrorist activities. On April 10, Greek police arrested six suspected RS members, including purported leadership figure Nikos Maziotis. In addition to the arrests, the Greek raid resulted in the seizure of a RPG launcher, possibly the one used against the U.S. Embassy in Athens in the 2007 attack. The six, plus two other suspected RS members, face charges for arms offenses, causing explosions, and multiple counts of attempted homicide. Their trial started in December 2011, and if found guilty, the suspects face up to 25 years in prison. However, Nikos Maziotis and one other accused RS conspirator disappeared in July 2012 after the Greek courts released them on bail.

Strength: Unknown but numbers presumed to be low.

Location/Area of Operation: Athens, Greece

Funding and External Aid: Unknown

AL-SHABAAB

aka The Harakat Shabaab al-Mujahidin; al-Shabab; Shabaab; the Youth; Mujahidin al-Shabaab Movement; Mujahideen Youth Movement; Mujahidin Youth Movement

Description: Designated as a Foreign Terrorist Organization on March 18, 2008, al-Shabaab was the militant wing of the former Somali Islamic Courts Council that took over parts of southern Somalia in the second half of 2006. Since the end of 2006, al-Shabaab and disparate militias led a violent insurgency using guerrilla warfare and terrorist tactics against the Transitional Federal Government (TFG) of Somalia; the group continues to fight the Government of Somalia. In February 2012, al-Qa'ida (AQ) announced that al-Shabaab leader Ahmed Abdi aw-Mohamed had pledged obedience to Ayman al-Zawahiri and AQ. Al-Shabaab has also developed ties to al-Qa'ida in the Arabian Peninsula (AQAP) and al-Qa'ida in the Islamic Maghreb (AQIM).

In some camps, AQ-affiliated foreign fighters often led the training and indoctrination of the recruits, while rank and file militia fighters from multiple clan and sub-clan factions that are aligned with al-Shabaab are predominantly interested in indigenous issues. The group's foreign fighters were generally intent on conducting attacks outside Somalia but since 2011 have seen their operational capacity reduced due to the military campaign against al-Shabaab. In 2012, al-Shabaab's capability to wage conventional attacks was greatly diminished. Somalia's TFG and its successor, the Federal Government of Somalia (elected indirectly in September) – with the assistance of the AU Mission in Somalia (AMISOM), as well as Ethiopian and allied Somali militia forces – secured areas neighboring Mogadishu and drove al-Shabaab from control of many of its urban strongholds in south-central Somalia. Most notably, the forces drove al-Shabaab from control of the port city of Kismayo on September 28. This led to al-Shabaab's greater reliance on indirect assaults and asymmetrical tactics against AMISOM, Somali, and Kenyan forces. These attacks included the increased use of more sophisticated improvised explosive devices (IEDs).

Activities: Al-Shabaab has used intimidation and violence to undermine the TFG and now the Government of Somalia, forcibly recruit new fighters, and kill activists working to bring about peace through political dialogue and reconciliation. The group has claimed responsibility for several high profile bombings and shootings throughout Somalia targeting AMISOM troops and Somali officials. It has been responsible for the assassination of numerous civil society figures, government officials, and journalists. Al-Shabaab fighters and those who have also claimed allegiance to the group have conducted violent attacks and have assassinated international aid workers and members of NGOs.

In its first attack outside of Somalia, al-Shabaab was responsible for the July 11, 2010 suicide bombings in Kampala, Uganda during the World Cup, which killed nearly 76 people, including one American citizen. Al-Shabaab's attacks continued apace in 2012, and resulted in the deaths of hundreds of people. Among al-Shabaab's most notable 2012 attacks in Somalia were a series of mortar attacks in March against the Somali presidential palace; an April suicide attack targeting Prime Minister Abdiweli Mohamed Ali at Mogadishu's National Theater, which killed five; a May suicide attack at a Café in Dusa Mareb, which killed seven people, including two Somali Members of Parliament; and a violent attack on the town near the Kenyan border in November, which left at least 12 dead. Outside of Somalia, al-Shabaab was also believed responsible for a number of deadly grenade attacks in Kenya.

There were frequent reports of al-Shabaab carrying out amputation of limbs for minor thievery offenses, stoning for suspected adultery, killing converts to religions other than Islam, and forced conscription of child soldiers. Al-Shabaab leaders frequently ordered beheaded corpses to be left in streets as a lesson to local communities. Shabaab forces also engaged in widespread rape and violence against women.

Location/Area of Operation: Al-Shabaab lost full control of significant areas of territory in 2011 and 2012. In September 2012, al-Shabaab lost control of Kismayo, a vital port it used to obtain supplies and funding through taxes. Despite these losses, al-Shabaab continued to control large sections of rural areas in the middle and lower Jubba regions, as well as Bay and Bakol regions, and augmented its presence in northern Somalia along the Golis Mountains and within Puntland's larger urban areas.

Strength: Al-Shabaab is estimated to have several thousand members, including foreign fighters, a force that is augmented by allied clan militias in some areas.

Funding and External Aid: Al-Shabaab saw its income diminish due to the loss of the strategic port cities of Kismayo and Merka; furthermore, it lost a general ability to freely levy taxes in certain urban areas in southern and central Somalia. Al-Shabaab continued to have sufficient financing available, however, including funds from illegal charcoal production and exports from smaller ports along the coast, taxation of local populations and areas under al-Shabaab control, and foreign donations.

Because al-Shabaab is a multi-clan entity, it receives significant donations from the global Somali diaspora; however, the donations are not all intended to support terrorism; but also to support family members.

SHINING PATH

aka SL; Sendero Luminoso; Ejercito Guerrillero Popular (People's Guerrilla Army); EGP; Ejercito Popular de Liberacion (People's Liberation Army); EPL; Partido Comunista del Peru (Communist Party of Peru); PCP; Partido Comunista del Peru en el Sendero Luminoso de Jose Carlos Mariategui (Communist Party of Peru on the Shining Path of Jose Carlos Mariategui); Socorro Popular del Peru (People's Aid of Peru); SPP

Description: Shining Path (SL) was designated as a Foreign Terrorist Organization on October 8, 1997. Former university professor Abimael Guzman formed SL in Peru in the late 1960s, and his teachings created the foundation of SL's militant Maoist doctrine. SL's stated goal is to destroy existing Peruvian institutions and replace them with a communist peasant revolutionary regime. It also opposes any influence by foreign governments. In the 1980s, SL was one of the most ruthless terrorist groups in the Western Hemisphere. The Peruvian government made dramatic gains against SL during the 1990s, capturing Guzman in 1992, and killing a large number of militants. In 2011, the Upper Huallaga Valley (UHV) faction of SL was largely reduced, and in December, the faction's leader publicly acknowledged defeat. Separately, the much larger and stronger rival SL faction in the Apurimac, Ene, and Montaro River Valley (VRAEM) expanded in 2012.

Activities: SL carried out 87 known attacks in 2012, killing one civilian and 18 members of the security forces. In April, SL combatants kidnapped 36 natural gas workers from the Camisea pipeline outside the VRAEM zone. During failed rescue attempts, eight security forces were killed, 10 were wounded and a U.S.-owned helicopter operated by the police was destroyed. All 36 workers were released unharmed within five days. In June, SL guerrillas briefly seized 18 Camisea pipeline workers from an area close to the April kidnapping site. The hostages were released unharmed. In August, SL ambushed a Peruvian army patrol in a remote part of the VRAEM, killing five soldiers and wounding six others. In September, SL combatants damaged the Camisea gas pipeline near Kepashiato and killed a soldier aboard the helicopter that came to inspect the damage. In Echarate, a district in the region of Cusco, SL members blew up three helicopters subcontracted by Camisea in October.

Strength: The two SL factions together are believed to have several hundred armed members.

Location/Area of Operation: Peru, with most activity in rural areas, specifically the Huallaga Valley and the Apurimac, Ene, and Montaro River Valley of central Peru.

Funding and External Aid: SL is primarily funded by the narcotics trade.

TEHRIK-E TALIBAN PAKISTAN

aka Pakistani Taliban; Tehreek-e-Taliban; Tehrik-e-Taliban; Tehrik-e Taliban Pakistan; Tehrik-i-Taliban Pakistan; TTP

Description: Designated as a Foreign Terrorist Organization on September 1, 2010, Tehrik-e Taliban Pakistan (TTP) is a Pakistan-based terrorist organization formed in 2007 in opposition to Pakistani military efforts in the Federally Administered Tribal Areas. Previously disparate militant tribes agreed to cooperate and eventually coalesced into TTP under the leadership of now deceased leader Baitullah Mehsud. The group officially presented itself as a discrete entity in 2007. Since August 2009, TTP has been led by Hakimullah Mehsud. TTP's goals include waging a terrorist campaign against the Pakistani military, as well as against NATO forces in Afghanistan, and overthrowing the Government of Pakistan. TTP uses the tribal belt along the Afghan-Pakistani border to train and deploy its operatives, and the group has a symbiotic relationship with al-Qa'ida (AQ). TTP draws ideological guidance from AQ, while AQ relies on TTP for safe haven in the Pashtun areas along the Afghan-Pakistani border. This arrangement gives TTP access to both AQ's global terrorist network and the operational experience of its members.

Activities: TTP has carried out and claimed responsibility for numerous terrorist acts against Pakistani and U.S. interests, including a December 2009 suicide attack on a U.S. military base in Khowst, Afghanistan, which killed seven U.S. citizens, and an April 2010 suicide bombing against the U.S. Consulate in Peshawar, Pakistan, which killed six Pakistani citizens. TTP is suspected of being involved in the 2007 assassination of former Pakistani Prime Minister Benazir Bhutto. TTP claimed to have supported the failed attempt by Faisal Shahzad to detonate an explosive device in New York City's Times Square on May 1, 2010. TTP's claim was validated by investigations that revealed that TTP directed and facilitated the plot.

Throughout 2011, TTP carried out attacks against the Government of Pakistan and civilian targets, as well as against U.S. targets in Pakistan. Attacks in 2011 included: a March bombing at a gas station in Faisalabad that killed 31 people; an April double suicide bombing at a Sufi shrine in Dera Ghazi Khan that left more than 50 dead; a May bombing of an American consulate convoy in Peshawar that killed one person and injured 12; a May siege of a naval base in Karachi; and a September attack against a school bus that killed four children and the bus driver.

TTP continued to utilize the same tactics against similar targets in 2012. In March, a suicide bomber struck at a mosque in Khyber Agency, and killed over a dozen people while injuring approximately 10 others. In May, an attack in the Bajaur tribal region killed 24 people when a suicide bomber detonated his explosives at a police checkpoint near a crowded market. In August, TTP stormed a Pakistani Air Force base in Kamra; five Pakistani soldiers were killed in the ensuing firefight. Also in August, TTP militants pulled 22 Shia Muslims off busses in the remote Pakistani district of Manshera before shooting them dead.

Strength: Several thousand.

Location/Area of Operation: Federally Administered Tribal Areas, Pakistan

Funding and External Aid: TTP is believed to raise most of its funds through kidnapping for ransom and operations that target Afghanistan-bound military transport trucks for robbery. Such operations allow TTP to steal military equipment, which it sells in Afghan and Pakistani markets.

UNITED SELF-DEFENSE FORCES OF COLOMBIA

aka AUC; Autodefensas Unidas de Colombia

Description: Designated as a Foreign Terrorist Organization on September 10, 2001, the United Self-Defense Forces of Colombia (AUC) – commonly referred to as the paramilitaries – was formed in April 1997. AUC was designed to serve as an umbrella group for loosely affiliated, illegal paramilitary groups retaliating against leftist guerillas. As the Colombian government increasingly confronted terrorist organizations, including the AUC, the group's activities decreased. In the years after the AUC declared a cease-fire in December 2002, the AUC's centralized military structure was dismantled and all of the top paramilitary chiefs have since stepped down.

Activities: The AUC has carried out political killings and kidnappings of human rights workers, journalists, teachers, and trade unionists, among others. As much as 70 percent of the AUC's paramilitary operational costs were financed with drug-related earnings. Some former members of the AUC never demobilized or are recidivists, and these elements have continued to engage heavily in criminal activities. The AUC did not carry out any terrorist attacks in 2012.

Strength: Unknown

Location/Area of Operation: Strongest in Northwest Colombia, with affiliate groups in Valle del Cauca, on the west coast, and Meta Department, in Central Columbia.

Funding and External Aid: None

Chapter 7.
Legislative Requirements and Key Terms

Country Reports on Terrorism 2012 is submitted in compliance with Title 22 of the United States Code, Section 2656f (the "Act"), which requires the Department of State to provide Congress a full and complete annual report on terrorism for those countries and groups meeting the criteria of the Act. Statutory excerpts relating to the terms used in this report and a discussion of the interpretation and application of those terms in this report are included below.

Excerpts and Summary of Key Statutory Terms:

Section 2656f(a) of Title 22 of the United States Code states as follows:
(a) ... The Secretary of State shall transmit to the Speaker of the House of Representatives and the Committee on Foreign Relations of the Senate, by April 30 of each year, a full and complete report providing -

(1) (A) detailed assessments with respect to each foreign country -

(i) in which acts of international terrorism occurred which were, in the opinion of the Secretary, of major significance;

(ii) about which the Congress was notified during the preceding five years pursuant to Section 2405(j) of the Export Administration Act of 1979; and

(iii) which the Secretary determines should be the subject of such report; and

(B) detailed assessments with respect to each foreign country whose territory is being used as a sanctuary for terrorist organizations;

(2) all relevant information about the activities during the preceding year of any terrorist group, and any umbrella group under which such terrorist group falls, known to be responsible for the kidnapping or death of an American citizen during the preceding five years, any terrorist group known to have obtained or developed, or to have attempted to obtain or develop, weapons of mass destruction, any terrorist group known to be financed by countries about which Congress was notified during the preceding year pursuant to section 2405(j) of the Export Administration Act of 1979, any group designated by the Secretary as a foreign terrorist organization under section 219 of the Immigration and Nationality Act (8 U.S.C. 1189), and any other known international terrorist group which the Secretary determines should be the subject of such report;

(3) with respect to each foreign country from which the United States Government has sought cooperation during the previous five years in the investigation or prosecution of an act of international terrorism against United States citizens or interests, information on -

(A) the extent to which the government of the foreign country is cooperating with the United States Government in apprehending, convicting, and punishing the individual or individuals responsible for the act; and

(B) the extent to which the government of the foreign country is cooperating in preventing further acts of terrorism against United States citizens in the foreign country; and

(4) with respect to each foreign country from which the United States Government has sought cooperation during the previous five years in the prevention of an act of international terrorism against such citizens or interests, the information described in paragraph (3)(B).

Section 2656f(d) of Title 22 of the United States Code defines certain key terms used in Section 2656f(a) as follows:

(1) the term "international terrorism" means terrorism involving citizens or the territory of more than one country;

(2) the term "terrorism" means premeditated, politically motivated violence perpetrated against non-combatant targets by subnational groups or clandestine agents; and

(3) the term "terrorist group" means any group practicing, or which has significant subgroups which practice, international terrorism.

Interpretation and Application of Key Terms. For purposes of this report, the terms "international terrorism," "terrorism," and "terrorist group" have the definitions assigned to them in 22 USC 2656f(d) (see above). The term "non-combatant," which is referred to but not defined in 22 USC 2656f(d)(2), is interpreted to mean, in addition to civilians, military personnel (whether or not armed or on duty) who are not deployed in a war zone or a war-like setting.

It should be noted that 22 USC 2656f(d) is one of many U.S. statutes and international legal instruments that concern terrorism and acts of violence, many of which use definitions for terrorism and related terms that are different from those used in this report. The interpretation and application of defined and related terms concerning terrorism in this report is therefore specific to the statutory and other requirements of the report, and is not intended to express the views of the U.S. government on how these terms should be interpreted or applied for any other purpose. Accordingly, there is not necessarily any correlation between the interpretation of terms such as "non-combatant" for purposes of this report and the meanings ascribed to similar terms pursuant to the law of war (which encapsulates the obligations of states and individuals with respect to their activities in situations of armed conflict).

Statistical Information. Pursuant to 22 USC § 2656f(b), this report should contain "to the extent practicable, complete statistical information on the number of individuals, including United States citizens and dual nationals, killed, injured, or kidnapped by each terrorist group during the preceding calendar year." This is satisfied through the inclusion of a statistical annex to the report that sets out statistical information provided by the National Consortium for the Study of Terrorism and Responses to Terrorism (START), a Department of Homeland Security Science and Technology Center of Excellence, based at the University of Maryland. The statistical annex includes a discussion of the methodology employed by START in compiling the relevant data. This report does not contain statistical information specifically concerning combatants. The focus of the terrorism report, as is clear from the definition of terrorism, is on violence against noncombatant targets. Further, it would not be practicable to provide such statistics, as the government does not maintain - and would have great difficulty maintaining - statistics that distinguish between incidents against combatants by terrorist groups and by others, including insurgents, in Iraq and Afghanistan.

Contextual Reporting. Adverse mention in this report of individual members of any political, social, ethnic, religious, or national population is not meant to imply that all members of that population are terrorists. Indeed, terrorists rarely represent anything other than a tiny fraction of such larger populations. It is terrorist groups--and their actions--that are the focus of this report.

Furthermore, terrorist acts are part of a larger phenomenon of violence inspired by a cause, and at times the line between the two can become difficult to draw. This report includes some discretionary information in an effort to relate terrorist events to the larger context in which they occur, and to give a feel for the conflicts that spawn violence.

Thus, this report will discuss terrorist acts as well as other violent incidents that are not necessarily "international terrorism" and therefore are not subject to the statutory reporting requirement.